Real-Time Shading

Real-Time Shading

Marc Olano
John C. Hart
Wolfgang Heidrich
Michael McCool

CRC Press
Taylor & Francis Group
Boca Raton London New York

CRC Press is an imprint of the
Taylor & Francis Group, an **informa** business

AN A K PETERS BOOK

First published 2002 by A K Peters, Ltd.

Published 2019 by CRC Press
Taylor & Francis Group
6000 Broken Sound Parkway NW, Suite 300
Boca Raton, FL 33487-2742

© 2002 by Taylor & Francis Group, LLC
CRC Press is an imprint of Taylor & Francis Group, an Informa business

First issued in paperback 2019

No claim to original U.S. Government works

ISBN 13: 978-0-367-44702-1 (pbk)
ISBN 13: 978-1-56881-180-2 (hbk)

Visit the Taylor & Francis Web site at
http://www.taylorandfrancis.com

and the CRC Press Web site at
http://www.crcpress.com

Library of Congress Cataloging-in-Publication Data

Real-time shading / Marc Olano ... [et al.].
   p. cm.
  Includes bibliographical references and index.
  ISBN 1-56881-180-2
  1. Computer graphics. 2. Real-time data processing. I. Olano, Marc.

T385 .R43413 2002
006.6'9--dc21

                              2002066286

Dedication

To Erin, who was done with the book long before I was.
—*M.O.*

To Patty, Chelsea and Hannah.
—*J.C.H.*

To Götz and Ingrid Heidrich.
—*W.H.*

To Monique.
—*M.M.*

Contents

Preface

The shading for real-time computer graphics has undergone a complete paradigm shift in recent years. The classical Gouraud-interpolated Phong shading model that dominated real-time graphics for three decades is no longer our only choice. It is interesting, and at first confusing, that we overcame this classical shading model not through the hardware interpolation of surface normals, as had been predicted. Instead, advanced shading methods were implemented through a combination of unusual texture coordinates, unexpected image combinations, and the complete perversion of the environment map.

These techniques were highly irregular and not covered in typical introductory computer graphics courses. Many of us who thought we were experts in computer graphics have had to relearn the subject from its fundamentals to understand how these new shading methods work.

This book serves as a primer and a repository for these off-the-wall algorithms and techniques. It is an instrument that those in computer graphics, who may have felt the field has past them by, can use as a tutorial to catch back up. Those who have tried to keep current may appreciate this book as a coherent collection of methods, many of which were only previously available in scattered papers, powerpoint slides, and course notes.

The book should be of interest to anyone who wants to use real-time shading. Game developers will find numerous techniques for making their characters and scenes appear more realistic, while still maintaining the interactivity of their games. As advanced shading continues to be a useful tool in scientific visualization, scientists and engineers will find these techniques useful for integrating more information into their visualizations. Implementing advanced shading in graphics hardware also allows more accurate display of objects in the preview window of modeling packages. This can aid the animator in lighting and texturing, and also assists the geometric designer to more efficiently design surfaces with aesthetic reflectance. This book is also a tutorial for researchers and students of both shading and graphics hardware, or anyone else wanting to experiment with their own shading algorithms or languages.

This book is dedicated to all levels of shading, but the true promise of real-time shading is found in high-level shading languages. RenderMan is a high-level shading language for non-real-time rendering, and its success is legendary. From Pixar's "Toy Story" to the work of ILM in Jurassic Park, the results of such powerful tools in the hands of capable artists are amazing.

It is no surprise that the most common phrases used to describe the ultimate goal of real-time shading are "real-time Toy-Story," "real-time Final Fantasy," "real-time ... ." This doesn't discount the importance of lower levels of real-time shading; they are a necessary part of building high-level shading into a real-time system. Yet, for the ultimate in usability and portability, there is no substitute for a high-level shading language.

We are writing this book amidst a flurry of new real-time shading methods and a torrent of new programmable shading hardware. We have tried to focus on the concepts and fundamentals of real-time shading while including some of the practical domain knowledge necessary to make it efficient. This book does not contain long and detailed specifications or code listings for the latest graphics accelerators. Instead, it contains shading algorithms that are suitable for running on graphics hardware, analysis of the programming languages and application programming interfaces for real-time shading, and information about how they work. As graphics accelerators evolve, and even after the current accelerators are distant memories (in, say, two or three years), the algorithms and concepts in this book will still apply.

The book is organized into four parts. The first, *Fundamentals*, covers background information on shading techniques and the structure of the modern graphics hardware this book targets. For those new to computer graphics, it provides a concise introduction to the science of shading, lighting, and texturing, but assumes some prior knowledge of the basics of linear algebra and calculus. Experienced readers may choose to skip this part, but might want to examine the end of the Introduction (which contains a new grammatical model used throughout the book to articulate a variety of shading pipelines), and the end of the Chapter 3 (texturing), which contains a multipass implementation of the Perlin noise function.

The second part, *Building Blocks for Shading*, describes a set of algorithms and approximations to the fundamental techniques to make them "suitable for hardware." These chapters document the unusual uses of texture coordinates, image compositing, and the environment map that have made modern shading methods possible. These are some of the basic pieces you can pull together into shaders for interesting real-world objects (and some not so real).

The third part, *High-Level Procedural Shading*, deals exclusively with shading languages for graphics hardware. What does it take to make one? What can they do? How do they compare? It highlights aspects of all real-time shading languages and compilers in existence at the writing of this book. Others will certainly come in the years to follow, but by nature they will likely be similar to the ones presented here. This part also covers shading APIs—the interfaces for using shaders from a real application.

The final part, *And Beyond*, looks to the near and far future of real-time shading.

Acknowledgments

Sometime around 1991, as part of a graduate research assistantship at UNC, I found myself rewriting some of the lighting code for Pixel-Planes 5. This involved SIMD array code quite similar in character to current vertex and fragment shaders. I came away with two insights: graphics machines had developed enough computational power to do all kinds of procedural shading (an insight shared by others on the Pixel-Planes project); and without a true high-level shading language, you needed superhuman effort to use it. Thus began ten years of research (so far) in creating and using real-time shading languages.

I was fortunate to be in the right place and time to influence the design of the PixelFlow machine at UNC. Everyone on the PixelFlow project deserves some credit for creating a machine that was almost ideal for shading, but I'd like to make specific mention of Steve Molnar, the lead architect of PixelFlow; Rob Wheeler and Voicu Popsecu, who assisted me with the shading compiler implementation; Jon Leech, who deserves much of the credit for the PixelFlow shading OpenGL extensions; and of course Anselmo Lastra, my dissertation advisor.

After leaving UNC, I came to SGI to work on shading languages targeting multipass rendering on conventional hardware. Of the many great people I've worked with at SGI, I'd like to give extra thanks to John Airey, Mark Peercy, Jeff Ungar, Thayer Andrews and Bob Kuehne. Mark Peercy, in particular, is responsible for defining the first version of the ISL language and OpenGL Shader API, and Thayer Andrews (among his many other contributions) created the shaders shown in Figures 9.2 and 14.2.

Marc Olano
Mountain View, California
April 2002

My research in real-time shading began in 1996 with a conversation with Steve Tibbitts, then president of Silicon Reality (RIP) when he was recruiting at Washington State University. He saw then that procedural shading could be a valuable feature in consumer graphics cards, and with Terry Coleman's help, we designed and patented the antialiased procedural solid texturing system described in this book. Grad students Nate Carr and Masaki Kameya also packaged it up into a nice OpenGL utility library software implementation. Evans & Sutherland purchased Silicon Reality and continued the research, which allowed me to work with Pete Doenges on analyzing procedural shading hardware, resulting in the shading pipeline grammar and the Evans & Sutherland Multitexturing Language. E&S also supported the atlas-based real-time procedural solid texturing methods, which were joint work with Nate Carr and Jerome Maillot at Alias|Wavefront.

John C. Hart
Champaign, Illinois
April 2002

I first became interested in realtime shading and lighting in 1996, when I started my Ph.D. studies at the University of Erlangen-Nürnberg, Germany. I owe much to Hans-Peter Seidel (my supervisor in Erlangen) and Philipp Slusallek (then a Post-Doc there), for their encouragement to pursue this line of research. Much of my work on this subject is also co-authored with Hans-Peter and Philipp. I am also indebted to a number of Ph.D students that I worked with in Erlangen as well as later at the Max-Planck-Institut für Informatik. Jan Kautz and I worked together on environment maps, light source representations (canned light sources), bump map shadows, and a number of smaller projects. Stefan Brabec worked with me on real-time shadow algorithms, and also prepared a nicely packaged up demo for the canned light source project. In addition, Katja Daubert, Michael Goesele, Hendrik Lensch, Hartmut Schirmacher, and Pere-Pau Vazquez contributed to various aspects related to realtime shading (as well as a variety of projects not related to this book).

Wolfgang Heidrich
Vancouver, BC
April 2002

I would like to thank Kevin Moule for his displacement map research and images, Mauro Steigleder for his last-minute work on implementing the Ashikhmin reflectance model, and Jason Ang, Anis Ahmad, and Jan Kautz for their work on BRDF representations. Funding for real-time rendering research at the University of Waterloo was provided by grants from the National Science and Engineering Research Council of Canada (NSERC) and the Centre for Information Technology Ontario (CITO). Facilities used to perform the work in the Computer Graphics Laboratory at the University of Waterloo were provided by the Bell University Laboratory initiative, hardware donations from NVIDIA, and a grant from the Canadian Foundation for Innovation and the Ontario Innovation Trust, as part of the Integrated Centre for Visualization, Design, and Manufacturing. The author would also like to thank his fellow CGL faculty Stephen Mann, William Cowan, Ian Bell, and Gladimir Baranowski, as well as other members of CGL and especially my graduate students, for picking up the slack and generally putting up with my distractedness while I was occupied with this project. Finally, I would like to thank Monique McCool, my mother, for encouraging me to get the best education I could and accepting the fact that I never *did* leave school.

Michael McCool
Waterloo, Ontario
April 2002

Part I

Fundamentals

In this part, we introduce notation used throughout the rest of the book, and give a brief background on the shading models, techniques and hardware that are the basis for the remainder of the book.

1

Introduction

Procedural shading and real-time rendering have long been considered to be at opposite ends of the quality/interactivity spectrum. Exciting advances in the past several years have changed this completely. Now it is not only possible, but common, to see real-time procedural shading on even the most inexpensive of graphics accelerators.

In graphics, one often reads that a given algorithm is suitable for "implementation on hardware." What that (usually) means is that the algorithm was designed to make use of the operations available on a graphics accelerator, not that the author was targeting a direct hardware implementation (again, usually). However, this is slightly misleading, since the graphics accelerator may have programmable (software-driven) components.

This book is, in large part, about shading algorithms suitable for "implementation on hardware." The algorithms that we will discuss have been designed to (a) be as simple and efficient as possible, (b) avoid operations not available on graphics accelerators, and (c) provide high-quality visual results even in the face of the shortcomings of current accelerators.

Unfortunately (and fortunately), graphics accelerators are constantly evolving. The available operations and the limitations of today's accelerators may not be true of tomorrow's accelerators.

We have done two things to address this problem. First, we made some predictions about how we expect hardware will evolve in the next few years. Key to this is the prediction that the current low-level interface for procedural shading hardware will be replaced by high-level shading languages. This allows us to address algorithms, not the shuffling of bits from one hardware register to another. Second, we have focused on fundamental issues and technologies, like representations of functions and compilation, that will likely be important even on this future hardware. What we have not done, for the most part, is provide overly specific examples of how to convert the algorithms we will present so they can run on such-and-such an accelerator. Such information would be useful in the short term but would quickly become obsolete. Instead, we have focused on the underlying mathematics and fundamental techniques useful for high-performance implementation of shaders on graphics accelerators.

This chapter lays the groundwork for later chapters. First we will define our goals as precisely as possible: Of course, this book is about real-time shading, but what do we mean by that, exactly? We will then review the basic concepts of programmable shading, and summarize the relationship of current real-time capabilities to them. These fundamental topics will be revisited many times through the course of the book—the remainder of this part covers basic graphics techniques that serve as the basis for many shaders, whether real-time or not; Part II includes more detail on algorithms that are specifically well-suited for use on graphics hardware; Part III deals with shading languages, shading language compilers, and APIs for shading; and finally, in Part IV, we make some educated predictions for what directions shading hardware will go in the future.

1.1   Terminology

In this book we will use a particular set of words in ways that are consistent with common usage in graphics. Unfortunately, some of our usages will conflict with the usages of these terms outside of graphics. We define these terms below.

1.1.1   Real Time

The word *real time* is often used when talking about interactive graphics to denote "fast", and when used in the context of graphics, tends to mean 30 frames per second (fps) or higher. However, there are large areas of computer science in which real time means "with bounded execution time"; for instance, real-time operating systems.

In graphics, of course, bounded execution time is a useful and often even mandatory requirement. Many game and flight simulator companies, for instance, write real-time code in the sense that they do not tolerate any technique (even otherwise useful things like adaptive tessellation) that might put a glitch in gameplay or simulation.

However, "bounded execution time" is not exactly our meaning. What we mean by real-time rendering in graphics specifically is that the rendering should be fast enough that we do not perceive it as taking any time at all;

it seems like it is a real object moving under our control. For different applications, this can mean anything from 15 fps to 60 fps, depending on the speed of the action being rendered. This also means that the latency should be low, on the same order as the frame rendering time.

A more reasonable name for this would be *interactive*, since that implies that the system could respond quickly to a user's input. Unfortunately, interactive has somehow acquired the meaning of "fast enough for previsualization," which might be as much as a few seconds per frame.

1.1.2 Shading

Shading is the assignment of colors—or more specifically—outgoing radiance, to points on a surface.

Shading can be done in a number of different ways, some physically realistic, some not. Physically realistic shading involves the combination of an illumination process (evaluation of incoming light, taking into account things like shadows) and a reflectance process.

Illumination processes can be varied, of course, and can include everything from simple point sources to integrating over a radiance field representing the result of a light transport simulation. Reflectance (even physically based reflectance) can be similarly varied. There are many different reflectance models, each a more-or-less valid approximation to the properties of some kind of surface.

Typically, when we try to approximate the real physical appearance of objects, we say we are implementing *photorealistic shading*. In the early history of graphics, this was done by eye, but there has been a recent movement to base reflectance models in particular on the underlying physics of reflectance, leading to a more rigorous form of shading: *physically based shading*. Often, but not always, the fastest way to photorealistic shading is via physically based shading.

It is also possible that a shading process could assign colors that do not correspond to a physical process, or even an approximation to the properties of a physical object. Instead of approximating the physics of light reflectance, we may want to use artistic conventions, such as cross hatching or emphasis of edges. Frequently, artistic conventions can lead to clearer representations, and so can be useful in visualization and technical contexts. This is called *Non-Photorealistic Rendering* (NPR), *artistic rendering*, or *stylized rendering* (the latter two are less commonly used, but more positive) [56].

As an example, a cartoon shader might be used that would make silhouette edges and prominent ridges and valleys in a surface black, while assigning a constant color to regions not in shadow and a darker but still constant color to regions in shadow [55]. Such a shading model has been used to integrate three-dimensional rendering with traditional cel animation [7]. Examples include the movies *Iron Giant*, *Atlantis*, and *Titan A.E.*. The highlighting of edges, in particular, is a common convention in non-photorealistic rendering but is just that: a convention. One of the characteristics of NPR is that it is not as rigorously defined as physically based rendering.

1.2 Representations of Shading

The shading in a scene can be described in several different ways, from fixed but parameterized formulas to sampled numerical approximations to procedural models. These are discussed in more detail in Chapter 9.

1.2.1 Parameterized Analytical Shading Models

If a simple mathematical relationship between the input parameters (the point location on the surface or in three-dimensional space; the normal and/or tangent at that point; the direction of the viewer; the direction(s) of the light source(s); texture map(s) applied to the object, etc.) can be found, then a single formula is sufficient for a complete description of the shading. This is most often the case for physically based shading; artistic rendering is usually more difficult to describe that way.

Most analytical models describe only the directional dependencies of materials. For example, they describe how light is reflected for different combinations of incoming (light) and outgoing (viewing) direction, but they do not describe how the material changes across a complex surface.

Analytical models are extremely compact representations of material properties. If an analytical model is built into a rendering system, its implementation can of course be highly optimized. Such a built-in model would usually support several parameters that would permit the look to be varied. However, good physically based models can be expensive to evaluate, and are limited in flexibility because every model applies only to a certain class of materials. If a new material is desired, a new and completely different analytical description has to be derived and implemented.

1.2.2 Procedural Shaders

Rather than using a parameterized analytical model of reflectance, it is often more convenient to provide the capability for the user of a system to describe the shading themselves by a (usually small) procedure. Such a procedure would implement a function that computes the radiance from given input parameters such as the point location on the surface or in three-dimensional space; the normal and/or tangent at that point; the direction of the viewer; the direction(s) of the light source(s); texture map(s) applied to the object, etc.

Procedural descriptions of this form are called *procedural shaders* (or just *shaders*). Of course, procedural shaders can be used to implement analytic lighting models, but they can also be used for many other purposes.

Because these shaders are not hardcoded into the rendering program, they must be generated by an artist or programmer who wants to achieve a specific effect. The shaders can then be loaded and interpreted dynamically by the system so that an unlimited number of different effects is possible with one rendering system.

Many systems actually support a whole network of different procedures that describe different aspects of a scene, or are applied at different stages of the rendering pipeline. In the literature, these are still called shaders, even though they don't necessarily compute surface shading. Some commonly used categories are:

Surface shaders: Describe the color of points on a surface (i.e., one point on a geometric object) for a given viewing direction and illumination setting. In most systems, a surface shader is provided only with local information (point, normal, etc.), and has no access to neighboring geometry. Surface shaders usually compute color values either based on a two-dimensional location on the geometry (i.e., based on texture coordinates provided with the geometric model), or based on the three-dimensional location of the point. The latter case is called a *solid texture*, because it is most useful for objects that are supposed to look like they have been carved out of a solid block of material, such as wood or marble.

Volume shaders: Describe the appearance of volumetric objects without clearly defined geometry, such as clouds or smoke. Their restrictions are very similar to those of surface shaders in that they usually have information about only a single point in space available.

Light shaders: Procedural descriptions of the light sources in the scene. Given a point in three-dimensions, they compute the amount of light each source contributes to that point.

This list describes only some of the most commonly used shader classes. A number of systems have other classes of shaders, for example, for describing local or global transformations and surface displacements, or imaging effects such as film transfer functions or lens glare. These will be described in more detail in Chapter 4.

In general, a procedural approach to shading has a number of significant advantages:

Flexibility: Procedural shading is extremely flexible. Every effect that can be computed can be described with this approach, including any analytical model.

Compactness: Procedural descriptions tend to be highly storage efficient. Very simple procedures can describe quite complex appearances.

Resolution independence: A procedural description can be used for a wide range of different image resolutions and object sizes. However, it has to be done right; specifically, the issue of antialiasing needs to be addressed.

On the other hand, procedural shading also has a number of disadvantages, especially when it comes to real-time systems:

Efficiency: More complex shaders can result in long execution times. In the extreme, it is quite possible that a shader may run into an infinite loop and not terminate at all. Clearly these issues have to be addressed for real-time rendering.

Content creation: While procedural shaders are extremely flexible and powerful, they are not always intuitive to write. Most artists prefer to draw or paint effects instead. Even for very skilled programmers the writing of a shader for a complex effect can be difficult and time consuming task.

1.2.3   Textures and Sampled Representations

In interactive or real-time applications, naturally the complexity of tasks that can be performed on the fly is limited. An alternative (or adjunct) to procedural shaders in this scenario is to precompute as much information as possible, and to store the result in tables or texture maps. These representations are also natural choices for data that has been measured or otherwise captured, for example, with a digital camera or flatbed scanner.

A *texture*, *texture map*, or *texture image* is a regularly spaced array of samples (called *texels*), from which a continuous function can be reconstructed using *interpolation*. Although the texture consists only of values at discrete locations, it is possible to use interpolation to obtain function

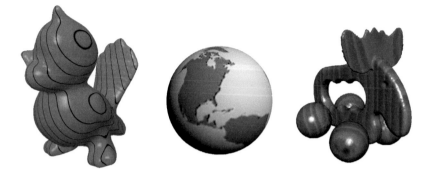

Figure 1.1. Left: A one-dimensional texture applied to a three-dimensional object to generate contour lines. Center: A world map applied as a two-dimensional diffuse texture. Right: A solid three-dimenional texture applied to a geometric model to make it look like it has been carved out of wood.

values at arbitrary positions. Commonly used interpolation schemes include linear and (primarily in software systems) cubic interpolation. Also, texture map hardware includes support for filtering algorithms, such as MIP-mapping [180].

Texturing or *texture mapping* [29] is the process of mapping images (textures) onto geometric primitives. Modulating the color of pixel fragments this way represents the most efficient way of increasing the visual complexity of a synthetic image without increasing the geometric complexity of the scene. Since very complex effects can be achieved at only moderate computational cost, texturing has become quite popular. It is used in both high-quality off-line rendering systems and interactive computer graphics.

Textures come in a variety of different flavors describing different kinds of detail information. For example, textures can simply contain color values to be applied to a surface, but they can also be used to perturb the surface normal and/or the surface point, or they can store information about the incoming illumination at a certain point in space. In real-time applications especially, the values contained in a texture map are often not related to colors at all, but rather just represent the results of an expensive computation in a tabular form.

The term *texture* is often used synonymous to *two-dimensional texture*, i.e., a two-dimensional grid of sample values. However, the same principles apply to textures of other dimensions. Just as a two-dimensional texture is an image that gets attached to a surface, a one-dimensional texture is a table that can be used, for example, to generate contour lines on objects, and a three-dimensional texture can be used for holding volumetric data such as clouds or smoke, or for representing solid textures as described above in a sampled form.

Like procedural shading, texture mapping is extremely flexible; textures can hold arbitrary shading effects (or partial results of their computation). In contrast to procedural shaders, however, textures usually require significantly more space than shaders, and they are not independent of resolution (i.e., there is only a certain maximum level of detail available that is determined by the resolution of the texture). On the positive side, texture mapping can be computationally much more efficient, and many artists prefer painting textures over writing shader programs.

The choice between procedural shaders and texture maps is therefore the usual tradeoff between memory and computational efficiency. In practical applications, it is often necessary to strike a balance between the two. This is possible, for example, by restricting procedural computations to simple and efficient calculations, or those where resolution independence is most desirable. Texture mapping and lookup tables are often used to store precomputed parts of shading models as well as smooth functions that can be represented well at low resolutions.

1.3   A Grammatical Model
for Shading Pipelines

Distilled to its essence, rendering is a process that converts geometry into images. The geometry is commonly specified as triangles in model coordinates, whereas the images are output in fragments. The term *fragment* denotes a sample that may contribute to a final image pixel. Fragments are the result of the rasterization of a triangle, whereas pixels are elements of an image array. Even though they correspond to the same location, it is important to understand the distinction. Fragments from the rasterization of several triangles may correspond to the same pixel. How fragments combine to color the pixel is a function of the depth test, antialiasing, stencil test, and yet other factors.

In order to process geometry as fast as possible, the rendering process has been pipelined. A variety of rendering pipelines have been developed, and even more have been investigated in the quest for making them work in real time. This book uses a grammar to describe and analyze a variety of graphics pipelines that perform this rendering process. The symbols used in this grammar are listed in Table 1.1.

$\mathbf{x}$	vertex in model coordinates
$\mathbf{u}$	surface parameterization (u, v)
$\mathbf{s}$	shading parameter vector, e.g. (N, V, R, H)
π	graphics pipeline from model to viewport coordinates
$\mathbf{x}_s$	fragment in viewport coordinates (xs,ys)
δ	rasterization (interpolation and sampling)
$\mathbf{c}$	color vector (R,G,B)
$\bigoplus$	color combination function
C	frame buffer
T	texture map
$\leftarrow$	assignment

Table 1.1. Operators in the shading pipeline grammar.

We denote a two-dimensional surface parameterization as $\mathbf{u} = (u, v)$. We denote the shading parameters as a vector $\mathbf{s}$ that can, for example, contain the light source and surface material constants, as well as the local coordinate frame and the view vector. We use the vector $\mathbf{x}$ to represent a triangle vertex with its position in model coordinates, and $\mathbf{x}_s$ to denote the same point in viewport (screen) coordinates.

These symbols can be combined to express other attributes in the rendering pipeline. The two-dimensional surface texture coordinates are an attribute of the vertex and are denoted $\mathbf{ux}$. Read this as the *surface parameterization* ($\mathbf{u}$) at *vertex* ($\mathbf{x}$). Likewise, the shading parameter vector is also a vertex attribute and is denoted $\mathbf{sx}$. Note that the pipeline symbols are more properly thought of as functions, $\mathbf{u}(\mathbf{x})$, but we eliminate the use of parentheses in favor of a grammatical expression.

We denote color $\mathbf{c} = (R, G, B)$. The map $\mathbf{p} : \mathbf{s} \rightarrow \mathbf{c}$ denotes a shader, a procedure that maps shading parameters $\mathbf{s}$ to a color $\mathbf{c}$. The operator $T : \mathbf{u} \rightarrow \mathbf{c}$ is a two-dimensional texture map that returns a color $\mathbf{c}$ given surface texture coordinates $\mathbf{u}$.

We use capital letters to denote maps that are implemented with a lookup table, such as the texture map T. We will use the $\leftarrow$ operator to denote assignment to this table. For example, the frame buffer $C : \mathbf{x}_s \rightarrow \mathbf{c}$ is a mapping from screen coordinates $\mathbf{x}_s$ to a color $\mathbf{c}$. The frame buffer is implemented as a table, and assignment of an element $\mathbf{c}$ into this table at index $\mathbf{x}_s$ is denoted as $C\mathbf{x}_s \leftarrow \mathbf{c}$: the frame buffer element at $\mathbf{x}_s$ gets the color $\mathbf{c}$.

Most of the standard graphics pipeline can be decomposed into a general projection π that maps vertices from three-dimensional model coordinates $\mathbf{x}$ to two-dimensional screen coordinates $\mathbf{x}_s$, and a rasterization that takes

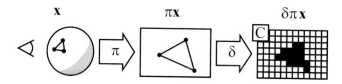

Figure 1.2. Addressing of fragments using $C\delta\pi\mathbf{x}$. In this example, the location of each pixel in the frame buffer (C) is found by projecting (π) vertices ($\mathbf{x}$) into screen space, and filling in (via the rasterization operator δ) the triangular region of fragments described by the vertices.

these screen coordinate vertices and fills in the fragments of the polygon they describe using linear interpolation. It will be useful for the analysis of the aliasing artifacts to know exactly when attributes are interpolated across a polygon, as this signals when continuous functions are discretely sampled. We will indicate that a continuous function has been discretely sampled by rasterization with a delta function operator δ.

As Figure 1.2 shows, $\mathbf{x}$ is a polygon vertex in model coordinates, $\pi\mathbf{x}$ is the screen coordinate corresponding to that point, and $\delta\pi\mathbf{x}$ reminds us that the coordinates of that fragment were discretely interpolated from the screen coordinates of the polygon's vertices. Shaders are techniques that produce candidate fragment values to place in the screen pixel $C\delta\pi\mathbf{x}$.

1.3.1 Gouraud Interpolation

The classical 90s hardware implementation of the graphics pipeline is dominated by the linear interpolation of vertex attributes at the end of the pipeline

$$C\delta\pi\mathbf{x} \leftarrow \delta\mathbf{psx} \qquad (1.1)$$

Lighting is computed per vertex ($\mathbf{psx}$), and the resulting color is interpolated across the fragments of the screen-space polygon by the rasterization engine, as shown in pixels of the screen-space polygon by the rasterization engine, as shown in Figure 1.3.

1.3.2 Deferred Shading

Deferred shading [120, 177] implements procedural shading in two phases. In the first phase

$$T\delta\pi\mathbf{x} \leftarrow \delta\mathbf{sx} \qquad (1.2)$$

such that the shading parameters are stored in a texture map T, which is the same resolution as the display. Once all of the polygons have been scan

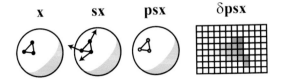

Figure 1.3.   Gouraud shading of fragments. In this example, the shading parameters s are the surface normals at each vertex **x**, which the procedure **p** turns into a per-vertex color that is interpolated across the face fragments by the δ rasterization operator.

converted, the second phase makes a single shading pass through every pixel in the frame buffer

$$C\mathbf{x}_s \leftarrow \mathbf{p}T\mathbf{x}_s \tag{1.3}$$

replacing the color with the results of the procedure applied to the stored solid texture coordinates. In this matter, the application of **p**, the shader, is deferred until all of the polygons have been projected, such that the shader is applied to only the visible fragments of the polygons.

Deferred shading applies all of the operations of the shader expression to a pixel before the next pixel is visited, and so suffers the same process limitations as fragment lighting. Unlike fragment lighting, deferred shading has a fixed number of pixels to visit, which provides a constant execution speed regardless of scene depth complexity.

In fact, the main benefit of deferred shading is the reduction of its shading depth complexity to one. This means that a shader is evaluated only once for each pixel, regardless of the number of overlapping fragments that project to that pixel. Since some shaders can be quite complex, applying them only to visible fragments can save a significant amount of rendering time.

The main drawback to deferred shading is the size of the texture map T. This texture map contains every variable used by the shader, including surface normals, reflection vectors, and the location/direction and color of each light source.

One possible offset to the large frame buffer is to generate the frame in smaller chunks, trading space for time. It is not yet clear whether the time savings due to deferred shading's unit depth complexity makes up for the multiple renderings necessary for this kind of implementation.

Antialiasing is another drawback of deferred shading since the procedural texture is generated in a separate step of the algorithm than the step where the samples have been recorded from the δ. Deferred shading thus precludes the use of efficient polygon rasterization antialiasing methods such as coverage masks. Unless a significant amount of auxiliary information is also recorded, previous procedural texturing antialiasing algorithms do not easily apply to deferred shading.

However, with the multi-sample antialiasing found in many recent graphics controllers, supersampling appears to be the antialiasing technique of choice, and is certainly the most directly and generally scalable antialiasing solution across all segments of the graphics market. While the deferred shading frame buffer would have to be as large as the sampling space, this still seems to be a feasible and attractive direction for further pursuit.

Since all of the information needed by shader is held per pixel by the texture map, the channels of the texture map would need to be signed and generally of higher precision than the resulting color to prevent error accumulation in complex shaders.

2

Reflectance

A lighting model is a specific algorithm or a mathematical formula for computing the color of a surface, the goal being some level of similarity to the real-world appearance of a physical surface. This can be compared to a shading model or *shader*, which implies something more arbitrary; lighting models are a subclass of all shading models. It is of course very, very common to write shaders that implement lighting models.

Shading by itself sometimes means the process of interpolation of inputs or outputs of lighting or shading models, for instance in Phong and Gouraud shading. Note that Phong *shading*, the interpolation of normals before evaluation of some (arbitrary) lighting model, is distinct from the Phong *lighting model*, which has a specific mathematical form. However, shading can also mean the application of some arbitrary per-pixel *shading program* in a renderer supporting programmable or procedural shaders.

Lighting models usually consist conceptually of two parts: illumination and reflectance. Illumination is the process of transporting light from the light source in the scene to the surfaces in the scene. Reflectance is what happens when the light reaches a surface: Some of it is absorbed (in computer graphics, we usually include absorption in the concept of *reflectance*) and some is bounced off in other directions.

Reflectance and illumination are related: global illumination, for instance, involves tracking the flow of light throughout a scene, including any and all surface interactions in the scene. The light reaching any given surface in a scene may have bounced many times off other surfaces. In real-time graphics, we may be forced to approximate global illumination, but even for direct illumination, a lighting model will frequently include effects that can be attributed to *both* illumination and reflectance.

In this chapter we will survey and discuss reflectance models that in some way are meant to approximate the appearance of physically realistic surfaces and materials. We will not focus on implementation here, just the mathematical theory. However, we have chosen reflectance models that happen to have some nice properties for real-time implementation, and will go into the details of several implementation techniques in later chapters.

Some lighting and reflectance models are based on physics, others were just made up out of thin air to "look right." Often the latter "made-up" models are called empirical models, but phenomological would be a better term. A phenomological model approximates the appearance of a phenomenon directly with a function that has approximately the right behavior. A phenomological model is not derived by analyzing root causes.

Phenomological models are important in computer graphics for historical reasons (they were the first models developed); because they are usually relatively easy to understand and implement; and because they often have been tuned for performance (or are simple enough to be fast). For instance, the phenomological Blinn-Phong model has been supported in hardware accelerators and the OpenGL API for a relatively long time. As a model of the physical process of reflection, it has some serious shortcomings, but it is easy to use, understand, and of course, it is already there.

More rigorous physically based models are also useful, and can be used to generate more interesting and accurate pictures than the basic phenomological models. Many of these more sophisticated models are actually not all that difficult to implement in real time, even using the limited kind and number of mathematical operations available on a graphics accelerator. We will present the basic concepts of physically based models and present and discuss some specific models. In practice, many practical reflectance models are hybrids with some phenomological factors and some physically based factors.

2.1 BRDFs and Lighting Models

When discussing physical reflection specifically, as opposed to non-photo-realistic shading, we will often use the BRDF (*Bidirectional Reflectance Distribution Function*). A BRDF f_r gives the ratio between the incoming irradiance E_i and outgoing radiance L_o at a single point $\mathbf{x}$ on a surface, as a function of both incoming (light) direction $\hat{\mathbf{l}}$ and outgoing (view) direction $\hat{\mathbf{v}}$:

$$f_r(\mathbf{x}; \hat{\mathbf{v}} \leftarrow \hat{\mathbf{l}}) \quad = \quad \frac{dL_o(\mathbf{x}; \hat{\mathbf{v}})}{dE_i(\mathbf{x}; \hat{\mathbf{l}})}.$$

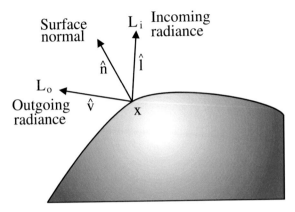

Figure 2.1. Local surface geometry for parameterization of the BRDF.

We can also express the BRDF in terms of incoming radiance L_i, rather than irradiance:

$$f_r(\mathbf{x}; \hat{\mathbf{v}} \leftarrow \hat{\mathbf{l}}) = \frac{dL_o(\mathbf{x}; \hat{\mathbf{v}})}{L_i(\mathbf{x}; \hat{\mathbf{l}}) \langle \hat{\mathbf{n}}, \hat{\mathbf{l}} \rangle \, d\omega(\hat{\mathbf{l}})}.$$

We will use the convention throughout this book that all vectors point *away* from the point on the surface being lighted. See Figure 2.1. Otherwise we would have to specify and remember which way each one goes, which would be a nuisance. This means that above, the flow of energy for $L_i(\mathbf{x}; \hat{\mathbf{l}})$ is actually in the direction of $-\hat{\mathbf{l}}$, whereas the flow of energy for $L_o(\mathbf{x}; \hat{\mathbf{v}})$ is in the direction of $\hat{\mathbf{v}}$. We also use the convention that $\hat{\mathbf{a}}$ is a unit-length vector (a "pure" direction) and $\vec{a}$ is a vector that may or may not have a unit length. Usually, if both forms appear together, this implies that $\hat{\mathbf{a}} = \text{norm}(\vec{a}) = \vec{a}/|\vec{a}|$. Finally, we will (mostly) show inner (dot) products using the notation $\langle \hat{\mathbf{a}}, \hat{\mathbf{b}} \rangle$. The notation $a \cdot b$ is occasionally used to disambiguate *scalar* multiplication where it otherwise might be confused with function application: $\cos \gamma \cdot F = (\cos(\gamma))(F)$. We will introduce more conventions in Section 2.4.

Local reflectance can be modeled with an integration against the incoming radiance at a point $\mathbf{x}$ and the BRDF. Formally, BRDFs can be used only inside such integrals:

$$L_o(\mathbf{x}; \hat{\mathbf{v}}) = \int_{\Omega(\hat{\mathbf{n}})} f_r(\mathbf{x}; \hat{\mathbf{v}} \leftarrow \hat{\mathbf{l}}) \, L_i(\mathbf{x}; \hat{\mathbf{l}}) \, \langle \hat{\mathbf{n}}, \hat{\mathbf{l}} \rangle \, d\omega(\hat{\mathbf{l}}). \tag{2.1}$$

This integral defines a mapping between the incoming radiance L_i in a hemisphere $\Omega(\hat{\mathbf{n}})$ above the reflection point (centered about the surface normal $\hat{\mathbf{n}}$) and the outgoing radiance L_o over the same hemisphere. The result of this integration, L_o, is a function that describes the radiance that travels away from point $\mathbf{x}$ in direction $\hat{\mathbf{v}}$.

This kind of mapping from one function (L_i) to another (L_o) is called a *functional operator*. In fact, this is a linear functional operator, since the output depends linearly on the input. The BRDF is the *kernel* of this operator. Think of a linear functional operator as a linear transformation and the kernel as the matrix that can be used to implement it. A BRDF is a kind of infinite-dimensional matrix that transforms an incoming irradiance function to an outgoing radiance function. Another way of thinking about the local reflectance integral is as a spherical convolution, and there is in fact some useful theory that backs up that interpretation [150].

A BRDF is not really a function itself, but a distribution or generalized function, sort of like a probability density. Like a probability density, a BRDF can contain impulses and other "special distributions" that make sense only inside integrals, but correspond to straightforward computational operations. For instance, a Dirac delta impulse $\delta(x)$ is a special distribution that when integrated against another function, corresponds to sampling the second function at a point. It is defined by this sampling process, but cannot itself be represented as a function, although it can be represented as a limit of a sequence of functions.

The dot product $\langle \hat{\mathbf{n}}, \hat{\mathbf{l}} \rangle$ in Equation 2.1 is required to convert between units, specifically from radiance to irradiance. These units arise from the geometry of light transport. Radiance and irradiance are standard units in radiometry. Understanding them is a big part of understanding light transport and the mathematical modeling of reflectance. It particular, it should be understood that this dot product is really part of the integral's measure, not the integrand. Sometimes in the literature you will see the "throughput" measure μ used instead, especially when light transport is given in point-to-point form:

$$
\begin{aligned}
d\mu(\mathbf{x}, \mathbf{y}) &= \frac{\langle \hat{\mathbf{n}}(\mathbf{x}), (\mathbf{y} - \mathbf{x}) \rangle \cdot \langle \hat{\mathbf{n}}(\mathbf{y}), (\mathbf{x} - \mathbf{y}) \rangle}{\langle \mathbf{y} - \mathbf{x}, \mathbf{x} - \mathbf{y} \rangle^2} \, dA(\mathbf{x}) \, dA(\mathbf{y}) \\
&= \frac{\cos\theta_x \cdot \cos\theta_y}{r^2} \, dA(\mathbf{x}) \, dA(\mathbf{y}) \\
&= \cos\theta_x \, dA(\mathbf{x}) \, d\omega(\hat{\mathbf{l}}),
\end{aligned}
$$

where $d\omega$ is the solid angle measure (which takes into account both the distance r to a source and the orientation of that source) and dA is the area measure.

Irradiance is the incoming radiance projected against the orientation of the surface. In other words, irradiance is the power density, per unit area, actually received by a surface:

$$E = \frac{d\Phi}{dA}.$$

Radiance is power density normalized by (relative to) the throughput, or rather, relative to the product of the projected area of the sending surface, the projected area of the receiving surface, and the square of the distance r between the two surfaces. As the throughput measure can be "factored" in a number of different ways, as shown above, there are a variety of seemingly different ways to define radiance that in fact all mean the same thing:

$$
\begin{aligned}
L &= \frac{d^2\Phi}{d\mu(\mathbf{x},\mathbf{y})} \\
&= \frac{d^2\Phi}{dA_\perp(\mathbf{x})\,d\omega(\mathbf{y})} \\
&= \frac{d^2\Phi}{dA(\mathbf{x})\,\langle\hat{\mathbf{n}}(\mathbf{x}),\hat{\mathbf{r}}\rangle\,d\omega(\mathbf{y})} \\
&= \frac{d^2\Phi}{d\omega(\mathbf{x})\,dA_\perp(\mathbf{y})} \\
&= \frac{d^2\Phi}{d\omega(\mathbf{x})\,dA(\mathbf{y})\,\langle\hat{\mathbf{n}}(\mathbf{y}),-\hat{\mathbf{r}}\rangle},
\end{aligned}
$$

where $d\omega$ again stands for the solid angle measure and $\hat{\mathbf{r}} = \text{norm}\,(\mathbf{y}-\mathbf{x})$. The solid angle measure gives the area covered on a unit sphere by an image of the source from the point it is viewed. This accounts for both the orientation of a source and its distance.

Such normalization by distance and orientation makes the actual value of the radiance *independent* of these considerations: Radiance is constant along a ray travelling in a vacuum. It is, effectively, what we see when we "look" at a surface. No matter how far away a surface is, for instance, it appears to be the same color when we observe it *at a point*—or rather, along a single specific view direction, or ray.[1] However, the *total* energy received from a surface will depend on how large it seems; in other words, its solid angle, and this solid angle, will decrease with distance.

The inner products in the reflectance integral, or the throughput measure, can be explained as follows. If a surface faces incoming light squarely,

---

[1] In a vacuum, anyway. Including the effects of participating media is something else; you need to solve a differential equation along the ray to update the radiance as it travels through the medium.

the full power of that light is captured and available for reflection. The more the surface tilts away from the direction of the flow of energy, the less power it receives, therefore the less it can reflect. When the surface normal is perpendicular to the flow of energy, the surface receives nothing and can reflect nothing. This variation can be modeled using a cosine of the incident angle, the angle between the normal and the incoming direction, which can be computed with a dot product. This is the source of Lambert's law for diffuse surfaces. Diffuse surfaces actually have a constant BRDF; the cosine in the Lambertian lighting model comes from the *geometry*, not the reflectance.

When the dot product $\langle \hat{n}, \hat{l} \rangle$ is negative the BRDF is irrelevant. A surface can't reflect light that comes from underneath. That's called "transmission" (and might be modelled with a BTDF, or *Bidirectional Transmission Distribution Function*, which we won't get into much). Frequently you will see the cosine term clamped to zero when it goes negative. This is equivalent to ignoring incoming radiance below the horizon of the surface and convenient computationally, and so is common practice in real-time implementations. Usually this clamping will be taken for granted and we will write down formulas for BRDFs that are nonzero for directions below the horizon of the surface. It is understood that these parts of the BRDF model are to be ignored or clamped to zero. Yet another way of putting this is that the integration is only over the upper hemisphere, and the outgoing radiance is also only supposed to be seen in the upper hemisphere. In theory, therefore, it should not matter what values the lighting model computes below the horizon. However, in real-time applications there are approximations that cause this to happen. For instance, both Phong shading and bump mapping force us to shade with "normals" that are not the true geometric normals of the surface, and it is possible in practice that this may cause lighting models to be evaluated in regions where they should not be. Implementations therefore should check for viewing and lighting vectors below the horizon and clamp the BRDF to zero or some suitable extrapolated value, depending on the visual needs of the application. Hard clamping can look bad, so sometimes a soft clamp is used instead. Sometimes we make approximations that extend the integral below the horizon. For instance, this happens in Phong lobe environment-map prefiltering, to be discussed in Chapter 7.

It is important to recognize that BRDFs are an approximation to reality. Light hitting a surface rarely leaves again from the exact point at which it arrived. Many interesting materials, such as skin, marble, and plastic, are in fact somewhat transparent and the light penetrates slightly under the surface, bounces around, and comes back out a small distance away [81]. However, the BRDF is a reasonable approximation to many reflectance processes if you are far enough away from an object, and has a big advantage: you can mostly[2] separate shape from reflectance if reflectance is purely local.

2.2 Physical Plausibility

A BRDF has to satisfy some basic physical properties to be physically valid. For instance, since light power cannot physically be negative, being proportional to the square of the amplitude of the electric field, neither can the BRDF. Two additional conditions, conservation and reciprocity, are also important because failure to adhere to these physical constraints can break certain illumination algorithms. They are also good checks to see if a reflectance model is at least a reasonable approximation to reality. When these three properties are satisfied, we say a BRDF is *physically plausible*. Just because a BRDF is nonnegative and satisfies energy conservation and reciprocity does not guarantee that it is physically *possible*, just that it is *plausible*. For instance, the Lambertian (diffuse) lighting model satisfies these constraints, but is in fact physically impossible; it leads to a discontinuous electric field, which is not permitted by the laws of nature.

A BRDF must be *conservative*: it must result in a reflectance process that conserves energy. Intuitively, reflectance processes can only redirect energy, not create it. For certain illumination algorithms, this property is crucial: iterative global illumination algorithms, for instance, may fail to converge if surfaces amplify the light that fall on them. A light transport solver might end up sending the light around in a loop, amplifying it each time, increasing the power each time, forever. This is not a numerical problem; if surfaces amplify light, a stable solution simply may not exist.[3]

Some reflectance processes may appear to create energy, such as fluorescence. Such a process is just transforming invisible ultraviolet energy to visible energy. A BRDF, as a formal model, does not include fluorescence; we would have to add an incoming and outgoing wavelength and another integration over incoming wavelength. We don't do this because it would

---

[2]Shape can still exert a local effect on reflectance, for instance, via curvature. But these parameters can always be computed with local differential operators and passed to a shader. With a BRDF model, reflectance is still fundamentally local, and depends only on the properties of the surface at a single point.

[3]Many algorithms for global light transport are related to algorithms for neutron transport. However, in constrast with light transport, neutron/matter interactions *can* amplify neutron flux, and certain neutron transport situations are actually engineered on purpose to have non-convergent physical solutions. They're called "nuclear weapons".

be too expensive and complex to deal with in practice. Fortunately, fluorescence is easily modeled with a hidden illumination process to distribute ultraviolet radiation and convert it into fixed-power sources of visible illumination in the scene [178]. Many common materials, such as almost all man-made dyes, are fluorescent, and daylight has a lot of ultraviolet radiation, so this is an important effect.

Secondly, BRDFs must result in reflectance processes that are *reciprocal*. This basically means that if the light flow were somehow made to reverse direction, it would transfer the same amount of power backwards as forwards. It is sufficient to define BRDFs that are symmetrical with respect to incoming and outgoing directions; exchanging the incoming direction vector $\hat{\mathbf{l}}$ and the view vector $\hat{\mathbf{v}}$ should give the same value and/or symbolic form for the BRDF. Certain common phenomological reflectance models, such as the Phong and Blinn-Phong reflectance models, are not in fact reciprocal.

2.2.1 Energy Conservation

To define energy conservation formally, we have to compare the power reaching a surface with the power leaving it. The ratio of these is known as the hemispherical reflectance, and can be computed as follows:

$$H(\mathbf{x}; \hat{\mathbf{l}}) \quad = \quad \int_{\Omega(\hat{\mathbf{n}})} f_r(\mathbf{x}; \hat{\mathbf{v}} \leftarrow \hat{\mathbf{l}}) \langle \hat{\mathbf{n}}, \hat{\mathbf{v}} \rangle \, d\omega(\hat{\mathbf{v}}). \tag{2.2}$$

In contrast with the local reflectance integral given in Equation 2.1, to compute the hemispherical reflectance we are integrating over the *outgoing* direction and scaling the BRDF by the inner product of the *outgoing* direction with the normal. In other words, we are using the outgoing throughput measure.

In the reflectance integral, we use $\langle \hat{\mathbf{n}}, \hat{\mathbf{l}} \rangle$ to convert incoming radiance to incoming irradiance. Here, we use $\langle \hat{\mathbf{n}}, \hat{\mathbf{v}} \rangle$ to convert outgoing radiance to outgoing irradiance, so that the value inside the integral is a ratio of differential incoming irradiance to differential outgoing irradiance. The integral computes the total power flowing outwards over the hemisphere around point $\mathbf{x}$, relative to the power arriving from direction $\hat{\mathbf{l}}$. The value of $H(\mathbf{x}; \hat{\mathbf{l}})$ must be less than one for all incoming direcions $\hat{\mathbf{l}}$ over the hemisphere $\Omega(\hat{\mathbf{n}})$ to guarantee that the BRDF will not violate conservation of energy.

2.2.2 Reciprocity

Maxwell's equations, which describe electromagnetic radiation and so light, have solutions that propagate backward in time as well as forward. In fact, one of the more interesting mysteries of physics is the existence in Maxwell's equations of solutions for electromagnetic radiation that flows from the future to the past, the so-called advanced solutions.

What the symmetrical form of these equations means in practice is that in order to have a particular power transfer in one direction, we must have the *same* power transfer for light flowing in the opposite direction. This is called the Helmholtz reciprocity condition, or reciprocity for short. To be consistent with this condition, the BRDF must be symmetrical:

$$f_r(\mathbf{x}; \hat{\mathbf{v}} \leftarrow \hat{\mathbf{l}}) = f_r(\mathbf{x}; \hat{\mathbf{l}} \leftarrow \hat{\mathbf{v}}).$$

This symmetry is especially important for algorithms that try to solve light transport problems by working both backward and forward, for instance, the combination of photon mapping "shooting" light out from light sources and of ray tracing "gathering" light into the eye. If BRDFs are not reciprocal, implementation of such hybrid algorithms have to be very careful to give the arguments to BRDFs in the correct order, or they will get inconsistent results.

Common phenomological lighting models, such as the Phong lighting model, are not reciprocal, and if a renderer supports procedural shaders, there is nothing stopping a user from defining a nonsymmetrical model. More recently defined physically based lighting models are usually reciprocal. However, renderers should be written assuming that BRDFs used in practice might not be symmetric. A reciprocity failure in general is less serious than a energy conservation failure. A renderer can be written to tolerate a nonreciprocal BRDF, but failure to conserve energy may cause global illumination algorithms to fail.

The reader may be thinking: "I'm doing real-time rendering, but global illumination is not real-time, so I don't have to worry about all this stuff." If this is the case, the reader is using insufficient imagination. Technology marches on, and real-time global illumination algorithms and systems supporting them are on the horizon.

For example, consider the technique of *instant radiosity* [88]. Such an algorithm has problems with dynamic range on current accelerators, but these limitations are likely to go away soon (floating-point fragment shaders, textures, and buffers are part of DX9) and similar algorithms can be imagined. Hardware-based algorithms have also been developed to simulate small-scale multiple scattering (global illumination) effects on bump maps to obtain better reflection models that capture these effects

[73]. However, these simulations must start with a physically plausible microscale reflectance model. It should even be possible to implement (possibly selective) path tracing on a programmable graphics accelerator in the near future. It would be best not to develop too many bad habits!

2.3 Isotropy and Anisotropy

The discussion so far has involved only abstract direction vectors, particularly $\hat{\mathbf{l}}$, $\hat{\mathbf{v}}$, and $\hat{\mathbf{n}}$. But to fully define the BRDF, you must pick a frame of reference on the surface—a set of axes to use as a common coordinate system for all three vectors. The BRDF is actually defined as a function of these vectors expressed in a surface-relative coordinate system.

A common choice for a surface-relative coordinate system puts $\hat{\mathbf{n}}$ along the z-coordinate axis, but what about the other two axes? How should the BRDF be oriented *about* the vector $\hat{\mathbf{n}}$, and does it even matter? For many BRDFs, it doesn't matter. They are called *isotropic*, because the reflection is the same for all orientations about $\hat{\mathbf{n}}$. For example, if you look at the cover of this book and spin it around its surface normal, the shapes of the highlights and overall reflectance don't change.

But other BRDFs do have some dependence on the orientation of the surface about its normal. These are known as *anisotropic* BRDFs. Examples include brushed metal, fabric (especially satin, but others as well to a greater or lesser extent), compact discs, or the formerly common example of vinyl records. Figure 2.2 gives an example; see also Figures 6.4, 6.5, and 6.6. The outgoing radiance L_o will change as you spin a piece of anisotropic material around its surface normal even if $\hat{\mathbf{v}}$, $\hat{\mathbf{l}}$, $\hat{\mathbf{n}}$ all stay the same relative to one another.

Figure 2.2. Anisotropic BRDF with fixed light and view as surface rotates.

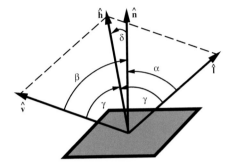

Figure 2.3.   Vectors and angles used to describe isotropic reflection models. These names are used throughout this text: $\hat{\mathbf{l}}$ points towards source of incoming light, $\hat{\mathbf{v}}$ points towards observer, $\hat{\mathbf{h}} = \text{norm}\,(\hat{\mathbf{v}} + \hat{\mathbf{l}})$, $\cos\alpha = \langle\hat{\mathbf{l}}, \hat{\mathbf{n}}\rangle$, $\cos\beta = \langle\hat{\mathbf{v}}, \hat{\mathbf{n}}\rangle$, $\cos\gamma = \langle\hat{\mathbf{v}}, \hat{\mathbf{h}}\rangle = \langle\hat{\mathbf{l}}, \hat{\mathbf{h}}\rangle$, and $\cos\delta = \langle\hat{\mathbf{h}}, \hat{\mathbf{n}}\rangle$.

2.4   Surface Coordinate Conventions

Before defining specific reflectance models we will have to introduce a few more basic conventions and definitions, the concept of the surface frame and surface-relative coordinates, and some important mathematical relationships. We will define in particular several standard direction vectors and angles, most of which are shown in Figure 2.3.

An anisotropic reflectance model requires at every point on a surface, in addition to a normal, some indication of the orientation about that normal. This is accomplished by providing two surface tangents, $\hat{\mathbf{t}}$ and $\hat{\mathbf{s}}$. Together $[\hat{\mathbf{t}}, \hat{\mathbf{s}}, \hat{\mathbf{n}}]$ should form a right-handed surface frame with $\hat{\mathbf{n}}$ in the same direction as $\hat{\mathbf{t}} \times \hat{\mathbf{s}}$.

A surface frame is also necessary for bump mapping. For bump mapping, $\hat{\mathbf{t}}$ and $\hat{\mathbf{s}}$ give the directions in which we should perturb the normal based on values stored in the bump map, or alternatively we can represent actual normals with respect to the local surface frame:

$$\hat{\mathbf{n}}'(u, v) \quad = \quad n'_x(u, v)\hat{\mathbf{t}} + n'_y(u, v)\hat{\mathbf{s}} + n'_z(u, v)\hat{\mathbf{n}}.$$

Then we would simply use the perturbed normal in the lighting model. Bump mapping is discussed in more detail in Chapter 3 and 6.

We will call the tangent vector $\hat{\mathbf{t}}$ the *primary tangent* and the tangent vector $\hat{\mathbf{s}}$ the *secondary tangent*. Often $\hat{\mathbf{s}}$ is called the *binormal*, after a similar vector in the Frenet frame defined for curves. However, the binormal in the Frenet frame, when used according to its exact definition for curves, actually gives a left-handed frame! To avoid inconsistent usage and confusion we therefore avoid this terminology. The term *bitangent* could be used instead, although this is not standard terminology. It makes sense, though: for curves, the Frenet frame *binormal* is in fact a second normal selected out of a plane of normals; for a surface, the vector $\hat{\mathbf{s}}$ is a second tangent selected out of a plane of tangents.

We define the spherical coordinates of an arbitrary unit vector $\hat{\mathbf{a}}$ as the angles θ_a and ϕ_a, called the elevation and azimuth angles respectively. In the case of an orthonormal frame we can compute the sines and cosines of these angles in terms of inner products:

$$
\begin{aligned}
\cos\theta_a &= \langle \hat{\mathbf{n}}, \hat{\mathbf{a}} \rangle, \\
\vec{\mathbf{a}}' &= \hat{\mathbf{a}} - \hat{\mathbf{n}}\langle \hat{\mathbf{n}}, \hat{\mathbf{a}} \rangle, \\
\hat{\mathbf{a}}' &= \mathrm{norm}\,(\vec{\mathbf{a}}') \\
&= \frac{\vec{\mathbf{a}}'}{\sqrt{1 - \langle \hat{\mathbf{n}}, \hat{\mathbf{a}} \rangle^2}}, \\
\cos\phi_a &= \langle \hat{\mathbf{t}}, \hat{\mathbf{a}}' \rangle, \\
&= \frac{\langle \hat{\mathbf{t}}, \hat{\mathbf{a}} \rangle}{\sqrt{1 - \langle \hat{\mathbf{n}}, \hat{\mathbf{a}} \rangle^2}}, \\
\sin\phi_a &= \langle \hat{\mathbf{s}}, \hat{\mathbf{a}}' \rangle \\
&= \frac{\langle \hat{\mathbf{s}}, \hat{\mathbf{a}} \rangle}{\sqrt{1 - \langle \hat{\mathbf{n}}, \hat{\mathbf{a}} \rangle^2}}.
\end{aligned}
$$

The angle ϕ_a is the angle of the vector $\hat{\mathbf{a}}$ with respect to the tangent vectors $\hat{\mathbf{t}}$ and $\hat{\mathbf{s}}$ after being projected onto the tangent plane defined by these two vectors. When $\theta_a = 0$, and the corresponding direction vector $\hat{\mathbf{a}}$ lines up with the surface normal $\hat{\mathbf{n}}$, we say $\hat{\mathbf{a}}$ has *normal incidence*.

Computing a vector from spherical coordinates, fortunately, is easier. Given an orthonormal frame $[\hat{\mathbf{t}}, \hat{\mathbf{s}}, \hat{\mathbf{n}}]$ and spherical coordinates (θ_w, ϕ_w), we can compute the corresponding unit vector $\hat{\mathbf{w}}$ as follows:

$$
\begin{aligned}
\hat{\mathbf{w}} &= \sin\theta_w \cdot \cos\phi_w \cdot \hat{\mathbf{t}} + \sin\theta_w \cdot \sin\phi_w \cdot \hat{\mathbf{s}} + \cos\theta_w \cdot \hat{\mathbf{n}} \\
&= w_t \hat{\mathbf{t}} + w_s \hat{\mathbf{s}} + w_n \hat{\mathbf{n}}.
\end{aligned}
$$

Here, (w_t, w_s, w_n) are the coordinates of $\hat{\mathbf{w}}$ with respect to the local surface frame $[\hat{\mathbf{t}}, \hat{\mathbf{s}}, \hat{\mathbf{n}}]$. We can write the change of coordinates from surface frame to world frame as

$$
\hat{\mathbf{w}} = [\hat{\mathbf{t}}, \hat{\mathbf{s}}, \hat{\mathbf{n}}] \begin{bmatrix} w_t \\ w_s \\ w_n \end{bmatrix}
$$

if we treat $[\hat{\mathbf{t}}, \hat{\mathbf{s}}, \hat{\mathbf{n}}]$ as a matrix with columns $\hat{\mathbf{t}}$, $\hat{\mathbf{s}}$, and $\hat{\mathbf{n}}$ (or a row vector with these elements) and the coefficient sequence $[w_t, w_s, w_n]^T$ as a column vector. We can also compute the coordinates with a similar matrix-vector product by inverting the above:

$$
\begin{aligned}
w_t &= \langle \hat{\mathbf{w}}, \hat{\mathbf{t}} \rangle, \\
w_s &= \langle \hat{\mathbf{w}}, \hat{\mathbf{s}} \rangle, \\
w_n &= \langle \hat{\mathbf{w}}, \hat{\mathbf{n}} \rangle, \\
\begin{bmatrix} w_t \\ w_s \\ w_n \end{bmatrix} &= [\hat{\mathbf{t}}, \hat{\mathbf{s}}, \hat{\mathbf{n}}]^T \, \hat{\mathbf{w}}.
\end{aligned}
$$

This symmetry is actually valid only if the frame $[\hat{\mathbf{t}}, \hat{\mathbf{s}}, \hat{\mathbf{n}}]$ is orthonormal, since the transpose of an orthonormal matrix is its inverse.

The change of variables required to convert an integration with respect to solid angle into an integration with respect to elevation and azimuth angles is given by the following:

$$
d\omega(\hat{\mathbf{w}}) = \sin\theta_w \, d\theta_w \, d\phi_w.
$$

For the upper hemisphere, the integration should be over $\theta_w \in [0, \pi/2]$ and $\phi_w \in [0, 2\pi]$. For the complete sphere, the integration should be over $\theta_w \in [0, \pi]$ and $\phi_w \in [0, 2\pi]$.

The half-vector $\hat{\mathbf{h}}$ is the direction vector midway between $\hat{\mathbf{v}}$ and $\hat{\mathbf{l}}$:

$$
\hat{\mathbf{h}} = \mathrm{norm}(\hat{\mathbf{v}} + \hat{\mathbf{l}}).
$$

Since $\hat{\mathbf{h}}$ is by definition directly between $\hat{\mathbf{v}}$ and $\hat{\mathbf{l}}$, it lies on the same plane as these two vectors and the following dot products are equivalent:

$$
\langle \hat{\mathbf{v}}, \hat{\mathbf{h}} \rangle = \langle \hat{\mathbf{l}}, \hat{\mathbf{h}} \rangle.
$$

We will use

$$
\begin{aligned}
\cos\gamma &= \langle \hat{\mathbf{v}}, \hat{\mathbf{h}} \rangle \\
&= \langle \hat{\mathbf{l}}, \hat{\mathbf{h}} \rangle
\end{aligned}
$$

in place of these dot products. This convention will help to point out symmetries in BRDFs that arise as the result of reciprocity. As a mnemonic, note that the symbol "γ" is (sort of) left-right symmetrical.

In addition, we will define the cosines of the following angles in terms of their corresponding inner products:

$$
\begin{aligned}
\cos \alpha &= \langle \hat{\mathbf{l}}, \hat{\mathbf{n}} \rangle, \\
\cos \beta &= \langle \hat{\mathbf{v}}, \hat{\mathbf{n}} \rangle, \\
\cos \delta &= \langle \hat{\mathbf{h}}, \hat{\mathbf{n}} \rangle.
\end{aligned}
$$

For mnemonics, remember that we *first* start with the incoming light at angle α, then *second* the light leaves the surface with angle β. The angle δ measures the *difference* between the normal $\hat{\mathbf{n}}$ and the normal of a perfect mirror $\hat{\mathbf{h}}$. These angles are also diagrammed in Figure 2.3, which we will refer to when necessary.

2.5 Basic Reflection Models

The most basic reflection models are for diffuse and pure specular (mirror) reflection. We also discuss how to compute the mirror direction and the Fresnel term that modulates physical specular reflections.

2.5.1 Diffuse Reflection

Diffuse reflection scatters light energy equally in all directions. A physically plausible BRDF for diffuse reflection is given by

$$
f_r(\mathbf{x}; \hat{\mathbf{v}} \leftarrow \hat{\mathbf{l}}) = \frac{k_d}{\pi}
$$

with $k_d \leq 1$. More generally, $k_d(\lambda)$ is a reflectance spectrum which is nowhere greater than one, or a color representation equivalent to such a spectrum. In the future we will usually just define reflectance models in terms of scalar quantities, with the understanding that in practice, wavelength dependence can be introduced by making appropriate factors and parameters in the models wavelength-dependent (e.g., by replacing scalar quantities with red, green and blue components).

The division by π is required here to ensure the hemispherical reflectivity is less than one for all incident angles.

Diffuse surfaces are view-independent, which is a significant advantage in certain contexts. For instance, global illumination can be precomputed and represented as a single color value at every point in a scene. A view-dependent solution would require a function to be stored at every point. Under direct lighting there is still some shading variation when using a diffuse shading model, due to the $\langle \hat{\mathbf{n}}, \hat{\mathbf{l}} \rangle$ factor in the reflectance integral. Lambert's cosine law comes from use of projected area to convert radiance to irradiance; it is not represented in the BRDF, but is present as a factor in *all* lighting models.

2.5.2   Specular Reflection

A pure specular reflection represents the reflection off a mirrored or highly polished surface. Specular reflection is basically a deterministic process. The outgoing radiance is based on a sample of the incoming radiance from one direction: the mirror direction.

To determine the mirror direction $\hat{\mathbf{r}}_{\hat{\mathbf{n}}}(\hat{\mathbf{v}})$ for a specular reflection, given a particular incoming direction $\hat{\mathbf{v}}$ and the surface normal $\hat{\mathbf{n}}$, we can use a *Householder transformation matrix* $\mathsf{R}_{\hat{\mathbf{n}}}$:

$$
\begin{aligned}
\hat{\mathbf{r}}_{\hat{\mathbf{n}}}(\hat{\mathbf{v}}) &= 2\hat{\mathbf{n}}\langle \hat{\mathbf{n}}, \hat{\mathbf{v}} \rangle - \hat{\mathbf{v}} \\
&= (2\hat{\mathbf{n}}\hat{\mathbf{n}}^T - \mathsf{I})\hat{\mathbf{v}} \\
&= \mathsf{R}_{\hat{\mathbf{n}}}\hat{\mathbf{v}}; \\
\mathsf{R}_{\hat{\mathbf{n}}} &= 2\hat{\mathbf{n}}\hat{\mathbf{n}}^T - \mathsf{I}.
\end{aligned}
$$

The matrix $\mathsf{R}_{\hat{\mathbf{n}}}$ is symmetric and independent of $\hat{\mathbf{v}}$—in essence, it's an elegant way to derive a matrix for a 180 degree rotation about $\hat{\mathbf{n}}$:

$$
\begin{aligned}
\mathsf{R}_{\hat{\mathbf{n}}} &= \begin{bmatrix} 2n_x^2 - 1 & 2n_x n_y & 2n_x n_z \\ 2n_x n_y & 2n_y^2 - 1 & 2n_y n_z \\ 2n_x n_z & 2n_y n_z & 2n_z^2 - 1 \end{bmatrix} \\
&= \mathsf{R}_{\hat{\mathbf{n}}}^T.
\end{aligned}
$$

Modeling pure specular reflection using a BRDF-based reflection integral requires the use of the spherical BRDF delta $\Delta(\vec{\mathbf{v}})$, which has the property that

$$
g(\hat{\mathbf{v}}) = \int_{\Omega(\hat{\mathbf{n}})} \Delta(\hat{\mathbf{v}} - \hat{\mathbf{l}})\, g(\hat{\mathbf{l}})\, \langle \hat{\mathbf{n}}, \hat{\mathbf{l}} \rangle\, d\omega(\hat{\mathbf{l}}).
$$

The above integral is simply a definition of deterministic sampling suitable for use in a BRDF representing perfect mirror reflection. We have chosen to define the spherical BRDF delta in a way that does not require normalization factors to account for the $\langle \hat{\mathbf{n}}, \hat{\mathbf{l}} \rangle$ term; you should be aware that other references may define the reflectance delta differently. The other way of thinking about this is that we have defined the Dirac delta with respect to the throughput measure rather than the solid angle measure.

Using this particular definition of the reflectance delta, the BRDF for specular reflection is given by

$$f_r(\mathbf{x}; \hat{\mathbf{v}} \leftarrow \hat{\mathbf{l}}) = \Delta(R_{\hat{\mathbf{n}}} \hat{\mathbf{v}} - \hat{\mathbf{l}})$$
$$= \Delta(\hat{\mathbf{r}}_{\hat{\mathbf{n}}}(\hat{\mathbf{v}}) - \hat{\mathbf{l}}).$$

2.5.3 Fresnel Effect

In reality, specular reflection is subject to the Fresnel effect, which leads to stronger specular reflections off polished surfaces at glancing angles, and stronger transmission into surfaces at normal incidence.

The Fresnel effect is a direct consequence of the electromagnetic nature of radiation, specifically the fact that the electric field cannot be discontinuous, even when it meets a discontinuity in refractive index (density) at a surface boundary [22, 49].

Suppose we have a polished surface with a refractive index of n_1 above the surface and a refractive index of n_2 below the surface. This gives a relative refractive index of $n = n_1/n_2$.

The Fresnel factor actually both depends on and influences the polarization of light. Polarization is the orientation of the electric field vector with respect to the surface. It is the Fresnel effect that tends to polarize outgoing light after a specular reflection even if the incoming light was unpolarized.

The Fresnel factor computes the fraction of power reflected as opposed to transmitted *through* a polished interface between two materials. Call the plane formed by $\hat{\mathbf{n}}$ and $\hat{\mathbf{l}}$ the *plane of incidence*. Define the following:

$r^{\perp}$: Ratio of amplitudes of reflected to incoming electric fields perpendicular to the plane of incidence.

$r^{\|}$: Ratio of amplitudes of reflected to incoming electric fields parallel to the plane of incidence.

$t^{\perp}$: Ratio of amplitudes of transmitted to incoming electric fields perpendicular to the plane of incidence.

$t^{\|}$: Ratio of amplitudes of transmitted to incoming electric fields parallel to the plane of incidence.

Let θ_q be the angle, relative to $-\hat{\mathbf{n}}$, of the refracted specular ray $\hat{\mathbf{q}}$ given by Snell's Law. Recall that we defined $\cos \alpha = \langle \hat{\mathbf{l}}, \hat{\mathbf{n}} \rangle$:

$$n_1 \sin \alpha = n_2 \sin \theta_q,$$

$$\hat{\mathbf{q}} = \hat{\mathbf{n}} \left(\frac{n_1}{n_2} \cos \alpha - \sqrt{1 - \left(\frac{n_1}{n_2}\right)^2 (1 - \cos^2 \alpha)} \right) - \frac{n_1}{n_2} \hat{\mathbf{l}},$$

$$\cos \theta_q = \langle -\hat{\mathbf{n}}, \hat{\mathbf{q}} \rangle.$$

If the value under the square root is negative, which can happen only if $n_1 > n_2$, then total internal reflection has occured and there can be no transmitted energy.

Assume we are reflecting off a surface with refractive index n_2 from a medium with refractive index n_1. Then:

$$r^{\perp} = \frac{n_1 \cos \alpha - n_2 \cos \theta_q}{n_1 \cos \alpha + n_2 \cos \theta_q},$$

$$r^{||} = \frac{n_2 \cos \alpha - n_1 \cos \theta_q}{n_2 \cos \alpha + n_1 \cos \theta_q},$$

$$t^{\perp} = \frac{2n_1 \cos \alpha}{n_1 \cos \alpha + n_2 \cos \theta_q},$$

$$t^{||} = \frac{2n_1 \cos \alpha}{n_2 \cos \alpha + n_1 \cos \theta_q}.$$

Because these terms are different for parallel and transverse polarizations, both transmitted and reflected light are polarized.

The power carried by an electromagnetic wave is proportional to the square of its amplitude. For refraction, the power density is increased by the reduced angle over which refracted ray can vary, when refracting into a denser medium. In graphics, we usually assume unpolarized light, which will have a uniform random orientation (uniform electric field amplitude in all directions perpendicular to the direction of propagation). Under the assumption of unpolarized incoming light, we can define the average fraction of reflected and transmitted power:

$$R_s = \frac{(r^{\perp})^2 + (r^{||})^2}{2},$$

$$T_s = \left(\frac{n_2 \cos \alpha}{n_1 \cos \theta_q}\right) \left(\frac{(t^{\perp})^2 + (t^{||})^2}{2}\right).$$

The outgoing light will be polarized, but if we are computing only direct illumination (one bounce from an unpolarized light source into a virtual camera which we can assume is insensitive to polarization) we can ignore this.

The Fresnel factor does *not* include absorption, so we will have

$$R_s + T_s = 1.$$

However, for many surfaces, the refracted ray is absorbed almost immediately (especially in metals). For others, the refracted ray is scattered by subsurface phenomena and comes out as "diffuse" reflection. Such "diffuse" reflection will not be constant; it should in fact be stronger at normal incidence, although still symmetrical about the normal if sufficient scattering takes place below the surface.

The Fresnel factor applies only to mirror-like specular reflections. Sometimes, however, we will be given both $\hat{\mathbf{v}}$ and $\hat{\mathbf{l}}$ and will need to compute the Fresnel factor for them. What this means is that we must find the normal of a mirror surface that reflects $\hat{\mathbf{l}}$ in the direction of $\hat{\mathbf{v}}$ and compute the factor for that surface orientation.

Recall that we defined $\cos\gamma = \langle \hat{\mathbf{v}}, \hat{\mathbf{h}} \rangle = \langle \hat{\mathbf{l}}, \hat{\mathbf{h}} \rangle$ with $\hat{\mathbf{h}} = \text{norm}\,(\hat{\mathbf{v}} + \hat{\mathbf{l}})$. The half-vector $\hat{\mathbf{h}}$ is the orientation of a perfect mirror that reflects light from direction $\hat{\mathbf{l}}$ into the direction of $\hat{\mathbf{v}}$ and vice versa.

The Fresnel reflectance factor can be reformulated as follows:

$$
\begin{aligned}
c &= \cos\gamma, \\
n &= \frac{n_1}{n_2}, \\
g^2 &= n^2 + c^2 - 1, \\
F(c) &= \frac{(g-c)^2}{2(g+c)^2}\left(1 + \frac{(c(g+c)-1)^2}{(c(g-c)+1)^2}\right).
\end{aligned}
\tag{2.3}
$$

We can also use $F(\langle \hat{\mathbf{l}}, \hat{\mathbf{n}} \rangle) = F(\cos\alpha)$ or $F(\langle \hat{\mathbf{v}}, \hat{\mathbf{n}} \rangle) = F(\cos\beta)$ with this same formula if $\hat{\mathbf{l}} = \hat{\mathbf{r}}_{\hat{\mathbf{n}}}(\hat{\mathbf{v}})$, which of course also implies that $\hat{\mathbf{v}} = \hat{\mathbf{r}}_{\hat{\mathbf{n}}}(\hat{\mathbf{l}})$, $\hat{\mathbf{n}} = \hat{\mathbf{h}}$, and $\cos\gamma = \cos\beta = \cos\alpha$.

The function $F(\cos\gamma)$ gives the variation away from the specular direction of the unpolarized average reflectance fraction. Let R_s be fraction of reflectance in the specular direction at normal incidence. This is a special case of the above; in this case the Fresnel factor is a function only of the relative refractive index:

$$
R_s = \left(\frac{n-1}{n+1}\right)^2.
$$

Since this value can be measured, we can use it to estimate the relative refractive index n of a real surface. The Fresnel term is wavelength-dependent since the relative index of refraction is usually wavelength-dependent. In practice, we often approximate the relative refractive index with a constant.

Frequently, the full Fresnel term is too expensive to compute in real-time applications. Schlick suggests the following approximation [157]:

$$
F(\cos\gamma) = R_s + (1 - R_s)(1 - \cos\gamma)^5.
$$

The approximation error in Schlick's approximation is less than the approximation error in going from polarized to unpolarized light, so in practice it is nearly as good as the full formula. This approximation also sometimes shows up in lighting models. When it does, you can replace the approximation with the full version if you are tabulating the function and real-time performance is not an issue.

2.6 Phenomological Reflectance Models

2.6.1 Phong Model

The original or "classic" Phong lighting model [141] is given as a sum of a diffuse part and a specular part. It is usually defined in terms of a point light source, and includes $1/r^2$ attenuation factors. We will give it directly in terms of radiance:

$$L_o(\mathbf{x}; \hat{\mathbf{v}}) = \left(k_d \langle \hat{\mathbf{n}}, \hat{\mathbf{l}} \rangle + k_s \langle \hat{\mathbf{r}}_{\hat{\mathbf{n}}}(\hat{\mathbf{v}}), \hat{\mathbf{l}} \rangle^q \right) L_i(\mathbf{x}; \hat{\mathbf{l}}).$$

We usually add the constraints $k_d \leq 1$ and $k_s \leq 1$ in practice, although in fact these constraints are *not* sufficient to ensure energy conservation.

The Phong lighting model can be expressed as a BRDF-like distribution:

$$f_r(\mathbf{x}; \hat{\mathbf{v}} \leftarrow \hat{\mathbf{l}}) = k_d + k_s \langle \hat{\mathbf{r}}_{\hat{\mathbf{n}}}(\hat{\mathbf{v}}), \hat{\mathbf{l}} \rangle^q / \langle \hat{\mathbf{n}}, \hat{\mathbf{l}} \rangle.$$

We can replace $\hat{\mathbf{r}}_{\hat{\mathbf{n}}}(\hat{\mathbf{v}})$ with the Householder transformation $\mathsf{R}_{\hat{\mathbf{n}}}$ and simplify:

$$\begin{aligned} f_r(\mathbf{x}; \hat{\mathbf{v}} \leftarrow \hat{\mathbf{l}}) &= k_d + k_s \langle \mathsf{R}_{\hat{\mathbf{n}}} \hat{\mathbf{v}}, \hat{\mathbf{l}} \rangle^q / \langle \hat{\mathbf{n}}, \hat{\mathbf{l}} \rangle \\ &= k_d + k_s (\hat{\mathbf{v}}^T \mathsf{R}_{\hat{\mathbf{n}}}^T \hat{\mathbf{l}})^q / \langle \hat{\mathbf{n}}, \hat{\mathbf{l}} \rangle \\ &= k_d + k_s (\hat{\mathbf{v}}^T \mathsf{R}_{\hat{\mathbf{n}}} \hat{\mathbf{l}})^q / \langle \hat{\mathbf{n}}, \hat{\mathbf{l}} \rangle. \end{aligned}$$

We can see from the appearance of the $\langle \hat{\mathbf{n}}, \hat{\mathbf{l}} \rangle$ term in the denominator of the specular term that the classic Phong model is not reciprocal. It is also not energy-conserving. Consider the diffuse term alone; it lacks the $1/\pi$ normalization factor. The problem is more than a simple scale factor will fix; the specular term is also too reflective at glancing angles, but not specular enough. However, the Phong model does have some useful properties. First, the cosine lobe $(\hat{\mathbf{v}}^T \mathsf{R}_{\hat{\mathbf{n}}} \hat{\mathbf{l}})^q$ is itself symmetrical in $\hat{\mathbf{v}}$ and $\hat{\mathbf{l}}$, since the Householder matrix is symmetric. This can be used to define modifications of the Phong model that *are* reciprocal. Second, the specular lobe of the Phong model is symmetric about the reflection vector. This turns out to be handy for some environment-map prefiltering techniques for real-time rendering, which we will discuss in Chapter 7.

2.6.2 Modified Phong Model

Modifications of the Phong model have been proposed [94] to fix the two major problems with it: lack of both reciprocity and energy conservation. The modified model has a BRDF given by

$$f_r(\mathbf{x}; \hat{\mathbf{v}} \leftarrow \hat{\mathbf{l}}) \quad = \quad \frac{k_d}{\pi} + \frac{k_s(q+2)}{2\pi}(\hat{\mathbf{v}}^T \mathsf{R}_{\hat{\mathbf{n}}} \hat{\mathbf{l}})^q,$$

where we have used a Householder transformation for the reflectance to emphasize the symmetric nature of the model. The constraints $k_d + k_s \leq 1$ are sufficient (but not necessary) to ensure energy conservation.

The parameters of the modified Phong BRDF mean slightly different things than in the classic model. First, raising the exponent makes the peak of the specular lobe higher, while maintaining the integral. In the classic model, the peak of the lobe (and so the brightness and color of the highlight) remained the same; it was only the width of the lobe that changed. Secondly, there are some scale factors applied to k_d and k_s, so, for given values of these constants, the modified Phong model will appear less reflective. This can be fixed, at least for the diffuse term for direct illumination, by multiplying the light source power by π.

2.6.3 Blinn-Phong Model

The Blinn-Phong model [18] is a variant of the classic Phong model and is often used in its place. It is defined in terms of the half-vector rather than the reflection vector:

$$f_r(\mathbf{x}; \hat{\mathbf{v}} \leftarrow \hat{\mathbf{l}}) \quad = \quad k_d + k_s \langle \hat{\mathbf{h}}, \hat{\mathbf{n}} \rangle^q / \langle \hat{\mathbf{n}}, \hat{\mathbf{l}} \rangle.$$

Whereas Phong's model is purely phenomological, the Blinn-Phong model can be somewhat justified by thinking of the $\cos \delta = \langle \hat{\mathbf{n}}, \hat{\mathbf{h}} \rangle$ factor as measuring the deviation of the normal $\hat{\mathbf{n}}$ of the surface from the vector $\hat{\mathbf{h}}$. Since $\hat{\mathbf{h}}$ is the normal of the ideal mirrored surface that would reflect $\hat{\mathbf{l}}$ into $\hat{\mathbf{v}}$, the closer $\hat{\mathbf{n}}$ and $\hat{\mathbf{h}}$ are, the brighter the specular highlight should be. The Blinn-Phong model is in fact related to microfacet models, such as the Cook-Torrance model. In these models, off-specular reflection is assumed to arise due to randomness at the microscopic level of the surface normal; there is some probabilty of a fraction of the microscopic normals being oriented in the correct direction to cause a mirror reflection.

The Blinn-Phong model is important chiefly because it is the "built-in" lighting model in standard OpenGL, and so is available as a standard feature on a wide range of graphics accelerators. However, it is also neither energy-conserving nor reciprocal.

This form of the cosine lobe is also symmetrical in $\hat{\mathbf{v}}$ and $\hat{\mathbf{l}}$ since $\hat{\mathbf{h}}$ is. Building a modified form of this model which is reciprocal is straightforward.

2.6.4 Lafortune Generalized Phong Model

Phong cosine lobes are symmetrical (reciprocal) and easy to compute. However, all the models we have considered so far are isotropic. How can we generalize these models to anisotropic BRDFs? We will actually look at two anisotropic variations of the Phong model: the Lafortune model and the Ashikhmin model. The Lafortune model is phenomological, while the Ashikhmin model includes consideration for effects such as the Fresnel factor. Therefore, we cover Lafortune's model here and Ashikhmin's in the next section.

Lafortune *et al.* [93] decided to use an arbitrary symmetric matrix in place of the Householder transformation $R_{\hat{\mathbf{n}}}$:

$$f_r(\mathbf{x}; \hat{\mathbf{v}} \leftarrow \hat{\mathbf{l}}) \;=\; k_s \left(\hat{\mathbf{l}}^T \mathbf{M} \hat{\mathbf{v}} \right)^q .$$

This reduces to the specular part of the modified Phong model if we set up k_s to include the appropriate normalization and let $\mathbf{M} = R_{\hat{\mathbf{n}}}$.

We can understand this model a little better if we take the SVD (singular value decomposition) of $\mathbf{M}$ to diagonalize it, as follows:

$$\mathbf{M} \;=\; \mathbf{Q} \mathbf{D} \mathbf{Q}^T .$$

In this decomposition $\mathbf{Q}$ is an orthonormal square matrix and $\mathbf{D}$ is diagonal. The matrix $\mathbf{Q}$ is change of coordinates; usually, in fact, we will use the local surface frame for $\mathbf{Q}$, so $\mathbf{Q}^T \hat{\mathbf{v}}$ amounts to finding the surface relative coordinates of $\hat{\mathbf{v}}$, and the same for $\hat{\mathbf{l}}^T \mathbf{Q}$. Then we have the following relationships:

$$
\begin{aligned}
\hat{\mathbf{l}}^T \mathbf{M} \hat{\mathbf{v}} &= \hat{\mathbf{l}}^T \mathbf{Q} \mathbf{D} \mathbf{Q}^T \hat{\mathbf{v}} \\
&= (\mathbf{Q}^T \hat{\mathbf{l}})^T \mathbf{D} (\mathbf{Q}^T \hat{\mathbf{v}}), \\
\mathbf{Q} &= \left[\hat{\mathbf{t}}, \hat{\mathbf{s}}, \hat{\mathbf{n}} \right], \\
\hat{\mathbf{l}}_S &= \mathbf{Q}^T \hat{\mathbf{l}}, \\
\hat{\mathbf{v}}_S &= \mathbf{Q}^T \hat{\mathbf{v}}, \\
\hat{\mathbf{l}}^T \mathbf{M} \hat{\mathbf{v}} &= \hat{\mathbf{l}}_S^T \mathbf{D} \hat{\mathbf{v}}_S .
\end{aligned}
$$

For *any* anisotropic model, we would need to change coordinates anyway to get the orientation of the lighting and viewing vectors relative to the local surface frame.

Let $\hat{\mathbf{l}}_S = [l_t, l_s, l_n]^T$ and $\hat{\mathbf{v}}_S = [v_t, v_s, v_n]^T$. Then in the surface-relative coordinate system, $\hat{\mathbf{l}}_S^T \mathsf{D} \hat{\mathbf{v}}_S$ represents a weighted inner product:

$$f_r(\mathbf{x}; \hat{\mathbf{v}} \leftarrow \hat{\mathbf{l}}) \quad = \quad k_s \left(d_t l_t v_t + d_s l_s v_s + d_n l_n v_n \right)^q .$$

By setting up D in various ways, with appropriate normalization factors in k_s, we can obtain a Phong-like model, a non-constant "diffuse" lobe centered around the normal, a retro-reflective lobe, and various other effects. By using a weighted sum of a number of these lobes, we can also approximate other BRDFs to arbitrary fidelity.

2.6.5 Banks Anisotropic Model

The Banks model [13, 167, 184] is an anisotropic reflectance model based on the Phong model. It assumes that light is reflected by microscopic cylinders embedded in the surface. An infinitesimal cylinder has, at every point, a whole plane of normals perpendicular to the tangent describing the direction of that cylinder. Given a lighting direction $\hat{\mathbf{l}}$, we choose the normal which is coplanar to $\hat{\mathbf{l}}$ and the tangent $\hat{\mathbf{t}}$ of the line, but perpendicular to $\hat{\mathbf{t}}$, and then apply the Phong lighting model.

The mathematical form of the Banks model is as follows:

$$L_o(\mathbf{x}, \hat{\mathbf{v}}) \quad = \quad \left(k_d \langle \hat{\mathbf{n}}', \hat{\mathbf{l}} \rangle^p + k_s \langle \hat{\mathbf{v}}, \hat{\mathbf{r}}_{\hat{\mathbf{n}}'}(\hat{\mathbf{l}}) \rangle^q \right) \cdot \cos \alpha \cdot L_i(\mathbf{x}, \hat{\mathbf{l}}).$$

The parameter q is the Phong exponent and the exponent p is used to combat the "excess brightness" due to the fact that we are *choosing* the normal rather than using a constant normal. A value of p from 1 to 10 or so is recommended. The "equivalent normal" $\hat{\mathbf{n}}'$ is the projection of $\hat{\mathbf{l}}$ onto the plane formed by $\hat{\mathbf{l}}$ and $\hat{\mathbf{t}}$ and perpendicular to $\hat{\mathbf{t}}$. This is the normal that forms the center of the specular highlight on the microcylinders assumed to be embedded in the surface. The factor $\cos \alpha = \langle \hat{\mathbf{n}}, \hat{\mathbf{l}} \rangle$ is used only when we are shading surfaces and a surface normal $\hat{\mathbf{n}}$ is available. For shading microcylindrical lines in free space it is omitted.

We do not actually have to explicitly compute the equivalent normal $\hat{\mathbf{n}}'$. The value $\langle \hat{\mathbf{n}}', \hat{\mathbf{l}} \rangle$ can be computed using

$$\langle \hat{\mathbf{n}}', \hat{\mathbf{l}} \rangle \quad = \quad \sqrt{1 - \langle \hat{\mathbf{l}}, \hat{\mathbf{t}} \rangle^2}$$

where $\hat{\mathbf{t}}$ is the tangent vector giving the direction of the microcylinders [167]. Likewise, $\langle \hat{\mathbf{v}}, \hat{\mathbf{r}}_{\hat{\mathbf{n}}'}(\hat{\mathbf{l}}) \rangle$ can be computed using

$$\langle \hat{\mathbf{v}}, \hat{\mathbf{r}}_{\hat{\mathbf{n}}'}(\hat{\mathbf{l}}) \rangle \quad = \quad \sqrt{1 - \langle \hat{\mathbf{l}}, \hat{\mathbf{t}} \rangle^2} \sqrt{1 - \langle \hat{\mathbf{v}}, \hat{\mathbf{t}} \rangle^2} - \langle \hat{\mathbf{l}}, \hat{\mathbf{t}} \rangle \langle \hat{\mathbf{v}}, \hat{\mathbf{t}} \rangle.$$

It is interesting to observe that after these manipulations, the equivalent BRDF depends on only two parameters, $\langle \hat{\mathbf{l}}, \hat{\mathbf{t}} \rangle$ and $\langle \hat{\mathbf{v}}, \hat{\mathbf{t}} \rangle$, a fact we exploit in Chapter 6.

The Banks model has some problems—for instance it is not reciprocal, and does not handle surface self-shadowing—but turns out to be easy to map onto hardware accelerators in a portable way. The use of the Banks model to shade lines as cylinders that are too small to resolve into surfaces is also occasionally very useful.

2.7 Physically Based Models

Physically based reflectance models are based, at least in part, on the underlying physics of reflection. Basing a reflection model on physics seems like a reasonable approach to obtaining a more accurate model of reflection. Unfortunately, reflection physics is complicated and combining all possible effects into a reasonably efficient and usable lighting model is difficult.

Physically based reflectance models should therefore not be considered perfect models of how the real world works. When setting up a physically based model, for various reasons, we may find it necessary to neglect or approximate certain factors. This is common in physical models in general. The real world is a complex place; you have to decide what's important and what isn't to the applications of the model.

For instance, recall that the BRDF model of reflectance makes the assumption that surface reflectance is completely local: the light energy is assumed to leave the surface at the same point that it enters. This is convenient for computer graphics, especially real-time graphics, since it means that we can define shading as a local operation and decouple surface shape from surface shading.

Even physically based models of BRDFs will share this fundamental approximation. Many other approximations are often made when deriving a physically based reflectance model; multiple scattering and polarization are usually neglected, for instance.

Multiple scattering can lead to major changes in the appearance of a surface, but is hard to compute and like subsurface scattering, nonlocal. Rather than neglecting it completely, though, some models do include an approximation.

Polarization is physically well-understood, and in the derivation of physical models via electromagnetic analysis it is natural to include it. In fact, real-world specular reflectance frequently polarizes light to some degree or another. You may have worn polarized sunglasses to block glare off water.

Polarized sunglasses selectively block specularly reflected light because the Fresnel effect, discussed earlier, happens to strongly polarize light.

Some simple extensions to the concept of flux [49, 168, 178, 182] can be used to model polarization. Representing polarization state does require carrying around some additional information with every ray and doing some additional computation at every reflection, but is not an unreasonable computational burden. Despite this, polarization effects are visually subtle, and so renderers in computer graphics rarely maintain polarization state. Usually even physically based models will assume unpolarized light on input and output. In most cases, this is a reasonable approximation, but it *is* an approximation.

Another approximation often made in renderers is the treatment of color. When deriving a physical model of reflectance, it is natural to derive formulas that give the reflection as a function of wavelength. A fine sampling of visible wavelengths[4] is a bit more than most real-time rendering systems can afford at present. Instead, since the human visual system can distinguish only three dimensions from all the visible wavelengths and computer monitors only display three colors, we'll typically use an RGB (*Red-Green-Blue*) model instead. How do we go from a reflectance spectrum to the RGB model? An easy but naive choice is to treat the RGB values as samples of the spectrum, one each in the red, green, and blue ranges. Yet three samples are pretty sparse and this could lead to aliasing [136]. A better choice is to treat the RGB components as *basis* colors, each with their own overlapping spectrum. This is closer to what our eyes actually perceive, and closer to the overlapping spectra produced by red, green and blue monitor phosphors. However, this is not correct either; each RGB component is the result of a weighted integral over the spectrum. But reflection is a multiplicative process, and the product of the integrals of two functions is not the same as the integral of the products. The only way to get spectral antialiasing *and* separability is to have non-overlapping RGB basis functions, such as square pulses. Usually, though, reflectance spectra are smooth, so just sampling them is not (usually) too horrible, but it *is* yet another approximation, and sometimes a big one.

The bottom line is that most physically based models should be taken more as reflectance models whose derivation was *guided* by physical principles, not as ground truths. Even if one starts with a good physical model,

---

[4]Actually, there is evidence that anything more than nine samples of the visible spectrum gives visually indistinguishable results in most cases. Three samples is minimal, and a bit too few for physical computations to be accurate. But you *could* sum three passes of a standard rendering system (with suitable color transformations on each pass) to get nine samples! You would also have to sample ultraviolet wavelengths if fluorescence is accurately modeled.

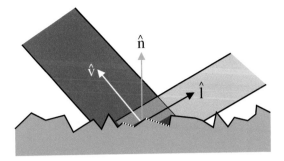

Figure 2.4.   Geometry assumed for microfacet BRDF models. The surface consists of microscopic perfectly reflective facets. $\hat{\mathbf{n}}$ is the surface normal and mean normal of the facets. The BRDF is derived from the probability of having facets with the right orientation to reflect $\hat{\mathbf{v}}$ to $\hat{\mathbf{l}}$ (dotted) and factors to account for facets blocking light or view from other facets.

by the time a renderer (without polarization and spectral sampling) is done with it, the result may deviate significantly from the reflectance of real surfaces.

2.7.1 Cook-Torrance Model

The Cook-Torrance reflectance model is a microfacet model. It is based on the assumption that variations in reflectivity are due to microscopically rough surfaces and randomly oriented specular facets. Under this kind of model, it is assumed that variation in reflection is due to the probability distribution of microfacet orientations, the Fresnel term on individual microfacets, and shadowing and masking (Figure 2.4).

The Cook-Torrance model is based in part on the earlier Torrance-Sparrow model; in fact there are several variations that all follow basically the same form. These models neglect multiple scattering, which is a potentially large effect.

The Cook-Torrance model is a combination of a diffuse and a specular term:

$$f_r(\mathbf{x}; \hat{\mathbf{v}} \leftarrow \hat{\mathbf{l}}) \quad = \quad k_d f_d + k_s f_s(\hat{\mathbf{v}} \leftarrow \hat{\mathbf{l}}).$$

To make sure that energy is conserved, we should follow the constraint that $k_d + k_s \leq 1$.

The diffuse term is a standard constant diffuse term:

$$f_d \quad = \quad \frac{1}{\pi}.$$

Recall that we had defined $\cos\gamma = \langle\hat{\mathbf{v}}, \hat{\mathbf{h}}\rangle = \langle\hat{\mathbf{l}}, \hat{\mathbf{h}}\rangle$. The specular term has the following general form:

$$f_s(\mathbf{x}; \hat{\mathbf{v}} \leftarrow \hat{\mathbf{l}}) \;\; = \;\; \frac{1}{\pi} \frac{F \cdot D \cdot G}{\langle\hat{\mathbf{n}}, \hat{\mathbf{v}}\rangle\langle\hat{\mathbf{n}}, \hat{\mathbf{l}}\rangle}.$$

Here, F represents the Fresnel factor, D represents the distribution of microfacet orientations, and G represents shadowing and masking (a *geometry factor*, defined below).

Recall that we have defined $\cos\delta = \langle\hat{\mathbf{n}}, \hat{\mathbf{h}}\rangle$. Blinn defined a Gaussian model for the distribution function

$$D(\cos\delta) \;\; = \;\; c\exp\left(-(\delta/m)^2\right)$$

where m is the root mean square slope of the facets (as an angle). Blinn says c is an *arbitrary constant*, but really, c should be chosen to normalize the BRDF... but how? A vector-based approximation to this distribution function can be made:

$$\delta^2 \;\; \approx \;\; \sin^2\delta,$$
$$\sin^2\delta \;\; = \;\; 1 - \langle\hat{\mathbf{h}}, \hat{\mathbf{n}}\rangle^2,$$
$$D(\langle\hat{\mathbf{n}}, \hat{\mathbf{h}}\rangle) \;\; \approx \;\; c\exp\left(\frac{\langle\hat{\mathbf{h}}, \hat{\mathbf{n}}\rangle^2 - 1}{m^2}\right).$$

The Beckmann distribution does not need the "arbitrary constant" in the Blinn model:

$$D(\cos\delta) \;\; = \;\; \frac{1}{m^2\cos^4\delta}\exp\left(-\frac{\tan^2\delta}{m^2}\right).$$

This function represents a distribution of slopes, with the slope represented as *tangents* of angles (i.e., in terms of $\Delta y/\Delta x$). There is therefore a slightly different meaning for m relative to Blinn's model. However, note that $\delta \approx \tan\delta$ for small angles δ.

The Beckmann distribution can also be implemented in vector form. First, we compute the squared tangent with ratio of dot products:

$$\tan^2\delta \;\; = \;\; \frac{\sin^2\delta}{\cos^2\delta}$$
$$= \;\; \frac{1 - \langle\hat{\mathbf{n}}, \hat{\mathbf{h}}\rangle^2}{\langle\hat{\mathbf{n}}, \hat{\mathbf{h}}\rangle^2}.$$

Substituting, we get

$$D(\langle \hat{\mathbf{n}}, \hat{\mathbf{h}} \rangle) \;\; = \;\; \frac{1}{m^2 \langle \hat{\mathbf{n}}, \hat{\mathbf{h}} \rangle^4} \exp \left(- \frac{1 - \langle \hat{\mathbf{n}}, \hat{\mathbf{h}} \rangle^2}{\langle \hat{\mathbf{n}}, \hat{\mathbf{h}} \rangle^2 m^2} \right).$$

We may want to model multiple scales of roughness. In that case we can use a multiscale roughness term:

$$D(\langle \hat{\mathbf{n}}, \hat{\mathbf{h}} \rangle) \;\; = \;\; \sum_j w_j D_j (\langle \hat{\mathbf{n}}, \hat{\mathbf{h}} \rangle),$$

$$\sum_j w_j \;\; = \;\; 1.$$

This corresponds to an idea of the surface roughness being due to "bumps on bumps". It is also possible to derive distribution functions directly from bump maps, a fact which is potentially useful when considering how to antialias bump maps. The correct answer is that bump maps should fade out to their corresponding BRDF when the highlights from the individual bumps can no longer be resolved without aliasing.

The geometry term represents the effect of shadowing and masking. Shadowing is when light is blocked by other features on the surface. Masking is when the view is blocked by other features on surface. Shadowing and masking are symmetrical, but *not* independent. If the incoming light and outgoing view directions are nearly the same, you can always see the same surfaces the light hits. We can also derive shadowing/masking functions from bump maps [9].

There are several analytical models of shadowing and masking. The model quoted by Torrance and Cook is based on the assumption of V-shaped microfacets:

$$G(\langle \hat{\mathbf{n}}, \hat{\mathbf{l}} \rangle, \langle \hat{\mathbf{n}}, \hat{\mathbf{h}} \rangle, \langle \hat{\mathbf{n}}, \hat{\mathbf{v}} \rangle, \cos \gamma) = \min \left(1, \frac{2 \langle \hat{\mathbf{n}}, \hat{\mathbf{h}} \rangle \cdot \langle \hat{\mathbf{n}}, \hat{\mathbf{v}} \rangle}{\cos \gamma}, \frac{2 \langle \hat{\mathbf{n}}, \hat{\mathbf{h}} \rangle \cdot \langle \hat{\mathbf{n}}, \hat{\mathbf{l}} \rangle}{\cos \gamma} \right).$$

In the original paper, we see $\langle \hat{\mathbf{v}}, \hat{\mathbf{h}} \rangle$ used in both denominators, but $\langle \hat{\mathbf{l}}, \hat{\mathbf{n}} \rangle$ gives the same answer, so this term really *is* symmetrical. To emphasize this, we have used $\cos \gamma$ above to represent this common value.

The model proposed by Smith [164] is more complex but is especially useful in real-time shading since it only depends on two angles:

$$\Lambda(\cot \theta) \;\; = \;\; \frac{1}{2} \left(\sqrt{\frac{2}{\pi}} \cdot \frac{m}{\cot \theta} \cdot e^{-\cot^2 \theta / 2m^2} - \mathrm{erfc} \left(\cot \theta / \sqrt{2} m \right) \right),$$

$$S(\theta) = \frac{1 - \frac{1}{2}\mathrm{erfc}\left(\cot\theta/\sqrt{2}m\right)}{\Lambda(\cot\theta) + 1},$$

$$G(\langle\hat{\mathbf{n}}, \hat{\mathbf{l}}\rangle, \langle\hat{\mathbf{n}}, \hat{\mathbf{v}}\rangle) = G(\cos\alpha, \cos\beta)$$

$$= S(\alpha) \cdot S(\beta), \tag{2.4}$$

where m has the same meaning (RMS mean slope) as in the Beckmann model and erfc is the complementary error function. This model, however, assumes that shadowing and masking are independent when, in fact, they are not.

2.7.2 Ashikhmin Model

The Ashikhmin model [10, 9] is related to models by Schlick, Neumann, and Lafortune [93, 125, 157] in the sense that it incorporates certain ideas from them. It is a modern version of the Phong model, more specifically the Blinn-Phong model. In particular, it uses the same exponentiated cosine lobe. However, the Ashikhmin model also includes enhancements to take into account the Fresnel effect, the energy tradeoff between diffuse and specular modes of reflection, and so forth. This reflectance model is also physically plausible, and is amenable to implementation in both hardware accelerators and off-line systems such as path tracers. So, despite the fact that it uses the Phong lobe, a phenomological technique, the Ashikhmin model can be considered to be physically based since it is physically plausible and models a number of important physical effects.

The specular lobe in the Ashikhmin reflectance model can also support anisotropy, and can be used in particular to give a reasonable approximation to the reflectance of brushed metal.

The Ashikhmin model is a sum of a "diffuse" part and a "specular" part:

$$f(\mathbf{x}; \hat{\mathbf{v}} \leftarrow \hat{\mathbf{l}}) = k_d(1 - k_s)f_d(\mathbf{x}; \hat{\mathbf{v}} \leftarrow \hat{\mathbf{l}}) + k_s f_s(\mathbf{x}; \hat{\mathbf{v}} \leftarrow \hat{\mathbf{l}}).$$

The specular part f_s does not represent a pure specular reflection, and is not an impulse. This part of the BRDF just represents the "glossy," view-dependent part of the BRDF that is *not* symmetric around the normal.

The diffuse part f_d of the Ashikhmin BRDF is not constant, and so is also view-dependent. It is, however, rotationally symmetric about the surface normal, which is what distinguishes it from the specular lobe. The Ashikhmin diffuse reflectance model is actually based on the assumption that "diffuse" reflectance modes are due to subsurface scattering. The diffuse reflectance depends on the specular reflectance; according to the

Fresnel effect, light that was not specularly reflected must have been transmitted into the surface, and so will contribute to the diffuse reflectance.

However, if desired, a constant diffuse part can be used in place of the one Ashikhmin suggests if view-independence is desired. In any case, for metals, the diffuse part should be set to zero.

It should be noted that our presentation of this model differs from that in the literature; in particular, we have changed the notation to be consistent with our notation in this book.

A color or spectrum k_s controls the color of the specular lobe. This value should be roughly equal to the reflectance of the BRDF at normal incidence, that is, looking directly down at the surface with the light also coming from the same direction. A second color or spectrum k_d controls the color of the diffuse lobe. This color can be measured away from the specular lobe, and represents the underlying color of the base surface. For metals, only the specular lobe is relevant and the diffuse part should be set to zero.

Two exponents, q_t and q_s, control the shape of the specular lobe. Two degrees of freedom are provided to support anisotropic reflectances. To render a surface with an anisotropic reflectance model, surface tangents are needed as well as normals. However, if the Ashikhmin model is used in an isotropic mode with $q_t = q_s$ (in which case we will use the notation q for the value of the exponent), then tangents are not required.

Let ϕ be the azimuth angle of $\hat{\mathbf{h}}$ with respect to $\hat{\mathbf{t}}$ and $\hat{\mathbf{s}}$. The Ashkhimin specular lobe f_s is given by

$$f_s(\mathbf{x}; \hat{\mathbf{v}} \leftarrow \hat{\mathbf{l}}) = \frac{\sqrt{(q_t + 1)(q_s + 1)}}{8\pi} \frac{\langle \hat{\mathbf{n}}, \hat{\mathbf{h}} \rangle^{q_t \cos^2 \phi + q_s \sin^2 \phi}}{\cos \gamma \cdot \max(\langle \hat{\mathbf{n}}, \hat{\mathbf{v}} \rangle, \langle \hat{\mathbf{n}}, \hat{\mathbf{l}} \rangle)} F(\cos \gamma).$$

In terms of vector dot products, this can be given as

$$f_s(\mathbf{x}; \hat{\mathbf{v}} \leftarrow \hat{\mathbf{l}}) = \frac{\sqrt{(q_t + 1)(q_s + 1)}}{8\pi} \frac{\langle \hat{\mathbf{n}}, \hat{\mathbf{h}} \rangle^{(q_t \langle \hat{\mathbf{h}}, \hat{\mathbf{t}} \rangle^2 + q_s \langle \hat{\mathbf{h}}, \hat{\mathbf{s}} \rangle^2)/(1 - \langle \hat{\mathbf{h}}, \hat{\mathbf{n}} \rangle^2)}}{\cos \gamma \cdot \max(\langle \hat{\mathbf{n}}, \hat{\mathbf{v}} \rangle, \langle \hat{\mathbf{n}}, \hat{\mathbf{l}} \rangle)} F(\cos \gamma)$$

where $\cos \gamma$ can be computed either as $\langle \hat{\mathbf{v}}, \hat{\mathbf{h}} \rangle$ or $\langle \hat{\mathbf{l}}, \hat{\mathbf{h}} \rangle$.

For isotropic reflectance, $q = q_t = q_s$, and we can make some simplifications:

$$f_s(\mathbf{x}; \hat{\mathbf{v}} \leftarrow \hat{\mathbf{l}}) = \frac{(q + 1)}{8\pi} \frac{\langle \hat{\mathbf{n}}, \hat{\mathbf{h}} \rangle^q}{\cos \gamma \cdot \max(\langle \hat{\mathbf{n}}, \hat{\mathbf{v}} \rangle, \langle \hat{\mathbf{n}}, \hat{\mathbf{l}} \rangle)} F(\cos \gamma).$$

Recall that this term is weighted by k_s, although the k_s term is used again (for R_s) in the definition of F.

An alternative formulation is possible [9], and turns out to be more convenient for real-time implementation:

$$f_s(\mathbf{x}; \hat{\mathbf{v}} \leftarrow \hat{\mathbf{l}}) = \frac{\sqrt{(q_t + 1)(q_s + 1)}}{8\pi} \frac{\langle \hat{\mathbf{n}}, \hat{\mathbf{h}} \rangle^{(q_t \langle \hat{\mathbf{h}}, \hat{\mathbf{t}} \rangle^2 + q_v \langle \hat{\mathbf{h}}, \hat{\mathbf{s}} \rangle^2)/(1 - \langle \hat{\mathbf{h}}, \hat{\mathbf{n}} \rangle^2)}}{\cos \gamma \cdot \langle \hat{\mathbf{n}}, \hat{\mathbf{v}} \rangle \cdot \langle \hat{\mathbf{n}}, \hat{\mathbf{l}} \rangle} F(\cos \gamma),$$

$$f_s(\mathbf{x}; \hat{\mathbf{v}} \leftarrow \hat{\mathbf{l}}) = \frac{(q + 1)}{8\pi} \frac{\langle \hat{\mathbf{n}}, \hat{\mathbf{h}} \rangle^q}{\cos \gamma \cdot \langle \hat{\mathbf{n}}, \hat{\mathbf{v}} \rangle \cdot \langle \hat{\mathbf{n}}, \hat{\mathbf{l}} \rangle} F(\cos \gamma).$$

The advantage of this formulation is that, after multiplication by $\langle \hat{\mathbf{n}}, \hat{\mathbf{l}} \rangle$, we can cancel the same factor in the denominator.

Finally, the directional diffuse lobe f_d is given by

$$f_d(\mathbf{x}; \hat{\mathbf{v}} \leftarrow \hat{\mathbf{l}}) = \frac{28}{23\pi}(1 - (1 - \langle \hat{\mathbf{n}}, \hat{\mathbf{v}} \rangle/2)^5)(1 - (1 - \langle \hat{\mathbf{n}}, \hat{\mathbf{l}} \rangle/2)^5).$$

The leading constant has been chosen to ensure energy conservation. Recall that this term is weighted by $k_d(1 - k_s)$. The form of the directional diffuse lobe comes from the Schlick approximation to the Fresnel factor. It is based on the assumption that diffuse reflectance is due to subsurface scattering. Under this assumption, diffusely scattered light is subject to the Fresnel effect twice: once going into the surface, and once coming out. This leads to a lower diffuse reflectivity at glancing angles, where the specular reflection is stronger.

3

Texturing

Texturing is the process of making surfaces appear more interesting by adding detail to their shading. It is among the most important means of increasing the visual complexity of a synthetic image. Most forms of texturing can be applied without increasing the geometric complexity of the surface. Since geometric complexity is an important factor in both the computational cost of rendering and the difficulty of making models, texturing has become an extremely popular technique in computer graphics.

Textures come in a variety of different flavors describing different kinds of detail information. For example, textures can simply contain color values to be applied to a surface, but they can also be used to perturb the surface normal (bump maps) and the surface position (displacement maps). Textures can also store information about the incoming illumination at a specific point in space (environment maps). Finally, textures can be used to store tabulated functions, which we will see is important in the implementation of sophisticated per-pixel lighting models. However, textures are much more than simple lookup tables. Their implementation also must include support for interpolation and filtering.

3.1 Texture Mapping

The term *texture mapping* [29] describes the process of mapping a two-dimensional image onto a geometric primitive or set of primitives. Texture mapping associates points in a texture image with the points of a geometric primitive. For the most part, in this chapter we will deal only with geometric primitives that represents two-manifolds, that is, surfaces. As the term *image* implies, we will also mostly consider two-dimensional textures.

The identification of texture samples in an image with points on a surface is achieved through the use of *texture coordinates*. A vector of texture

Figure 3.1. The result of projective texture mapping for both color and shadow. Here the texture coordinates are a projective transformation of world-space position. (Image courtesy of Stefan Brabec, Max-Planck-Institut für Informatik, after a method by Heidrich et al. [74].)

coordinates $\mathbf{u} = (u, v)$ must first be specified for each point on the surface to be texture mapped. Each texture coordinate indicates the value from the texture image $T(\mathbf{u})$ that should be looked up and associated with that point on the surface during rendering.

Given any parameteric surface $S(s, t) = [x(s, t), y(s, t), z(s, t)]^T$, such as a spline patch, the texture coordinates (u, v) of the surface can be defined in turn as a function $(u, v) = P(s, t)$ of the surface parameters s and t:

$$P(s, t) \quad = \quad [u(s, t), v(s, t)]^T.$$

Very often the function P is simply the identity, and then the parametric values (s, t) can be used directly as texture coordinates. This binds the texture directly to the model, so transformations of the model carry the texture along. An affine or projective projection of the spatial coordinates of the model can also be used, which lets textures be used for illumination purposes, as in Figure 3.1. These are called *projective textures*, since they project images onto the geometry using a perspective transformation. This approach can be used as a slide projector effect to project color images onto geometry as depicted in Figure 3.1, and is also used to cast shadows onto geometry using the shadow map approach (see Section 3.2.5). In this case, transformation of the model with respect to world space could change which texture coordinates are applied to every vertex of the model.

The only geometric primitive we will consider in this chapter is the triangle. Usually we will bind texture coordinates to vertices of polygonal models and interpolate them in model space, but other ways of associating texture coordinates with surfaces are possible. Considering only triangles makes the discussion more straightforward, but the techniques can be applied to general polygons or higher order curved surfaces.

Because triangles are mapped onto screen space under a projective transformation, texture coordinates only need to be computed at the polygon vertices and can then be interpolated across the polygon. Non-orthographic projections such as perspective require a per-pixel division for correct interpolation of texture coordinates, but this is straightforward. Quite often more complex primitives are tessellated into triangles, which simplifies the treatment of the texture coordinates.

We can use the notation of Section 1.3 to model the texture-mapping process. The texture mapping of triangles is performed in screen coordinates. Texture coordinates are assigned per-vertex ($\mathbf{ux}$) and interpolated across the pixels of the screen-space polygon by the rasterization engine ($\delta\mathbf{ux}$). Interpolated texture coordinates are then used as an index into a texture map to determine a per-pixel texture color

$$C\delta\pi\mathbf{x} \leftarrow T\delta\mathbf{ux}. \qquad (3.1)$$

Aliasing artifacts can be introduced by texture mapping when the sampling rate of the delta function on the LHS (*Left-Hand Side*) of (3.1) (the resolution of the polygon's screen projection) disagrees with the sampling rate of the delta function on the RHS (*Right-Hand Side*) (the texture's resolution). Methods for resampling the texture map based on the MIP map [180] or the summed-area table [36] fix this problem by adjusting the sampling density on the RHS of (3.1) to match that of the LHS. These (and other) resampling techniques are described in more detail later in this chapter, in Section 3.3.2.

An additional though subtle issue with the δ function on the RHS of (3.1) is perspective correction. Since the projection δ on the LHS performs a perspective divide, then the δ rasterization function on the RHS must also perform a per-pixel perspective divide during interpolation of texture coordinates.

We have assumed so far that a texture is a two-dimensional image. However, as we have seen in Section 1.2.3, we can extend the texture-mapping concept to a regular grid of point samples of arbitrary dimension. For example, we could have three-dimensional textures that can be interpreted as volumes, or a one-dimensional texture such as the one used for rendering contour lines in Figure 1.1.

3.2 Shading Techniques Based on Texture Mapping

Texture mapping is a extremely versatile tool that can be used for a whole range of different shading algorithms. In the following, we will describe some of the most commonly used techniques. More sophisticated examples are given in Chapters 6 and 7 and throughout this book.

3.2.1 Ambient and Diffuse Textures

A simple and efficient way of increasing the visual complexity of an object is to apply a texture map to it. This can be either a painted image, or a (possibly processed) photograph that is used to define the view-independent part of the illumination. If the texture is simply used to set the color of points on the object without changes, the texture mapping is said to be *ambient*, or illumination-independent. If the texture map is multiplied by the local illumination from one or more light sources such that the texture is brighter in areas where the light hits the surface almost perpendicular and dark in areas where the light arrives at grazing angles, according to Lambert's cosine law, the result is a diffuse texture map.

In addition, one can add a specular reflection on top of the ambient and/or diffuse texture. This specular reflection is usually not modulated by the diffuse texture map, but is simply added on top. Sometimes an additional texture, called a *gloss map*, is used to modulate the specular component separately. This is typically done to simulate two similar surfaces with different reflectivity on a single object. This idea can be extended to *material mapping*, a technique which uses textures to blend between multiple lighting models, as described in Section 6.7.1.

Figure 3.2.   Texture mapping with ambient, diffuse, and specular reflection models.

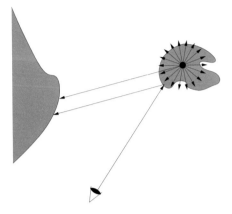

Figure 3.3.   Environment maps hold the light arriving at *one point* in space from *all directions*. They can be used to render approximate reflections on curved objects, providing that the environment is far from the reflecting object.

3.2.2 Environment Maps

Environment maps are textures that describe for all directions the incoming or outgoing light at one point in space. The main use of these maps is to simulate reflections off curved objects, but they can do much more than that. In particular in hardware-accelerated rendering engines, environment maps are often used to store precomputed directional information that is too expensive to compute on the fly.

The basic idea of environment maps is that if a reflecting object is small compared to its distance from the environment, the incoming illumination on its surface really depends strongly only on the *direction* of the reflected ray. The *origin* of reflected rays, that is the actual position on the surface where reflected rays begin, can often be neglected. When this approximation is valid, the incoming illumination at the object can be precomputed and stored in a relatively compact two-dimensional texture map indexed only by direction.

If the environment map parameterization is cleverly chosen, the illumination for reflections off the surface can be looked up very efficiently. Of course, the assumption of a small object compared to the environment often does not hold, but environment maps are a good compromise between rendering quality and the need to store the full four-dimensional (or five-dimensional) radiance field that would describe the appearance of every surface point from any viewing direction.

Both off-line [65] and interactive hardware-based renderers [159] have used the environment mapping approach to simulate mirror reflections, often with amazing results.

Parameterizations of environment maps

Since environment maps must represent directionally dependent information in a two-dimensional texture, it is necessary to decide how to map from directions (vectors on a unit sphere) to actual texture coordinates in order to define a concrete representation of environment maps. This mapping, which is also called the *parameterization* of the environment map, should fulfill a few properties in order to be most useful for real-time, hardware-accelerated rendering:

1. The method for computing the texture coordinates should be simple and efficient, and it should be easy to implement in hardware. This means that complicated and expensive mathematical functions like trigonometric functions should be avoided.

2. For walkthroughs of static environments, it should not be necessary to create a new environment map every frame. This means that:

   (a) The computation of texture coordinates should be possible for all viewing directions from a single map.

   (b) All light directions need to be represented equally well in the environment map. Although some light directions are more important than others for certain viewing directions, all directions are equally important for a walkthrough, where the viewing direction is not known in advance. This property is called the *uniformity* of the parameterization.

3. For interaction with dynamic environments, it should be easy and inexpensive to create a new environment map from perspective images of the scene, because this is what the hardware can generate.

There are three major parameterizations for environment maps in use today. The *spherical environment map* [63]is based on the analogy of a small, perfectly mirrored metal ball centered around the object. The image that an orthographic camera sees when looking at such a ball from a certain viewing direction is stored as the environment map. An example environment map from the center of a colored cube is shown on the left of Figure 3.5. It can be seen that one face, corresponding to the region directly behind the sphere, is represented only by a very narrow strip around

Figure 3.4. An example of environment mapping.

the silhouette of the sphere. This indicates that the the sampling rate for spherical environment maps is highly non-uniform. In fact, the sampling rate varies by a factor of $1 : \infty$. Spherical environment maps therefore fail to satisfy the second criteria and are best used for moving objects with a static view. Generating spherical environment maps from rendered views is not difficult, but does require an extra warping or rendering pass. However, spherical maps do have the advantage that standard OpenGL supports a built-in texture coordinate generation mode for them that can even support local viewers.

The second parameterization, that of *cubical environment maps* or *cube maps* [59, 173], consist simply of six independent perspective images from the center of a cube through each of its faces. From this description it is clear that the generation of such a map simply consists of rendering the six necessary perspective images with $90°$ fields of view. A warping step, as required for spherical maps, is not necessary before a cube map can be used for rendering. The variation in sampling rate across cube maps is fairly good. It can be shown that the sampling rates for all directions differ by a factor of $\sqrt{3}^3 : 1 \approx 5.2$. Cube maps also have two more advantages: first, a lookup in a cube map can be designed to tolerate non-unit-length vectors, and so includes an implicit normalization; second, linear interpolation of vectors sweeps out a great circle. The biggest disadvantage of cube maps is that they are not supported on all platforms, and special hardware support is necessary to use them.

Finally, *parabolic maps* [76, 77],often used in pairs as *dual paraboloid maps* when representing a function over a full sphere, are based on an analogy similar to the spherical environment maps: each parabolic map is an image of a metallic reflecting paraboloid. Assume that the reflecting object lies at the origin, and that the viewing direction is along the negative z-axis. The image seen by an orthographic camera when looking at the paraboloid given by

$$f(x, y) = \frac{1}{2} - \frac{1}{2}(x^2 + y^2), \quad x^2 + y^2 \le 1 \tag{3.2}$$

contains the information about the hemisphere facing towards the viewer. A complete environment must be stored in two separate textures, each containing the information of one hemisphere, with a small amount of overlap. The geometry is depicted in Figure 3.5. Parabolic maps are the most uniform parameterization with differences in sampling rate of only 4 : 1. A further advantage of parabolic maps is that cones of directions (i.e., all directions within a cone around a certain reference direction) map to roughly circular areas. This property, which we call *symmetry,* is useful for environment map prefiltering as described in Section 7.2.4. A single parabolic map is also a useful representation when we only need to represent a function

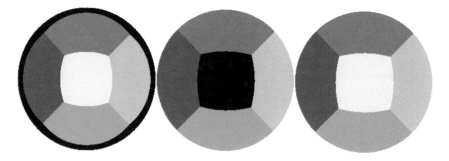

Figure 3.5. Left: A spherical environment map from the center of a colored cube. Note the poor sampling of the cube face directly in front of the observer (directly behind the sphere). Center and right: Two images comprising a parabolic map of the same scene. The cube map for this scene would consist of just six square images with the colors of the six faces.

	Spherical	Cube	Parabolic
Number of images	1	6	2
View independent	-	+	+
Difference in sampling rate	$1 : \infty$	$5.2 : 1$	$4 : 1$
Symmetry	-	-	+
Ease of creation	-	+	-
Hardware support	+	+	+
Autonormalizing	-	+	-
Great Circle interpolation	-	+	-

Table 3.1. Advantages and disadvantages of the different environment maps.

over a hemisphere, as when evaluating reflectance models. Parabolic maps do not require any special hardware beyond projective transformations, but the fact that two maps are needed to represent a full sphere may be that multiple passes may be required to environment map an object.

A summary of the advantages and disadvantages of the different maps is provided in Table 3.1.

Environment maps for non-photorealistic rendering

Not only can environment maps hold actual reflections, but they can be used for a number of non-photorealistic effects as well. Figure 3.6 shows some examples of this.

The first example uses simply a sketch of a window frame and was inspired by a RenderMan shader. Although the image only consists of two

Figure 3.6. Environment used for non-photorealisitc rendering. Left: Hand painted window reflection. Center: Cold-warm shading [57]. Right: Rendering silhouettes using spherical environment maps [57]. (See Color Plate I.)

colors, black and white, the shape of the object can be understood quite well, especially when manipulating the object interactively.

The second example shows cold-warm shading, again with a very simple, hand drawn environment map. This method has been described by Gooch et al. [57]. The environment map consists merely of two triangles—one blue, one yellow—and one white circle. The resulting image has been blurred with fairly large blur filter. The cold color blue looks like a shadowed region, while the warm color yellow, including the white "highlight," looks like parts lit by the sun.

The third column shows a final environment mapping technique, also from Gooch et al [57]. This technique is designed to render silhouettes black and everything else white. This is achieved by having a thin ring of black pixels in the outer regions of the environment map. Silhouette areas with a small curvature will have a fairly wide black stripe, while areas with a strong curvature have a very narrow one. This can be evened out somewhat by making the silhouette line constant width in each MIP level of the environment map.

3.2.3 Displacement Maps

So far, we have seen textures and shaders represent ambient and diffuse color, as well as incoming light. In general, however, there is no reason why they should not be used for something completely different than color or light.

Displacement maps [33] take a point on the original surface geometry, and move it to a new location. For shading, a new surface normal (and tangent direction) is computed at the new point location from the way points in the neighborhood move. This is done by computing the par-

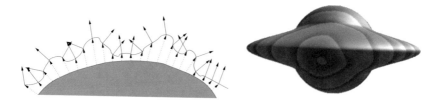

Figure 3.7. Left: Displacement mapping moves points from an existing surface along the local surface normal (dotted arrows). New normals (solid arrows) are then computed at every point for shading. Right: Displacement mapping applied to a sphere.

tial derivatives of the displaced points in the proximity of the point to be shaded.

Displacement mapping often works slightly differently for procedural shaders than for texture maps. In the latter case, the displacement is usually given in terms of a scalar displacement distance. Every surface point is then moved by that distance along its previous surface normal. Procedural shaders, on the other hand, often allow for arbitrary displacements that are not restricted to the normal direction.

The problem with displacement mapping is that the displacements can be arbitrarily large, which complicates rendering algorithms and often requires retessellation of the underlying geometry to represent features well. For this reason, displacement maps are usually not implemented in real-time systems, although some researchers have recently investigated solutions involving current hardware [86] or changes to the hardware itself [40]. An example of an adaptive tessellation of a displacement map generated by a real-time system is shown in Figure 3.9, where it is also compared to bump mapping.

3.2.4 Bump Maps

An alternative to displacement mapping is to not actually displace the surface point, but to perturb the local shading normal *as if* the point had been displaced. This method is called *bump mapping* [19]. As before, bump maps can be either procedurally defined or taken from a texture map.

Bump mapping, as originally formulated [19], perturbs the normal of the surface according to a given height field $B(s,t)$, which describes a slight movement of the surface point for each location (s,t) in the parameter

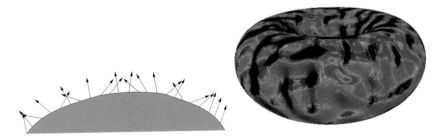

Figure 3.8.   Left: Rather than actually displacing the surface points, bump mapping simply perturbs the normal *as if* the surface had been displaced. Right: A bump-mapped torus. Note that the silhouettes are still those of the original torus; only the shading normals have been changed at every point.

domain. The height field defines the spatial position of the displaced point $\mathbf{P}'$ as an offset along the surface normal $\hat{\mathbf{n}}$. For simplicity, we assume unit-length normals in the following:

$$\mathbf{P}' = \mathbf{P} + B(s, t) \cdot \hat{\mathbf{n}}. \tag{3.3}$$

The perturbed normal of the displaced surface is given as the cross product of the two tangent vectors in $\mathbf{P}'$:

$$\hat{\mathbf{n}}' = \frac{d\mathbf{P}'}{ds} \times \frac{d\mathbf{P}'}{dt} \approx \hat{\mathbf{n}} + \underbrace{\left(\hat{\mathbf{n}} \times \frac{d\mathbf{P}}{ds}\right) \cdot \frac{dB(s, t)}{dt} + \left(\frac{d\mathbf{P}}{dt} \times \hat{\mathbf{n}}\right) \cdot \frac{dB(s, t)}{ds}}_{\hat{\mathbf{d}}}.$$

$$\tag{3.4}$$

This formula includes an approximation which assumes that the bump height is small compared to the dimensions of the surface. The details of this approximation, and the derivation of the formula, can be found in [19].

One difficulty with implementing bump maps in hardware is the expensive tangent vector computation $\hat{\mathbf{t}}_s := \hat{\mathbf{n}} \times (d\mathbf{P}/ds)$ and $\hat{\mathbf{t}}_t := (d\mathbf{P}/dt) \times \hat{\mathbf{n}}$, which normally has to be performed for each pixel. Alternatively, these vectors could be interpolated across polygons, but even this is quite expensive, since it requires a normalization step per pixel. The partial derivatives of the bump map itself, on the other hand, can be precomputed and stored in a texture.

Several ways have been proposed to simplify the computation of $\hat{\mathbf{t}}_s$ and $\hat{\mathbf{t}}_t$ by making additional assumptions, or by using a completely different, simpler coordinate system. For example, Schilling et al. [156] proposed building a local coordinate frame in each point using a global reference direction $\hat{\mathbf{m}}$, while Fournier [47, 48], among other approaches, suggests that we should precompute the normal in object space for each pixel, and store *it* in a texture map. This is sometimes called a *normal map*.

Normal maps have the advantage that the expensive operations (computing the local surface normal by transforming the bump into the local coordinate frame) have already been performed in a preprocessing stage. This makes them a popular choice for hardware rendering [79, 77]. In the most straightforward implementation, where the normals in a normal map are stored in object space, they possess the disadvantage that the representation is dependent on the surface geometry, so a different texture is required for each object and objects cannot be easily deformed. In contrast, bump maps can be shared across different objects and it is possible to deform objects.

The difficulties with ordinary normal mapping can be overcome by *tangent space normal mapping* [137], an approach where the normals in the texture are actually specified relative to a *local coordinate frame*, which is interpolated from the vertices of a triangle. This works as follows: the local reflection models applied to a bump map are functions of the angles between different vectors such as the surface normal, the light direction, and the viewing direction. Rather than expressing these vectors in a common global coordinate frame, they are expressed relative to a varying local surface frame. To this end, a local coordinate frame consisting of a normal $\hat{\mathbf{n}}$, a tangent $\hat{\mathbf{t}}$, and a secondary tangent $\hat{\mathbf{s}}$ is specified at every vertex. Vector shading parameters such as the light and viewing direction are transformed into this coordinate frame at every vertex. The resulting surface-relative coordinates get linearly interpolated to yield per-pixel light and viewing directions in the local coordinate frame for every surface point. Bump mapping is then performed by combining these interpolated vectors with normals or tangents [85] from the normal map:

$$\hat{\mathbf{n}}'(u,v) = n'_t(u,v)\hat{\mathbf{t}} + n'_s(u,v)\hat{\mathbf{s}} + n'_n(u,v)\hat{\mathbf{n}}.$$

Bump maps are useful by themselves, of course, but prove to be even better when combined with coarse displacement mapping. The results shown in Figure 3.9 are actually a combination of relatively coarse displacement mapping combined with a hardware implementation of bump mapping, using the surface frame technique. If a surface is already bump-mapped, the displacement mapping algorithm only has to worry about displacing the surface where the error due to parallax would otherwise be visible. The lighting is taken care of by the bump map, and so is consistent even if the tessellation changes. Per-pixel bump mapping can also hide ill-formed triangles in tessellations so that a relatively simple adaptive tessellation scheme can be used.

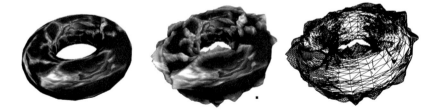

Figure 3.9. Left: Bump mapping alone. Center: A bump-mapped and displaced surface. The small black square shows the screen-space error bound used. Right: The underlying adaptive mesh used for the displacement. (Images courtesy Kevin Moule and Michael McCool of the University of Waterloo Computer Graphics Lab.)

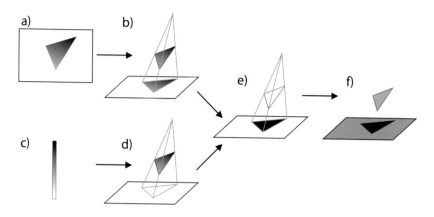

Figure 3.10. Shadow mapping. In a first rendering pass, a depth image (a) of the scene as seen from the light source is generated. This map is then applied as a projective texture to the scene as seen from the camera, yielding image (b). In parallel, the *actual* distance of every scene point seen visible from the camera is determined. For example, this can be achieved by applying a one-dimensional texture (c) to the whole scene, resulting in image (d). A comparison of (b) and (d) yields a mask (e) of all pixels which are in shadow. Applying a lighting model only in those areas that are marked as lit results in the final image (f).

3.2.5 Shadow Maps

Yet another kind of information that can be stored in two-dimensional textures is the visibility of light sources. *Shadow maps* [179] are an efficient means for computing shadows. A shadow map contains the depth values of a scene as seen from the light source. To test whether a specific object point is illuminated by the light source, the three-dimensional location of the point is projected into the local coordinate system of the light source, and the depth value is compared with the result from applying the shadow map as a projective texture. If distance of the point is larger than the depth stored in the map, the point lies in shadow. Otherwise, it is illuminated.

Shadow map rendering therefore requires (at least) two rendering passes per light source: First, the shadow map has to be created by rendering the scene from the light source. Second, the scene has to be rendered from the viewpoint of the camera, while both the projective texturing and the one-dimensional texturing are performed, the results are compared to form a mask, and the lit regions are illuminated using the object's material properties. On modern graphics hardware this second step can be performed in a single rendering pass, while older hardware may require this step to be further split into additional passes. Yet more passes may be required to cover a wider range of directions from the light source, since the full 360° field of view cannot be represented in a single perspective shadow map. Ideally, hardware vendors would combine cube maps and shadow maps, but this has not yet been done.

3.3 Image Texture Antialiasing

When using texture mapping for generating images, correct filtering becomes a crucial issue. This subject is very complex, and a comprehensive treatment would unfortunately exceed the scope of this book. Therefore, we will limit our discussion to the methods that are most widespread in practice. A more detailed overview of the topic with additional pointers to other literature can be found in Heckbert's survey article [69].

Textures, like digital images in general, are meant to represent continuous functions over the image plane, but in fact consist only of a finite number of sample values spaced at regular intervals. These discrete samples are called *pixels*, or (in the case of texture maps) *texels*. In order to obtain the color value of any point on the image plane that does not lie on this regular grid, we need to apply a reconstruction procedure. This is done by convolving the discrete samples (texels) with a low-pass filter that removes the high frequencies due to the sampling pattern. Texture mapping then takes the resulting continuous function, maps it onto a geometric object, and from there onto the screen. In order to obtain a final image, we take this continuous function, and evaluate it at other discrete sample positions (i.e., the pixels). To do this without introducing artifacts, we again have to remove frequencies that are too high for the output image resolution. This is achieved with another low-pass filter. This final filtering step is called texture antialiasing.

Conceptually, the process for generating a digital image from texture-mapped geometry can be summarized as follows:

- Given a texture $T[i, j]$, generate the continuous image $T(u, v)$ via low-pass filtering in texture space.

- Map $T(u, v)$ onto the surface.

- Project the surface onto the image plane using a projective transformation.

- Low-pass filter the resulting continuous function according to the desired image resolution in image space.

- Sample the resulting continuous function by evaluating it at pixel positions.

This idealized treatment is not typically feasible exactly as stated due to the use of continuous functions. In practice, we have to make some form of approximation to this ideal image formation process.

One observation is that the above algorithm contains two low-pass filters: one performed in the texture coordinate space, and one in the image coordinate space of the final output image. If, instead of performing both of these filter operations, we perform only the one with the lower cut-off frequency, we can expect that the image quality will not degrade much, since this filter will also remove all frequencies above the threshold of the other filter operation.

To understand why this is the case, consider the locations of the texels projected onto the image plane. If these samples are spaced further apart then the pixels of the final image, then it suffices to perform only the low-pass reconstruction filter in texture coordinate space. This case is called *texture magnification*, because the texture appears to be enlarged on the screen.

The other case is that the projected texels are closer together in the image plane than the pixel locations. In this case, which is called *texture minification*, it is approximately sufficient to perform only the image-space antialiasing filter. Both cases are depicted in Figure 3.11.

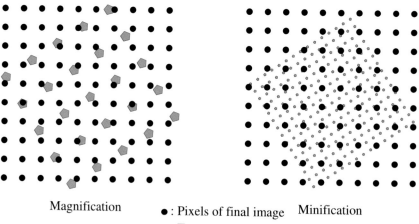

Magnification   ● : Pixels of final image   Minification

● : Texels of texture map

Figure 3.11. Left: Texture magnification. Right: Texture minification.

Unfortunately, both texture magnification and minification still require the application of a low-pass filter. The ideal low-pass filter cannot be implemented easily, having very wide support, so approximations have to be made. Different approximations are commonly used for texture magnification and minification.

3.3.1 Texture Magnification

The simpler of the two cases is magnification, since we can ignore the sampling rate of the pixels in the image plane. All we need to do is to approximate the low-pass reconstruction filter in texture space. For each pixel, this requires us to find the corresponding texture coordinates s and t to center the filter kernel of the low-pass filter. The ideal low-pass filter, which passes all frequencies below a cutoff and blocks all frequencies above, has a sinc function as the kernel ($\operatorname{sinc}(x) := \sin(x)/x$). To filter an image with an ideal low-pass filter, we must either transform the image to the frequency domain, chop the high frequencies, and transform back (not practical for real-time rendering); or, alternatively, for each pixel we must sum contributions from every other pixel, weighted by the positive or negative value of the sinc function centered at the target pixel (also not practical for real-time rendering). Because the ideal low-pass filter combines contributions from all other pixels (and, in fact, all of space), it is said to have *infinite support*. For practical purposes, we need a filter with *finite support*, that compute only a weighted sum of the texels in some neighborhood around s and t.[1] Several choices exist:

Figure 3.12. Texture magnification filters, applied in the extreme to a 4 x 4 texture: nearest neighbor, linear, and cubic.

---

[1] Not to mention the problem that while a perfect low-pass reconstruction filter is *ideal* in a signal-processing sense, it introduces "ringing" around sharp edges that are less than ideal in a visual sense, and may even create negative values that cannot be displayed. A tent or Gaussian filter often gives better results in practice.

Nearest neighbor reconstruction: The simplest form of reconstruction is nearest neighbor sampling. For each pixel in the image, the texture lookup proceeds as follows: Let s and t be the texture coordinate for a given pixel, let $I[s, t]$ be the texture, $I'[x, y]$ the digital image we are computing, and let s and t be the texture coordinates corresponding to pixel $(x, y)^T$.

The texel closest to that pixel is given by the indices $i_s = \text{round}(s \cdot (P_s - 1))$ and $i_t = \text{round}(t \cdot (P_t - 1))$ in a discrete texture of resolution $P_s \times P_t$. The reconstructed value for a pixel is then given by the value of that texel:

$$I'[x, y] := I[i_s, i_t].$$

This assigns the value of the closest texel to the pixel of the image. Nearest neighbor sampling results in a very poor quality reconstruction, leading to severe reconstruction artifacts. Nearest neighbor sampling can be interpreted as a convolution of the discrete samples with a box filter, which is a very coarse approximation of a sinc filter. Obviously, this approximation will cause some reconstruction artifacts. On the other hand, the nearest neighbor sample technique is very efficient, since it requires only a single access to the texture map. Nearest neighbor reconstruction is shown on the left in Figure 3.12.

Linear interpolation: A better reconstruction is the linear interpolation of samples. Here, we define

$$i_s := \lfloor s \cdot (P_s - 1) \rfloor, i_t := \lfloor t \cdot (P_t - 1) \rfloor$$

and

$$\Delta s := s \cdot (P_s - 1) - i_s, \Delta t := t \cdot (P_t - 1) - i_t.$$

With these definitions, the texture coordinate at the pixel location resides somewhere between the four texels located at indices (i_s, i_t), $(i_s + 1, i_t)$, $(i_s, i_t + 1)$, and $(i_s + 1, i_t + 1)$. The values $\Delta s, \Delta_t \in 0 \ldots 1$ are the weights for a bilinear interpolation between these four values:

$$\begin{aligned}I'[x, y] \quad := \quad & (1 - \Delta t)\left((1 - \Delta s)I[i_s, i_t] + \Delta s \cdot I[i_s + 1, i_t]\right) \\ & + \Delta t\left((1 - \Delta s)I[i_s, i_t + 1] + \Delta s \cdot I[i_s + 1, i_t + 1]\right).\end{aligned}$$

$$(3.5)$$

This means that four texture accesses are required for a two-dimensional texture. Linear interpolation corresponds to a convolution with a linear tent kernel, which could be interpreted as a linear approximation to the "ideal" sinc reconstruction kernel. Obviously, this approach is more expensive than nearest neighbor sampling, but the reconstruction quality is significantly improved. Linear reconstruction is shown in the center of Figure 3.12.

Higher order reconstruction: As we move to even higher order interpolations, the cost gets even higher. Nonetheless, these methods are often mandatory for high-quality reconstructions. Since the human eye is particularly sensitive to discontinuities in the first derivative of color values, at least quadratic interpolation is required to avoid artifacts (so-called Mach bands). In practice, bicubic and Gaussian filters are frequently used for very high quality applications in image processing. Both bicubic and Gaussian filters offer a relatively good approximation of the ideal low-pass filter, although at significantly increased cost: A bicubic filter, for example, requires access to a block of $4 \times 4 = 16$ texels. Bicubic reconstruction is shown on the left in Figure 3.12.

3.3.2 Texture Prefiltering for Minification

With texture minification, we have to apply a low-pass filter in image space rather than texture space. As for the case of magnification, the optimal filter is in practice approximated by a filter with finite support. In theory, it is possible to take the same approximations that are used in the case of magnification, for example a bilinear or a bicubic filter. However, in the minification case an arbitrarily large number of texels may be mapped to the support of the reconstruction filter for a single pixel. For example, if a texture-mapped object appears smaller in the image than the distance between two pixels (e.g., when the textured object is very far away), then a weighted sum of all $P_s \times P_t$ texels has to be computed in order to obtain the value of a single pixel.

This would be too expensive, especially for interactive applications. For this reason, several different resolutions of textures are typically used. Starting with a high-resolution texture, several lower-resolution textures are generated. This process is called *prefiltering*. Each of the prefiltered textures is well-suited for a minifications by a specific factor, and other minification factors are interpolated from these precomputed textures. The commonly used prefiltering schemes are:

MIP-maps: *MIP-mapping* is probably the most important multiresolution filtering scheme in practice. MIP stands for *Multum In Parvo*, which is Latin for "many things in one place" [180]. With MIP-mapping, the resolution of the original texture is restricted to powers of two. From this original texture, a *pyramid* of textures is generated, where the resolution in each level of the pyramid is reduced by a factor of two in each dimension. Ideally, the reduction of resolution should be performed as another low-pass filter, but most often it is simply achieved by averaging 2×2 neighboring texture values. This simple averaging can be interpreted as a convolution with a box function; however, the MIP-maps allow the use of arbitrary filters to generate the pyramid of textures. Storing the complete MIP pyramid of a two-dimensional texture requires only one-third more memory than storing the original texture.

For reconstruction, it first has to be determined which level of the pyramid is to be used for texturing. To this end, the texture coordinates corresponding to four neighboring pixels in the image plane are computed. These texture coordinates form an arbitrary quadrilateral in texture space. Finding an appropriate level in the pyramid corresponds to approximating this quadrilateral with a square [69]. Typically, the quadrilateral will not fit exactly to one level in the MIP-map hierarchy. Rather, there will be one level that has a somewhat too-large resolution, and a neighboring level with a somewhat too-small resolution.

MIP-mapping first performs a bilinear interpolation in each of the two MIP-map levels using the method used for texture magnification. The resulting two texture values are interpolated to form the final value at the pixel location in the image plane. The cost of this method is eight texel lookups.

It should be noted that MIP-mapping is widely implemented on hardware accelerators, and we can actually load the different levels with arbitrary images if we want (rather than images that are related by filtering). This flexibility can lead to useful methods for nonlinear filtering as well (for instance, the bump-map antialiasing method described in Section 6.7.2), by loading in a texture that simply selects a different shading technique by the level-of-detail index given by the MIP-map lookup. Several non-photorealistic real-time rendering techniques are also based on "abuses" of MIP-mapping.

Summed-area tables: One of the core problems of MIP-mapping is that it is an *isotropic* filtering method, which means that the size of the texture is reduced by the same factor in all parametric directions. However, there are many situations where the quadrilateral in texture

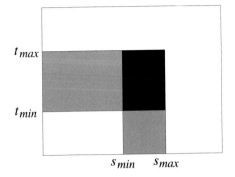

Figure 3.13. In a summed-area table the sum over an arbitrary axis-aligned rectangle can be computed from the sums of four precomputed and stored rectangular regions.

space is a long, thin polygon that cannot be approximated well by a square.[2] This situation requires *anisotropic* texture filtering.

One of the oldest techniques for anisotropic prefiltering is the summed-area table [36]. Instead of the actual texture value $I[s, t]$, the sum of all texels in the rectangle below s and t is stored, given by following two-dimensional table:

$$S\left[i_s, i_t\right] := \sum_{i=0}^{i_s} \sum_{j=0}^{i_t} I\left[i, j\right].$$

Note that this produces only $P_s \times P_t$ values, the same as in the original texture. However, each sample has to be represented with a larger number of bits for numerical stability, and the number of bits required grows with the resolution of the original texture.

From these values, the sum over an arbitrary, axis-aligned rectangular region ($s_{min} \leq s \leq s_{max}, t_{min} \leq t \leq t_{max}$) (see Figure 3.13) can be computed simply as

$$S\left[s_{max}, t_{max}\right] - S\left[s_{min}, t_{max}\right] - S\left[s_{max}, t_{min}\right] + S\left[s_{min}, t_{min}\right].$$

To compute the value of a pixel in the image plane, a quadrilateral is computed as in the case of MIP-mapping. This quadrilateral is then approximated as closely as possible with an axis-aligned rectangle.

---

[2]This is more common than you might think. Anywhere you can see a large stretch of ground near the horizon, you have a situation that is poorly filtered by MIP-maps.

The average over this rectangle (i.e., the corresponding sum divided by the number of texels contained in this region) is used as the pixel value. This means that summed-area tables are restricted to using a constant filter kernel.

Unfortunately, summed-area tables give better filtering only when the texture filter shape mismatch aligns with the s or t directions. If the filter covers a diagonal swath through the texture, a summed-area table performs as poorly as a MIP-map.

RIP-map: RIP-maps are an image pyramid similar to MIP-maps [96]. In addition to the MIP-map pyramid of images scaled by one-half in both P_s and P_t at each level, a RIP-map also prefilters textures independently scaled in s and t. So a MIP-map hierarchy may have sizes

$$\begin{bmatrix} (P_s, P_t) & & \\ & (\frac{P_s}{2}, \frac{P_t}{2}) & \\ & & (\frac{P_s}{4}, \frac{P_t}{4}) \end{bmatrix}.$$

The corresponding RIP-map hierarchy has sizes

$$\begin{bmatrix} (P_s, P_t) & (P_s, \frac{P_t}{2}) & (P_s, \frac{P_t}{4}) \\ (\frac{P_s}{2}, P_t) & (\frac{P_s}{2}, \frac{P_t}{2}) & (\frac{P_s}{2}, \frac{P_t}{4}) \\ (\frac{P_s}{4}, P_t) & (\frac{P_s}{4}, \frac{P_t}{2}) & (\frac{P_s}{4}, \frac{P_t}{4}) \end{bmatrix}.$$

RIP-maps provide the same coverage as summed-area tables and have the same problems with off-axis filter kernels.

Footprint assembly: Summed-area tables can deal only with anisotropy along the major axes of the texture coordinate system. The method of footprint assembly can handle filter anisotropy in arbitrary directions [156]. The fundamental concept behind footprint assembly is to approximate the shape of the quadrilateral in texture coordinate space with a sequence of squares. The total value for a pixel is then the sum of the contributions from each square. These are, in turn, looked up from a normal MIP-map hierarchy. For the details of the algorithm, please refer to [156]. Footprint assembly can be considered a combination of MIP-mapping and supersampling, as it sums several MIP-map filtered samples.

Figure 3.14. Solid textured wood plank. Using the spatial coordinates after warping causes the plank to "swim" through the solid texture. Assigning texture coordinates *before* positions are warped properly simulates a warped plank.

3.4 Solid Texturing

Peachey [133] and Perlin [139] introduced solid texturing as a method for simulating the sculpting of objects (of arbitrary detail and genus) out of a solid material such as wood or stone. Solid texturing creates the illusion that a shape is carved out of a solid three-dimensional substance. The details in a solid texture align across the edges and corners of an object's surface regardless of its surface complexity. Depending on the detail and genus of the object, similar alignment of two-dimensional image texture maps can be very tricky.

Solid texturing identifies each point on a surface with a point in a three-dimensional solid texture space. The solid texture coordinates $\mathbf{s} = (s, t, r)$ of a surface point are often given by the point's spatial coordinates $\mathbf{x} = (x, y, z)$ or an affine transformation of its spatial coordinates.[3] This simulates the effect of embedding the surface in the texture space, thereby sculpting the surface out of a block of the solid texture material.

Figure 3.14 shows an example of a plank sculpted from a solid wood texture. Special care must be taken when deforming the object to ensure that the deformation does not cause the object to swim through the texture space.

---

[3]Modern graphics cards are actually capable of supporting projective transformations of solid texture coordinates.

Current graphics hardware supports solid texturing with the management of homogeneous three-dimensional texture coordinates and three-dimensional texture volumes that can be MIP-mapped to support anti-aliasing. However, the addition of a third array dimension can quickly consume available texture memory resources. It seems to be a waste of valuable texture memory to store an entire three-dimensional texture space when only a two-dimensional surface slice will ever be viewed. It was no coincidence that the first solid texturing systems were based on procedural texturing. One can also sample a solid texture beforehand and store the samples in ordinary two-dimensional textures, something that we discuss at length in Chapter 8, but this has all the parameterization problems of two-dimensional texturing of arbitrary objects.

3.5 Procedural Texturing

Procedural textures require much less memory than stored image textures, and unlike image textures their resolution depends only on computation precision. Procedural textures can fill a sky full with clouds without repeating any details, and without consuming any memory. Procedural textures can generate planets whose features can be investigated to seemingly infinite levels of detail. Procedural textures also make solid texturing practical. One simple classical procedural texture is the wood texture. Wood can be modeled using a cylindrical classification of space by the function

$$f(s, t, r) = (s^2 + t^2) \bmod 1. \tag{3.6}$$

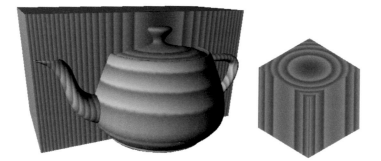

Figure 3.15. A teapot partially sculpted from a block of perfectly grown wood (left), procedurally textured using a family of concentric cylinders (right).

This function models the growth rings of a tree. The quadratic function is an accurate model of the growth rate as a first-order approximation since the later rings will be more closely spaced than the earlier rings. The function f is used to index a wood color map that ranges from a light "earlywood" color to a darker "latewood" color.

Figure 3.15 demonstrates this cylindrical wood procedural texture. This is a solid texture, and the features of the woodgrain meet across each of the areas of the model. Perhaps the most distracting aspect of the texture is that it is too regular. This regularity can be removed by the noise function described in the next section.

3.6 Noise Functions

One of the most common components of a procedural shading system is the noise function [139]. A noise function is a correlated three-dimensional field of "random" values. We don't actually use real random values, but a hash function of spatial position; noise functions are in fact completely deterministic. The spectrum of a noise function exists over a narrow band which can be used to control aliasing artifacts. These narrow bands can be scaled and summed to match the spectral properties of a variety of phenomena.

The most popular noise function used in graphics is Perlin noise [139]. The Perlin noise function defines random quantities at the integer coordinate locations in three dimensions, and interpolates the quantities across the cubic cells of the lattice. *Value noise* returns a random value at each integer lattice point, and interpolates these corner values across the edges,

Figure 3.16. The Perlin noise function over the domain $[-1, 1]^3$.

Figure 3.17. Left: Linear interpolation of random lattice value. Center: Cubic interpolation. Right: DNoise implemented by interpolating random lattice colors. (See Color Plate II.)

faces and interior of each cube. At each integer lattice point of gradient noise, the value is set to zero but the gradient is set to a random direction[4]. An interpolation method based on these gradients, such as Hermite interpolation, fills in the intermediate values across each cube, smoothly interpolating the zeros at the corners into their gradient directions. Value noise is easier to implement than gradient noise and both have similar appearances so we will limit the remainder of our discussion to value noise and call this function $\text{Noise}(s, t, r)$.

The interpolation of the random values (or derivatives) at the lattice vertices can be linear or cubic, as shown in Figure 3.17. Linear interpolation results in distracting artifacts of square features, whereas the features of the cubic interpolation are more rounded and natural. However, noise functions are commonly scaled and summed to achieve a desired frequency distribution, and this summing tends to disguise the artifacts of the individual noise functions.

The derivative of the noise function is called $\text{DNoise}(s, t, r)$ and is defined as the gradient of the noise function $\nabla \text{Noise}(s, t, r)$. It is often implemented as the interpolation of the gradients at the integer coordinate corners. An implementation of the DNoise function created by interpolating random colors placed at the lattice vertices is shown in Figure 3.17(right).

The spectrum of the noise function is ideally a narrow band. Hence noise functions can be scaled and summed to simulate a random process with any spectrum. The spectrum of natural processes tends to be $1/f$, which means that large events (e.g., mountains) occur at low frequencies, whereas small events (e.g., hills) occur more frequently. Figure 3.18 shows how a noise function can be summed to create a solid texturing space of natural randomness.

---

[4]This is Perlin's original formulation

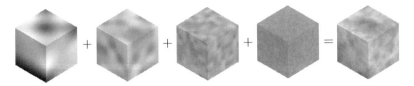

Figure 3.18.   Fractal $1/f$ noise constructed from the sum of noise functions whose amplitude is inversely proportional to their frequency.

3.6.1   Implementations

The Rayshade ray tracer has a nice implementation of the Perlin noise function. It creates its own pseudorandom numbers by hashing integer solid texture coordinates with a scalar function `Hash3d(i,j,k)`, then interpolates these random values with a simple smooth quasi-Gaussian s-curve cubic interpolant $S(u) = 3u^2 - 2u^3$ to yield the final result.

Given solid texture coordinates s, t, r, the Rayshade noise function effectively returns noise as the value

$$\sum_{i,j,k=0}^{1} \text{rand}(\lfloor s \rfloor + i, \lfloor t \rfloor + j, \lfloor r \rfloor + k)w(s,i)w(t,j)w(r,k) \qquad (3.7)$$

where

$$w(s,i) = S(s \bmod 1)^i(1 - S(s \bmod 1))^{1-i}. \qquad (3.8)$$

Because the Perlin noise function has become a ubiquitous but expensive tool in texture synthesis, it has been implemented in highly optimized forms on a variety of general and special purpose platforms. Several fast host-processor methods exist for synthesizing Perlin noise. Goehring et al. [54] implement a smooth noise function in Intel MMX assembly language, evaluating the function on a sparse grid, and use quadratic interpolation for the rest of the values. Kameya et al. [82] use streaming SIMD instructions that forward-difference a linearly interpolated noise function for fast rasterization of procedurally textured triangles.

One can also generate solid noise with a three-dimensional texture array of random values using hardware trilinear interpolation to correlate the random lattice values stored in a volumetric texture. Fractal turbulence functions can be created using multitexture/multipass modulate and sum operations. A texture atlas of solid texture coordinates would then be replaced with noise samples using the OpenGL pixel texture extension.

The vertex-shader programming model found in Direct3D 8.0 and the recent NVIDIA OpenGL vertex-shader extensions can support procedural solid texturing. A Perlin noise function has been implemented as a vertex program. But a per-vertex procedural texture produces vertex colors that are Gouraud-interpolated across faces, such that the frequency of the noise function must be at, or less than half, the frequency of the mesh vertices. This severely restricts the use of turbulence resulting from $1/f$ sums of noise. Hence the Perlin noise vertex shader is (currently) limited to low-frequency displacement mapping or other noise effects that can be mesh frequency bound.

3.6.2 A Multipass Implementation

Perlin noise can also be implemented as a multipass program [67]. The input to the multipass implementation is an image colored by its solid texture coordinates $(R, G, B) = (s, t, r)$, as shown in Figure 3.19. The noise value $\text{Noise}(s, t, r)$ for each pixel in this image will be constructed by weighting eight random values at the corners of the integer lattice cube containing (s, t, r).

We need eight images to represent these corners. The color of each pixel in these eight images is the (integer) solid texture coordinate of the corresponding corner. We first find the lower-left-rear corner by finding the integer part of the (s, t, r) color stored in the input image. We then find the eight other corners images' by adding one to the appropriate channels of the lower-left-rear image. (In early implementations of this algorithm, these operations were performed in eight-bit fixed point, with four bits integer and four bits fractional. Hence adding one meant adding the value 16 to the byte of the appropriate color channels.)

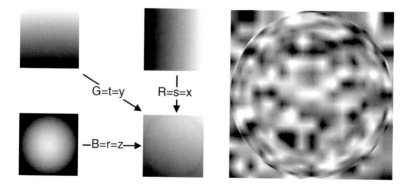

Figure 3.19. Left: An image of a sphere bulging from a plane, plotted as $(R, G, B) = (s, t, r) = (x, y, z)$. Right: A noise function has been applied to the solid texture coordinates stored in the color components of each pixel. (See Color Plate III.)

Figure 3.20. An example input image of solid texture coordinates (left) where s and t vary from zero to one, and $t = 0$. This input image is decomposed into an integer part (center) and a fractional part (right). (See Color Plate IV.)

Given the eight images whose pixels hold the integer coordinates of the cell corners of the corresponding pixel in the input image, we then need to generate random values. One simple method is to hash the color channels of a pixel into a single value by logically combining its bits in an arbitrary order. Then this hashed value can be used to index into a dependent texture, pixel texture, or PixelTransfer function, which references a precomputed list of random values. The pixels of the eight corner images are replaced by the random value they each index.

The eight corner images now need to be interpolated to create the value of the noise function corresponding to the input image. The percentages of each of the eight corner images will vary per pixel. Hence, we will use eight weighting images to determine, per pixel, the correct percentage of the eight corner-value-indexed images to include in the final result. We use the fractional portion of the color components of the input (s, t, r) image to define the weight of the corner random image indexed by the lower-left-rear corner integer value. The weighting images of the other seven corners are obtained by complementing the appropriate colors of this lower-left-rear weighting image.

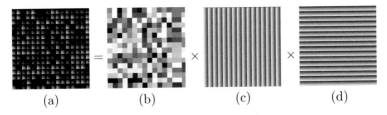

(a)   (b)   (c)   (d)

Figure 3.21. A corner image (a) generated by a random image (b) indexed by the corner integer solid texture coordinates, weighted by the fractional solid texture components $s - \lfloor s \rfloor$ (c) and $t - \lfloor t \rfloor$ (d).

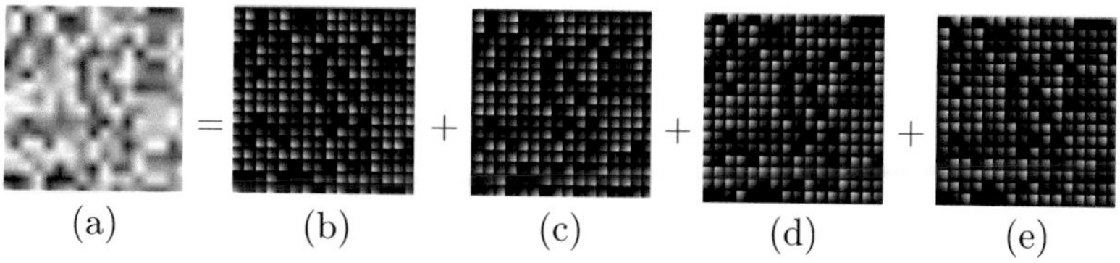

Figure 3.22. The noise image (a) corresponding to the noise function applied to the input image, generated by summing the weight corner random images (b–e).

Hence, the final noise function, shown in Figure 3.19 (right) is produced as the sum of the eight random corner images modulated by the eight corresponding weighting images. We can also create a vector-values DNoise implementation by having the pixels of the eight corner images index into a precomputed list of random colors instead of random values.

4

Procedural Shaders

As mentioned previously, a procedural shader is a program written in a high-level language designed to describe the appearance of a material or a light source. Shaders can be described graphically with networks of shading nodes [2], or textually with programs [65]. The shader allows an appearance to be encapsulated procedurally in a uniform device-independent manner.

In the literature, the term *shader* has been adopted for all types of procedures within the pipeline, not just materials and lights, but also transformations, fog, and others.

Shaders (of any type) can be compiled to a variety of different target graphics architectures. For example, the RenderMan interface has been implemented using both scan-line rendering and ray tracing.

Shaders also offer benefits of software reuse and integration. Shaders for different tasks can be written independently, but used together. For example, one could combine a shiny reflectance model with a bumpy texture, even if they were written by different people at different times with no knowledge that they would ever be used together. Shaders are also somewhat invulnerable to the problems of the bleeding edge of graphics architecture innovation. Shaders need not be rewritten; their compiler needs to be retargetted.

4.1 Logical Model

Procedural shaders can often be implemented in a variety of ways on a given graphics architecture. In addition to translating the high-level shading language into low-level graphics operations, a shading language compiler has the freedom to assign computation from one procedure to multiple units in the hardware pipeline or multiple procedures to a single unit in the hardware pipeline. The computational divisions chosen for the hardware don't have to be reflected in the shading language, which can be chosen to match the needs of the artists and programmers who will write the shaders.

Since the organization of shading procedures doesn't have to match that of the graphics system or software (and often won't), a central question is how the procedures are connected. This chapter deals with this *logical model* of the rendering process—the view of the system presented to a shader-writer.

To support procedural interfaces (i.e., shaders) throughout the rendering process, we need a reasonable decomposition into stages where the user-defined procedures could go. As stated above, these stages represent the programmer's view of the system and may not directly correspond to the hardware pipeline stages. Individual shader stages are implemented by the system designers to look like a stage of an *abstract pipeline*.

The benefit of shaders is that the abstract pipeline need not have any direct connection to the physical pipeline being used. A hardware implementation is free to add additional hidden stages or change the execution order of the stages; split procedures between multiple hardware stages; or join procedures on a single hardware stage. Pretty much anything is OK, as long as the procedure inputs and outputs don't change.

Every current shading system makes a different choice of logical model. To understand and compare them, we need a simple notation to describe the models. We'll use simple block diagrams, where each block is one shader or procedure, and the links between the blocks indicate how data flows. Figure 4.1 shows a simple, but functional, logical model. We imagine geometric information (vertex positions, normals, shading parameters, etc.) flowing in the top link. Vertices and normals are transformed by the

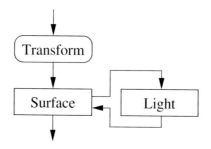

Figure 4.1.   Sample logical model. Each block is handled by an independent procedure. The rounded block indicates that *Transform* is a proposed procedure that is not yet fully programmable, while the *Surface* and *Light* blocks are.

transform shader in the first block. The results are used in some rendering process that isn't programmable in this example, producing pixels that are processed by the surface shader. The surface shader may use the results of one or more light shaders (hanging off to the side), to produce final pixel colors at the bottom.

In these diagrams, data flows from top to bottom. The data types between blocks need not match, whatever extra processing is necessary to convert (say from vertex data to pixel data) is not programmable and assumed to happen on the links between the blocks.

Since real-time shading systems are a moving target, we will also indicate the creator's overall plan using rounded and square boxes. Rounded boxes, such as the one for the transform stage, will indicate a stage that is proposed, but not implemented (at least as of this writing), while squared boxes like the ones for surface and light stages indicate stages that are fully functional.

Varying degrees of programmability have been provided in the years of software renderer development. The examples range from low-level prototype *testbed* graphics systems designed to be reprogrammed only by the original author to high-level production *shading languages* designed to support communities of graphics programming professionals. Both can shed light on what to choose as a good set of procedure types.

4.2   Procedural Shading Testbeds

Most experiments with programmability, even for software renderers, have been testbed systems. These are designed to allow the system creator to experiment with a variety of shading and rendering techniques. Creating and using a testbed system requires a certain sophistication in graphics. A useful testbed requires a good characterization of the common themes of all of the rendering or shading techniques that will be explored, yet must not be so restrictive that new ideas cannot be tried. The testbed is created as a modular rendering system based on these assumptions. New shaders, primitives, or transformations are implemented as replacement modules, generally in the same programming language used for the rest of the testbed. As long as the new modules obey the assumptions of the testbed, they are easy to create and investigate. To some degree, every rendering system that is not implemented entirely in hardware is part testbed, but we're interested in the ones that were planned that way.

Whitted and Weimer published a description of one of the earliest systems designed explicitly as a testbed [177]. They supported experimental primitives and shaders. Each primitive supplied the first scan-line where it would become active. At this scan-line, it could either be rendered directly using a scan-line algorithm or split into simpler pieces, each with its own starting scan-line. For shading, the primitive would interpolate arbitrary *shading parameters*, producing values at each pixel. A separate shading process would compute a color for each pixel. Since rendering could be slow and costly, a single set of rendered shading parameters could be reused for tests of several different shading algorithms.

Hall and Greenberg [64] and Trumbore, Lyttle and Greenberg [169] produced testbed systems for Cornell's global illumination research. These frameworks allowed easy testing of different *light transport* algorithms. The Hall and Greenberg system was based on ray tracing, and was similar to the ray-tracing testbeds that will be described next (though admittedly with different goals). The Trumbore, Lyttle, and Greenberg system was interesting in its reversal of the normal testbed organization. It provided a collection of library routines that could be called by user code. This places the user's code in charge of the scheduling of the different rendering tasks. This makes it more like the data-flow testbeds described later in this section.

A modular framework is almost guaranteed for any ray tracer. Rays are shot into the scene. Each primitive reports its closest intersection with a ray. Once a closest intersection has been chosen from among the primitives, either a color or shading parameter values are produced at the intersection point. As a result of this built-in framework, there have been a number of testbed ray tracers.

The 1983 Hall and Greenberg system already mentioned is one of these. Rubin and Whitted provided an environment for testing bounding volume hierarchies and surfaces defined through recursive subdivision (i.e., the surface can be split into smaller pieces, which can be split into still smaller pieces, which eventually can be converted into triangles or some other directly ray-traceable primitive) [153]. Wyvill and Kunii have a system for ray tracing complex CSG (*Constructive Solid Geometry*) objects. The complex objects are built of Boolean combinations of simpler objects, in their case, defined implicitly (by an arbitrary function—the surface is the locus of points where a function is zero) [183]. Kuchkuda created a simple modular ray tracer in C, which was expanded by Kolb into his popular, free Rayshade ray tracer [90, 91].

Finally, there have been a number of data-flow testbeds, allowing the pipeline order to be changed to experiment with different organizations for the flow of rendering data through the system. This effectively allows a single testbed renderer to support several different rendering algorithms.

Hedelman created a data-flow test bed allowing procedural models, transformations, and shaders to be connected together [70]. For example, you could apply a transformation before both model and shader, or between them. The shader could be applied across several models or on just one. The basic blocks of shader, transform and model were connected together into a tree, not unlike our logical model diagrams.

Fleischer and Witkin wrote a conceptually elegant LISP system, allowing fully programmable LISP modules to be connected together arbitrarily [45]. It represents each procedural transformation as a set of four functions that compute the transformation and inverse transformation for points and vectors. This system also requires all surfaces to have both implicit and parametric formulations so the system can be free to choose either ray-tracing or scan-line rendering. Nadas, Glassner and Trumbore have all produced other interesting data-flow testbed systems, all of which allow C or C++ procedures to be connected together in arbitrary ways [53, 124, 170].

4.3 RenderMan

The RenderMan standard was presented by Hanrahan and Lawson in 1990 [65] and described in detail by Upstill [171]. RenderMan provides a geometry description library similar to OpenGL [159], a geometric file format (called RIB), and a shading language. The library API (application program interface) is used by application developers to describe the geometry to be rendered. There is a one-to-one correspondence between the library function calls and the lines in a RIB file. In Pixar's PhotoRealistic RenderMan, calls to the library generate the RIB file. The renderer reads the RIB file to render the scene. RIB files are also used by other animation and modeling applications to create geometric descriptions that can be rendered with a RenderMan renderer.

Several implementations of the RenderMan standard exist, though all are software renderers. The first implementation, and the one against which all others are judged, is Pixar's own PhotoRealistic RenderMan. PhotoRealistic RenderMan uses the *REYES* rendering algorithm [34]. A few of the other RenderMan implementations include a free one using ray-tracing (the Blue Moon Rendering Tools or BMRT) [61], and another created for experiments with global illumination [162], plus at least a few other commercial RenderMan compatible software renderers (e.g., from Exluna or RenderDotC). Each implementation has its own strengths, but the same application, RIB files, or shaders will work on all of them, without change, to

produce comparable, if not identical, images. RenderMan effectively hides
the details of the implementation. Not only does this have the advantage
of allowing multiple implementations using completely different rendering
algorithms, but it also means that the user writing the application and
shaders doesn't need to know anything about the rendering algorithm being used. Knowledge of basic graphics concepts suffices. This is a huge
departure from normal testbed systems, where the programmer who writes
the procedural pieces needs to know both details of the rendering algorithm
and details of the implementation.

One key to this generality is the shading language. The shading language is a high-level language, similar to a subset of C, with extensions
useful for shading and other procedures. It is designed to handle transformations, deformations (small-scale perturbations of the actual geometry),
lighting, surface shading, and atmospheric effects.

The logical model for RenderMan shading language procedures is shown
in Figure 4.2. The procedural model stage doesn't use the shading language, and was proposed well before it was fully implemented on any RenderMan implementation. Since the RIB file format lists only the name of
the procedural model where it is used, the model itself is created in a library form that can be loaded by the renderer at run-time. The overall
procedural model interface appears more like what we are calling a *testbed*
interface, similar to the one used by Whitted and Weimer [177], with one
function returning a bounding box for the primitive, one to subdivide it
into other primitives, and one to free its data.

The procedural transformation stage has been documented since the
early versions of RenderMan, though no implementations supported it and
it has been deprecated in the RenderMan 3.2 specification [143]. As originally defined, it computes a new position and normal for any input point.
Many of the instances where a procedural transformation might be used are
done with displacement instead. Displacement has the same output (new
position and normal), but has more information about the local surface at
its disposal, including surface tangents, texture coordinates, eye position,
and incident viewing ray direction.

Surface and light procedures are similar to those described previously
and in more detail in Sections 4.4.6 and 4.4.7. Especially for ray-tracing
implementations, where a ray can bounce from object to object or be refracted through objects, there can be multiple surfaces interspersed with
volume shaders. The volume shader models the attenuation of the light
passing through objects or open space.

The atmosphere shader is another volume shader, intended to model
any fog or other effects between surfaces and the eye. Finally, the *imager*

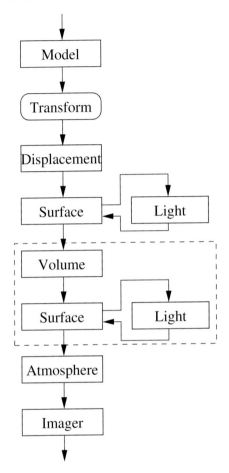

Figure 4.2. RenderMan logical model.

block allows changes to the final pixel color before it is displayed or stored into a file.

Pixar also uses a procedural interface for animation, called MENV or Marionette. MENV has been described by Leffler, Reeves and Ostby [98], though its details are outside the scope of this book.

4.4 Elements of Procedural Shaders

A fairly extensive analysis was done for the PixelFlow graphics system before deciding on a logical model for its procedures [129]. Since no PixelFlow

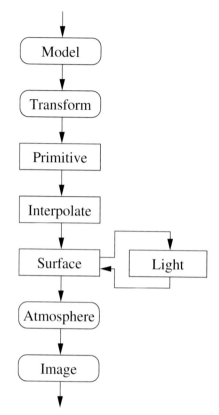

Figure 4.3. Logical model developed for PixelFlow.

systems are still running, its practical details are not likely to be of much use to any but the most dedicated readers of this book. However, since it was a fully programmable machine and some effort was made to choose a reasonable set of procedures, it provides a good starting point for looking at organization of the elements used for real-time shading.

The shading procedure writer's interface for PixelFlow described a pipeline in which every stage was programmable. Figure 4.3 shows this overall pipeline. The procedures were designed to be *orthogonal*, so that a new procedure for one stage would not require any changes to the procedures for the other stages. A particular hardware implementation could therefore just allow procedural access to those stages that it is able to support. The PixelFlow hardware was physically capable of supporting procedures at all of the suggested stages, but only primitive, interpolate, shade, and light were implemented.

In the following sections, we provide a brief description of each of the stages in the PixelFlow logical model. We also provide a brief survey of prior work for each procedure classification—the justification for dividing the rendering task into the blocks that were chosen.

4.4.1 Maps

Maps are not a stage, per se, but a type of procedure that may be used by any of the stages. Image maps are common in graphics. For example, a texture map is a two-dimensional image. The texture map is pasted onto a surface like a decal. The mapping is accomplished through a pair of texture coordinates that parameterize the surface (covered in detail in Chapter 3). The same two-dimensional texture coordinates can be used to map a bump map onto the surface. Instead of color, the bump map has information that is used to perturb the surface normal to change the surface shading [19].

Other mapping techniques don't rely on texture coordinates, but use another method to map values onto the surface. Like texture maps, reflection or environment maps also determine a color to apply to the surface (see Section 3.2.2). However, with environment mapping, the location in the two-dimensional image is determined by the direction of a reflection off of the surface, allowing simulatation of shiny objects [180]. Shadow maps are projected onto the surface from a light in the scene, and determine whether each point of the surface is lit or in shadow [179].

All of these techniques have a common theme. You start with a two- or three-dimensional array of values (the texture). Any one of a variety of techniques is used to decide where to look in the texture for each point on the surface (mapping the texture onto the surface). The resulting value is used as a parameter to the shading model. Procedural maps are just the programmable version of this idea. A procedural map is a function instead of an image. Instead of looking up texture results in an image map, any stage can call a map function to obtain the parameter value.

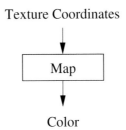

Figure 4.4. Procedural map.

With image texture maps, the same shader can be used with many different image textures to get many different effects. Similarly, the exact same shader could be used with any matching procedural map for an even greater variety. Procedural maps can be used wherever image maps would be. Procedural maps can also be generalized beyond simple replacements for two-dimensional image maps. The procedural maps can be functions of a different size (e.g., one-, three-, four-, or nine-dimensional instead of just two-dimensional), though only procedural maps of the same input and output dimensions can be substituted for each other. In other words, a procedural map is just a function that can be replaced under application control.

The hardware procedural shading capability on Pixel-Planes 5, described by Rhoades et al. [152] is really just an instance of procedural maps in a fixed Phong shader. The map function complexity was limited by the pixel memory on Pixel-Planes 5 (208 bits). The shading language was also not very high-level. It included simple operations (add, multiply, copy) and some more complicated built-in functions (wood, Julia set, Gardner textures, Perlin noise).

So, procedural maps are essentially just procedural replacements for the more common image texture maps. Other than the Pixel-Planes 5 system, procedural maps have not been well explored. In many cases, the procedure could be run in advance to create two-dimensional images from the map, which can be used by current hardware to simulate the same results.

4.4.2 Modeling

Modeling is the construction of objects and scenes out of basic geometric primitives. Usually, objects are defined as a rigid set of primitives. A procedural interface can be used to define rigid models, but it is more interesting for models that move, change shape, possess awareness of their

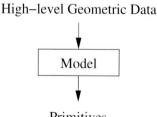

Figure 4.5. Procedural models.

Figure 4.6. Example of a procedural model.

environment and automatically interact with it, or possess awareness of their viewing conditions and change accordingly.

Procedural models use a set of control parameters to generate a description of the model in terms of geometric primitives or other procedural models. Most polygon-based systems implement spline patches in this way. These smooth patches are defined by a small set of control points. For rendering, the patch is first split into smaller patches. When the patches become small enough, they are rendered as polygons. A few other possibilities for procedural models are particle systems [151], fractals [68, 109], L-systems [147], hypertextures [140], and generative models [165].

The graphics API library itself usually serves as a procedural model interface. However, several systems have been created that provide an alternate form for defining procedural models. PixelFlow's procedural model interface was influenced by work done by Newell, Hedelman, Amburn, Green, and Perlin, as well as the procedural model interface in RenderMan.

Newell did some of the earliest work in codifying procedural models in 1975. His *procedure models* were an object-oriented representation (in the data-structures sense) of the objects in the scene [126]. Each model is an opaque entity, capable of responding to two messages: draw the object and provide an approximate three-dimensional extent for the object. Those two messages serve as the only connection between the rendering system and the models themselves, and within those rather broad constraints, a model procedure could do almost anything to decide which pixels to draw.

In 1984, Hedelman added the idea of procedural models capable of smart culling [70]. Such a model can use viewing information to choose one of several representations at different levels of detail. His models could also be linked together in arbitrary order with transformations and shaders into a tree. Thus a shader might be transformed before application to a model, or one shader might be applied across several models.

Amburn, Grant, and Whitted described two ideas for procedural modeling in a paper published in 1986 [6]. They presented a generalization of the subdivision used in Whitted and Weimer's testbed system [177], where a representation is subdivided until a transition test triggers a change to a different representation. The new representation can be another procedural model or a set of primitives. The spline algorithm mentioned previously is one example of such a model—it subdivides into similar spline patches until some test triggers the change to a polygonal representation. They also used communication between procedural models. Two interacting model procedures send messages to each other.

Green and Sun used a preprocessor to C, called MML, to generate rule-, or grammar-based, models [58]. This is similar to Prusinkiewicz' work on L-systems for modeling trees [147]. For example, a tree might be defined with a rule to split a branch into a trunk and two branches. By recursively applying the rules, they can create a large model.

In 1989, Perlin and Hoffert presented *hypertexture*, a modeling technique where an ordinary surface is thickened into a region of space with some density. A procedure modulates the density, creating a three-dimensional texture effect on the surface. The hypertexture surface can then be rendered by traditional volume-rendering techniques.

Finally, RenderMan includes procedural model interface (discussed in more detail in Section 4.3). While defined by the RenderMan standard from the beginning, it was not supported by Pixar's PhotoRealistic RenderMan until 1997 in version 3.7.

Why the delay for something that seems to have been studied so well? The application and RenderMan API library communicate with the renderer through a RIB file, and may not even run at the same time. This makes it is difficult for the renderer to call the procedural model functions. Only once dynamic loading of libraries became a common OS feature, was it feasible for a renderer like RenderMan to handle procedural models cleanly.

PixelFlow's procedural models were proposed to follow this latter mold, though under control of a shading-language procedure rather than C code. Models would either subdivide into simpler models or emit primitives to be passed further down the pipe. These types of models can handle many things, but cannot easily handle hypertexture, unless the final primitives are volume-based (they were not), or the hypertexture modeler can produce an isosurface of simpler primitives.

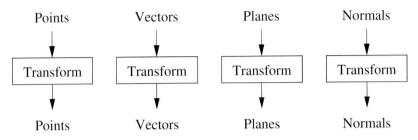

Figure 4.7. PixelFlow procedural transformation.

4.4.3 Transformation

Transformations are mappings of an object from one coordinate system to another. They are used to build models from component parts, for object motion, and ultimately to find the object's projection onto the screen. A transformation procedure takes a three-dimensional point or vector as its input and produces a new 3D point or vector.

The most common set of transformations used for graphics are the simple linear mappings of homogeneous points. For three-dimensional points, (x, y, z), the basic linear mappings create a new set of x, y, and z coordinates as a linear combination of the original x, y, and z. These linear mappings allow rotation and scaling of objects. With a homogeneous representation, $(x, y, z, 1)$, the linear mappings can be extended to include translation and perspective projection [46].

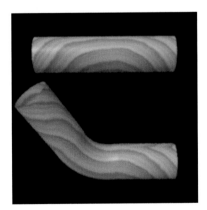

Figure 4.8.   Example of a procedural transformation, as rendered through a RenderMan displacement shader.

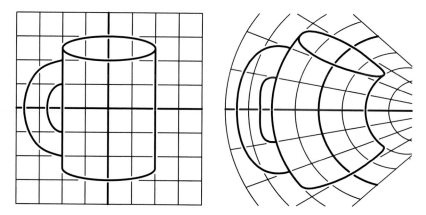

Figure 4.9. Local deformation.

Since transformation is just a mapping between coordinate systems, there is no reason to use only linear mappings. Because they deform the objects, nonlinear transformations are more commonly known as deformations. Two different kinds of deformations are in fairly common use [14, 158]. These are sometimes used for static modeling (positioning and sculpting of the parts of a model), but more often for animation of flexible objects.

Barr defined global and local deformations based on standard linear transformations, where the transformation parameters are simple functions of position. For example, a twist around the y-axis is defined as a rotation around the y-axis where the rotation angle is proportional to the y coordinate. This is more easily seen in a two-dimensional example (Figure 4.9). This figure shows a bend of the y-axis, defined as a rotation around a point on the x-axis, where the rotation angle depends on the y coordinate. This illustration also shows one of the common features of all transformations and deformations. The transformation deforms the space itself. The object is transformed only by virtue of its embedding in the space.

Sederberg defines *Free Form Deformations* (FFDs) as a spline warping of the space around an object. Just as a spline patch defines a mapping from a two-dimensional parameter space to positions on the patch, a spline volume defines a mapping from a three-dimensional parameter space to a 3D point in the volume. Thus, it is a mapping from three-dimensions to three-dimensions, and can be used as a transformation (Figure 4.10).

The full range of deformations is much larger than the subset covered by these two types. In addition, the Barr and Sederberg deformations do

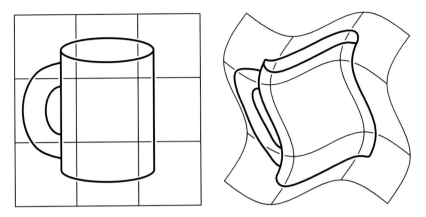

Figure 4.10. Free-form deformation.

not always provide very intuitive control. A tricubic FFD has 64 control points (4^3). In practice, simplified parameterization of their controls are preferred [98, 175]. For example, a single bending parameter might control the positions of the FFD control points. Procedural transformations can support the full set of possible transformations, while also providing more intuitive controls. Procedural transformation handles fixed rotations and transformations, local and global deformations, free form deformations, parameterized control point motion, and more.

Fleischer and Witkin defined true user-accessible programmable transformations as a set of four functions [45]. These four functions provide transformations for points and vectors, and the inverse transformation for each. The inverse transformations are necessary for correctly transforming planes and surface normals [131]. They are also useful for transforming from the distorted space back to the undistorted object.

The RenderMan specification defines transformation shaders [171]. As discussed in Section 4.3, they have never been implemented, and have since been removed from the RenderMan specification. The transformation shaders specified by RenderMan included only transformations of points and normals, not vectors or planes. Version 3.5 of Pixar's PhotoRealistic RenderMan added vector and normal transformation functions for use by the shading procedures; however, the procedural transformation specification did not change accordingly. In a pinch, RenderMan's displacement mapping can be used as a form of procedural transformation. Though it can cause rendering performance problems, it is often used in this way. Pixar's MENV system allows procedural control of the parameters of the classic types of deformations [98].

PixelFlow proposed to adopt the four-function Fliescher and Witkin transformation functions. The requirement to write four functions for each procedural transformation is rather onerous and could be prone to error.

4.4.4 Primitives

Primitives are the basic building blocks—the atoms—of the graphics system. They are the basic units that are rendered directly. A primitive procedure decides which pixels are inside the primitive. It may also use a specialized method to compute values for some shading parameters.

The Pixel-Planes 5 graphics system provides good anecdotal support for the need for procedural primitives. No user-level support was provided for writing primitives, yet a number of users went through the trouble to write their own custom primitives [129].

Given the number of primitive types currently available, the chances are good that any given rendering system will have missed several of them. A few possibilities are polygons, spline patches, subdivision surfaces, spheres, quadrics, superquadrics, metaballs, and other implicit models, generative models, smart points, and volume elements.

Ray tracing renders by shooting rays into the scene and rendering the closest intersection with the ray. New primitives in a ray tracer only have to support a ray-object intersection test, so procedural primitives are easily supported [64, 90, 91, 153, 183]. Examples are harder to find for non-ray-traced renderers. A handful of test bed systems have provided some degree of primitive programmability [35, 45, 64, 124, 177]. These testbeds require the new primitive to be created in the language of the testbed, using some general internal interface.

PixelFlow had an interface for writing procedural primitives in the pfman language. This interface allowed subdivision into other primitives or direct Z-buffered rendering. The direct rendering interface was fairly prim-

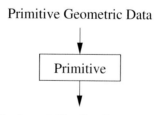

Figure 4.11. Procedural primitive.

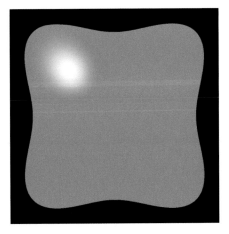

Figure 4.12. Example of a procedural primitive with a profile defined by a polynomial, as rendered interactively on PixelFlow.

itive and difficult to use since it was tightly bound to the interpolation stage (described next).

4.4.5 Interpolation

Interpolation is the computation of shading parameter values across each primitive, such as surface normals, colors, or texture coordinates. Some of the prior work in procedural shading (discussed next) demonstrates that this interpolation is independent of the shading procedure or its parameters. Since all that is important to the surface shader is the resulting parameter values at each pixel, any method may be used to compute the values. Thus, a procedural interpolator must produce shading parameter values for the set of pixels determined by the primitive.

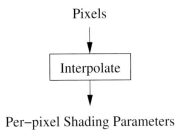

Figure 4.13. Procedural interpolation.

Figure 4.14. Example of procedural interpolation, embedding object in cylindrical coordinates, as rendered within a RenderMan shader.

The OpenGL API allows the texture coordinates to be interpolated using *texture coordinate generators* [159]. These texture coordinate generators include planar projection, spherical projection, or cylindrical projection. Any of these methods can be used to project the texture coordinates onto any primitive. Ebert allows arbitrary procedural interpolation with his *solid spaces* [41]. A solid space defines values throughout a three-dimensional volume. Ebert uses solid space to construct procedural models of smoke and fog.

The texture coordinate generators found in OpenGL are not an example of procedural interpolation, but they do demonstrate that more flexible interpolation techniques have been found useful enough to appear in interactive graphics hardware systems. It is easy to see how the fixed set of texture coordinate generators can be extended to other shading parameters or made as flexible as Ebert's solid spaces.

Procedural interpolation in PixelFlow followed this model. This provides general projection and embedding of objects in a parameter space for volume shading, but any surface-based interpolation is tightly bound to one particular procedural primitive.

4.4.6 Surface Shading

Since surface shading is one of the primary subjects of this book, it needs little introduction here. In this context, we are concerned with shading functions that compute a color for one point on a surface based on the lighting, surface properties, and the raw surface color. Unlike some of the other procedure types, surface shading appears in essentially the same form in any kind of rendering, whether Z-buffer, ray tracing, or volume rendering. After modeling (at least at the level provided by a graphics API), surface shading is the facet of the rendering process that is most often attacked by procedural methods.

Procedural shading describes the shading of a surface through a simple function to turn the surface attributes and shading parameters into a color. Over the past several years there has been a trend among high-quality rendering programs to include shading languages and procedural shading capabilities.

In early systems, programmability was supported by rewriting the shading code for the renderer. Whitted and Weimer explicitly allowed this in their testbed system [177]. Their *span buffers* are an implementation of a technique now called *deferred shading*. In this technique, the parameters for shading are scan-converted, producing an image-buffer full of shading parameters. Shading is done after all of the primitives have been scan-converted. For their software system, this allowed them to run multiple shaders on the same scene without having to spend the time to rerender.

More recently, easier access to procedural shading capability has been provided to the graphics programmer. Cook's *shade trees* [33] are the base of most later shading works. He turned simple expressions describing the shading at a point on the surface into a parse tree form, which was interpreted. A powerful set of precompiled library functions helped produce a reasonable rendering speed. He introduced the name *appearance parameters* for the parameters that affect the shading calculations. He also proposed an orthogonal subdivision of types of programmable functions into surface shade trees, light trees, and atmosphere trees. This corresponds exactly to the shading, lighting, and fog stages of Figure 4.15. Abram and Whitted created an implementation of Cook's shade trees called *building*

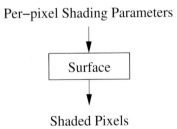

Figure 4.15. Procedural shader.

Figure 4.16. Example of procedural shading, showing a three-dimensional wood shader as rendered interactively on PixelFlow.

block shaders [2]. They had a graphical interface to construct the trees by plugging blocks together instead of using an expression parser.

Perlin's image synthesizer made the jump from simple expressions in Cook's shade trees to a full language with control structures [139]. He also introduced the powerful Perlin noise function, which produces random numbers with a band-limited frequency spectrum. This style of noise plays a major role in many procedural textures (see Section 3.6).

The RenderMan shading language (discussed in some detail earlier in this chapter and later in Chapter 12) extends the work of Cook and Perlin even further. They extend the procedure types introduced by Cook to include displacement mapping, transformations, image operations, and volume effects. The RenderMan shading language was originally presented as a standard so that shaders can be portable to any conforming implementation.

4.4.7 Lighting

Procedural lighting functions determine the intensity and color of light that hits a surface point from a light source. They can be used for a variety of shadow and slide projector techniques.

Surface Position

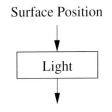

Light Color and Direction

Figure 4.17. Procedural light.

RenderMan and Cook's shade trees make an important conceptual distinction between lighting and shading. The same light procedure may be used by all of the shading procedures. A prime example of the power of lighting procedures is the window pane light in Pixar's *Tin Toy* [171]. A version of this light, rendered on PixelFlow, is shown in Figure 4.18.

Slusallek and collaborators at the University of Erlangen [163] created a graphical tree of *LightOps*, similar to the building-block shader representation [2]. Each LightOp represents a light or surface that reflects light in the scene. The connections between the LightOps represent the light that bounces from surface to surface. The resulting lighting network, which may include cycles, describes all of the light interactions as light bounces from object to object in a global illumination simulation.

PixelFlow lighting pretty faithfully copied the lighting provided by RenderMan. Multiple bounces were not supported.

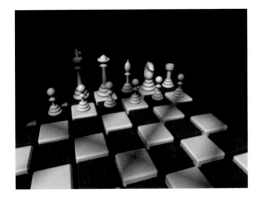

Figure 4.18.   Example of a window pane light shader, as rendered interactively on PixelFlow. (See Color Plate V.)

Color and Position

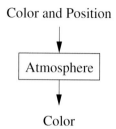

Color

Figure 4.19. Procedural atmospheric effects.

4.4.8 Volume and Atmospheric Effects

Procedural volume and atmospheric shaders handle the behavior of light as it passes through a medium, normally the space between a visible surface and the viewer. A few examples are fog, haze, atmospheric color shift, and density thresholding.

Cook defines atmospheric shade trees to handle fog and similar color effects between the surfaces and the viewer [33]. RenderMan extends this to two types of shaders, volume and atmospheric, to handle the passage of light through and outside of objects in the scene [65]. PixelFlow's model was similar to both. The atmospheric shaders take in a color produced from a surface in the scene and modify it to account for attenuation through the atmosphere between that surface and the eye.

Figure 4.20. Example of a procedural atmospheric shader, as rendered interactively on PixelFlow.

Pixels

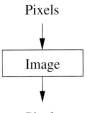

Pixels

Figure 4.21. Procedural image warp and filter.

4.4.9 Image Warping and Filtering

Procedural warping can be used to support a host of video-warping special effects: water droplets on a camera lens, for example. Procedural warping can also compensate for the barrel distortion caused by the lenses used in some head-mounted displays. Image warping effects require grabbing the final pixel color for one place in the image from another place in the image.

For image filtering the image pixels do not move, but are combined to achieve effects like blurring, sharpening, or brightening. Warping and filtering are similar because both use the values of one or more pixels in the input image to compute the value of each pixel in the output image.

Simple image modifications can be done with the RenderMan *imager shaders* [65]. As with all RenderMan procedures, imager shaders are written from the point of view of a single pixel. Since they do not allow access to the color results of other pixels, imager shaders do things like change the image brightness, but cannot do either filtering or warping effects, or even simple tone mapping.[1]

Better procedural warping and filtering capabilities can be found in image manipulation programs. Adobe Photoshop has a plug-in interface, which allows new filtering and warping functions to be written in C [89]. The GIMP (Gnu Image Manipulation Program) has a similar C plug-in interface, and also has both Scheme and Perl scripting interfaces [92].

The main form of filtering present in interactive graphics systems is antialiasing. The results of several image samples are combined to create the result color for a single pixel. By incorporating the procedural methods present in image manipulation software, we can provide a rich set of post-processing alternatives for three-dimensional images.

---

[1]Tone mapping is the process of scaling colors based on global or local intensities across an image to simulate the viewing of images with values beyond the range of intensities that a monitor or other display device can produce. For example, the tone mapping algorithm by Gregory Ward Larson compresses contrast on areas of an image based on the local image area [95].

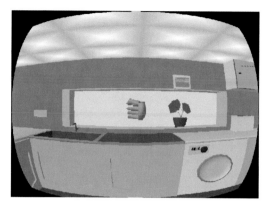

Figure 4.22. Example of a procedural image warp.

4.4.10 Shading Capabilities

Since surface shading is the most explored procedural method, we have a good understanding of the capabilities provided by procedural shading that are not possible with image texturing or other simple models previously used in interactive graphics systems. These include animated shaders, volume shaders, shaders with great computed detail, and shaders that do automatic antialiasing.

Procedural shading allows animated shaders, where the appearance of the surface changes with time. In animated shaders, time is just another control parameter for the shader. The animated ripple shown in Figure 4.23 is an example of this. It is possible to get similar effects by flipping through a set of image textures, but the animated procedural texture can react to changes on the fly. This animated ripple shader creates ripples under interactive user control.

Figure 4.23. Animated ripple shader.

Figure 4.24.   A surface shader that computes the Mandelbrot set, a function with infinite detail.

Procedural shading also allows volume shaders, where the surface appearance is derived from the position of the surface. This can be contrasted to typical image texturing techniques that attempt to map a two-dimensional image onto a surface. Sometimes this mapping can be quite difficult. The wood texture, show in Figure 4.16 is an example of a procedural volume texture. Image volume textures, as a stack of two-dimensional image textures, have appeared in interactive graphics hardware. For good results, they require stacking a large number of two-dimensional textures. A procedural volume texture has no additional cost for extra depth since all detail is computed.

Since procedural shaders are only computed for a limited number of samples, they can contain much greater detail than image textures. As we zoom closer to the surface, we can see more of the detail, but the additional detail computation only has to be done for a limited portion of the surface. For example, the Mandelbrot shader shown in Figure 4.24 is based on a mathematical function that has infinite detail. The shader cannot have truly infinite detail, but it does have visible detail to the precision limits of the computations involved. It would be prohibitively expensive to compute and store an image texture at the resolution limit (consisting of about $1.8 * 10^{19}$ pixels); a procedural shader computes only the subset of those pixels that appear in each frame.

Procedural shaders also have the ability to do automatic antialiasing, as is seen in Figure 4.25. Some procedural shaders do no antialiasing, and as a result are only useful at a limited range of distances. Others do much more sophisticated antialiasing. Both procedural shaders and image textures have a tradeoff between cost and antialiasing quality. The point along this

Figure 4.25. Antialiasing steps for a procedural shader (zoomed in to see detail). Antialiasing was done manually in the shader source.

spectrum typically chosen for interactive graphics systems is antialiasing using the MIP-mapping technique. MIP-maps contain a pyramid of filtered texture images, each level a quarter of the size of the one above it. This takes just 33% more space than the original full-size texture and provides good antialiasing at any distance as long as the textured surface is directly faces the viewer, with some degree of over-blurring if the texture is tilted away from the viewer. Antialiasing of shaders is discussed in more detail in the next section.

4.5   Antialiasing

The aliasing problem for procedural shaders is different from that for image textures. In particular, the procedural shader itself already describes a function at every point on the image plane, which means that this function does not have to be reconstructed from discrete samples as in the case of texture maps. There is therefore no analogy to the texture magnification problem with procedural shaders.

However, procedural shaders can potentially suffer from minification problems since they can procedurally define arbitrarily high frequencies. Theoretically, procedural textures could be prerendered into image texture maps and then MIP-mapped. But such precomputation defeats the purpose and benefits of procedural texturing. When procedural textures are used for solid textures, this would require storage of three-dimensional texture volumes at decreasing resolutions.

Several techniques have been used to antialias surface shaders. Since the surface shader can be an arbitrarily complex function, correct antialiasing has the potential to be much more difficult than for image texturing. The major techniques are analytical filtering, attenuation of high-frequency elements, and super sampling. Much of the work in this area is covered by Ebert et al. [41].

4.5.1 Analytical Filtering

Analytical filtering attempts to convolve a simple shader with a filter kernel. If this can be done exactly, the result is as good an antialiased shader as possible. The basic approach is presented by Peachy [41]. First if's and other conditional expressions are replaced by step functions (step(t) is 0 for t<0 and 1 for t>0). Then the step functions are replaced by a filtered form. RenderMan provides boxstep, smoothstep, and filterstep; versions of step convolved with different filter kernels.

Perlin discusses replacing conditionals with filtered step functions automatically [41]. Heidrich, Slusallek and Seidel extend this idea by also using affine arithmetic to keep track of the possible range values for all of the expressions in the shader [78]. This provides information on the possible error in the resulting filtered shader.

4.5.2 Frequency Attenuation

The second technique for antialiasing shaders is to selectively attenuate high-frequency elements in the shader, as discussed by Peachy [41]. This method is assisted by the use of a *band-limited noise* function introduced by Perlin [139]. Band-limited noise is a common building block for shaders. It can be thought of as white noise that has been put through a band-pass filter to limit the frequencies to the octave between a base frequency and half the base frequency. As the base frequency approaches the pixel size, the shader fades the noise function to zero. Other features can also be smoothly removed. For example, the mortar lines in a brick wall might fade to match the color of the brick as the mortar thickness approaches the width of a pixel.

Band-limiting the output of the procedure removes aliases by prefiltering the texture before sampling [127]. Some textures, such as fractal $1/f$ noise, are constructed by spectral synthesis, e.g.,

$$f(x) = \sum_{i}^{n} 2^{-i} n(2^i \mathbf{x}), \tag{4.1}$$

where $n()$ is any periodic function like *sine* or the Perlin noise function [139]. Band-limiting uses the derivative that represents the change in texture coordinates across the screen with respect to texture coordinates across space to determine what is the maximum frequency across space the screen can support. It then sets the value n in Equation 4.1 such that it does not generate frequencies above this maximum. In other words, a lot of the responsibility for avoiding aliasing is offloaded to the shader itself. The programmer who develops the shader will have to make sure the shader does not produce higher frequencies than appropriate for the current image resolution.

While Equation 4.1 generates a variety of procedural textures, this is just one method used by general procedural shaders. Band-limiting is difficult to implement in a generalized procedural shading environment.

4.5.3 Super Sampling

The final technique is shader *super sampling*. Super sampling is a common technique for antialiasing geometry, both in interactive and off-line rendering. With super sampling, several samples are rendered for each pixel, then combined to produce the final pixel color. Shader super sampling is discussed by both Peachy and Worley [41]. In this method, the shading procedure itself takes several samples at slightly perturbed points, which it blends to produce the color for a single image sample or pixel.

Super sampling is relatively easy, but only moves the aliases to higher frequencies. Sharp edges will continue to alias no matter how many samples are taken. In addition, super sampling is costly, degrading time performance proportionately to the number of additional samples.

5

Graphics Hardware

Recently, programmable commodity graphics hardware has become available. This chapter describes in general terms the structure of modern PC graphics accelerators. This chapter tries to provide a general framework for graphics processor programming that will not soon be obsolete but is specific enough to describe how it can be targeted by the compilers described later in the book.

5.1 Graphics Accelerators

Graphics accelerators are often, but not always, used in real-time graphics. A graphics accelerator is a special piece of hardware, separate from the CPU, that implements specific graphics algorithms more efficiently (hopefully) than the CPU. Conceptually, graphics accelerators are organized as pipelines, as in Figure 5.1. Geometry goes in one end, and pixels are written to the frame buffer at the other. Each stage of the pipeline implements a specific graphics algorithm and passes its results onto the next stage in the pipeline. The vast majority of graphics accelerators are based on the z-buffer hidden surface removal algorithm; the major performance enhancements provided by an accelerator are in the implementation of the rasterization and compositing steps. Lower-cost accelerators implement the earlier stages of the pipeline: transformation, lighting, and clipping on the host.

Up until the last five years or so, commodity graphics accelerators were conceived as fixed in function. High-end graphics hardware has gone through periodic cycles of programmability (previous commercially available programmable graphics accelerators include [43, 144]). However, except for a few mode changes here and there in the pipeline, conventional wisdom was that low-cost graphics accelerators could not be adapted to the implementation of arbitrary algorithms. Two things changed this.

First, it was found that with a few small evolutionary changes (specifically, texture lookups using pixel values as coordinates and floating-point computations) even a conventional graphics hardware architecture could be used to evaluate arbitrary arithmetic expressions for the computation of color at each pixel [130]. Secondly, hardware vendors introduced new graphics accelerators with programmable functions at specific stages of the pipeline. Rather than relying on, for example, a fixed per-vertex lighting model, you could now download your own microcode to the vertex processor and use it for your own purposes. Such user-programmable graphics accelerators are called GPUs. They still include direct hardware implementation of important algorithms like rasterization and texture filtering, but also include more specific general-purpose programmable capabilities.

5.2   Programmable Shading Hardware

Figure 5.1 illustrates a general model for the programmable elements of modern graphics accelerators. Triangles are sent down a geometry pipeline represented by the vertex shader. The triangles are transmitted as vertex positions with associated attribute data such as colors and texture coordinates. The figure represents the transmission of the triangles as horizontal line segments, and the transmission is made to appear serial, from top to bottom.

To achieve high throughput, and high polygon-per-second rendering rates, vertex processing is parallelized. This can be done through parallel units, with appropriate bookkeeping to re-sort the results in serial rendering order after processing. It can also be done by performing vertex operations in a deep pipeline. For example, an accelerator may pipeline each simple vertex shader operation in a pipeline hundreds of (simple) units long. Of course an accelerator could also combine these approaches with several parallel deep pipelines.

Once a triangle's vertices have been processed, the triangle is rasterized. This process figures out which pixels in the frame buffer the viewport-coordinate triangle covers. During rasterization, the triangle's vertex attribute data is interpolated across the pixels that it covers. This interpolation is linear but perspective correct, which means the linearly interpolated texture coordinates are divided by a linearly interpolated homogeneous coordinate per pixel.

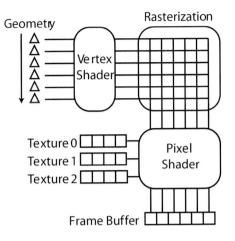

Figure 5.1. Modern graphics accelerators include programmable vertex and pixel shading processors.

Many graphics accelerators actually distinguish *pixels* in the frame buffer from *fragments* passing through the pipe. There may be a one-to-one relationship between fragments and pixels, or many fragments may contribute to a single pixel for antialiasing, or a fragment may be dropped and not contribute to any pixel.

As each fragment that the current triangle covers is rasterized, the fragment or pixel shader is invoked to determine its color. The pixel/fragment shader performs arithmetic on the texture coordinates, uses the texture coordinates to access texture memory, and performs arithmetic on the fetched texture values.

Our model assumes there are an arbitrary number of textures. Hardware available at this writing supports as many as six simultaneous textures. Accessing multiple textures to compute shading is called multitexturing.

Some have termed the arithmetic performed on texture coordinates *texture shading*. However, pixel shaders are evolving such that they do not differentiate between operations on texture coordinates and fetched texture values, hence the distinction between the *texture shader* and pixel shader is no longer important. Furthermore, we prefer the term texture shader to denote the task of precomputing shading expressions and storing them in a texture map.

Our model assumes arbitrary precision. At the time of this writing, vertex shaders and texture coordinate arithmetic are performed in 32-bit floating point, but fetched texture arithmetic is still performed in low precision (between eight- and 16-bit) fixed point.

To achieve high throughput at this stage and high pixel-fill rates, these stages are also parallelized. As with vertex shading, this parallelization may use parallel units, deep instruction-level pipelines, or both.

5.3   Vertex Shaders

The vertex shader replaces the geometry pipeline. These stages of the graphics pipeline are responsible for converting vertices from model coordinates to clip coordinates. Vertices at the end of the vertex shader are then clipped and transformed into viewport coordinates.

The vertex shader changes the vertex attributes including position, color, and texture coordinates.

The vertex shader does not change the number of vertices passing through it. But since its output is clipped, it can delete vertices by moving them outside the clipping region.

In the notation of Chapter 1.3, vertex shaders implement the pipeline

$$C\delta \mathbf{px} \leftarrow \delta \mathbf{psx}. \tag{5.1}$$

This pipeline resembles the Gouraud shading pipeline of Equation (1.1). Shading is computed at the vertices $\mathbf{psx}$, and the result is then interpolated across the face of the polygon by the rasterization operator δ.

The difference from Gouraud shading is that the LHS of Equation (5.1) replaces the projection π that represents the geometry pipeline of classical graphics systems with a general procedure $\mathbf{p}$ that can relocate the vertices to implement, for example, displacement mapping.

5.4   Pixel Shaders

The pixel (or fragment) shader generalizes the per-pixel access and application of texture. The pixel shader can perform arithmetic operations on the texture coordinates before they index into the texture, and can then perform additional arithmetic operations with the fetched texture result.

In a single pass, the pixel shader computes each pixel in isolation, and cannot access data stored at other pixels in the framebuffer.

Pixel shaders implement the pipeline

$$C\delta \pi \mathbf{x} \leftarrow \mathbf{p}\delta \mathbf{sx}. \tag{5.2}$$

The shader parameters stored at each vertex are interpolated across the pixels of the polygon's projection, and a procedure at each pixel synthesizes the color of that pixel. Methods for Phong shading in hardware [17, 137] are based on fragment shading, as are a variety of procedural shaders, both production [65] and real time [66]. Note that fragment shading (5.2), which supports Phong shading interpolation, is a permutation of (1.1), which supports Gouraud shading interpolation. The juxtaposition of sampling δ and shader evaluation $\mathbf{p}$ suffices to change the representation from interpolating shader results (color) with shader parameters (e.g., surface normals).

Fragment shading applies the entire procedure to each pixel before moving to the next. The main drawbacks to this technique is that interpolated vectors, such as the surface normal, need to be renormalized, which requires an expensive per-pixel square root operation. If this renormalization is approximated or ignored, the resulting artifact can be incorrect shading, and this error increases with the curvature of the surface the polygon approximates.

The sampling rate of the δ in the LHS of Equation (5.2) (the resolution of the polygon's projection) matches the sampling rate of the RHS (the resolution of the polygon sampling the shader). Hence aliasing occurs when this rate insufficiently samples the shader $\mathbf{p}$. With the exception of the obvious and expensive supersampling technique, procedural shaders can be antialiased by band-limiting [127] and a gradient magnitude technique [66, 152]; both modify the texture procedure $\mathbf{p}$ to generate eonly signals properly sampled by the coordinates discretized by the δ.

5.4.1 Dependent Texturing

Dependent texturing is the ability to use values of a pixel as texture coordinates. This is an important feature for shading since it allows per-pixel computed values to be used as texture coordinates, something that could not be done any other way within OpenGL. This feature was originally called *pixel texture*, and was available as an OpenGL extension on some SGI workstations. The pixel texture extension allowed the pixels in the frame buffer to be replaced by texture values indexed by the pixel's color components. Expressed as a pipeline, the pixel shader pipeline is

$$C\mathbf{x}_s \leftarrow TC\mathbf{x}_s. \tag{5.3}$$

Modern consumer hardware implementations operate on the texture map instead of the frame buffer. Dependent texturing was a new feature available in the NVidia GeForce3 and ATI Radeon 8500. It allowed the color components of a fetched texture sample to be used as texture coordinates for an additional texture fetch. It can be expressed in the pipeline notation as

$$C\delta\pi\mathbf{x} \leftarrow T'T\mathbf{u} \qquad (5.4)$$

where, for example, its result is simply assigned in the frame buffer. The texture T is used as coordinates into the texture T'.

These two implementations offer the same basic ability for shading, and a shading language compiler can target the same operation to either (more on shading compilers in the next part). It is possible to convert from pixel texturing to dependent texturing by rendering the first texture to the framebuffer before applying Equation (5.3). It is also possible to convert dependent texturing to pixel texturing by copying the frame buffer to a texture before applying Equation (5.4). The pixel texture extension has been used in multipass implementations of line integral convolution, shadow mapping, layered fog, and bump mapping [79].

A very specific form of dependent texturing was available in Direct3D 6.0 called *Environment-Mapped Bump Mapping* (EMBM). This early implementation of bump mapping used a texture of displacements based on the bump map to offset the indexing of an environment map. The reflection vector would index into an environment map, but its index would be perturbed by the EMBM offset texture. This form of offsetting remains available as a special dependent texturing mode, and yields the pipeline

$$C\delta\pi\mathbf{x} \leftarrow T'(\mathbf{u}' + T\mathbf{u}). \qquad (5.5)$$

5.5   Performance

The speed of modern graphics accelerators is indicated by vertex rate, which measures the vertical bandwidth of Figure 5.1, and its pixel rate, which measures the horizontal bandwidth. The pixel rate is an order of magnitude faster than the vertex rate on modern graphics cards.

5.6   Logical Models for Consumer Hardware

Commercially available procedural shading hardware is much simpler than the PixelFlow system described at the introduction of our logical model diagrams in Chapter 4. The current consumer graphics systems don't have shading languages, providing lower-level access to their shading capabilities, but we can still look at the logical model of programmable stages they present.

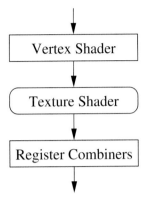

Figure 5.2. Logical models for NVIDIA.

With the GeForce3, NVIDIA added a simple shading model consisting of three stages (Figure 5.2). Vertex shaders (programmed with an assembly-level interface) contain operations that occur per model vertex, including transformations, texture coordinate generation, and per-vertex color and normal computations. Texture shaders contain operations to control texture access. We have marked this stage as proposed but not truly programmable since, at the time of this writing, it is controlled by choosing one of several texturing options. Finally, the register combiners control operations on pixel and per-pixel texture data. This is programmed by selecting inputs for each combiner stage from a set of registers, choosing an input and output mapping functions, and operations to apply.

The model used by DirectX 8 and shared by ATI's Radeon is similar in logical layout (Figure 5.3). It consists of two stages, vertex and fragment

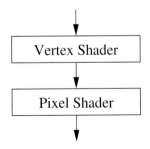

Figure 5.3. Logical models for DirectX (and ATI).

operations. Both are programmed with an assembly language interface. The vertex stage is virtually identical in form and function to NVIDIA's, while the fragment stage encompasses both texture and register combiner NVIDIA stages.

Part II

Building Blocks for Shading

This part provides details of those algorithms that are well suited to graphics hardware. These algorithms may be used to good effect on any programmable shading system, whether hand-coded multipass OpenGL, low-level vertex or fragment shaders, or a real shading language.

6

Texture Shading

Texture shading [72, 77, 114] is a real-time shading implementation technique that precomputes a complex lighting model (or part of a complex lighting model) and stores it into one or more texture maps. The real-time implementation then consists only of per-vertex texture parameter calculations, one or more texture lookups, and possibly a small amount of post-texture arithmetic to combine multiple texture lookups.

For example, any complex function $\mathbf{c} = f(s, t)$ that returns a color from any two real parameters can be encoded into a two-dimensional texture map, assuming the error due to sampling, quantization, and interpolation can be tolerated. With a small additional amount of arithmetic (supported via compositing or fragment shader operations in practice), a small number of texture look-ups can often be combined into complete and surprisingly sophisticated lighting models. For instance, if a four-dimensional function $g(s, t, u, v)$ can be decomposed into a product $g_1(s, t) \cdot g_2(u, v)$, only two two-dimensional texture lookups and a multiply are needed to evaluate it. We will use the term "texture shading" loosely to refer to any shader implementation technique that depends primarily, but not necessarily entirely, on values stored in textures rather than per-fragment arithmetic.

Traditional implementations of hardware lighting are usually restricted to the Phong or Blinn-Phong reflection models. As we have seen in Chapter 2 these simple models violate the laws of physics [18, 102] and are thus not suitable for more highly realistic rendering. Usually these models are evaluated only at vertices anyway and the colors interpolated; however, ideally, we would like to have per-pixel lighting.

We can use the shading grammar to articulate the goal of per-pixel lighting as

$$C\delta\pi\mathbf{x} \leftarrow \mathbf{p}\delta s\mathbf{x}. \tag{6.1}$$

The rasterization operator δ on the left indicates that the projection π of the polygon vertices $\mathbf{x}$ is filled in with fragments, whereas the rasterization operator on the right indicates that the shading parameters **s** (e.g. the surface normal) associated with each vertex **x** are interpolated before being sent to the shading procedure **p**.

Graphics systems supporting full procedural shading such as, for example, [130], can support arbitrary lighting and shading models, but the full power of these system is not (quite) yet available in widely available accelerators, at least at the pixel/fragment level. However, almost all current accelerators support per-pixel texture mapping and compositing operations.

Shading using pretabulated full or partial shading models provides a simple technique for using more sophisticated lighting models in the context of hardware renderers with good support for texture mapping but limited real-time arithmetic capabilities. These methods can easily be combined with other local illumination algorithms, such as shadow mapping and environment mapping, but in this chapter we will focus on point-source lighting models.

Texture shading precomputes the shading for all possible shading parameters **s** and stores the precomputed results in the texture map T using the pipeline

$$T\delta\mathbf{us} \leftarrow \delta\mathbf{ps}. \tag{6.2}$$

The expression **us** indicates that shading parameters **s** are converted into texture coordinates **u**. The pipeline iterates over all texture coordinates **s** that correspond to unique texture map locations. The δ operator on the LHS indicates that the texture coordinates are discretized, and on the RHS indicates that the shading result may be quantized before being stored in the texture map.

The texture shader is applied by assigning the shading parameters as texture coordinates when rendering a surface. This process is represented by the pipeline grammar

$$C\delta\pi\mathbf{x} \leftarrow T\delta\mathbf{usx}. \tag{6.3}$$

This resembles the pipeline for standard texture mapping (Equation 3.1) except that the texture coordinates, which are ordinarily explicitly assigned per vertex, are now a function of the shading parameters assigned per vertex.

Texture shading provides a method that allows us to use a wide variety of different shading models so that the most appropriate model can be chosen for each application. To achieve this flexibility without relying on full procedural shading, a sample-based representation of lighting models is used. For point sources of illumination, this amounts to sampling the BRDF or possibly the outgoing radiance at a surface (if the illumination is simple, such as hemispherical lighting).

Unfortunately, a faithful sampling of three-dimensional isotropic or four-dimensional anisotropic BRDFs requires too much storage to be useful on contemporary graphics accelerators. Even if we had enough memory, three-dimensional texture maps are not supported on all platforms, while four dimensional texture maps are not supported at all (unless you count MIP-mapped three-dimensional texture maps). Memory consumption could be a big concern if we want to support scenes with a large number of different materials and shading models. Instead of using brute-force three-dimensional or four-dimensional storage, we will rely on additive or multiplicative decompositions of BRDFs into lower-dimensional functions. Such decompositions can be stored in the more standard and memory-conserving two-dimensional texture maps.

A final advantage of texture shading is that support for texture filtering, already widely deployed in hardware accelerators, can be used to filter shading models. When the curvature of a glossy surface is high, per-pixel sampling of the lighting model could cause the highlight to break up, which looks terrible. Implementations of lighting models should take this into account, and blur and dim the highlight when the curvature is too high. This approximates what should happen, an integral over the pixel area. Procedural lighting models should ideally take this into account, for instance, by clamping the Phong highlight as a function of surface curvature [5]. With texture shaders, we already have techniques such as MIP-map filtering selecting an alternative lower-resolution form of a texture map when the derivatives of the texture interpolation functions are large. We can use this to bootstrap effective highlight antialiasing, the simplest technique being just applying ordinary MIP-mapping to the individual factors of a decomposed model. This is wrong—you can't filter a product by filtering its factors individually—but is *way* better than doing nothing, and is certainly easy. A more formally justified filtering model would be to use an alternative and less specular BRDF in high-curvature situations, and store the decomposition of this BRDF in the coarser levels of the MIP-map hierarchy.

6.1 One-Texture Shading

We will begin with a simple one-texture example.

Consider Figure 6.1, which was rendered using OpenGL. While the sphere on the right in this figure may appear to be rendered by OpenGL's built-in lighting model, in fact lighting has been completely disabled. The lighting is a texture decal (i.e., the color comes directly from the texture)

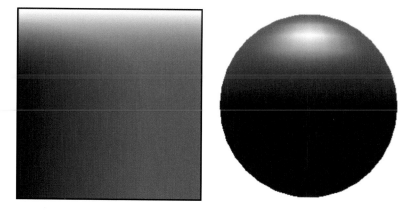

Figure 6.1.   Texture computed as $g(s,t) = (.3,0,0) + s(1,0,0) + t^9(1,1,1)$ applied to sphere with texture coordinates $s = \langle \hat{\mathbf{n}}, \hat{\mathbf{l}} \rangle$ and $t = \langle \hat{\mathbf{v}}, \hat{\mathbf{r}} \rangle$, where $\hat{\mathbf{r}}$ is the reflection direction for $\hat{\mathbf{l}}$.

using the texture map shown on the left. The texture coordinates are assigned as

$$(s,t) = (\langle \hat{\mathbf{n}}, \hat{\mathbf{l}} \rangle, \langle \hat{\mathbf{v}}, \hat{\mathbf{r}}_{\hat{\mathbf{n}}}(\hat{\mathbf{l}}) \rangle)$$

where $\hat{\mathbf{n}}$ is the surface normal, $\hat{\mathbf{l}}$ is the light vector, $\hat{\mathbf{v}}$ is the view vector, and $\hat{\mathbf{r}}_{\hat{\mathbf{n}}}(\hat{\mathbf{l}})$ is the reflected light vector, given by

$$\hat{\mathbf{r}}_{\hat{\mathbf{n}}}(\hat{\mathbf{l}}) = 2\langle \hat{\mathbf{n}}, \hat{\mathbf{l}} \rangle \hat{\mathbf{n}} - \hat{\mathbf{l}}.$$

The texture $g(s,t)$ is precomputed using the formula

$$g(s,t) = (.3,0,0) + s(1,0,0) + t^9(1,1,1)$$

for $(s,t) \in [0,1]^2$. This effectively uses texture mapping to implement a Phong-like reflection model.

This simple example demonstrates how texture mapping might be useful to simulate much more complex reflection models. In fact we could have easily used a much more sophisticated lighting model in the above, as long it depended only on two values, which could be computed at vertices and interpolated.

6.2   Parameterization and Interpolation

In practice, we have to be careful when selecting a parameterization for interpolation. Not all lighting model parameters interpolate in the correct way. In the example given in the previous section, for orthographic cameras and directional lights (that is, when light and viewing vectors are assumed constant), the interpolation of the texture coordinates across a polygon corresponds roughly to a linear interpolation of the normal without renormalization. Since the reflection model itself is highly nonlinear, this is much better than simple Gouraud shading, but not as good as evaluating the illumination in every pixel (Phong shading). Interpolation of normals without renormalization is commonly known as *fast Phong shading* [17].

The problem with using an unnormalized normal $\vec{n}$ with the usual Phong lobe $\langle \hat{v}, \hat{r}_{\vec{n}}(\hat{l}) \rangle^q$, especially when implemented procedurally, is that the highlight is dimmer than it should be when $|\vec{n}| < 1$. In the case of texture shading, we can sometimes sneak the normalization into how we parameterize, index, or set up our texture maps. For instance, cube maps, a kind of texture map which is indexed by a vector directly, include an implicit renormalization.

Linear interpolation of vector parameters can also lead to non-uniform angular speed, but this is reasonable, given that "Phong" interpolation is an approximation to start with. In fact, to interpolate normals in particular we *should* be using a higher-order interpolation that takes the tangent plane into account [172]. Hardware accelerators that support PN patches (Bézier patches based on triangle vertices and vertex normals) do this implicitly, although they also change the geometry to match.

A remaining problem is that certain parameterizations of unit vectors don't interpolate along the shortest arc joining two unit vectors on the hemisphere, as we often want. For example, direct use of spherical coordinates (θ, ϕ) is not recommended because texture mapping does not have the right periodicities. It is better to use local surface coordinates or parts of local surface coordinates, since these vary more slowly and give the right "topology" to the interpolation. These coordinates will typically appear as inner products of a parameter of interest, $\hat{v}$, $\hat{l}$, $\hat{h}$, etc., with one of the vectors of the local surface frame $(\hat{t}, \hat{s}, \hat{n})$: $\langle \hat{v}, \hat{n} \rangle$, $\langle \hat{h}, \hat{t} \rangle$, etc. An advantage of local surface coordinates is that the coordinates (and functions) of interest vary only over a hemisphere, and it is easier to put a function over a hemisphere into a two-dimensional texture map than a function over a sphere. Another advantage of these surface inner-product parameterizations is that they are often easy to compute in the texture matrix transformation, or, more recently, in vertex shaders.

For instance, to parameterize a unit vector $\hat{a}$ over a hemisphere, we might use just its projection down onto the unit disk given by

$$(u, v) \;=\; (\langle \hat{a}, \hat{t} \rangle, \langle \hat{a}, \hat{s} \rangle).$$

A related parameterization used specifically for unit vectors over the hemisphere is the parabolic parameterization [76], given by

$$(u, v) \quad = \quad \frac{(\langle \hat{\mathbf{a}}, \hat{\mathbf{t}} \rangle, \langle \hat{\mathbf{a}}, \hat{\mathbf{s}} \rangle)}{1 + \langle \hat{\mathbf{a}}, \hat{\mathbf{n}} \rangle}.$$

This is only slightly more expensive to compute than the hemispherical projection, since we can sneak the division into the projective normalization required for correct interpolation of texture coordinates under perspective, i.e., into the homogeneous coordinate of the corresponding texture coordinate. The parabolic parameterization also suffers less from compression near the horizon.

Of course, in both these cases (hemispherical and parabolic), we would shift the $[-1, 1]$ ranges defined above to the $[0, 1]$ range of texture map arguments with an appropriate scale and bias, and we might "shrink" the function toward the center of the map to avoid edge effects in near-horizon conditions.

6.3   Normal Lighting

To derive a more sophisticated one-texture example, recall the Blinn-Phong lighting model, and apply it to a point source:

$$L_o(\mathbf{x}; \hat{\mathbf{v}}) \quad = \quad \left(k_d \langle \hat{\mathbf{n}}, \hat{\mathbf{l}} \rangle + k_s \langle \hat{\mathbf{h}}, \hat{\mathbf{n}} \rangle^q \right) L_i(\mathbf{x}; \hat{\mathbf{l}}).$$

Now suppose $\hat{\mathbf{l}}$ and $\hat{\mathbf{v}}$ are fixed. This is often a reasonable approximation if the light and viewer are both far from the surface. In this case, $\hat{\mathbf{h}}$ is also fixed, and the above model depends only on the normal $\hat{\mathbf{n}}$. This will be true of *any* isotropic lighting model.

A classic technique for reshading prerendered images stores normals in an indexed color frame buffer, and then uses the color lookup tables to apply dynamic lighting changes [52]. We can do the same thing with a texture dependent only on the normal:

$$g(\hat{\mathbf{n}}) \quad = \quad k_d \langle \hat{\mathbf{n}}, \hat{\mathbf{l}} \rangle + k_s \langle \hat{\mathbf{h}}, \hat{\mathbf{n}} \rangle^q.$$

The only real difficulty here is how to encode the normal so that we can interpolate it and parameterize a texture map with it conveniently. Unfortunately, the normal can vary over a full sphere, even though we are only interested (roughly speaking) in normals that point towards the eye.

Some hardware accelerators support cube maps, which can be indexed directly by a (possibly) denormalized vector and returns a color for each possible direction. In this case you could use the (transformed) normal directly as a texture coordinate and the cube-map look-up would implicitly take care of any denormalization. If the accelerator you're using does not support cube maps, you could use a standard OpenGL spherical environment map, but index it with the (x, y) components of the normal (relative to axes perpendicular to the view direction) rather than the usual reflection vector. Setting up such a map amounts to rendering a sphere with the desired lighting. This technique has also been used with art-based lighting, with an artist first drawing a shaded sphere [161] whose lighting can be extended to an entire surface.

This technique can also be used conveniently with bump maps, as long the rendering system can perform dependent texture look-ups (a dependent texture look-up uses the result of a previous computation or buffer value as a texture address). To implement bump mapping, we would first compute a per-pixel normal, then use the above technique to do the lighting. A similar technique can be (and has been) used for lighting in other situations, such as during volume rendering.

The main disadvantage of this technique is its limitation to fixed light and view vectors.

6.4 Factored Multitexture Models

It turns out that many lighting models used in computer graphics can be factored into independent components that depend only on one or two local surface frame coordinates. We can store these factors in separate one- or two-dimensional texture maps, then combine them with appropriate arithmetic operations during rendering. In this case, a little bit of per-pixel arithmetic can go a long way.

Recall the specular lobe of the Cook-Torrance BRDF model presented in Section 2.7.1:

$$f(\mathbf{x}; \hat{\mathbf{v}} \leftarrow \hat{\mathbf{l}}) \quad = \quad \frac{1}{\pi} \frac{F \cdot D \cdot G}{\langle \hat{\mathbf{n}}, \hat{\mathbf{v}} \rangle \langle \hat{\mathbf{n}}, \hat{\mathbf{l}} \rangle},$$

where we have suppressed the arguments of F, D, and G for clarity. We will use several angles and vectors which are shown in Figure 2.3 and conventions described in Section 2.1.

For a fixed index of refraction, the Fresnel term F, which was presented in Section 2.5.3, depends only on the cosine of the angle γ between the light direction $\hat{\mathbf{l}}$ and the microfacet normal $\hat{\mathbf{h}}$, which is the normalized

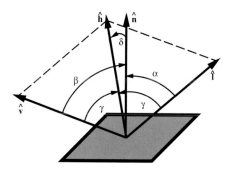

Figure 6.2. Geometric entities for the Cook-Torrance reflection model.

vector halfway between $\hat{\mathbf{l}}$ and $\hat{\mathbf{v}}$:

$$
\begin{aligned}
F(\cos \gamma) &= F(\langle \hat{\mathbf{v}}, \hat{\mathbf{h}} \rangle) \\
&= F(\langle \hat{\mathbf{l}}, \hat{\mathbf{h}} \rangle).
\end{aligned}
$$

The microfacet distribution function $D(\langle \hat{\mathbf{n}}, \hat{\mathbf{h}} \rangle)$, which defines the percentage of facets oriented in direction $\hat{\mathbf{h}}$, depends on the cosine of the angle δ between $\hat{\mathbf{h}}$ and the surface normal $\hat{\mathbf{n}}$, as well as a roughness parameter. This is true for all widely used choices of distribution functions, including the Gaussian angle distribution, the Gaussian height distribution, and the Beckmann distribution. Since the roughness is generally assumed to be constant for a given surface, this is again a univariate function.

Finally, the geometry term G describes the shadowing and masking of light by microfacets. For surfaces with a Gaussian microfacet distribution, the term developed by Smith [164] (given in Equation 2.4) can be used. It requires only two parameters: $G(\langle \hat{\mathbf{n}}, \hat{\mathbf{l}} \rangle, \langle \hat{\mathbf{n}}, \hat{\mathbf{v}} \rangle) = G(\cos \alpha, \cos \beta)$.

The reflected radiance from a surface due to a single point or directional light source with incoming radiance L_i at point $\mathbf{x}$ is given as

$$
\begin{aligned}
L_o(\mathbf{x}; \hat{\mathbf{v}}) &= k_s f(\mathbf{x}; \hat{\mathbf{v}} \leftarrow \hat{\mathbf{l}}) \langle \hat{\mathbf{n}}, \hat{\mathbf{l}} \rangle L_i \\
&= k_s \frac{1}{\pi} \frac{F(\cos \gamma) \cdot D(\langle \hat{\mathbf{n}}, \hat{\mathbf{h}} \rangle) \cdot G(\langle \hat{\mathbf{n}}, \hat{\mathbf{l}} \rangle, \langle \hat{\mathbf{n}}, \hat{\mathbf{v}} \rangle)}{\langle \hat{\mathbf{n}}, \hat{\mathbf{v}} \rangle \langle \hat{\mathbf{n}}, \hat{\mathbf{l}} \rangle} \cdot \langle \hat{\mathbf{n}}, \hat{\mathbf{l}} \rangle \cdot L_i \\
&= k_s \frac{1}{\pi} \frac{F(\cos \gamma) \cdot D(\langle \hat{\mathbf{n}}, \hat{\mathbf{h}} \rangle) \cdot G(\langle \hat{\mathbf{n}}, \hat{\mathbf{l}} \rangle, \langle \hat{\mathbf{n}}, \hat{\mathbf{v}} \rangle)}{\langle \hat{\mathbf{n}}, \hat{\mathbf{v}} \rangle} L_i.
\end{aligned}
$$

Here we have cancelled out the $\langle \hat{\mathbf{n}}, \hat{\mathbf{l}} \rangle$ term. It should be noted that the $\langle \hat{\mathbf{n}}, \hat{\mathbf{l}} \rangle$ term in practice is frequently clamped to zero to clamp the lighting model to zero when the surface shadows itself. During rendering we will have to find some other way to account for self-shadowing.

If the material properties are assumed to be constant over a surface, this lighting model can be split into two bivariate factors, which can be stored in two texture maps $f(s_f, t_f)$ and $g(s_g, t_g)$:

$$
\begin{aligned}
f(s_f, t_f) &= F(s_f) \cdot D(t_f), \\
s_f &= \langle \hat{\mathbf{v}}, \hat{\mathbf{h}} \rangle \\
&= \langle \hat{\mathbf{l}}, \hat{\mathbf{h}} \rangle \\
&= \cos \gamma, \\
t_f &= \langle \hat{\mathbf{n}}, \hat{\mathbf{h}} \rangle, \\
&= \cos \delta, \\
g(s_g, t_g) &= G(s_g, t_g)/(\pi t_g), \\
s_g &= \langle \hat{\mathbf{n}}, \hat{\mathbf{l}} \rangle \\
&= \cos \alpha, \\
t_g &= \langle \hat{\mathbf{n}}, \hat{\mathbf{v}} \rangle \\
&= \cos \beta.
\end{aligned}
$$

The values of (s_f, t_f) and (s_g, t_g) would be computed at the vertices and interpolated. Two-dimensional texture mapping can then be used to implement the lookup process during rendering. To account for self-shadowing, we should arrange for $g(s_g, t_g)$ to equal zero for $s_g < 0$, for instance by providing a suitable texture border.

If all vectors are normalized, the texture coordinates are simple dot products between the surface normal, the viewing and light directions, and the microfacet normal. These vectors and their dot products can be computed in software (or in vertex shaders, should the graphics accelerator support them) and assigned as texture coordinates to each vertex of the object.

Under standard OpenGL 1.2, to implement this lighting model the object needs to be rendered at least twice. On the first pass, we would texture the model using $f(s_f, t_f)$ and place this image in the frame buffer. On the second pass, we would texture the model with $g(s_g, t_g)$ and multiply the frontmost fragments with the value currently in the frame buffer. It is important to use the less-than-or-*equal* depth test here to eliminate all but the frontmost fragments so that the multiplication applies only to the visible surfaces. The factor $k_s L_i$ can be specified as a per-vertex color and multiplied with the results from texturing using standard texture blending operations during the second pass. Optionally, we can perform a third pass

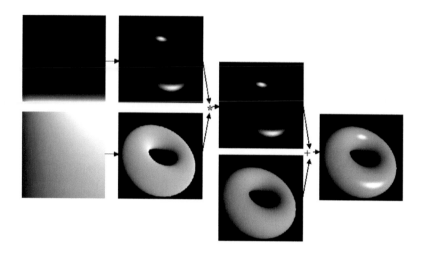

Figure 6.3. Cook-Torrance texture shader: Two separate two-dimensional textures (left column) represent the terms FD and G of the Cook-Torrance BRDF. When independently applied to some geometry, they result in two images whose product is the desired result. A diffuse component can be added in to form the complete reflection model.

to add in a diffuse component to the lighting model, using the standard OpenGL lighting model.

Recent PC accelerators can look up more than one texture in a single pass and combine the results with simple arithmetic operations. The standard OpenGL API to this is called multitexturing, but various vendors have defined other models, such as NVIDIA's register combiners. The advantage of using these extensions is that fewer passes over the geometry will be required, and so the result will be obtained more quickly. However, the visual result is the same. In this text we will refer to the use of one texture look-up per pass and the use of compositing operators to perform arithmetic as a multipass implementation. Regardless of the extension used (register combiners, etc.) we will refer to the use of multiple texture look-ups as a multitexturing implementation.

If the light and viewing directions are assumed to be constant, that is, if a directional light and an orthographic camera are assumed, the computation of the texture coordinates can actually be performed using the standard OpenGL texture coordinate transformation matrix. To implement this, light and viewing direction, as well as the halfway vector between

them, are used as row vectors in the texture transformation matrix for the
two textures:

$$
\begin{bmatrix}
0 & 0 & 0 & \cos\gamma \\
h_x & h_y & h_z & 0 \\
0 & 0 & 0 & 0 \\
0 & 0 & 0 & 1
\end{bmatrix}
\cdot
\begin{bmatrix}
n_x \\
n_y \\
n_z \\
1
\end{bmatrix}
=
\begin{bmatrix}
\cos\gamma \\
\cos\delta \\
0 \\
1
\end{bmatrix},
\qquad (6.4)
$$

$$
\begin{bmatrix}
l_x & l_y & l_z & 0 \\
v_x & v_y & v_z & 0 \\
0 & 0 & 0 & 0 \\
0 & 0 & 0 & 1
\end{bmatrix}
\cdot
\begin{bmatrix}
n_x \\
n_y \\
n_z \\
1
\end{bmatrix}
=
\begin{bmatrix}
\cos\alpha \\
\cos\beta \\
0 \\
1
\end{bmatrix}.
\qquad (6.5)
$$

On modern programmable hardware [103] the accelerator provides a
means of specifying per-vertex shader programs. Vertex programs can perform short computations at every vertex, based on any parameters bound
to each vertex. The vertex shader outputs values that will be used for
interpolation. With vertex shader programs, we can easily perform the
necessary computations to support both local viewers and local point light
sources right on the accelerator.

The use of textures for representing this lighting model introduces an
approximation error: while the term $F \cdot D$ is bounded by the interval
$[0, 1]$, the second term $G/(\pi \cos\beta)$ exhibits a singularity for grazing viewing
directions ($\cos\beta \to 0$). Since contemporary graphics hardware typically
uses a fixed-point or scaled-integer representation of textures, the texture
values are clamped to the range $[0, 1]$. When these clamped values are
used for the illumination process, areas around the grazing angles can be
rendered too dark, especially if the surface is very shiny.

The problem of singularities can arise in other factorizations of BRDFs.
Due to the limited resolution and range of texture maps, we want to find
factorizations that give gently varying factors with bounded range. Generally we also want to multiply values stored in textures by appropriate
constants so that the (bounded) values in each texture span the full dynamic range of the storage format to maximize precision. The reciprocals of
these scale factors can ultimately by multiplied onto the final result. This
can be a problem if the scale factors are larger than one, since standard
graphics accelerator APIs do not permit scaling by values outside the $[0, 1]$
range. Fortunately, we can scale up a frame buffer by 2^n by adding it to
itself n times, and multitexturing extensions, such as register combiners,
also provide ways to scale by powers of two. Of course, if the desired scale
factor C is not a power of two, we still have to account for some factor
$C/2^n$ elsewhere in the system. We may also want to apply different scale
factors to different color channels.

Even with this rearrangement, the limited range and precision of frame buffer arithmetic is a problem in general, as some computations naturally lead to a wide dynamic range that cannot be predicted easily. Fixed dynamic range and clamping makes it hard to include $1/r^2$ attenuation, for instance, in factored texture shader computations. In such cases it is possible to lose enough precision in intermediate computations that, after scaling, serious quantization artifacts become visible. Future hardware with floating-point fragment operators should alleviate these difficulties.

The same methods can be applied to all kinds of variations of the Cook-Torrance model, using different distribution functions and geometry terms, or the approximations proposed in [157]. With varying numbers of terms and rendering passes, it is also possible to find similar factorizations for many other models. For example, the Phong, Blinn-Phong and Lafortune Cosine Lobe models (Sections 2.6.1 and 2.6.4) can all be rendered in a single pass with a single texture. Such a texture can even include an ambient and a diffuse term in addition to the specular one.

Last but not least, the factorization approach allows for the use of measured or simulated factors. For example, the shadowing and masking of surfaces with a Gaussian height distribution has been simulated numerically and data for an appropriate function found [24]. The results could be directly applied as a geometry factor.

6.5   Anisotropic Models

Although the treatment of anisotropic materials is somewhat harder, similar factorization techniques can be applied here. For anisotropic models, both the microfacet distribution function and the geometrical attenuation factor may also depend on the angle ϕ between the facet normal and a reference direction in the tangent plane. This reference direction is given in the form of a tangent vector $\hat{\mathbf{t}}$.

For example, the elliptical Gaussian model [174] introduces an anisotropic facet distribution function specified as the product of two independent Gaussian functions, one in the direction of $\hat{\mathbf{t}}$, and one in the direction of a secondary, orthogonal tangent $\hat{\mathbf{s}} = \hat{\mathbf{n}} \times \hat{\mathbf{t}}$. This makes D a bivariate function in the angles δ and ϕ. Consequently, the texture coordinates can be computed in software in much the same way as described above for isotropic materials. This also holds for many other anisotropic models in computer graphics literature. We will study two anisotropic models in greater detail: the Banks model and the Ashikhmin model. The Banks model is simple, and therefore efficient (it requires only one texture). The

Ashikhmin model is more complex, but can still be implemented efficiently on modern programmable accelerators.

6.5.1 Banks Model

Since anisotropic models depend on both a normal and a tangent that varies per vertex, it is usually necessary to have a larger number of texture maps that cover the dependence on all these variables. One simple example that only needs one texture, however, is the model by Banks [13]. The algorithm outlined in the following has been published by Heidrich [71, 75]. As discussed in Section 2.6.5, the Banks model defines the reflection off an anisotropic surface as

$$L_o(\mathbf{x}, \hat{\mathbf{v}}) \;=\; (k_d \langle \hat{\mathbf{n}}', \hat{\mathbf{l}} \rangle^p + k_s \langle \hat{\mathbf{v}}, \hat{\mathbf{r}}_{\hat{\mathbf{n}}'}(\hat{\mathbf{l}}) \rangle^q) \cdot \cos\alpha \cdot L_i(\mathbf{x}, \hat{\mathbf{l}}) \qquad (6.6)$$

where the "equivalent normal" $\hat{\mathbf{n}}'$ is the projection of the light vector $\hat{\mathbf{l}}$ into the plane containing both $\hat{\mathbf{n}}$ and the tangent vector $\hat{\mathbf{t}}$. This vector is then used as a shading normal for a Blinn-Phong lighting model with diffuse and specular coefficients k_d and k_s, and specular exponent q. The exponent p, which should be between two and five, is used to correct for excess brightness.

It has been pointed out [167, 184] that this model is really only a function of the two angles between the tangent and the light direction, as well as the tangent and the viewing direction:

$$f_d(\langle \hat{\mathbf{l}}, \hat{\mathbf{t}} \rangle) \;=\; \sqrt{1 - \langle \hat{\mathbf{l}}, \hat{\mathbf{t}} \rangle^2}, \qquad (6.7)$$

$$f_s(\langle \hat{\mathbf{l}}, \hat{\mathbf{t}} \rangle, \langle \hat{\mathbf{v}}, \hat{\mathbf{t}} \rangle) \;=\; \sqrt{1 - \langle \hat{\mathbf{l}}, \hat{\mathbf{t}} \rangle^2} \sqrt{1 - \langle \hat{\mathbf{v}}, \hat{\mathbf{t}} \rangle^2} - \langle \hat{\mathbf{l}}, \hat{\mathbf{t}} \rangle \langle \hat{\mathbf{v}}, \hat{\mathbf{t}} \rangle, \qquad (6.8)$$

$$f(\langle \hat{\mathbf{l}}, \hat{\mathbf{t}} \rangle, \langle \hat{\mathbf{v}}, \hat{\mathbf{t}} \rangle) \;=\; k_d f_d^p(\langle \hat{\mathbf{l}}, \hat{\mathbf{t}} \rangle) + k_s f_s^q(\langle \hat{\mathbf{l}}, \hat{\mathbf{t}} \rangle, \langle \hat{\mathbf{v}}, \hat{\mathbf{t}} \rangle), \qquad (6.9)$$

$$L_o(\mathbf{x}, \hat{\mathbf{v}}) \;=\; f(\langle \hat{\mathbf{l}}, \mathbf{t}(\hat{\mathbf{x}}) \rangle, \langle \hat{\mathbf{v}}, \mathbf{t}(\hat{\mathbf{x}}) \rangle) \cdot \cos\alpha \cdot L_i(\mathbf{x}, \hat{\mathbf{l}}). \qquad (6.10)$$

A similar formula has been used for the illumination of "microcylindrical" lines [167]. For lines, however, we would omit the $\cos\alpha = \langle \hat{\mathbf{n}}, \hat{\mathbf{l}} \rangle$ term since we do not have a surface normal.

Applied to anisotropic reflection models, the fact that f can be parameterized by only two values means that it can be precomputed and stored in a two-dimensional texture. For fixed view and light vectors, if the tangent $\hat{\mathbf{t}}$ is specified as a texture coordinate, the texture transformation can be set up to compute the lighting model (here we have not included scales and biases to map the natural parameterization of this model over $[-1, 1]^2$ into the range $[0, 1]^2$, but this is easy to do):

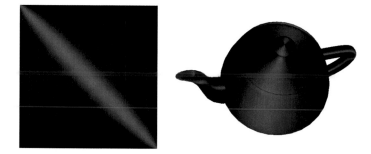

Figure 6.4.   Left: A two-dimensional texture holding the Banks model. The x-coordinate holds the describes the variation of the light direction, while the y-coordinate describes the change in the viewing direction. Right: Teapot rendered with this texture.

$$
\begin{bmatrix} \langle \hat{\mathbf{l}}, \hat{\mathbf{t}} \rangle \\ \langle \hat{\mathbf{v}}, \hat{\mathbf{t}} \rangle \\ 0 \\ 1 \end{bmatrix}
=
\begin{bmatrix} l_x & l_y & l_z & 0 \\ v_x & v_y & v_z & 0 \\ 0 & 0 & 0 & 0 \\ 0 & 0 & 0 & 1 \end{bmatrix}
\begin{bmatrix} t_x \\ t_y \\ t_z \\ 1 \end{bmatrix}
$$

The additional factor $\cos \alpha$ in Equation 6.6, which is applied only when we are shading surfaces as opposed to lines, can be computed by standard diffuse lighting with a directional light source and a purely diffuse material. With this approach the Banks model can be rendered with one texture and one pass per light source even under standard OpenGL, however with the limitation of fixed view and light source directions. If vertex shaders or host computation are used to compute $\langle \hat{\mathbf{l}}, \hat{\mathbf{t}} \rangle$ and $\langle \hat{\mathbf{v}}, \hat{\mathbf{t}} \rangle$, then of course variable light and view vectors can be used. Figure 6.4 shows the two-dimensional texture arising from this approach, and its application to a teapot model.

6.5.2 Ashikhmin Model

The Ashkhimin model is an anistropic model with a Phong-like specular lobe, but with various enhancements to improve its physical accuracy [9, 10]. It was described in detail in Section 2.7.2, but is basically a weighted sum of a diffuse part and a specular part:

$$
f(\mathbf{x}; \hat{\mathbf{v}} \leftarrow \hat{\mathbf{l}}) \;=\; k_d (1 - k_s) f_d(\mathbf{x}; \hat{\mathbf{v}} \leftarrow \hat{\mathbf{l}}) + k_s f_s(\mathbf{x}; \hat{\mathbf{v}} \leftarrow \hat{\mathbf{l}}).
$$

The diffuse part models subsurface scattering, and is nonconstant but symmetric about the normal:

$$
f_d(\mathbf{x}; \hat{\mathbf{v}} \leftarrow \hat{\mathbf{l}}) \;=\; \frac{28}{23\pi} \left(1 - (1 - \langle \hat{\mathbf{n}}, \hat{\mathbf{v}} \rangle / 2)^5 \right) \left(1 - (1 - \langle \hat{\mathbf{n}}, \hat{\mathbf{l}} \rangle / 2)^5 \right).
$$

Since this term depends on only two parameters, $\langle \hat{\mathbf{n}}, \hat{\mathbf{v}} \rangle$ and $\langle \hat{\mathbf{n}}, \hat{\mathbf{l}} \rangle$, it can be sampled and stored in a two-dimensional texture map directly. No other parameters of the lighting model appear inside this function and so this texture map never needs to be regenerated.

There are two variations on the specular part; we will discuss both, but will begin with the most recently introduced version. The vector form is most useful:

$$f_s(\mathbf{x}; \hat{\mathbf{v}} \leftarrow \hat{\mathbf{l}}) = \frac{\sqrt{(q_t + 1)(q_s + 1)}}{8\pi} \frac{\langle \hat{\mathbf{n}}, \hat{\mathbf{h}} \rangle^{(q_t \langle \hat{\mathbf{h}}, \hat{\mathbf{t}} \rangle^2 + q_s \langle \hat{\mathbf{h}}, \hat{\mathbf{s}} \rangle^2)/(1 - \langle \hat{\mathbf{h}}, \hat{\mathbf{n}} \rangle^2)}}{\cos\gamma \cdot \max(\langle \hat{\mathbf{n}}, \hat{\mathbf{v}} \rangle, \langle \hat{\mathbf{n}}, \hat{\mathbf{l}} \rangle)} F(\cos\gamma).$$

A factorization of this model has recently been developed by Michael Mc-Cool and Mauro Steigleder at the University of Waterloo. Taking advantage of the separability of the exponential in the Blinn-Phong lobe, we obtain the following:

$$
\begin{aligned}
f_s(\mathbf{x}; \hat{\mathbf{v}} \leftarrow \hat{\mathbf{l}}) &= \frac{\sqrt{(q_t + 1)(q_s + 1)}}{8\pi} \\
&\quad \cdot \left[\langle \hat{\mathbf{n}}, \hat{\mathbf{h}} \rangle^{q_t \langle \hat{\mathbf{h}}, \hat{\mathbf{t}} \rangle^2 /(1 - \langle \hat{\mathbf{h}}, \hat{\mathbf{n}} \rangle^2)} \right] \left[\langle \hat{\mathbf{n}}, \hat{\mathbf{h}} \rangle^{q_s \langle \hat{\mathbf{h}}, \hat{\mathbf{s}} \rangle^2 /(1 - \langle \hat{\mathbf{h}}, \hat{\mathbf{n}} \rangle^2)} \right] \\
&\quad \cdot \left[\frac{F(\cos\gamma)}{\cos\gamma} \right] \left[\frac{1}{\max(\langle \hat{\mathbf{n}}, \hat{\mathbf{v}} \rangle, \langle \hat{\mathbf{n}}, \hat{\mathbf{l}} \rangle)} \right] \\
&= C_a \cdot g_s(\langle \hat{\mathbf{n}}, \hat{\mathbf{h}} \rangle, \sqrt{q_t} \langle \hat{\mathbf{t}}, \hat{\mathbf{h}} \rangle) \cdot g_s(\langle \hat{\mathbf{n}}, \hat{\mathbf{h}} \rangle, \sqrt{q_s} \langle \hat{\mathbf{s}}, \hat{\mathbf{h}} \rangle) \\
&\quad \cdot g_f(\cos\gamma) \cdot g_m(\langle \hat{\mathbf{n}}, \hat{\mathbf{v}} \rangle, \langle \hat{\mathbf{n}}, \hat{\mathbf{l}} \rangle), \\
g_s(u, v) &= u^{v^2/(1 - u^2)}, \\
g_f(u) &= F(u)/u, \\
g_m(u, v) &= 1/\max(u, v)
\end{aligned}
$$

where C_a will account for both the normalization factor in the original model and any scale factors required to normalize the texture map ranges. We would normally also include $\langle \hat{\mathbf{n}}, \hat{\mathbf{l}} \rangle$ in g_m to account for the radiance/irradiance conversion and clamping to zero for self-shadowing. This factorization requires three unique textures, but four texture look-ups.

We can do a little better if we use the alternative form of this model. Here we include the $\langle \hat{\mathbf{n}}, \hat{\mathbf{l}} \rangle$ term from the beginning:

$$
\begin{aligned}
f_s(\mathbf{x}; \hat{\mathbf{v}} \leftarrow \hat{\mathbf{l}}) &= \frac{\sqrt{(q_t + 1)(q_s + 1)}}{8\pi} \\
&\quad \cdot \frac{\langle \hat{\mathbf{n}}, \hat{\mathbf{h}} \rangle^{(q_t \langle \hat{\mathbf{h}}, \hat{\mathbf{t}} \rangle^2 + q_s \langle \hat{\mathbf{h}}, \hat{\mathbf{s}} \rangle^2)/(1 - \langle \hat{\mathbf{h}}, \hat{\mathbf{n}} \rangle^2)}}{\cos\gamma \cdot \langle \hat{\mathbf{n}}, \hat{\mathbf{v}} \rangle \cdot \langle \hat{\mathbf{n}}, \hat{\mathbf{l}} \rangle} F(\cos\gamma),
\end{aligned}
$$

$$
\begin{aligned}
f_s(\mathbf{x}; \hat{\mathbf{v}} \leftarrow \hat{\mathbf{l}}) \langle \hat{\mathbf{n}}, \hat{\mathbf{l}} \rangle \;=\; & \frac{\sqrt{(q_t + 1)(q_s + 1)}}{8\pi} \\
\cdot \; & \left[\langle \hat{\mathbf{n}}, \hat{\mathbf{h}} \rangle^{q_t \langle \hat{\mathbf{h}}, \hat{\mathbf{t}} \rangle^2 / (1 - \langle \hat{\mathbf{h}}, \hat{\mathbf{n}} \rangle^2)} \right] \left[\langle \hat{\mathbf{n}}, \hat{\mathbf{h}} \rangle^{q_s \langle \hat{\mathbf{h}}, \hat{\mathbf{s}} \rangle^2 / (1 - \langle \hat{\mathbf{h}}, \hat{\mathbf{n}} \rangle^2)} \right] \\
\cdot \; & \left[\frac{F(\cos\gamma)}{\cos\gamma \cdot \langle \hat{\mathbf{n}}, \hat{\mathbf{v}} \rangle} \right] \\
=\; & C_a \cdot g_s(\langle \hat{\mathbf{n}}, \hat{\mathbf{h}} \rangle, \sqrt{q_t}\langle \hat{\mathbf{t}}, \hat{\mathbf{h}} \rangle) \cdot g_s(\langle \hat{\mathbf{n}}, \hat{\mathbf{h}} \rangle, \sqrt{q_s}\langle \hat{\mathbf{s}}, \hat{\mathbf{h}} \rangle) \\
\cdot \; & g_p(\cos\gamma, \langle \hat{\mathbf{n}}, \hat{\mathbf{v}} \rangle).
\end{aligned}
$$

which requires only two unique textures and three look-ups. Unfortunately, it does not include self-shadowing, and does not include any term that depends on $\langle \hat{\mathbf{n}}, \hat{\mathbf{l}} \rangle$, so we will have to include an appropriate clamping factor somehow during implementation. For instance, we might compute the sign of this dot product and set the illumination to zero when it is negative. If shadows are computed (for instance, via shadow maps), they would take care of this too.

The $1 - \langle \hat{\mathbf{h}}, \hat{\mathbf{n}} \rangle^2$ factor in the denominator of the exponent in g_s normalizes the projected tangent vector to unit length, so interpolation of it has the desired effect. This is true even after we factorize the model. The inclusion of this factor causes a numerical singularity at $u = \langle \hat{\mathbf{n}}, \hat{\mathbf{h}} \rangle = 1$ in $g_s(u, v)$. Fortunately, this singularity is removable, and we can find the appropriate limit symbolically and replace evaluation of $g_s(1, v)$ with its limit:

$$
\lim_{u \to 1} \left(u^{v^2 / (1 - u^2)} \right) \;=\; e^{-v^2 / 2}.
$$

The "repaired" function g_s then has a nice bounded range. We also add in some scale factors and represent only the "interesting" part of this function to get a clean highlight even with low-resolution (32×32) textures. We can factor out the exponents q_t and q_s, and so can reuse the same texture for different materials with different specularities.

The term g_p also has potential problems at $\cos\gamma = 0$ and $\langle \hat{\mathbf{n}}, \hat{\mathbf{v}} \rangle = 0$, where the denominator goes to zero. This unfortunately gives this function unbounded range. We therefore approximate it using

$$
g_p(\cos\gamma, \langle \hat{\mathbf{n}}, \hat{\mathbf{v}} \rangle) \;=\; \frac{F(\cos\gamma)}{\varepsilon + \cos\gamma \cdot \langle \hat{\mathbf{n}}, \hat{\mathbf{v}} \rangle}
$$

with $\varepsilon \approx 1/256$, which results in a "soft clamp" at these extremes. The conditions $\cos\gamma = 0$ and $\langle \hat{\mathbf{n}}, \hat{\mathbf{v}} \rangle = 0$ occur only at near-grazing angles anyway, so this approximation still results in a very close visual approximation to the desired model. It isn't important to get this model exactly right, as

it is phenomological.   The Fresnel term in this model also has a hidden
dependence on k_s. Using the Schlick approximation, this term expands
into

$$F(\cos\gamma) \;=\; k_s + (1 - k_s)(1 - \cos\gamma)^5.$$

Unfortunately, there doesn't seem to be any easy way to get rid of the
dependence on k_s, so we need to regenerate the texture map for g_p for each
different k_s used in a scene.

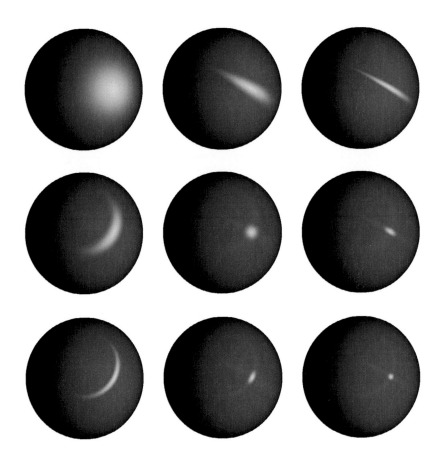

Figure 6.5. Anisotropic Ashikhmin reflectance model. Exponents of 10, 200, and
1000 in all combinations. Rendered using hardware acceleration, a three-texture
factorization of the anisotropic specular lobe, and a precomputed one-texture
nonconstant diffuse lobe.

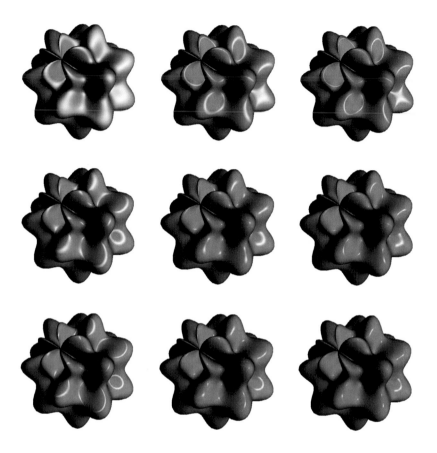

Figure 6.6.   Anisotropic Ashikhmin reflectance model. Exponents of 10, 200, and 1000 in all combinations. Rendered using hardware acceleration, a three-texture factorization of the anisotropic specular lobe, and a precomputed one-texture nonconstant diffuse lobe. (See Color Plate VII.)

Examples of renderings made in real time with this model are shown in Figure 6.5 and Figure 6.6.

The anisotropic Ashikhmin model requires a tangent frame, which is not always convenient and can cause singularities in the parameterization. For a true anisotropic model, these singularities are natural and cause a reasonable visual effect. For isotropic BRDFs with $q_t = q_s$, however, the tangent frame is not necessary, and we can in fact simplify the factorization:

$$f_s(\mathbf{x}; \hat{\mathbf{v}} \leftarrow \hat{\mathbf{l}})\langle \hat{\mathbf{n}}, \hat{\mathbf{l}} \rangle \;=\; C_a \cdot \left[\langle \hat{\mathbf{n}}, \hat{\mathbf{h}} \rangle^q \right] \cdot g_p(\cos\gamma, \langle \hat{\mathbf{n}}, \hat{\mathbf{v}} \rangle)$$

$$=\; C_a \cdot g_q(\langle \hat{\mathbf{n}}, \hat{\mathbf{h}} \rangle, q) \cdot g_p(\cos\gamma, \langle \hat{\mathbf{n}}, \hat{\mathbf{v}} \rangle),$$

$$g_q(u, v) \;=\; u^v.$$

Use of a two-dimensional map for the g_q parameter permits reuse of the same texture map for different specularities q. An alternative would be to use a one-dimensional MIP-mapped texture, with fewer specular highlight functions stored at the coarser levels. This implements both highlight antialiasing and, assuming MIP-map level clamping is supported, selection of different specularities for different materials.

6.6 Numerical Factorization

So far we have considered symbolic factorization of analytic lighting models. However, there are situations when an analytic model is not available, yet we still want to derive a real-time texture shader. For instance, we may have measured data for a particular BRDF, or we may have run a simulation and derived data that way. Unfortunately certain physical phenomena, such as multiple scattering, lead to significant changes in reflectivity but are not amenable to closed-form mathematical modeling.

In these cases we can turn to numerical factorization techniques. Given some samples of a BRDF (or even a full lighting model), we first propose a particular symbolic form for the texture shader, then solve for the free degrees of freedom in that form. In the case of texture shaders, all the texels are in fact degrees of freedom that we can optimize over.

The choice of symbolic form includes the number of texture maps, their parameterization, and how they are combined. This choice can be guided by the data; if the material *looks* like a Cook-Torrance model, for instance, we might use the same parameterization as the Cook-Torrance model, but solve directly for the entries in the texture maps rather than evaluating analytic formulas. There are other approximation approaches that try to optimize for parameters in given analytic models. For instance, a few measurements with a glossmeter can be used to estimate parameters for the Cook-Torrance model [176]. These methods are useful when it is feasible to make only a few measurements. However, when a lot of data is available, solving for *all* the degrees of freedom in a texture shader is possible and lets us approximate effects that might not be captured by a small number of measurements. Changing the values stored in texture maps, like parameter fitting, does not affect the real-time performance of a texture shader. Another possible approach would be to project the data against a prechosen set of basis functions. The problem with this is that the basis functions have to be stored somewhere for reconstruction, i.e., in texture maps. Again, we are not taking advantage of all the degrees of freedom available to us in the texture maps.

There are two useful techniques for fitting a texture shader to data: the singular value decomposition and homomorphic factorization.

6.6.1 Singular Value Decomposition

The *Singular Value Decomposition* (SVD) fits data to a texture shader of the form

$$f(\hat{\mathbf{v}} \leftarrow \hat{\mathbf{l}}) = \sum_{k=1}^{K} g_{k,1}(\rho_1(\hat{\mathbf{v}}, \hat{\mathbf{l}})) \cdot g_{k,2}(\rho_2(\hat{\mathbf{v}}, \hat{\mathbf{l}})).$$

Here the functions ρ_j are projections that represent the parameterization of the texture maps $g_{i,j}$ in terms of the four-dimensional parameter space $(\hat{\mathbf{v}}, \hat{\mathbf{l}})$. The projection functions can be combined into a single projection $\rho = [\rho_1, \rho_2]$ from four dimensions to four dimensions. Given enough terms in this series and an independent set of projections (in other words, with an invertible combined reparameterization function ρ), this approximation can be arbitrarily close to the original BRDF. In practice, if a suitable parameterization is chosen, as few as three or four terms can result in an approximation indistinguishable from the original [83]. The same parameterization is used for each term, which in practice is an advantage as the parameters only have to be computed once. However, the terms are signed, which can be a disadvantage on older accelerators.

The SVD approximation is found as follows. First, the BRDF samples are organized into an array. The samples of the BRDFs should be organized so that columns project down onto texels in $g_{k,1}$ using ρ_1, and rows project down onto texels in $g_{k,2}$ using ρ_2. This may require interpolating and resampling the BRDF data. For convenience, we may also want to use a different parameterization of the factors for the SVD than what we eventually use for the texture maps. For example, suppose we use

$$\rho_1(\hat{\mathbf{v}}, \hat{\mathbf{l}}) = \hat{\mathbf{v}},$$
$$\rho_2(\hat{\mathbf{v}}, \hat{\mathbf{l}}) = \hat{\mathbf{l}},$$

and use spherical coordinates

$$(\theta_v(i_v), \phi_v(j_v)) = \left(\frac{\pi}{2} \frac{i_v}{V_1}, 2\pi \frac{j_v}{V_2} \right)$$

for $\hat{\mathbf{v}}$ and

$$(\theta_l(i_l), \phi_l(j_l)) \quad = \quad \left(\frac{\pi}{2}\frac{i_l}{L_1}, 2\pi\frac{j_l}{L_2}\right)$$

for $\hat{\mathbf{l}}$. Then, by varying (i_v, j_v) over $[0, V_1] \times [0, V_2]$ and (i_l, j_l) over $[0, L_1] \times [0, L_2]$ and resampling the BRDF at corresponding values of $\hat{\mathbf{v}}(i_v, j_v)$ and $\hat{\mathbf{l}}(i_l, j_l)$, we can generate the matrix

$$\mathsf{F} = \begin{bmatrix} f_{1,1,1,1} & f_{1,1,1,2} & \cdots & f_{1,1,1,L_2} & f_{1,1,2,1} & \cdots & f_{1,1,L_1,L_2} \\ f_{1,2,1,1} & f_{1,2,1,2} & \cdots & f_{1,2,1,L_2} & f_{1,2,2,1} & \cdots & f_{1,2,L_1,L_2} \\ \vdots & \vdots & \ddots & \vdots & \vdots & \ddots & \vdots \\ f_{1,V_2,1,1} & f_{1,V_2,1,2} & \cdots & f_{1,V_2,1,L_2} & f_{1,V_2,2,1} & \cdots & f_{1,V_2,L_1,L_2} \\ f_{2,1,1,1} & f_{2,1,1,2} & \cdots & f_{2,1,1,L_2} & f_{2,1,2,1} & \cdots & f_{2,1,L_1,L_2} \\ \vdots & \vdots & \vdots & \vdots & \vdots & \ddots & \vdots \\ f_{V_1,V_2,1,1} & f_{V_1,V_2,1,2} & \cdots & f_{V_1,V_2,1,L_2} & f_{V_1,V_2,2,1} & \cdots & f_{V_1,V_2,L_1,L_2} \end{bmatrix}$$

where

$$f_{i_v, j_v, i_l, j_l} \quad = \quad f(\hat{\mathbf{v}}(i_v, j_v) \leftarrow \hat{\mathbf{l}}(i_l, j_l)).$$

Now we apply the singular value decomposition to this matrix to obtain the factorization

$$\mathsf{F} = \mathsf{USV}^T$$
$$= \sum_{k=1}^{K} s_k \mathsf{u}_k \mathsf{v}_k^T$$

where U and V are orthonormal, u_k and v_k are columns of U and V, and, finally, S is a diagonal matrix with diagonal elements s_k. A given element f_{i_v, j_v, i_l, j_l} of the matrix F can now be reconstructed using

$$f_{i_v, j_v, i_l, j_l} \quad = \quad \sum_{k=1}^{K} s_k \mathsf{u}_k(i_v, j_v) \cdot \mathsf{v}_k(i_l, j_l).$$

By "unpacking" the elements of u_k and v_k and placing them in texture maps, reparameterizing and resampling as necessary (for instance, to convert from spherical coordinates to parabolic maps), we can obtain texture maps that can be used for point-wise evaluation of f. We assume that interpolation of the samples in these texture maps can be used to obtain samples of f in between the original samples, and in practice this works well.

In the above we could have avoided the second resampling step and could have used samples on, for example, a parabolic parameterization of the texture maps to set up the matrix. In general, the projection functions, taken together as a single vector function, need to be invertible. We also need the ability to take samples of the original BRDF f at arbitrary locations, and this is a disadvantage of this technique. Another disadvantage is that we only get two factors per term, although in theory we could repeat the factorization on individual factors of a term. Finally, the SVD technique finds the minimum RMS fit to the original data. It tends to overemphasize the fit to the specular peak at the expense of the base color. This sort of behavior is good for BRDFs used as global illumination operators, but not for direct viewing. We could try to fit nonlinearly transformed data, but then we would have to invert this nonlinearity after reconstruction, at run time.

6.6.2 Homomorphic Factorization

The SVD technique is very powerful and can give an arbitrarily good approximation. However, it can be a nuisance to set up due to the need to sample the BRDF at specific locations in four-dimensional space given by the parameterization of the texture maps. Measured BRDF data, for instance, is often given at sparse locations that may not map conveniently onto the parameterization used for the final representation, and interpolating sparse four-dimensional data is nontrivial.

In practice, it usually turns out that one or two terms of a factorized representation are adequate, and given real-time constraints may be all that we can afford. In this case, we simply may want to find the best single-term factorization that we can.

Homomorphic factorization [113] finds approximations of the form

$$f(\hat{\mathbf{v}} \leftarrow \hat{\mathbf{l}}) \;\approx\; \prod_{k=1}^{K} g_k(\rho_k(\hat{\mathbf{v}}, \hat{\mathbf{l}}))$$

where the ρ_k projection functions are again arbitrary. Define $\tilde{f} = \log f$. To find samples of the g_k texture maps from samples of f, we first take the logarithm of both sides of the above equation, to obtain

$$\tilde{f}(\hat{\mathbf{v}} \leftarrow \hat{\mathbf{l}}) \;\approx\; \sum_{k=1}^{K} \tilde{g}_k(\rho_k(\hat{\mathbf{v}}, \hat{\mathbf{l}})).$$

This is a linear equation, and from it we can set up a number of linear constraints on the elements of $\tilde{g}_k$. Once we have enough equations, we can solve the system to derive the texture maps. In practice, we need to add some additional equations to ensure the smoothness of the solution.

Consider a specific case:

$$f(\hat{\mathbf{v}} \leftarrow \hat{\mathbf{l}}) \approx g_1(\hat{\mathbf{v}}) \cdot g_2(\hat{\mathbf{h}}) \cdot g_3(\hat{\mathbf{l}}),$$
$$\tilde{f}(\hat{\mathbf{v}} \leftarrow \hat{\mathbf{l}}) \approx \tilde{g}_1(\hat{\mathbf{v}}) + \tilde{g}_2(\hat{\mathbf{h}}) + \tilde{g}_3(\hat{\mathbf{l}}).$$

In order to ensure reciprocity, g_1 and g_3 must be the same. Renaming the factors to $g_1 = g_3 = p$ and $g_2 = q$, we have

$$f(\hat{\mathbf{v}} \leftarrow \hat{\mathbf{l}}) \approx p(\hat{\mathbf{v}}) \cdot q(\hat{\mathbf{h}}) \cdot p(\hat{\mathbf{l}}),$$
$$\tilde{f}(\hat{\mathbf{v}} \leftarrow \hat{\mathbf{l}}) \approx \tilde{p}(\hat{\mathbf{v}}) + \tilde{q}(\hat{\mathbf{h}}) + \tilde{p}(\hat{\mathbf{l}}).$$

If we are given a specific sample of f, say $f_j = f(\hat{\mathbf{v}}_j \leftarrow \hat{\mathbf{l}}_j)$, we can set up a single constraint equation as follows:

$$\tilde{f}(\hat{\mathbf{v}}_j \leftarrow \hat{\mathbf{l}}_j) \approx \tilde{p}(\hat{\mathbf{v}}_j) + \tilde{q}(\hat{\mathbf{h}}_j) + \tilde{p}(\hat{\mathbf{l}}_j)$$

where of course $\hat{\mathbf{h}}_j = \text{norm}\,(\hat{\mathbf{v}}_j + \hat{\mathbf{l}}_j)$. Unfortunately, in general the samples of f will not project exactly to the positions of samples in p and q, so we will have to interpolate. In that case, we can just set up the constraint to equal the sum of the interpolated values in p and q; we still have a linear equation relating a sample of f to samples in p and q. These linear interpolations do *not* correspond to the interpolation that will later occur during texture look-up, since we are doing the interpolation in log space. It's just a way to get subpixel precision when setting up the constraints.

We can represent all the data constraints in matrix form:

$$\tilde{\mathbf{f}} = \begin{bmatrix} A_p & A_q \end{bmatrix} \begin{bmatrix} \tilde{\mathbf{p}} \\ \tilde{\mathbf{q}} \end{bmatrix}$$

where $\tilde{\mathbf{f}}$ contains the samples of the log BRDF, $\tilde{\mathbf{p}}$ contains log samples of the texture map p, $\tilde{\mathbf{q}}$ contains log samples of the texture map q, and A_p and A_q are sparse matrices containing the coefficients of the data constraints between them.

In theory, now we can solve this system of linear equations to find the unknowns. Unfortunately, in practice, we may not have enough equations, or may have gaps. We also would like to encourage a smooth solution. We can augment the system with second-derivative operators L acting on the texture maps, the outputs of which we set to zero, as follows:

$$\begin{bmatrix} \tilde{\mathbf{f}} \\ 0 \end{bmatrix} = \begin{bmatrix} A_p & A_q \\ \lambda L & 0 \\ 0 & \lambda L \end{bmatrix} \begin{bmatrix} \tilde{\mathbf{p}} \\ \tilde{\mathbf{q}} \end{bmatrix}.$$

Figure 6.7.   Homomorphic factorization can be used to approximate arbitrary
functions. Here is a two-dimensional example. Left: The original function. Middle: An approximation using two projections in x and y. Right: An improved
approximation using three projections: x, y, and $x - y$ (a diagonal projection).

The operator is a mask which estimates the magnitudes of the second
derivatives in p and q, such as

$$
\begin{array}{rrr}
1 & -2 & 1 \\
-2 & 4 & -2 \\
1 & -2 & 1.
\end{array}
$$

The convolution of this mask against p and q generates one equation in L
for each possible output of the convolution.

The addition of these smoothness constraints augments the system with
a square submatrix so we that are sure the system is overdetermined. We
then must solve this system in a least-squares sense, to select $\tilde{p}$ and $\tilde{q}$ to
minimize the magnitude of the residual error vector e:

$$
\mathsf{e} \;=\; \begin{bmatrix} \tilde{f} \\ 0 \end{bmatrix} - \begin{bmatrix} \mathsf{A}_p & \mathsf{A}_q \\ \lambda\mathsf{L} & 0 \\ 0 & \lambda\mathsf{L} \end{bmatrix} \begin{bmatrix} \tilde{p} \\ \tilde{q} \end{bmatrix}.
$$

The value λ controls the relative importance of smoothness. We could
also weight rows in the data constraints to give some data samples more
importance than others.

There are many ways to solve this equation. The matrix given above is
very large, but sparse. Many sparse matrix solvers exist; we have used the
QMR technique, for which public-domain code exists in IML, available from
NIST. It would also be possible to factorize the above matrix using the SVD
and use the SVD to find the pseudoinverse. This would be a very, very large
factorization, but once we had this factorization we could factorize many
sets of data quickly, as long as they all had the same sampling pattern.

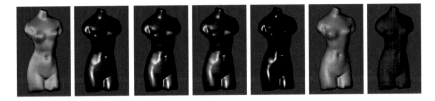

Figure 6.8.   Homomorphic factorization examples.   A model rendered at real-time rates (approximately half the speed of plain diffuse shading) using various factored BRDFs. The factorizations of these BRDFs were found numerically using homomorphic factorization. From left to right: Satin (using the anisotropic Poulin-Fournier model), Krylon Blue, Garnet Red, Cayman Blue, and Mystique paints (from the Cornell data set), leather, and velvet (from the CURET database). All but the first are measured data. Figure 6.9 gives the corresponding texture maps. (See Color Plate IX.)

Figure 6.8 and Figure 6.9 gives some examples. Data for these factorizations was chosen from public-domain databases, and in one case, was sampled from an analytic model.

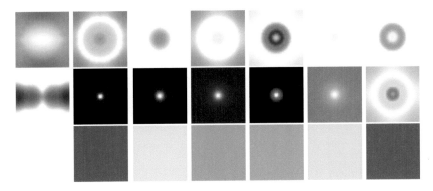

Figure 6.9.   Homomorphic factorization texture maps, using a parabolic representation of functions defined over a hemisphere. Top to bottom: $p'(\hat{\omega})$, $q'(\hat{\mathbf{h}})$, and the correction color α. Figure 6.8 gives some examples rendered using these texture maps; the materials are given in the same order here. (See Color Plate X.)

6.7 Texture Mapping Revisited

As we have shown in this chapter, texture mapping, when interpreted as a table look-up operation, can be used to implement sophisticated reflectance models. But how do we use these fancy lighting models with the traditional use of texture mapping, that is, to provide surface detail?

Of course, we could use textures that depend on texture coordinates (u, v) that parameterize a surface in the usual way to control parameters of our lighting models. For instance, if we wanted to vary the specularity of a Phong model, we could have a texture map that returned an exponent $q = t(u, v)$. However, this turns out to be a bad idea: Filtering operations in texture look-up units assume that the fragments ultimately written to the frame buffer depend linearly on texture values. If you use a texture map to control a parameter which is nonlinearly related to final fragment colors you risk aliasing.

The traditional textured lighting model in OpenGL is the sum of a diffuse and specular lobe. Under multitexturing and with recent ARB extensions to compute a separate specular color, we can separately texture the diffuse and specular parts of the lighting model:

$$f(u, v; \hat{\mathbf{v}} \leftarrow \hat{\mathbf{l}}) \quad = \quad t_d(u, v) f_d(\hat{\mathbf{v}} \leftarrow \hat{\mathbf{l}}) + t_s(u, v) f_s(\hat{\mathbf{v}} \leftarrow \hat{\mathbf{l}}).$$

Use of a texture to control the specular component of a lighting model separately from the diffuse part is called *gloss mapping*, which turns out to have good filtering properties. As the textures become blurrier with filtering, they tend to create a weighted average of diffuse and specular reflectivities, which gives the correct specular effect.

It should be noted that this filtering is only correct to the extent that the value returned by the BRDF does not depend on the surface position given by (u, v). In general, though, the BRDF's parameterization depends on surface normals and tangents which will vary with surface position, so separately filtering the masking textures is only an approximation. However, in most cases it seems to be a reasonable one.

6.7.1 Material Mapping

Gloss mapping uses textures to control the contribution of different lobes of one BRDF. This is naturally extended to summing several BRDFs:

$$f(u, v; \hat{\mathbf{v}} \leftarrow \hat{\mathbf{l}}) \quad = \quad \sum_{m=1}^{M} t_m(u, v) \cdot f_m(\hat{\mathbf{v}} \leftarrow \hat{\mathbf{l}}).$$

We call this generalization *material mapping*, since it permits us to place different materials at different places on a surface without adding more polygons. An example is given in Figure 6.10.

Like gloss mapping, material mapping behaves (mostly) correctly when the weighing textures are blurred by filtering, resulting in an average BRDF.

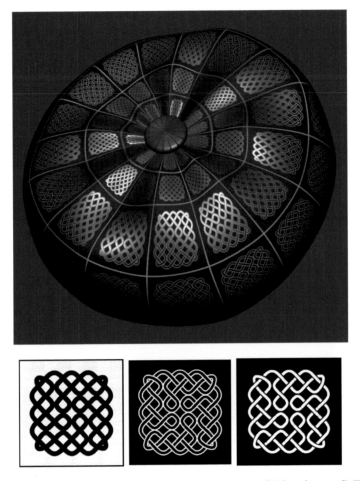

Figure 6.10. Material mapping. Rendered in real time (60fps+) on a GeForce3. The textures shown were used to blend between three homomorphically factorized BRDFs: velvet, garnet red, and anisotropic "brushed metal". The metal was also colored yellow on the trim around the knot by coloring the appropriate parts of the mask yellow. The textures were MIP-mapped. Notice the lack of aliasing at the center of the button. Here the filtered textures cause the BRDFs to blend together as desired. (See Color Plate XI.)

You could also think of material mapping as creating a sum of basis functions with coefficients that vary per texel, so that in theory, with a small number of "basis BRDFs" you could simulate more than that number of materials. You would also separate out the lobes of BRDFs that have diffuse and specular parts. If each lobe and the multiplication by a texture can be accomplished in a single pass, then the summation can be performed in the frame buffer over multiple passes. In this way, material mapping provides a simple architecture that scales to a large number of materials even on current hardware.

6.7.2 Bump, Twist, and Frame Mapping

Bump mapping with arbitrary BRDFs can also be implemented simply by looking up the normal in a texture map before evaluating the reflectance model. Normally we would store normals in surface-relative coordinates and would use the local surface frame to convert these normals into world space for shading, using

$$\hat{\mathbf{n}}'(u, v) \quad = \quad n_x(u, v)\hat{\mathbf{t}} + n_y(u, v)\hat{\mathbf{s}} + n_z(u, v)\hat{\mathbf{n}}.$$

With anisotropic models, we can do one better: we could store tangents at every texel as well, using exactly the same change-of-basis approach:

$$\hat{\mathbf{t}}'(u, v) \quad = \quad t_x(u, v)\hat{\mathbf{t}} + t_y(u, v)\hat{\mathbf{s}} + t_z(u, v)\hat{\mathbf{n}},$$
$$\hat{\mathbf{s}}'(u, v) \quad = \quad s_x(u, v)\hat{\mathbf{t}} + s_y(u, v)\hat{\mathbf{s}} + s_z(u, v)\hat{\mathbf{n}}.$$

We could also imagine perturbing the "twist" of the surface about the normal, but not the normal itself. This could be used to implement swirled brushed metal, for instance. Call this *twist mapping*. If we perturb both the normal and the tangents at every point on a surface, we have a new surface frame at every point; call this *frame mapping*. In theory we could store a representation of a frame in as few as three numbers using unit quaternions, so frame mapping would take hardly any more space than bump mapping! However, use of quaternions would require special interpolation hardware, so we might have to settle in practice for storing two tangents and computing the normal with a cross product.

One difficulty that arises with bump maps, particularly when the bumps are shaded with a glossy reflectance model, is how to antialias them. Applying normal MIP-map filtering to a bump map is incorrect; a bumpy surface might become smooth in the distance, but if the surface is glossy this would cause a sharper highlight than would be expected from the normal distribution of the bump map.

The solution is that bump maps should turn into BRDFs in the distance. It turns out that this behavior can be implemented on current graphics hardware with an intelligent combination of material mapping and MIP-mapping. Suppose you have two materials, one bump-mapped with BRDF f_1 using normals $\hat{\mathbf{n}}_1(u, v)$, the other just given by BRDF f_2 relative to the surface normal $\hat{\mathbf{n}}$. However, we set up BRDF f_2 to capture the overall reflectivity of the bump map when seen in the distance. Now suppose we material map between these two materials using a complementary set of texture maps:

$$\begin{aligned}
f(u, v; \hat{\mathbf{v}} \leftarrow \hat{\mathbf{l}}) &= t(u, v) \cdot f_1(\hat{\mathbf{n}}_1(u, v); \hat{\mathbf{v}} \leftarrow \hat{\mathbf{l}}) \\
&+ (1 - t(u, v)) \cdot f_2(\hat{\mathbf{n}}; \hat{\mathbf{v}} \leftarrow \hat{\mathbf{l}}).
\end{aligned}$$

Now, suppose texture t is MIP-mapped. We can set it to a constant value of one for the finer level of the MIP-map hierarchy where the scale of the bump map is valid, but to zero at coarser levels. This will fade out the bumps as they become invalid and fade in the BRDF that represents the overall response of the bumps that are too difficult to see. In general, we might have to frame-map or twist-map the new BRDF, and/or vary its properties using material mapping (for instance, to vary specularity):

$$\begin{aligned}
f(u, v; \hat{\mathbf{v}} \leftarrow \hat{\mathbf{l}}) &= t(u, v) \cdot f_1(\hat{\mathbf{n}}_1(u, v); \hat{\mathbf{v}} \leftarrow \hat{\mathbf{l}}) \\
&+ (1 - t(u, v)) \\
&\quad \cdot \left(\sum_{m=1}^{M} t_m(u, v) f_{2,m}(\hat{\mathbf{n}}_2(u, v), \hat{\mathbf{t}}_2(u, v), \hat{\mathbf{s}}_2(u, v); \hat{\mathbf{v}} \leftarrow \hat{\mathbf{l}}) \right).
\end{aligned}$$

This would be necessary to capture changes in reflectance due to variation of the invisible bumps if the bump texture had nonstationary behavior. In general, we could also have several layers of bumps, fading one out in favor of another as the scale changes, and might even want to include multiple levels of displacement mapping, and finally might use frame maps instead of bump maps at each level of the hierarchy.

Implementing this in full would of course require a large number of texture look-ups, per-pixel computations, and passes on current graphics hardware. In practice, we might change which materials are "active" based on the overall distance of the object to the viewer, to avoid spending passes computing the reflectivity of materials which will ultimately be multiplied by zero.

7

Environment Maps for Illumination

Basic environment mapping was discussed in Chapter 3. An environment map represents a function over a sphere that gives the radiance arriving at a single point from all possible directions. Once an environment map is available, it can be used to compute an (approximate) mirror reflection term for an object. Using multipass rendering and alpha blending, this mirror reflection term can be added to local illumination terms, such as point-source lighting models, that are computed via other means.

A true mirror reflection requires only a point sample of the incoming radiance, but correctly computing environmental illumination effects for surfaces with more general BRDFs requires an integration. Real-time integration of the local illumination integral over the hemisphere of incoming illumination directions with exact BRDFs is in general not computationally feasible. In order to efficiently incorporate true environmental illumination effects into reflection models other than a perfect metallic mirror, we need to perform some precomputations and take advantage of some special cases.

The two fundamental techniques for using environment maps with more general reflection models are

Decomposition: The reflection model is decomposed into simpler contributions, which can be treated separately. For example, a reflection model may be separated into a diffuse and a specular term, where the specular term is represented as a mirror reflection using an environment map and is multiplied with an viewing-angle-dependent Fresnel term. More generally, we could use a factorized model for the non-mirror terms of the BRDF. This approach has the disadvantage, mentioned above, that we are not actually using the same representation of the illumination for both parts of the reflectance.

Prefiltering: For certain reflection models, a filtered reflection of an environment map can be analytically precomputed and stored into a new texture map. The latter is called a *prefiltered environment map* or *radiance environment map*, so called because it actually holds the outgoing radiance instead of the reflected environment.

If the original environment map is given in a high-dynamic range format such as [38], then the prefiltering technique allows for effects similar to the ones described in [37]. For instance, a bright source in the scene can cause an extended highlight even if the surface looks like a mirror, if the BRDF has small but nonzero "tails" away from the specular peak. In general, a filtered and smoothed image will have a lower dynamic range than an unfiltered one.

In the following we will describe these two classes of techniques and demonstrate some applications for them.

7.1   Decomposition

Decomposition of a reflection model means separating its terms into simpler expressions that can be handled individually. The most fundamental example is a separation into additive diffuse and specular contributions. Decomposition can include a decomposition of a BRDF into a sum of lobes more general than this, however. For example, another possible term in an additive decomposition is a lobe to handle retroreflection. A retroreflective lighting model reflects energy back directly into the direction of incoming light, and so its BRDF would have a large value in the direction of $\hat{\mathbf{l}}$. We might also add up a number of basis functions to generate the exact shape of a BRDF; this would also be a decomposition.

Once we have decomposed the lighting model, we can deal with the individual terms in different ways. The main differences between techniques will depend on how terms are parameterized, and whether they are meant for representing high-frequency or low-frequency functions. A diffuse term in a BRDF is low-frequency and damps out high-frequency contributions from the illumination; a specular term is high-frequency and retains fine details from the illumination [150]. In general, if either the illumination or the BRDF is low-frequency the outgoing radiance will be low-frequency.

We will show in Section 7.2 that the diffuse term as well as certain specular terms can be treated with prefiltering. A diffuse surface in particular will blur out the incoming illumination enough that a crude approximation to it (such as a point source) will do. However, a pure specular term can also be handled efficiently via point sampling, for instance, using ordinary environment mapping.

Even for specular reflections, we may not have the same strength of reflection in all directions. In particular, we may want to factor the specular component of the lighting model into a standard environment map and an angularly dependent Fresnel term. This is described in the following section.

7.1.1 Generalized Mirror Reflections Using a Fresnel Term

The Fresnel term is a physical term describing the reflectivity of a material off a polished surface in the mirror direction of the incoming light. The Fresnel term depends on the relative optical density n (relative index of refraction) of the medium and the surface material and the angle of incoming light. The Fresnel term was covered in detail in Section 2.5.3. The formula for the average of both polarized terms (Equation 2.3, page 32) is repeated here:

$$ F(c) \;=\; \frac{(g-c)^2}{2(g+c)^2} \left(1 + \frac{(c(g+c)-1)^2}{(c(g-c)+1)^2} \right) $$

with $c = \langle \hat{\mathbf{h}}, \hat{\mathbf{v}} \rangle = \langle \hat{\mathbf{h}}, \hat{\mathbf{l}} \rangle$ and $g^2 = n^2 + c^2 - 1$. Here $\hat{\mathbf{h}}$ is the normal of a mirror surface that reflects $\hat{\mathbf{l}}$ in the direction of $\hat{\mathbf{v}}$. Sometimes you see the Fresnel term used with $\langle \hat{\mathbf{h}}, \hat{\mathbf{v}} \rangle$ or $\langle \hat{\mathbf{h}}, \hat{\mathbf{l}} \rangle$ as an argument. It's really just a question of whether you compute the mirror normal as the normalized average of $\hat{\mathbf{l}}$ and $\hat{\mathbf{v}}$ or whether, given $\hat{\mathbf{n}}$ and $\hat{\mathbf{v}}$ (or $\hat{\mathbf{l}}$), you compute $\hat{\mathbf{l}} = \hat{\mathbf{r}}_{\hat{\mathbf{n}}}(\hat{\mathbf{v}})$ (or $\hat{\mathbf{v}} = \hat{\mathbf{r}}_{\hat{\mathbf{n}}}(\hat{\mathbf{l}})$). In any case, to apply the Fresnel term we need the symmetrical angular relationship of a mirror reflection.

A regular environment map without prefiltering describes the incoming illumination at a point in space. If this information is directly used as the outgoing illumination, with suitable reparameterization by the reflection vector, only polished metallic surfaces can be modeled. This is because for metallic surfaces, which have a high optical density, the Fresnel term is almost a constant of one, independent of the angle between light direction and surface normal. Thus, for a perfectly smooth (i.e., polished to mirror smoothness) metal surface, incoming light is reflected in the mirror direction with a constant reflectance.

For nonmetallic materials (materials with a smaller relative optical density) however, the specular reflectance strongly depends on the angle of the incoming light. Mirror reflections on these materials should be weighted by the Fresnel term for the angle between the normal $\hat{\mathbf{n}}$ and the reflected viewing direction $\hat{\mathbf{r}}_{\hat{\mathbf{n}}}(\hat{\mathbf{v}})$ which is, of course, the same as the angle between the normal and viewing direction $\hat{\mathbf{v}}$.

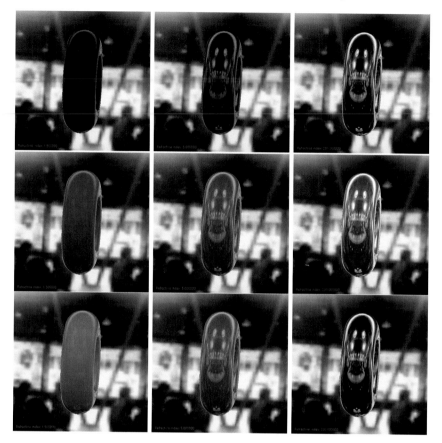

Figure 7.1.   Top row: Fresnel-weighted mirror term. Center row: Fresnel-weighted mirror term plus diffuse illumination. Bottom row: Fresnel blending between mirror and diffuse term. The indices of refraction are (from left to right) 1.5, 5, and 200.

For any given material with a given refractive index n, the Fresnel term $F(\cos\gamma)$ for the mirror direction $\hat{\mathbf{r}}_{\hat{\mathbf{n}}}(\hat{\mathbf{v}})$ can be stored in a one-dimensional texture map, and rendered to the frame buffer's alpha channel in a separate rendering pass. The mirror part is then multiplied with this Fresnel term in a second pass, and a third pass is used to add the diffuse part. If we have a reflection model consisting of a mirror component L_m and a diffuse component L_d, this yields an outgoing radiance of

$$L_o \;\; = \;\; F(\cos\gamma) \cdot L_m + L_d.$$

In addition to simply adding the diffuse part to the Fresnel-weighted mirror reflection, we can also use the Fresnel term for *blending* between diffuse and specular reflection modes:

$$L_o = F(\cos\gamma) \cdot L_m + (1 - F(\cos\gamma)) \cdot L_d.$$

This allows us to simulate diffuse surfaces with a transparent coating; the mirror term describes the reflection off the coating. Only light *not* reflected by the coating hits the underlying surface and is there reflected diffusely. This behavior is typical of high-gloss paints, for instance.

Figure 7.1 shows images generated using these two approaches. In the top row, the Fresnel-weighted mirror term is shown for indices of refraction of 1.5, 5, and 200. In the center row, a diffuse term is added, and in the bottom row, mirror and diffuse terms are blended using the Fresnel term. For low indices of refraction, the object is specular only for grazing viewing angles, while for high indices of refraction we get a metal-like reflection.

7.2 Prefiltered Environment Maps

Generally speaking, prefiltered environment maps capture the reflected *exitant* radiance travelling *outwards* in all directions $\hat{\mathbf{v}}$ from a fixed position $\mathbf{x}$. We will then apply the standard environment-map approximation of using this function as an approximation to the reflection (and outgoing radiance) for points near $\mathbf{x}$.

Recall the local illumination integral:

$$L_o(\mathbf{x}; \hat{\mathbf{v}}) = \int_{\Omega(\hat{\mathbf{n}})} f_r(\mathbf{x}; \hat{\mathbf{v}} \leftarrow \hat{\mathbf{l}}) L_i(\mathbf{x}; \hat{\mathbf{l}}) \langle \hat{\mathbf{n}}, \hat{\mathbf{l}} \rangle \, d\omega(\hat{\mathbf{l}}). \tag{7.1}$$

To be more exact, we will show the reparameterization into local surface coordinates implicit in the parameterization of the BRDF. At every point $\mathbf{x}$ on a surface, let there be a local surface frame given by an orthonormal triple of vectors: a primary tangent $\hat{\mathbf{t}}(\mathbf{x})$; a secondary tangent $\hat{\mathbf{s}}(\mathbf{x})$; and a normal $\hat{\mathbf{n}}(\mathbf{x})$. To avoid clutter we don't usually bother putting in the argument $\mathbf{x}$ to the elements of the local surface frame. However, we will do so in the following discussion to emphasize that the vectors of the local surface frame, and the coordinates of other vectors computed relative to this frame, are in fact functions of $\mathbf{x}$.

We can combine the elements of the surface frame into a row vector. If each frame vector is expressed as a column vector with respect to world-space coordinates, the result is the matrix $\mathsf{S}((\hat{\mathbf{x}}))$:

$$\mathsf{S}(\mathbf{x}) = [\hat{\mathbf{t}}(\mathbf{x}), \hat{\mathbf{s}}(\mathbf{x}), \hat{\mathbf{n}}(\mathbf{x})].$$

Suppose we are given an arbitrary vector $\hat{\mathbf{a}}$ expressed as a column vector in world-space coordinates. We can compute its surface-relative coordinates at $\mathbf{x}$, which we will denote as $\hat{\mathbf{a}}_s(\mathbf{x})$, using a matrix-vector product:

$$
\begin{aligned}
\hat{\mathbf{a}}_s(\mathbf{x}) &= \mathsf{S}^{-1}(\mathbf{x})\hat{\mathbf{a}} \\
&= \mathsf{S}^T(\mathbf{x})\hat{\mathbf{a}} \\
&= \begin{bmatrix} \langle \hat{\mathbf{t}}(\mathbf{x}), \hat{\mathbf{a}} \rangle \\ \langle \hat{\mathbf{s}}(\mathbf{x}), \hat{\mathbf{a}} \rangle \\ \langle \hat{\mathbf{n}}(\mathbf{x}), \hat{\mathbf{a}} \rangle \end{bmatrix}.
\end{aligned}
$$

Here we use the fact that the inverse of an orthonormal matrix is its transpose. We normally want an orthonormal surface frame so that we can correctly calculate angles in surface-relative coordinates. Due to interpolation of tangents and normals, it is possible that per-pixel frames will not be orthonormal, but we will treat them as if they were. This may introduce some error but is common practice; we often may not even start with orthonormal tangents. For homogeneous surfaces, the only dependence of the BRDF on $\mathbf{x}$ is the variation of $\mathsf{S}(\mathbf{x})$ with $\mathbf{x}$.

Given these conventions, we can now rewrite the local surface reflectance equation as follows:

$$
\begin{aligned}
L_o(\mathbf{x}; \hat{\mathbf{v}}) &= \int_\Omega f_r(\hat{\mathbf{v}}(\mathbf{x}) \leftarrow \hat{\mathbf{l}}(\mathbf{x}))\, L_i(\mathbf{x}; \hat{\mathbf{l}}) \langle \hat{\mathbf{n}}, \hat{\mathbf{l}} \rangle\, d\omega(\hat{\mathbf{l}}); \\
L_o(\mathbf{x}; \hat{\mathbf{v}}, \mathsf{S}(\mathbf{x})) &= \int_{\Omega(\hat{\mathbf{n}}(\mathbf{x}))} f_r(\mathsf{S}^T(\mathbf{x})\hat{\mathbf{v}} \leftarrow \mathsf{S}^T(\mathbf{x})\hat{\mathbf{l}})\, L_i(\mathbf{x}; \hat{\mathbf{l}}) \langle \hat{\mathbf{n}}(\mathbf{x}), \hat{\mathbf{l}} \rangle\, d\omega(\hat{\mathbf{l}}).
\end{aligned}
$$

Here we have explicitly written the outgoing radiance as a function of the surface frame $\mathsf{S}(\mathbf{x})$ at $\mathbf{x}$.

A prefiltered environment map or radiance map stores the radiance of light reflected towards the viewing direction $\hat{\mathbf{v}}$. It is computed by weighting the incoming light L_i from all directions $\hat{\mathbf{l}}$ with the BRDF f_r. The incoming radiance function L_i is stored in an unfiltered original environment map. In the general case we have a dependence on the viewing direction as well as on the orientation of the reflective surface, i.e., the local coordinate frame $[\hat{\mathbf{t}}(\mathbf{x}), \hat{\mathbf{s}}(\mathbf{x}), \hat{\mathbf{n}}(\mathbf{x})]$, which is in turn a function of $\mathbf{x}$.

A prefiltered environment map or radiance map is in general five-dimensional. Two degrees of freedom are needed to represent the viewing direction $\hat{\mathbf{v}}$ (a unit vector in world coordinates) and three more degrees of freedom are necessary to represent the orthonormal coordinate frame. For the latter, three angles can be used to specify the orientation of an arbitrary coordinate frame using three successive axis-oriented rotations, or we could use a unit quaternion, which also has three degrees of freedom.

Of course, five-dimensional textures would have enormous memory requirements, and at any rate aren't supported in current hardware. The prefiltered environment maps which we will examine drop some dependencies and make some further simplifications in the name of practicality. Usually, we drop the dependency on the tangents and so the orientation around the normal. The remaining degrees of freedom are often reparameterized; for instance, we may not index the outgoing radiance field with the viewing direction $\hat{\mathbf{v}}$, but with the reflected viewing direction.

Because this reduction in dimensionality also removes some of the generality of the approach, an additional decomposition method is often required to combine several simplified models. Frequently this takes the form of a summation of several different reduced-dimensionality representations, but there are other possibilities.

7.2.1 Diffusely Prefiltered Maps

As we have demonstrated, we can combine a mirror reflection term using an ordinary environment map with local illumination terms that are generated using some other form of lighting (the built-in lighting model, factorized BRDFs, whatever). It is also possible to add a diffuse global illumination term through the use of precomputed colors or textures. For the generation of such a representation, there are two approaches.

In the first approach, a global illumination algorithm such as radiosity or path tracing is used to compute the total irradiance of every surface point. This irradiance (which is just a single color at every point) could then be stored in a texture map attached to the surface and added to the outgoing radiance during rendering, after being scaled by a constant approximation to the BRDF for each surface.

The second approach is purely image-based, and uses a prefiltered environment map [59, 118]. The environment map used for the mirror term contains information about the incoming radiance $L_i(\mathbf{x}; \hat{\mathbf{l}})$, where $\mathbf{x}$ is the point for which the environment map is valid, and $\hat{\mathbf{l}}$ the direction of the incoming light. The outgoing radiance for a diffuse BRDF is then:

$$L_o(\mathbf{x}; \hat{\mathbf{n}}) = k_d \cdot \int_{\Omega(\hat{\mathbf{n}})} L_i(\mathbf{x}; \hat{\mathbf{l}}) \cdot \langle \hat{\mathbf{n}}, \hat{\mathbf{l}} \rangle \, d\omega(\hat{\mathbf{l}}).$$

Due to the constant BRDF of diffuse surfaces, L_o is a function only of the surface normal $\hat{\mathbf{n}}$ and the illumination L_i stored in the environment map, but not of the outgoing direction $\hat{\mathbf{v}}$. Thus, it is possible to precompute a map containing the diffuse illumination for all possible surface normals. For this map, like for the mirror map, any parameterization from Section 3.2.2

Figure 7.2.   Left: Diffusely prefiltered environment map of the café scene. Center: Diffusely illuminated torus. Right: Same torus illuminated with both a diffuse and a mirror term. (See Color Plate XII.)

can be used. The only difference is that diffusely prefiltered maps are always referenced via the normal of a vertex in environment map space, instead of via the reflection vector. Figure 7.2 shows such a prefiltered map, a torus with diffuse illumination only, as well as a torus with diffuse and mirror illumination.

The functions stored in such maps will have vary relatively slowly. It has been shown, in fact, that these functions can be characterized within a 9% maximum relative error with only nine numbers, using the first nine spherical harmonic basis functions [149, 150]. These basis functions can be written in terms of the cosines of the angles the normal makes with each coordinate axis, which of course are also its coordinates with respect to the world frame. This leads to a very convenient and compact procedural definition of a diffuse irradiance map:

$$E(n_x, n_y, n_z) \approx a_1(n_x^2 - n_y^2) + a_2 n_z^2 + a_3 n_x n_y + a_4 n_y n_z + a_5 n_x n_z$$
$$+ a_6 n_x + a_7 n_y + a_8 n_z + a_9.$$

Using these basis functions to compute the coefficients is also convenient since they are orthonormal. In effect, we can replace one integration for every pixel of a sampled irradiance map with nine similar integrations for computing the coefficients a_i of the above representation. This representation is simple enough that we could store nine volumes of coefficients for representing the variation of irradiance through a volume [60]:

$$E(x, y, z; n_x, n_y, n_z) \approx a_1(x, y, z)(n_x^2 - n_y^2) + a_2(x, y, z)n_z^2 + a_3(x, y, z)n_x n_y$$
$$+ a_4(x, y, z)n_y n_z + a_5(x, y, z)n_x n_z + a_6(x, y, z)n_x$$
$$+ a_7(x, y, z)n_y + a_8(x, y, z)n_z + a_9(x, y, z).$$

A very similar technique for representing irradiance on a surface has also been introduced recently, called *polynomial texture mapping* [107]. Suppose $\hat{\mathbf{l}}$ is a light vector, and

$$
\begin{aligned}
l_u &= \langle \hat{\mathbf{l}}, \hat{\mathbf{t}} \rangle, \\
l_v &= \langle \hat{\mathbf{l}}, \hat{\mathbf{s}} \rangle
\end{aligned}
$$

are the local surface frame coordinates of this vector with respect to the tangents $\hat{\mathbf{t}}$ and $\hat{\mathbf{s}}$ of a local surface frame. Then we can approximate the irradiance at every point of a surface parameterized by (u, v) with

$$
\begin{aligned}
E(u, v; l_u, l_v) &\approx a_1(u,v)l_u^2 + a_2(u,v)l_v^2 + a_3(u,v)l_ul_v \\
&+ a_4(u,v)l_u + a_5(u,v)l_v + a_6(u,v).
\end{aligned}
$$

Although the lighting variation can vary only gradually, the texture maps $a_i(u, v)$ can vary rapidly. This seems to be a good combination for diffuse illumination. This representation can also be used to represent bump-map diffuse lighting and self-shadowing, where it gives pleasingly soft and realistic results. Polynomial texture maps can be acquired with a simple apparatus that illuminates a surface from several directions, takes a number of aligned images for each direction of illumination, and fits the polynomial to the variation seen in each pixel. This technique can also be seen as a variation on material mapping, presented in Section 6.7.1.

7.2.2 Glossy Prefiltering of Environment Maps

A simplification similar to the one used for diffuse materials is also possible for certain specular reflection models [72, 77, 118], most notably the Phong model. Voorhies et al. [173] have used a similar approach to implement Phong shading for directional light sources.

The BRDF of the specular part of the classic Phong lighting model [102] is given by

$$
\begin{aligned}
f_r(\mathbf{x}; \hat{\mathbf{v}} \leftarrow \hat{\mathbf{l}}) &= k_s \cdot \frac{\langle \hat{\mathbf{r}}_{\hat{\mathbf{n}}}(\hat{\mathbf{l}}), \hat{\mathbf{v}} \rangle^q}{\cos \alpha} \\
&= k_s \cdot \frac{\langle \hat{\mathbf{r}}_{\hat{\mathbf{n}}}(\hat{\mathbf{v}}), \hat{\mathbf{l}} \rangle^q}{\cos \alpha} \\
&= k_s \cdot \frac{(\hat{\mathbf{v}}^T R_{\hat{\mathbf{n}}} \hat{\mathbf{l}})^q}{\cos \alpha}
\end{aligned}
$$

where $\hat{\mathbf{r}}_{\hat{\mathbf{n}}}(\hat{\mathbf{l}})$, and $\hat{\mathbf{r}}_{\hat{\mathbf{n}}}(\hat{\mathbf{v}})$ are the reflected light directions and viewing directions, respectively, $\cos \alpha = \langle \hat{\mathbf{n}}, \hat{\mathbf{l}} \rangle$, and $R_{\hat{\mathbf{n}}}$ is the symmetric Householder reflection matrix. In the following and in the captions of our figures, we will refer to the "roughness" r as the reciprocal of the Phong exponent: $r = 1/q$.

Specular global illumination using the Phong model can be approximated by

$$L_o(\mathbf{x}; \hat{\mathbf{r}}) = k_s \cdot \int_{\mathcal{S}^\in} \langle \hat{\mathbf{r}}, \hat{\mathbf{l}} \rangle^{1/r} L_i(\mathbf{x}; \hat{\mathbf{l}}) \, d\omega(\hat{\mathbf{l}}), \qquad (7.2)$$

for some roughness $r = 1/q$. The outgoing radiance here is a function only of the reflection vector $\hat{\mathbf{r}} = \hat{\mathbf{r}}_{\hat{\mathbf{n}}}(\hat{\mathbf{v}})$ and the environment map containing the incoming radiance $L_i(\mathbf{x}, \hat{\mathbf{l}})$. However, an approximation is required: We cannot afford to add a parameter for $\hat{\mathbf{n}}$, and so integrate over the entire unit sphere $\mathcal{S}^\in$ of incoming directions. If the specular peak is reasonably sharp, however, far from the reflection vector direction the integrand will be very close to zero, and negligible energy will be picked up from below the horizon.

Using this approximation, it is possible to take a map containing $L_i(\mathbf{x}, \hat{\mathbf{l}})$, and generate a filtered map containing the outgoing radiance $L_o(\mathbf{x}, \hat{\mathbf{r}}_{\hat{\mathbf{n}}}(\hat{\mathbf{v}}))$ for a glossy Phong material. This can be combined with a prefiltered map for the diffuse lobe to obtain a complete real-time simulation of the Phong reflection model.

The second image in Figure 7.3 shows such a map generated from the original cafe environment to the left, as well as a glossy sphere and torus textured with this map.

A Fresnel weighting of these prefiltered environment maps along the lines of Section 7.1.1 is only possible with some approximation. The exact Fresnel term for the glossy reflection cannot be used, since this term would have to appear inside the integral of Equation 7.2. However, for glossy surfaces with a low roughness, the Fresnel term can be assumed constant

Figure 7.3.   The second image is a prefiltered version of the map on the left with a roughness of 0.01. The two rightmost images are applications of this map to a reflective sphere and torus.

over the whole specular peak, which is very narrow in this case. Then the Fresnel term can be moved out of the integral, and the same technique as for mirror reflections applies.

The use of a Phong model for the prefiltering is somewhat unsatisfactory, since the classic Phong model is not physically valid. However, this method works for all reflection models having lobes that are rotationally symmetric about the reflected viewing direction, and whose shape does not depend on the angle to the surface normal. We can also approximate other BRDFs with sums of Phong-like lobes.

7.2.3 Approximations of General Isotropic BRDFs

Based on this concept, Kautz and McCool [84] extended the prefiltered Phong environment map idea to the   approximation of reflectances due to other isotropic BRDFs by approximating them with a special class of BRDFs:

$$f_r(\hat{\mathbf{v}} \leftarrow \hat{\mathbf{l}}; \hat{\mathbf{r}}_v) \;\; = \;\; p(\langle \hat{\mathbf{n}}, \hat{\mathbf{r}}_v \rangle, \langle \hat{\mathbf{r}}_v, \hat{\mathbf{l}} \rangle)$$

where p is an approximation to a given isotropic BRDF, which is not only isotropic, but also radially symmetric about the reflection vector $\hat{\mathbf{r}}_v = \hat{\mathbf{r}}_{\hat{\mathbf{n}}}(\hat{\mathbf{v}})$, and therefore only depends on two parameters.

Now consider Equation 7.2 using this form of reflectance function:

$$L_o(\mathbf{x}; \hat{\mathbf{v}}, \hat{\mathbf{n}}) = \int_{\Omega(\hat{\mathbf{n}})} p(\langle \hat{\mathbf{n}}, \hat{\mathbf{r}}_v \rangle, \langle \hat{\mathbf{r}}_v, \hat{\mathbf{l}} \rangle) \cdot L_i(\mathbf{x}; \hat{\mathbf{l}}) \langle \hat{\mathbf{n}}, \hat{\mathbf{l}} \rangle \; d\omega(\hat{\mathbf{l}}).$$

The authors then make the assumption that the BRDF is fairly specular, i.e., the BRDF is close to zero almost everywhere, except for $\hat{\mathbf{r}}_v \approx \hat{\mathbf{l}}$. Using this assumption they reason that $\langle \hat{\mathbf{n}}, \hat{\mathbf{r}}_v \rangle \approx \langle \hat{\mathbf{n}}, \hat{\mathbf{l}} \rangle$. Now the equation can be reparameterized and rewritten the following way:

$$L_o(\mathbf{x}; \hat{\mathbf{r}}_v, \langle \hat{\mathbf{n}}, \hat{\mathbf{r}}_v \rangle) = \langle \hat{\mathbf{n}}, \hat{\mathbf{r}}_v \rangle \int_{\Omega(\hat{\mathbf{n}})} p(\langle \hat{\mathbf{n}}, \hat{\mathbf{r}}_v \rangle, \langle \hat{\mathbf{r}}_v, \hat{\mathbf{l}} \rangle) \cdot L_i(\mathbf{x}; \hat{\mathbf{l}}) \; d\omega(\hat{\mathbf{l}}), \quad (7.3)$$

which leads to a three-dimensional representation. The third dimension is used to vary the diameter of the lobe with the angle between reflection vector and surface normal. This way, it is possible to have materials that are almost mirror-like at grazing viewing angles, while they are matte if looked at perpendicularly. This is a behavior that can be seen quite often with real materials.

In addition to this, Kautz and McCool also proposed an approximation technique that generates a BRDF with rotationally symmetric lobes from an arbitrary BRDF. This is done by averaging the lobes for different viewing directions. It is also possible to use lobes that are rotationally symmetric about any direction vector, not just the reflection vector.

This technique has the advantage that it can use approximations of arbitrary isotropic BRDFs and achieves interactive frame rates. Off-specular peaks can also be incorporated into this technique by indexing maps using vectors other than the reflection vector. An additional Fresnel factor as Miller [118] and Heidrich [77] proposed is not needed because it can be incorporated into the dependency on the viewing angle, i.e., the third dimension of the map. On the down side, three-dimensional textures are quite space consuming and can be relatively slow to render. Fortunately, only low resolution is usually needed for the dependency on viewing angle, and so interpolation between a small number of two-dimensional slices can be used instead of a full three-dimensional texture.

Depending on the BRDF, the quality of the approximation varies. For higher quality approximations Kautz and McCool also propose to use a multilobe approximation, which basically results in several prefiltered environment maps which are parameterized differently and have to be summed.

For instance, if a BRDF is to be used which is based on several separate surface phenomena (e.g., has retroreflections, diffuse reflections, and glossy reflections) each part has to be approximated separately, since no radially symmetric approximation can be found for the whole BRDF. This again means a decomposition of the reflection model into several parts. Unfortunately, while it is theoretically possible to approximate reflectances due to anisotropic BRDFs in this manner, many lobes would be needed to get a visually pleasing approximation.

7.2.4 Hardware-Accelerated Prefiltering

For interactive applications it would be nice if environment map prefiltering could be done on the fly. This means that if the scene changes, glossy reflections change accordingly. Kautz et al. [87] described a method with which it is possible to perform Phong filtering similar to that described in Section 7.2.2 on the fly using graphics hardware.

In a prefiltered environment map, every texel is a weighted sum of all pixels in a source environment map. This means we can think of the filtering process as applying the BRDF as a "filter kernel" to some unfiltered source map. Kautz et al. mapped this filtering operation to the operations provided by the OpenGL imaging subset. This subset supports only shift-invariant two-dimensional filters of certain sizes. In a shift-invariant filter, the filter size and shape must be the same across the image. We would like to use this feature to perform BRDF filtering over (hemi-)spherical para-

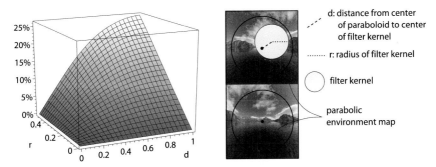

Figure 7.4. Distortion of a circle when projected from a parabolic map back to the sphere. (Image courtesy of Kautz et al. [87].)

metric domains. For hardware-accelerated prefiltering we have to choose an environment map technique that uses only two-dimensional environment maps and an environment map representation that keeps the filter shift-invariant over this representation.

The Phong model has a shift-invariant filter kernel over the hemisphere, since its cosine lobe is constant for all reflected viewing directions $\hat{r}_v$. It is also radially symmetric about $\hat{r}_v$. The filter size can also be decreased if smaller values are clamped to zero (this is necessary due to restrictions of the filter size imposed by the graphics hardware). The filter shape is obviously circular on the hemisphere, since it is radially symmetric. Therefore Phong environment maps seem to fulfill the necessary requirements for hardware-accelerated prefiltering. We still need to find an environment map representation that maps the shift-invariant circular filter kernel on the hemisphere to a shift-invariant circular filter kernel in texture space.

It turns out that the parabolic maps come close to this desired property. A filter kernel with circular footprint which is mapped from the parabolic environment map back to the hemisphere is also (almost) circular. A distortion occurs depending on the radius and the position of the filter. To visualize the distortion, we project a circular filter kernel with a radius of r ($r = 1$ is half the width of the parabolic map) from the parabolic map back to the sphere and measure the error; see the right side of Figure 7.4. The resulting distortion of the circle is given on the left side of the same figure. It depends on the radius of the filter kernel and also on the distance d of the filter's center from the parabolic map's center (i.e., the center of the front- or back-facing paraboloid). The distortion goes up to 25% for large radii, but in these cases the prefiltered environment map will be very blurry, so that the distortion will not lead to visible errors. For smaller radii the distortion remains fairly small.

Unfortunately, a shift-invariant filter kernel on the sphere still does not completely map to a shift-invariant filter in the parabolic space. Besides the slight distortion, the size of the filter kernel varies with the distance d to the center of the map. The ratio between the smallest filter radius and largest filter radius is 1:2, since the ratio for the areas is 1:4, as shown in Section 3.2.2. To adjust for this, we generate two prefiltered environment maps, one with the smallest filter size (this yields map S) and one with the largest necessary filter size (this yields map L). Then we blend between both prefiltered environments. The value with which we need to blend between both maps is different for different pixels in the parabolic environment map, but it depends only on the distance d and is always d^2. For a pixel in the center of the paraboloid this means that we use 0% of map L and a 100% of map S; for a pixel with distance $d = 0.5$ to the center of the parabolic map, we use 25% of map L and 75% of map S, and so on.

The actual algorithm is fairly simple. First we create a Mip-map of the parabolic environment map, then we load the environment map (plus the Mip-map) into texture memory. The user has to specify the Phong exponent to be used and a limit when BRDF values from the Phong model can be clamped to zero, which is used to restrict the kernel size. Then we compute the two necessary filter radii, r_s for the small filter and r_l for the large filter. Now we get to the actual rendering part:

1. Set the camera to an orthographic projection (so that we can draw the environment map seen from the top).

2. Draw alpha texture with d^2 to alpha channel.

3. For both radii r_s and r_l:

4.   While r_s (resp. r_l) < hardware supported filter size:

5.   Divide r_s (resp. r_l) by 2. Double the shrink factor.

6.   Draw environment map shrunken by the shrink factor (uses Mip-mapping).

7.   Sample the Phong model into the filter kernel

8.   Filter the environment map (OpenGL convolution).

9.   Store the result as texture map (RGBα texture).

10. Draw environment map S.

11. Blend environment map L with it (using d^2).

12. Store the result again as a texture map.

13. Set up real camera.

14. Draw reflective object with generated environment map.

One problem arises when the center of the filter kernel is close to the border of the environment map. Part of the filter kernel will be outside the hemisphere covered by the core parabolic map, thus including values from outside the environment map. Fortunately, parabolic maps can easily be extended to include an arbitrary border of texels over the hemispherical horizon, texels that would be shared with the other half of the parabolic map if both hemispheres were required for rendering.

Some renderings that were done using an SGI O2 at interactive rates (16-25 fps), are depicted in Figure 7.5. All the renderings were done with parabolic environment maps with 512×1024 pixels. The border was 64 pixels in each direction (for each face). The maximum filter size we used was 7.

Please note that filtering was performed for *every* frame for test purposes, even though the Phong exponent did not change. We have included timings for the hardware convolution, the filter sizes that would have been required (the BRDF clamp value was set to 0.1) and the necessary shrink factor to get filter sizes with a maximum size of 7. You can see that for small Phong exponents hardware prefiltering is very fast. For larger Phong exponents the rendering speed is slower, because filtering then is done with a larger environment map. (For a visual comparison, see Figure 7.6). Due to the way convolutions work in OpenGL, the hardware method generates dark borders, but this does not pose a problem since these are not used

N = 50. 20 Hz.   N = 500. 9 Hz.   N = 50. 20 Hz.   N = 500. 9 Hz.

Figure 7.5. Two scenes rendered with a glossy reflective torus. Filtering is done with the Phong model (exponent of 50 and 500) for every frame, but interactive rates are still achieved. The original environment maps are 512×1024 pixels in size with a border of 64 pixels. Images courtesy of Kautz et al. [87]. (See Color Plate XIV.)

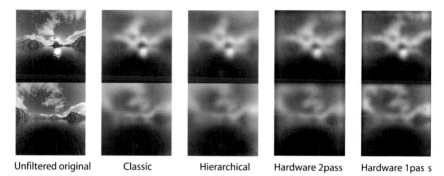

Unfiltered original   Classic   Hierarchical   Hardware 2pass   Hardware 1pas s

Figure 7.6. Comparison of the different filtering methods. Filtering was done with the Phong model and an exponent of 100. From left to right: Unfiltered, the classic method, our new hierarchical method, the hardware-accelerated method. The original environment map is 128×256 pixels in size with a border of 16 pixels. Images courtesy of Kautz et al. [87]. (See Color Plate XIII.)

for rendering (they replicate information present in the other hemisphere). Figure 7.5 shows renderings with different environment maps and different Phong exponents; they all run at interactive rates.

Using the same arguments as in Section 7.2.2, we can not only use Phong materials for this hardware prefiltering, but any BRDF with radially symmetric lobes. Unfortunately, the OpenGL Imaging subset is not widely available on consumer graphics cards. However, with multitexturing support and programmable pixel shading, the convolution can be simulated by multiple texture accesses with slightly offset texture parameters. Essentially, this uses footprint assembly to construct the convolution filter from multiple taps (Section 3.3.2).

7.3 Environment Map Interpolation

A different technique which makes similar assumptions (isotropic BRDFs) was presented by Cabral et al. [25]. They prefilter environment maps for several different fixed viewing directions, resulting in a set of view-dependent environment maps. An alternative to the prefiltering process is to take photographs from different viewing directions of a sphere made of the same material one would like to represent (producing spherical environment maps for the sample material).

In contrast to the previous approach, this actually results in a four-dimensional map L_o:

$$L_o(\mathbf{x}; \hat{\mathbf{v}}, \hat{\mathbf{n}}) \quad = \quad \int_{\Omega(\hat{\mathbf{n}})} p(\langle \hat{\mathbf{n}}, \hat{\mathbf{r}}_v \rangle, \langle \hat{\mathbf{r}}_v, \hat{\mathbf{l}} \rangle) \cdot L_i(\mathbf{x}; \hat{\mathbf{l}}) \langle \hat{\mathbf{n}}, \hat{\mathbf{l}} \rangle \, d\omega(\hat{\mathbf{l}}).$$

Each texel in the environment maps represents the integral of BRDF and all incoming light for one surface orientation, $\hat{\mathbf{n}}$. The two dimensions of surface orientations are sampled densely by the map. The two dimensions representing the viewing direction, $\hat{\mathbf{v}}$, are only sampled very coarsely, with a different environment map for each new viewpoint. Published results used only twelve samples for $\hat{\mathbf{v}}$ in the form of twelve spherical environment maps. Since the space of view directions is sampled so coarsely, the quality of the reconstruction for a new view direction becomes quite important.

Before rendering from a new view direction, a new environment map is constructed, representing L_o for surface orientations from that new view. The map is built by a linear blend of the sample maps closest to the new view, but with each sample map warped to align key features of each map with the new view. The new view-dependent environment map is then applied to an object. The warping compensates for the undersampled viewing directions, and minimizes visible artifacts. Although creating the texture does require hardware accelerated copy-to-texture or render-to-texture to achieve interactive frame rates, the final rendering can be done with standard sphere mapping. This is one major reason for generating the intermediate sphere map. The same algorithm could be applied through multiple environment look-ups on the actual shaded objects with per-vertex computation of warped environment map texture coordinates.

Warping is done based on an assumed direction for the central reflection of the BRDF (the mirror-reflected viewing direction and the surface normal are mentioned as examples in [25]). For example, if a primarily specular BRDF is assumed, then the warping maps highlight locations from the source maps to the right position on the destination map, at the expense of factors in the BRDF that don't line up along the specular reflection direction.

In the case of a primarily specular BRDF, a parabolic or cube representation for the original sampled maps is better than the original spherical map representation, since they don't need any additional warping at all! You would still need to blend several source maps, since the reason for using this method is not to get view-independent environment mapping based only on sphere maps, but to enable rendering of BRDFs with significant view-dependent effects in addition to their central reflection.

The warp itself is most easily understood as a composition of simple transformations: First, from a texel location in the new map to its surface orientation (whether working with sphere maps or not, this can be visualized as a point on a reflective sphere in a space convenient for computation).

This mapping from a sphere map to a sphere with view direction down the z-axis is:

$$g_{normal}(s, t) = \begin{bmatrix} 2s - 1 \\ 2t - 1 \\ \sqrt{1 - (2s - 1)^2 + (2t - 1)^2} \end{bmatrix}. \qquad (7.4)$$

Then, from that normal we find the corresponding central reflection direction. For the case of a primarily specular BRDF, this is:

$$g_{mirror}(x, y, z) = \begin{bmatrix} 2xz \\ 2yz \\ 2z^2 - 1 \end{bmatrix}. \qquad (7.5)$$

This direction is rotated by a simple rotation matrix, T, from the space with z down the destination map's view direction to one with z down the source map's view direction. Then the reflection direction to sphere normal transformation is reversed:

$$g_{mirror}^{-1}(x, y, z) = \left(\frac{[\begin{array}{ccc} x & y & z + 1 \end{array}]^T}{\sqrt{x^2 + y^2 + (z + 1)^2}} \right). \qquad (7.6)$$

Finally, the sphere normal to texture coordinate transformation is reversed:

$$g_{normal}^{-1}(x, y, z) = [\begin{array}{cc} x/2 + .5 & y/2 + .5 \end{array}]^T. \qquad (7.7)$$

This chain, $g_{normal}^{-1} \circ g_{mirror}^{-1} \circ T \circ g_{mirror} \circ g_{normal}$, generates the texture coordinate of the source map for a point in the destination map. By applying this as a per-vertex computation on a spherical mesh (or even a flat disk), we can warp the source sphere map to destination sphere map with a simple textured draw. Similar equations can be derived for other map representations (parabolic, cube, etc.) and other choices of central reflection. This method also allows the source maps and destination map to be of different forms by choosing a different set of functions to get to and from the central reflection.

Factors that determine the weighting of each warped map are shown in Figure 7.7. The weights are the ratio of spherical triangle areas. This makes the weight one when the destination view lines up directly with a source view, and it drops to zero for a destination view along the opposite triangle edge. For a triangle with angles α, β and γ, the area is:

$$a = \alpha + \beta + \gamma - \pi. \qquad (7.8)$$

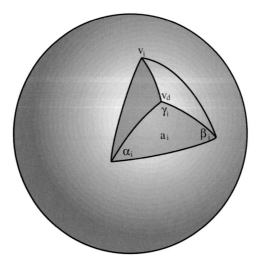

Figure 7.7. Configuration for spherical barycentric weighting. Sphere represents the tips of the unit vectors for all possible viewing directions. Three closest sample views are for viewing directions at vertices of the large triangle. New novel view is at the center vertex. The weight for the map from view direction v_i is the ratio of area a_i to the area of the large triangle.

The dihedral angles, α_i, β_i and γ_i for use in weighting view $\hat{\mathbf{v}}_i$ can be derived geometrically through cross and dot products of the view vectors involved. $\hat{\mathbf{v}}_d$ is the destination view vector, $\hat{\mathbf{v}}_h$ is the vertex before $\hat{\mathbf{v}}_i$ and $\hat{\mathbf{v}}_j$ is the vertex after it (i.e., view vectors $\hat{\mathbf{v}}_d$, $\hat{\mathbf{v}}_i$ and $\hat{\mathbf{v}}_h$ are vertices for the triangle with area a_i).

$$\alpha_i = \cos^{-1}(\hat{\mathbf{v}}_d \times \hat{\mathbf{v}}_h \cdot \hat{\mathbf{v}}_j \times \hat{\mathbf{v}}_h), \tag{7.9}$$

$$\beta_i = \cos^{-1}(\hat{\mathbf{v}}_j \times \hat{\mathbf{v}}_d \cdot \hat{\mathbf{v}}_j \times \hat{\mathbf{v}}_h), \tag{7.10}$$

$$\gamma_i = \cos^{-1}(\hat{\mathbf{v}}_j \times \hat{\mathbf{v}}_d \cdot \hat{\mathbf{v}}_h \times \hat{\mathbf{v}}_d). \tag{7.11}$$

The assumption of a single, predominant reflection direction fails for BRDFs that have off-specular reflections, like strong diffuse components or retroreflection. Similarly, since radially symmetric BRDFs are used, this method has the same difficulties with complex BRDFs as the previous method. To overcome these problems, the method can be combined with a decomposition approach.

As mentioned before, the generated two-dimensional environment map is view-dependent, so effects that are not well-modeled by the chosen warp

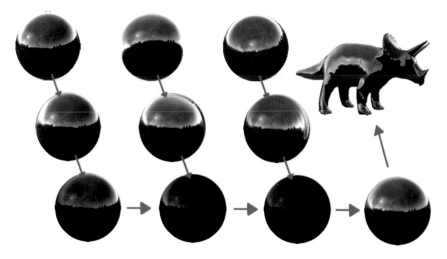

Figure 7.8.   Warping of the environment maps is done by taking three source maps corresponding to close-by viewing directions (top row). Each source map is then warped to the desired viewing direction by assuming a mirror reflection for the feature correspondences (i.e., matching the highlights, center row). Finally, all warped maps are weighted by considering how similar the viewing direction of the corresponding source map is to the desired viewing direction (bottom row). After summing up the contributions, a new spherical map is obtained that can be applied to an object.

will be incorrect unless a large number of source maps are used. For example, this method works well for materials with a Fresnel reflectance term since it varies slowly enough to be well-represented by a handful of maps. However, if the material contains a strongly varying Fresnel term, it cannot be represented efficiently in this form, because too many source maps would be required to get good coverage of the space of view directions.

8

The Texture Atlas

Components of real-time shaders can be view-dependent or view-independent.When the view of the object changes, the independent components of its shading remain constant. When the object and its lighting remain fixed, its diffuse reflection is view-independent whereas its specular reflection is view-dependent. Texturing, when used to represent the color variation of a homogeneous material, is view-independent. The surface normals of an object are view independent. Diffuse bump mapping is view-independent for fixed lighting, but specular bump mapping is view-dependent.

A view-dependent component needs to be recomputed when the view of the object changes, whereas a view-independent component need only be recomputed when the object or its lighting changes. View-independent components of a shader can be isolated, precomputed and stored. View-independent information needs to be stored across the entire object surface. One structure that supports the storage of shading components sampled across a surface is the texture atlas.

A texture map $\mathbf{c} \leftarrow T\mathbf{ux}$ is a prestored table of colors indexed by (surface) texture coordinates $\mathbf{u}$. The indices into this table are defined across an object surface by a texture coordinate function $\mathbf{u} : \mathbf{x} \rightarrow \mathbf{u}$ which maps surface points $\mathbf{x}$ to texture coordinates $\mathbf{u}$. This map is usually constructed by interpolation of texture coordinates stored at the vertices of each polygon. If the map $\mathbf{u}$ is one-to-one, then it is called a texture atlas.

8.1   Shading with a Texture Atlas

Apodaca and Gritz [7] describe how a texture atlas can store the shading of a model. This technique shades a mesh in world coordinates, but stores the resulting colors in a second "reference" copy of the mesh embedded in a two-dimensional texture map. The mesh could then be later shaded by applying the texture map instead of computing its original shading.

The texture atlas has been used for appearance-preserving simplification [15, 31, 32, 112, 155, 166]. First, a texture atlas is defined for the simplified version of the object. Then the shading of the original unsimplified object is stored in the atlas. When the texture is applied to the simplified object, shading from the features of the original object appear.

The texture atlas can also be used to facilitate multipass rendering of transparent objects. The problem with multipass rendering of transparent objects is that a single pixel is required to represent the shading of multiple overlapping surfaces. One proposed solution for multipassed shading of transparent surfaces is the *fragment buffer* [111]. The fragment buffer (a.k.a. f-buffer) is a method for storing a triangle's fragments in order of rasterization in a FIFO buffer, which can be later accessed as a fragment lookup when rasterizing the triangle into the frame buffer. Since there is no overlap in the FIFO fragment buffer, the fragments are kept distinct from each other, even if they correspond to the same pixel projected from overlapping transparent polygons. The texture atlas can be used as a form of a fragment buffer since it can similarly keep all fragments distinct from each other. For the atlas to avoid resampling, the triangles would need to be sheared and packed such that they covered the same number of pixels in the texture map as they do in the frame buffer.

The texture atlas can also be used for procedural solid texturing [28, 31]. In this case, the shading parameters are solid texture coordinates $\mathbf{s} = (s, t, r)$ stored at the vertices of a meshed object. First, the texture atlas is rasterized in texture memory, interpolating the solid texture coordinates across the polygon faces. A procedural texturing pass applies the texturing procedure to the interpolated solid texture coordinates at each pixel of the texture atlas, and stores the resulting color in that pixel. This results in a texture map that, when applied to the object, results in a procedural solid texturing.

The texture atlas is integrated into a shading pipeline in three phases. The first phase rasterizes each polygon into the texture map

$$T\delta\mathbf{ux} \leftarrow \delta\mathbf{sx} \tag{8.1}$$

using its surface texture coordinates $\mathbf{u}(\mathbf{x})$. The data it places in the texture map (the data that gets interpolated across the face of the rasterized polygon) are the shading parameters $\mathbf{s}(\mathbf{x})$.

The second phase applies the shading procedure to the shading parameters $\mathbf{s}(\mathbf{x})$ stored at each pixel in the rasterization of the atlas in the texture

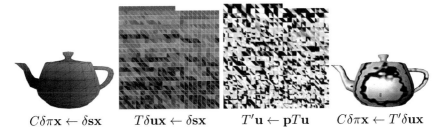

$$C\delta\pi\mathbf{x} \leftarrow \delta\mathbf{sx} \qquad T\delta\mathbf{ux} \leftarrow \delta\mathbf{sx} \qquad T'\mathbf{u} \leftarrow \mathbf{p}T\mathbf{u} \qquad C\delta\pi\mathbf{x} \leftarrow T'\delta\mathbf{ux}$$

Figure 8.1. The steps involved in texture atlas shading. (See Color Plate VI.)

map

$$T\mathbf{u} \leftarrow \mathbf{p}T\mathbf{u}. \tag{8.2}$$

The result stored at each pixel in the texture map T at surface texture coordinates $\mathbf{u}$ is synthesized by the procedural shader $\mathbf{p}$ on the shading parameters $\mathbf{s}$ in the texture atlas T located at the same texture coordinates $\mathbf{u}$.

The texture map T now contains a surface texture. The third phase uses a standard texture-mapping pass to reintegrate the procedural shading results stored in the texture map back onto the object as it is projected and rasterized.

Because the atlas shading Equations (8.1) and (8.2) resemble the deferred shading Equations (1.2) and (1.3), atlas shading can be considered a form of deferred shading in the texture map instead of the display. However, one benefit of deferred shading is that it reduces the shading depth complexity to one; only the visible parts of polygons are shaded. The texture atlas contains all of the model's polygons without overlap, so every polygon is "visible" in the atlas and needs to be textured, regardless of whether it is visible in the display.

Unlike deferred shading, atlas shading is view-independent. The triangles are rasterized and the procedural texture is rendered onto them in the texture buffer only once. The surface texture mapping of the atlas can occur any number of times from arbitrary viewpoints.

The real benefit of atlas shading instead comes from the fact that the procedure is executed as a second pass, independent of the display rasterization of the model. This allows a graphics process to rasterize polygons and a host processor to synthesize the texture for them. By separating rasterization from texture synthesis, atlas shading can be implemented in modern pipelined graphics API's, such as OpenGL.

The aliasing artifacts introduced by this method occur when the sampling rate of the LHS of Equation (8.1) (the surface texture coordinates) disagrees with the sampling rate of the RHS (the solid texture coordinates). This aliasing is dependent on the layout of the texture atlas.

8.2   Texture Atlas Layout

The only requirement for a texture map to be an atlas is that it be one-to-one. The layout of the atlas controls the non-overlapping placement of the triangles of the object surface in the atlas. There are a variety of different methods for texture atlas layout, designed from a variety of different application domains.

Often a mesh can be cut into a few pieces which can then be easily flattened into complex polygons. Figure 8.2 shows an atlas constructed by flattening the polygons onto the most appropriate face of a cube.

Once flattened, the complex polygons must be packed into a texture map. Such packing techniques have been researched by the textile industry, where the goal of layout is to avoid wasted fabric. Automatic methods for laying out complex patterns on fabric that avoid wasted fabric are

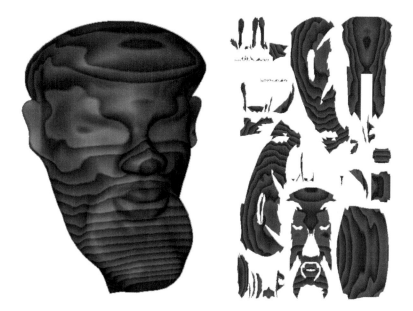

Figure 8.2.   A wood textured head. Right: Its texture atlas. (Image courtesy Jerome Maillot, Alias|Wavefront.)

complicated and efficient [117], but it is interesting that they are not yet as good as human experts.

Texture atlases used for simple texture mapping try to minimize distortion, which can deform an image when it is mapped onto a surface. Previous techniques for creating atlases have focused on reducing the distortion either by projection [16], optimization [101, 105, 154] or user-guided interactive placement [106, 134, 135]. When a texture atlas is used for shading, its contents are computed per pixel. Hence, the distortion of the atlas does not deform the shading, but it can affect the distribution of texture samples across the surface [15].

Texture atlases are discontinuous along the boundaries of their individual charts. These discontinuities sometimes result in a rendering artifact known as a seam. Some have reduced seams by maximizing the size and connectivity of the chart images in the texture atlas [155, 160].

We have found it easiest to construct a texture atlas by mapping all of the object's triangles into right triangles, and laying out these triangles in an alternating toothed pattern. A *uniform mesh atlas* layout maps all of the triangles to equally sized right triangles. Its results are demonstrated in Figure 8.1 (left).

The number of texture samples we have on the surface corresponds to the number of texture pixels the atlas layout covers. Hence we want the atlas to cover as much of the texture map as possible. These strips of right triangles can be sized to make use of nearly the entire texture map, and these atlases waste much less space than do other atlas methods. The wasted space in the atlases shown in Figure 8.3 is shown in solid black.

Often objects are constructed with triangles of different sizes. Mapping all of the surface triangles to right triangles of the same size means that all triangles on the surface will receive the same number of texture map samples. This causes some of the jagged edge artifacts in the woodgrain in the middle of Figure 8.3.

An alternative layout maps larger surface triangles to larger right triangles in the atlas, forming an *area-weighted mesh atlas*. In this layout, surface triangles are sorted in order of nonincreasing area. The largest triangles are packed into a strip of large right triangles. The next strip contains smaller triangles approximately the size of the next set of sorted surface triangles. Strips of still smaller triangles are packed until the atlas is filled. The background of Figure 8.4 demonstrates this layout. Right triangles in the atlas never shrink below the size of a single texture pixel.

The area-weighted atlas provides a more even distribution of available texture samples across the surface of the object. It distributes texture samples proportional to the area of each triangle. The impovement can

Figure 8.3.   Wood teapot (foreground) whose procedural solid texture was stored
in a uniform mesh atlas (background).

Figure 8.4.   Wood teapot (foreground) whose procedural solid texture was stored
in an area-weighted mesh atlas (background).

be seen by comparing the large triangles in the centers of the teapots in Figures 8.3 and 8.4.

Seams are one potential problem when discretely mapping individual triangles. These problems are overcome through careful control of atlas rasterization and texture magnification filtering using techniques described in Section 8.3.

8.3   Avoiding Seam Artifacts

Seams appear because the rasterization rules differ from the sampling rules of the texture magnification filter. The rules of polygon scan conversion are designed with the goal of plotting each pixel in a local polygonal mesh neighborhood only once. The rules for texture magnification are designed to appropriately sample a texture when the sample location is not the center of a pixel, usually either the nearest-neighbor sample or bilinear interpolation of the nearest four samples.

Figure 8.5 demonstrates the disparity between the rasterization and sampling of two triangles A and B. Assume for the moment that integer coordinates in the texture map correspond to the centers of texture samples (the pixels of the texture map) as shown in (a). Since these integer pixel coordinates occur at the center of the grid cells, the grid cell indicates the set of points whose nearest neighbor is the sample located at the cell's center. Two triangles with integer coordinates are rasterized into the texture map, as shown in (b) using the standard rules [46]. The texture sampling

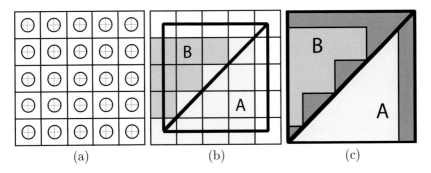

(a)   (b)   (c)

Figure 8.5.   Texture pixel samples are located at the center of grid cells (a). The rasterization of triangles A and B (shown textured) does not cover their entire domain (shown by their boundaries) (b). Because of this difference, nearest-neighbor sampling misclassifies the pixels shown in (c) resulting in seam artifacts.

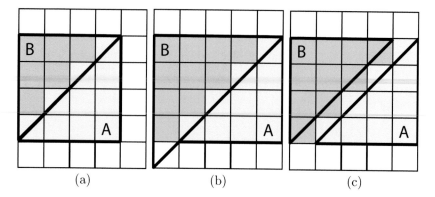

Figure 8.6.   Moving the texture coordinate vertices one half pixel diagonally aligns the rasterization with the sampling (a), except along the hypotenuse. Rasterizing a shifted A and an enlarged B (b) results in a rasterization that can be by nearest-neighbor sampled correctly by the shifted A and original B (c) at the cost of an extra column of pixels.

process needs to reconstruct an approximate sample for any point in these chart image regions. The nearest sample for some points in both regions A and B are background pixels, and the nearest sample for some points near the shared hypotenuse in region A are pixels rasterized from plotting B. These points are indicated in (c).

A common solution is to overscan the polygons in the texture map, but surrounding all three edges of each triangle with a one-pixel safety zone wastes valuable texture samples.

Figure 8.6 illustrates a better solution, adapted from [166]. The surface texture coordinates of the triangles in (a) have been offset by one half pixel. The rasterization of this configuration generates the same pixels as in Figure 8.5, but the nearest neighbor of any point within A and B never evaluates to a pixel outside of A or B. However, some pixels in A are the nearest neighbors of some points in B near its hypotenuse. This can be fixed by using different coordinates for rasterization and sampling. The rasterization in (b) shifts triangle A right by one pixel, and enlarges triangle B by one pixel. Points in the triangles A and B shown in (c) now draw their samples from the correct nearest neighbors.

Figure 8.7 shows that contracting the triangles by one half pixel yields a result that supports bilinear interpolation of samples. We rasterize the triangles shown in (a) but sample the triangles shown in (b). For any point in both triangles the nearest four samples used by bilinear interpolation are also drawn from the correct triangle.

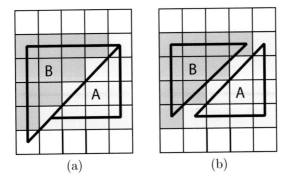

(a) (b)

Figure 8.7. Reducing the rasterization of the triangles by one half pixel yields the same rasterization (a). Similarly reducing the texture regions (b) leads to partial support for bilinear reconstruction.

The overscanning solution that shifts the rasterization of one of the triangles costs one column of pixels for each triangle pair. If a pair of triangles share an edge, then they can be organized in the atlas to share their hypotenuse and can be rasterized without shifting one of the triangles right one pixel. Meshed models are often organized into triangle strips for efficient display. Such strips can be more easily laid out into horizontal rows of right triangles in the texture atlas that do not require overscanning.

Plate I. Environment used for non-photorealistic rendering: cold-warm shading [57]. (See also Figure 3.6.)

Plate II. Cubic interpolation of random lattice colors. (See also Figure 3.17.)

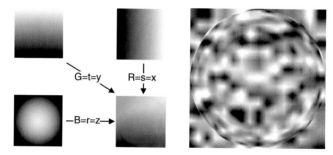

Plate III. Left: An image of a sphere bulging from a plane, plotted as $(R, G, B) = (s, t, r) = (x, y, z)$. Right: A noise function has been applied to the solid texture coordinates stored in the color components of each pixel. (See also Figure 3.19.)

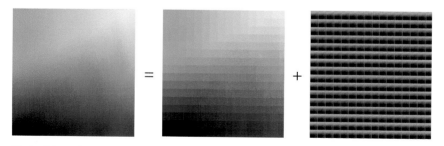

Plate IV. An example input image of solid texture coordinates (left) where s and t vary from zero to one, and $t = 0$. This input image is decomposed into an integer part (center) and a fractional part (right). (See also Figure 3.20.)

Plate V. Example of a window pane light shader, as rendered interactively on PixelFlow. (See also Figure 4.18.)

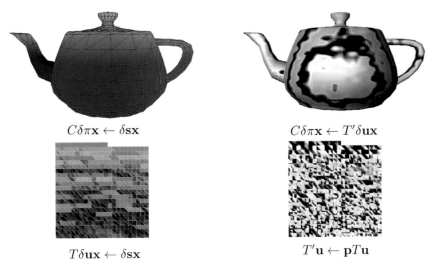

$C\delta\pi\mathbf{x} \leftarrow \delta\mathbf{sx}$

$C\delta\pi\mathbf{x} \leftarrow T'\delta\mathbf{ux}$

$T\delta\mathbf{ux} \leftarrow \delta\mathbf{sx}$

$T'\mathbf{u} \leftarrow \mathbf{p}T\mathbf{u}$

Plate VI. The steps involved in texture atlas shading. (See also Figure 8.1.)

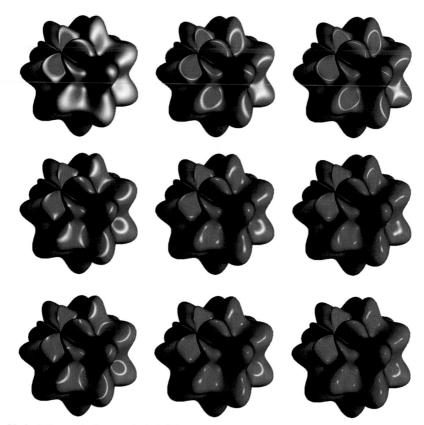

Plate VII.   Anisotropic Ashikhmin reflectance model. Exponents of 10, 200, and 1000 in all combinations. Rendered using hardware acceleration, a three-texture factorization of the anisotropic specular lobe, and a precomputed one-texture nonconstant diffuse lobe. (See also Figure 6.6.)

Plate VIII.   Car model using ISL shader for paint BDRF, glossy Fresnel reflectance, and combined paint with glossy layer. (See also Figure 14.3.)

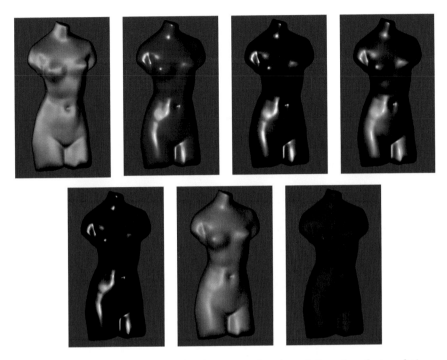

Plate IX.   Homomorphic factorization examples. A model rendered at real-time rates (approximately half the speed of plain diffuse shading) using various factored BRDFs. Plate X gives the corresponding texture maps. (See also Figure 6.8.)

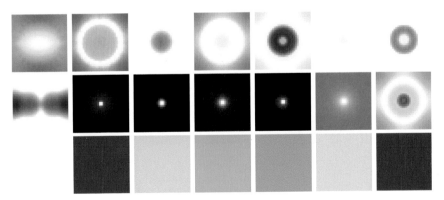

Plate X.   Homomorphic factorization texture maps, using a parabolic representation of functions defined over a hemisphere. Top to bottom: p', q', and the correction color α. Plates VIII, IX, and XI give some examples rendered using these texture maps. (See also Figure 6.9.)

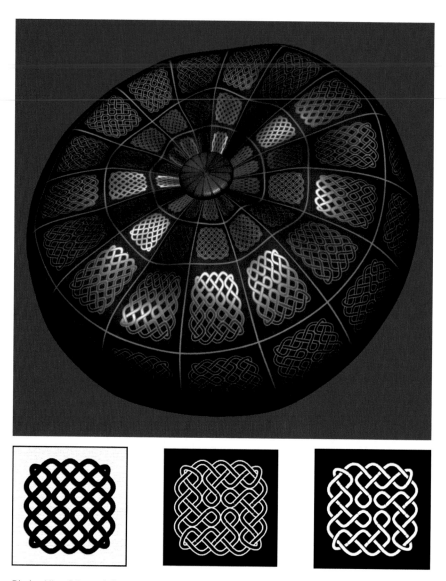

Plate XI. Material mapping. Rendered in real time (60fps+) on a GeForce3. The textures shown were used to blend between three homomorphically factorized BRDFs: velvet, garnet red, and anisotropic "brushed metal." The metal was also colored yellow on the trim around the knot by coloring the appropriate parts of the mask yellow. The textures were MIP-mapped. Notice the lack of aliasing at the center of the button. Here the filtered textures cause the BRDFs to blend together as desired. (See also Figure 6.10.)

Plate XII. Top left: Diffusely prefiltered environment map of the café scene. Bottom left: Diffusely illuminated torus. Right: Same torus illuminated with both a diffuse and a mirror term. (See also Figure 7.2.)

Unfiltered Original | **Classic** | **Hardware 2-pass**

Hierarchical | **Hardware 1-pass**

Plate XIII. Comparison of the different filtering methods. Filtering was done with the Phong model and an exponent of 100. From left to right: Unfiltered, the classic method, a new hierarchial method, the hardware-accelerated method. The original environment map is 128 x 256 pixels in size with a border of 16 pixels. Images courtesy of Kautz et al. [87]. (See also Figure 7.6.)

 N = 50. 20 Hz

 N = 500. 9 Hz

Plate XIV. Two scenes rendered with a glossy reflective torus. Filtering is done with the Phong model (exponent of 50 and 500) for every frame, but interactive rates are still achieved. The original environment maps are 512 x 1024 pixels in size with a border of 64 pixels. Images courtesy of Kautz et al. [87]. (See also Figure 7.5.)

Plate XV. Procedural fire that can be animated by varying one of its parameters. (See also Figure 10.4.)

Plate XVI. A procedural planet whose continents follow the same statistical distribution as the Earth. (See also Figure 10.5.)

Plate XVII. A moonrise faked by procedurally texturing a disk and a plane. The reflection is simulated by a noise function ranging from white to blue. (See also Figure 10.6.)

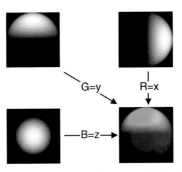

Plate XVIII. Sphere map of normal vectors. (See also Figure 16.1.)

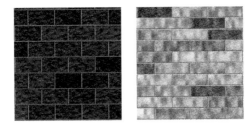

Plate XIX. Two instances of the same brick shader. (See also Figure 18.2.)

Part III

High-Level Procedural Shading

In this part, we explore the different levels of shading, what factors influence real-time shading language design, how these are expressed in some existing shading languages, and how real-time shading languages are implemented.

9

Classifying Shaders

Any graphics system can be braodly classified as using "high-" or "low-" level shading We can further classify the shading capability of any system (real-time or not) into four broad categories. For the purposes of this book, we'll call these four *fixed-function shading, parameterized shading, programmable shading* and *procedural shading.*

9.1   Fixed-Function Shading

Fixed-function shading is the lowest-level, most restrictive of the four categories. It is also the style of shading that first appeared on graphics hardware and was prevalent for decades. It provides a single fixed-function to determine the color of rendered objects. This function can be something simple, like "interpolate the colors given at each triangle vertex", or something more complicated, like "combine this texture with these diffuse and specular lighting terms". Fixed-function shading is good enough for quite a few tasks, but anything not included in the one fixed function cannot be done. A fixed-function shading model is not designed to do different things, beyond a little tweaking. It is designed to do one thing, period.

9.2   Parameterized Shading

Parameterized shading goes slightly beyond single-function fixed shading models. It is still based on one (or a choice of several) fixed shading functions, but much more flexible ones. The distinguishing feature of a parameterized shader is a model complex and flexible enough that its users can

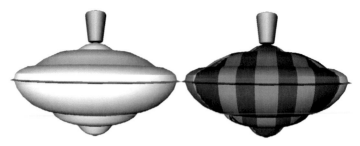

Figure 9.1. Left: A model with fixed-function shading using OpenGL. Right: Simple diffuse shading and more complex (but still fixed-function) diffuse shading with a texture.

create effects that were never directly envisioned by the designers. It is a shading model designed from the ground up to be tweaked and repurposed.

A good example of this is *Antialiased Parameterized Solid Texturing* (APST) [66], which is capable of producing a number of noise-based functions typically associated with more capable procedural shading systems. APST is described in much more detail in Chapter 10. Its basis is a fast hardware-evaluated band-limited noise function. This is a simplified primitive operation similar to the well-known Perlin noise function, which is described in more detail in Section 3.6. The APST system allows several octaves of this noise primitive to be combined together, with general matrices to specify the relationships between the noise octaves. This allows each octave of noise to be independently scaled and rotated. The noise sum is passed through a general color lookup table to map the grayscale noise values into colors. Many realistic textures, like wood, marble, water, or fire, can be constructed in this manner. The result is a flexible shading model, but limited to things that can be constructed by octaves of noise and a final color table. On the other hand, since the texture generation function is mathematically well-defined, the APST system can automatically antialias any textures generated with it.

Another example of a system that would qualify for this category, should it be implemented directly in a hardware accelerator, would be Lafortune's generalized Phong lobe model, which has a small number of shape parameters which can be used to approximate a wide variety of effects (Section 2.6.4). Sums of generalized Phong lobes could be used to approximate arbitrary BRDFs, as well as other directionally dependent functions, such as diffuse radiance maps. Other examples of useful parameterized shaders could include polynomial texture maps (Section 7.2.1) and material textures (Section 6.7.1). Many of these systems have in common the ability to approximate arbitrary functions while performing correct antialiasing.

They are the kinds of things you'd like to have in a "standard shader function library," just like the noise function. Parameterized shaders may start life designed to stand on their own, but the current trend is to provide a small number of powerful operators and some small amount of programmability to combine them, which leads us to the next category: programmable shaders.

9.3 Programmable Shading

Programmable shading is the minimum necessary for truly flexible shading. In a programmable system, a large range of shading functions can be programmed, but they must be written, at best, as low-level (often called *assembly level*) programs. Sometimes, the programmability is in the form of a sequence of configurable pipeline stages (multitexturing) or is hidden in operations intended originally for other things (multipass). Generally, the idea is that it can be done, but it isn't necessarily easy.

A number of graphics hardware platforms have been created that are specifically designed to be programmable at a low level, either in assembler, microcode, specialized languages, or C written to work with their original internal library code. Two typical examples were the Ikonas [43] and the AT&T Pixel Machine [144]. These machines were not designed to support programmable shading per se, but did expose the relatively general purpose processors used internally. These processors could be re-programmed to extend the capabilities of the standard software libraries, but only if you had a good idea of what those libraries were already doing and how.

We are most interested in systems that provide programmable shading as an expected part of the end-user interface. This form of codified programmable shading was first seen on graphics hardware in 1992 on the Pixel-Planes 5 research graphics machine at the University of North Carolina [152]. Similar shading ability first appeared in commodity graphics hardware in 2001 with the NVIDIA GeForce3 [103].

Both of these systems demonstrate why this is often called assembly-level shading. The end-user interface closely resembles a microprocessor assembly language. Additional operators are available for operations common in shading but not as important for general purpose processing, like dot product or vector normalize. None the less, the shading language itself maintains the assembly-language style of a sequence of instructions of the form

```
operator operand, operand, operand
```

with a register-based model of storage.

We also place general multipass rendering in the programmable but not procedural class. There is a long history of multipass rendering algorithms that combine results over several rendering passes to achieve a more complex effect than the rendering hardware can achieve alone. Multipass algorithms include three basic classes: algorithms that render the scene from multiple viewpoints (e.g., to create an environment map or shadow map before final rendering [21, 179]), algorithms that render some or all of the objects in a scene from a single viewpoint (e.g., for transparency [108]), and algorithms that render just a single object multiple times from a single viewpoint (e.g., for complex reflectance models [39, 79, 77]). The last class of algorithms provides the capabilities seen in other shading methods. Running counter to most people's gut instincts, rendering an object with multiple simple rendering passes can be quite efficient. This is due to the focus of rendering hardware development for many years on polygons per second and pixel fill performance at the expense of more complex shading. That multipass rendering is a form of programmable shading was recognized by Peercy et al. [138], and is a basis for the procedural shading languages described in Chapters 14 and 15.

9.4   Procedural Shading

Procedural shading is the ultimate in flexible shading. It has all the capabilities of programmable shading in a pretty package. Procedural shaders are written in a high-level language (many shading languages have been modeled after C) instead of the low-level assembly language equivalent offered by programmable shading. RenderMan is the most well-known example of a rendering system with support for procedural shading, but it is mostly used for off-line rendering.

The first software system to provide a simple procedural shading interface was Cook's Shade Trees [33], which, however, allowed only simple expressions with a C-like syntax and many built-in functions. The first fully capable procedural shading system was Perlin's Image Synthesizer [139], which added loops, if-branches, and everything else normally associated with a full programming language. We lump languages with and without control constructs into a single procedural shading category, but the difference is quite significant. With all the control constructs of a traditional language, a shader can do anything you can program. For example, using a language with control constructs, you can construct a shader with effectively infinite detail—you can write shaders so that the closer you get to the surface the more detail the shader potentially could generate. Without control constructs, you're limited to a fixed (though potentially large) level of detail.

The first true real-time procedural shading hardware appeared in the PixelFlow system at the University of North Carolina [130]. PixelFlow is described in more detail in Chapters 4 and 13. Later systems that provide procedural shading on less-specialized graphics hardware are described in Chapters 14 and 15.

9.5   Why Use Procedural Shading?

Procedural and programmable shading expose the same hardware capabilities. So why would anyone need or want the higher-level interface that real-time procedural shading languages provide if low-level programmable shading will do the trick? There are three primary reasons: ease of use, portability and optimization. Not surprisingly, all three of these are not specific to procedural shading, but apply equally well to recommend any high-level programming language (like C) over assembler.

Ease of use has a couple of facets. First, the shading capabilities are accessible to more people when the shading tools are easier to learn. This is one of the primary reasons RenderMan has succeeded when testbed off-line renderers that allowed users to rewrite part of the rendering system did not.

The experience with programmable shading on Pixel-Planes 5 [152] offers anecdotal support of this. As mentioned in Section 9.3, Pixel-Planes 5 was a research graphics machine, designed and built at the University of North Carolina at Chapel Hill. Among its features was an assembly-level programmable shading language. This is shading closer in spirit to vertex shaders [103] than register combiners [128]. Despite the existence of this language, *no one* that was not an author on the 1992 Pixel-Planes 5 shading paper ever wrote a Pixel-Planes 5 shader!

The other aspect of ease of use is the length and maintainability of the shading code. An assembly-level shader may use tens or hundreds of lines of code to achieve the same effect as a couple of lines of high-level shading code. This translates into a longer development time for the low-level shader and a corresponding reluctance to make changes to improve or modify the look if this would involve large-scale changes to the code. Figures 9.2 and 9.3 show a shader in both high-level form and the corresponding low-level code. Which would you rather write and maintain?

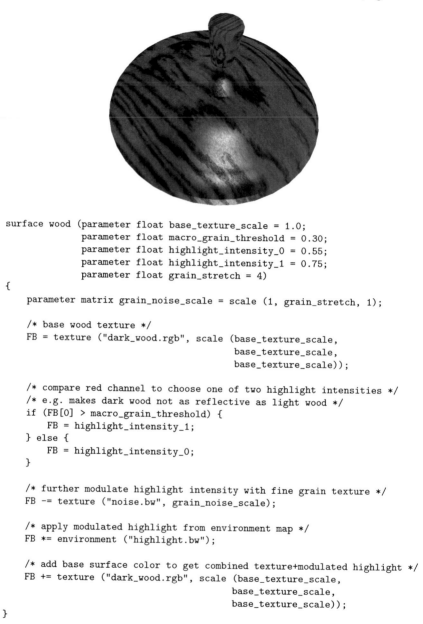

```
surface wood (parameter float base_texture_scale = 1.0;
              parameter float macro_grain_threshold = 0.30;
              parameter float highlight_intensity_0 = 0.55;
              parameter float highlight_intensity_1 = 0.75;
              parameter float grain_stretch = 4)
{
    parameter matrix grain_noise_scale = scale (1, grain_stretch, 1);

    /* base wood texture */
    FB = texture ("dark_wood.rgb", scale (base_texture_scale,
                                          base_texture_scale,
                                          base_texture_scale));

    /* compare red channel to choose one of two highlight intensities */
    /* e.g. makes dark wood not as reflective as light wood */
    if (FB[0] > macro_grain_threshold) {
        FB = highlight_intensity_1;
    } else {
        FB = highlight_intensity_0;
    }

    /* further modulate highlight intensity with fine grain texture */
    FB -= texture ("noise.bw", grain_noise_scale);

    /* apply modulated highlight from environment map */
    FB *= environment ("highlight.bw");

    /* add base surface color to get combined texture+modulated highlight */
    FB += texture ("dark_wood.rgb", scale (base_texture_scale,
                                           base_texture_scale,
                                           base_texture_scale));
}
```

Figure 9.2. A Simple ISL wood shader. OpenGL code for the same wood shader is shown in Figure 9.3.

Figure 9.3. OpenGL code implementing the same wood as the ISL shader in Figure 9.2. This font is admittedly too small to read, but it is presented here primarily as a size comparison of high-level and low-level representations for the same shader.

The second reason to use procedural shading, portability, is not strictly a feature of procedural shading alone. The shading capabilities in Direct X [115] demonstrate that it is possible to have a low-level programmable shading interface that operates on multiple different graphics architectures. However, a common interface at this level dictates quite a bit about the graphics hardware design. A high-level language can provide a shading interface that is portable across a wider range of platforms and that can remain useful and usable over a longer period of time, despite changes in hardware designs.

The final reason to use procedural shading is optimization. A high-level shading language is processed by a shading language compiler into whatever form is used directly by the graphics hardware. Like any compiler, it can perform optimizations on the generated code. Yes, a sufficiently motivated and knowledgeable programmer could write code as well or better optimized than that produced by a compiler. But this is significant work for each shader if done by hand, or at most a couple minutes work by a shading compiler for each and every shader written.

It should be noted in closing that our usage of the words *procedural* and *programmable* is not reflected in the literature, where the two words are used interchangeably. However, no other terms have developed to distinguish these two distinct types of shading, and since procedural and programmable are evocative of the difference, we adopt them here.

10

APST: Antialiased Parameterized Solid Texturing

The previous chapter described the difference between fixed function, parameterized, programmable and procedural shaders. This chapter describes a parameterized shader capable of synthesizing the most commonly used textures found in procedural shaders.

Procedural solid texture mapping uses a mapping from solid texture coordinates $\mathbf{s} = (s, t, r)$ into a color space (R, G, B). Often procedural solid textures incorporate a color map. In such cases, $\mathbf{p}(\mathbf{s}) = \mathbf{c}(f(\mathbf{s}))$ consisting of an implicit classification of the texture space $f(\mathbf{s})$ and a color map $\mathbf{c}(f)$. The color map $\mathbf{c}$ associates a color (R, G, B) with each index returned by the classification function f. The value returned by f can either be clamped or cycled to fall within the bounds of the color map. We assume that values of f from zero to one map to the extremes of the color table.

This section uses a single function f to generate a variety of procedural solid textures. This function is defined

$$f(\mathbf{s}) = q(\mathbf{s}) + \sum a_i n(T_i(\mathbf{s})) \tag{10.1}$$

where $q(\mathbf{s})$ is a quadric classification function and $n(\mathbf{s})$ is the Perlin noise function. The combination of quadrics and noise yields a specification sufficient to generate a wide variety of commonly used procedural solid textures. The affine transformations T_i control the frequency and phase of the noise functions.

The function $q()$ in Equation (10.1) is the quadric

$$q(s, t, r) = As^2 + 2Bst + 2Csr + 2Ds + Et^2 + 2Ftr + 2Gt + Hr^2 + 2Ir + J \tag{10.2}$$

which can be also represented as

$$q(\mathbf{s}) = \mathbf{s}^T Q \mathbf{s} = [s\ t\ r\ 1] \begin{bmatrix} A & B & C & D \\ B & E & F & G \\ C & F & H & I \\ D & G & I & J \end{bmatrix} \begin{bmatrix} s \\ t \\ r \\ 1 \end{bmatrix} \tag{10.3}$$

using a homogeneous 4×4 matrix of coefficients [20]. This classification function allows texture grains to be modeled as concentric spherical or cylindrical shells.

The function $n()$ in Equation (10.1) is an implementation of the Perlin noise function [139]. The values a_i control the amplitude of the noise function, whereas the affine transformation T_i controls the frequency and phase of each noise component. There are a fixed number of noise components available, and this limit is typically between four and eight in typical texturing examples.

10.1 Examples

The space of solid textures spanned by Equation (10.1) covers the textures most commonly found in procedural solid texturing. The four fundamental procedural solid textures are: wood, clouds, marble, and fire.

Wood: The texture model generated the wood texture shown in Figure 10.1, by using the quadratic function to classify the texture space into

Figure 10.1. Teapot sculpted from a wood solid texture space.

a collection of concentric cylinders [133]. Waviness in the grain is created
by modulation of a noise function

$$f(s,t,r) = s^2 + t^2 + n(4s, 4t, r).\tag{10.4}$$

The color map consists of a modulo-one linear interpolation of a light "earlywood" grain and a darker "latewood" grain. The quadric classification
makes the early rings wider than the later rings, which is to a first approximation consistent with tree development.

Clouds: Cloudy skies are made with a fractal $1/f$ sum of noise

$$f(\mathbf{s}) = \sum_{i=0}^{N} 2^{-i} n(2^i \mathbf{s}).\tag{10.5}$$

The texture described by Equation (10.5) is mapped onto a very large high-
altitude polygon parallel to the ground plane in Figure 10.2, resulting in
clouds that become more dense in the distance due to perspective-corrected
texturing coordinate interpolation. The color map is a clamped linear

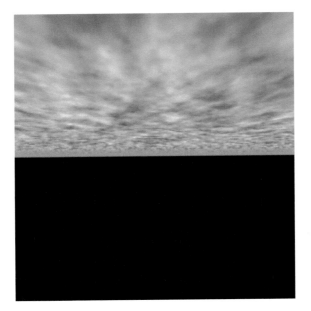

Figure 10.2.   Sky and water with infinite non-repeating detail generated by
procedural textures.

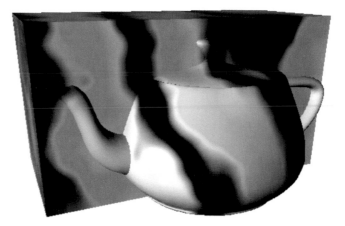

Figure 10.3. Teapot sculpted from a marble solid texture space.

interpolation from blue to white. The water is the same procedural texture
with a blue-to-black colormap.

Marble: Marble uses the noise function to distort a linear ramp function
of one coordinate [139]

$$f(s,t,r) = r + \sum_{i=0}^{N} 2^{-i} n(2^i s, 2^i t, 2^i r). \tag{10.6}$$

The color map consists of a modulo-one table of colors from a cross section
of the marble. Figure 10.3 demonstrates the marble texture on a cube,
and the solid texturing again aligns the texture details on the edges of the
cube. Continuously increasing the noise amplitude animates the formation
of the ripples in the marble, simulating the pressure and heating process
involved in the development of marble [41].

Fire: Like marble, fire is simulated by offsetting a texture coordinate with
fractal noise [123]. The fire example shown in Figure 10.4 was textured onto
a single polygon and modeled as

$$f(s,t,r) = r + \sum_{i=0}^{N} 2^{-i} n(2^i s, 0, 2^i r + \phi). \tag{10.7}$$

Continuously varying the noise phase term ϕ animates the fire texture.

Figure 10.4. Procedural fire that can be animated by varying one of its parameters. (See Color Plate XV.)

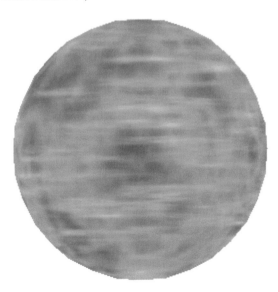

Figure 10.5. A procedural planet whose continents follow the same statistical distribution as the Earth. (See Color Plate XVI.)

Figure 10.6.   A moonrise faked by procedurally texturing a disk and a plane. The reflection is simulated by a noise function ranging from white to blue. (See Color Plate XVII.)

Planet: A wide variety of different worlds, such as the one shown in Figure 10.5, can be generated by applying fractal textures, such as Equation (10.5), to spheres. This simulates the sculpting of a world out of a solid texturing space consisting of rocks suspended in water. The color map for such images resembles a cartographic legend. The cloudy atmosphere was rendered on the same sphere "over" the planet in a second pass using a color map with varying opacity values.

Moonrise: The moonrise in Figure 10.6 was rendered completely using synthesized textures, without any other kind of shading. The moon is a sphere with a fractal texture. The clouds were rendered on a single polygon perpendicular to the viewer and imposed over the moon. The water was rendered with a single polygon extending off to infinity. The highlight on the water was faked with two triangles textured using Equation (10.6) with a partially transparent color map.

10.2   Antialiasing

One method for antialiasing a procedural texture is to determine the width of a box filter that would eliminate the aliasing frequencies from the spectrum of the synthesized texture. Several have described techniques for antialiasing procedural textures by antialiasing the textures' colormaps [41, 152].

For a given polygon, $\mathbf{s}(\mathbf{x}) = (s(x), t(x), r(x))$, the texture coordinate functions, indicates the range of the texture coordinates with respect to screen coordinates $\mathbf{x} = (x, y)$. Hence, the fixed function (10.1) can be evaluated with respect to screen coordinates as $\mathbf{p}(\mathbf{x}) = \mathbf{c} \circ f \circ \mathbf{s}(\mathbf{x})$.

Consider a domain D on the screen consisting of pixels whose color is determined solely by the projection of a single procedurally texture mapped polygon. We assume the color map indices generated by the procedural texture are continuous across the polygon. Let $a = \min_D f(\mathbf{x})$ be the least possible color map index used in the pixels in D, and let $b = \max_D f(\mathbf{x})$ be the greatest such index. Then we assume in the equation

$$\frac{\int_D \mathbf{p}(\mathbf{x})d\mathbf{x}}{\int_D d\mathbf{x}} \approx \frac{\int_a^b \mathbf{c}(f)df}{b - a} \tag{10.8}$$

that the average color in D is sufficiently approximated by the average of the color table entries between indices a and b. As shown in Figure 10.7, we provide a first-order approximation of the bounds a and b used in the RHS of Equation (10.8) by differentiating the texture function $f(\mathbf{x})$ and setting $a = f(\mathbf{x}) - \|f(\mathbf{x})\|/2$ and $b = f(\mathbf{x}) + \|f(\mathbf{x})\|/2$. If either a or b or both fall outside the bounds of the color table, then the boundary of the color table is appropriately extended.

The magnitude of the gradient $\nabla f = (\partial f/\partial x, \partial f/\partial y)$ indicates the width of the filter on the color map. The gradient of Equation (10.1) is

$$\nabla f = \nabla q + \sum a_i \nabla n_i \tag{10.9}$$

where n_i is the noise function $n(T_i \mathbf{s})$. The gradient of Equation (10.3) is

$$\nabla q(\mathbf{x}) = \mathbf{s}^T Q \frac{d\mathbf{s}}{d\mathbf{x}} + \left(\frac{d\mathbf{s}}{dx}\right)^T Q\mathbf{s}, \tag{10.10}$$

$$= 2\mathbf{s}^T Q \frac{d\mathbf{s}}{d\mathbf{x}}, \tag{10.11}$$

$$= 2[s\ t\ r\ 0] \begin{bmatrix} A & B & C & D \\ B & E & F & G \\ C & F & H & I \\ D & G & I & J \end{bmatrix} \begin{bmatrix} \frac{\partial s}{\partial x} & \frac{\partial s}{\partial y} \\ \frac{\partial t}{\partial x} & \frac{\partial t}{\partial y} \\ \frac{\partial r}{\partial x} & \frac{\partial r}{\partial y} \\ 0 & 0 \end{bmatrix} \tag{10.12}$$

since Q is symmetric.

The derivative of the noise terms are given by

$$a_i \nabla n(T_i \mathbf{s}(\mathbf{x})) = a_i \frac{dn(T_i \mathbf{s}(\mathbf{x}))}{d\mathbf{s}} T_i \frac{d\mathbf{s}}{d\mathbf{x}}. \tag{10.13}$$

The gradient $dn/d\mathbf{s}$ is also known as the function DNoise [139].

The value $d\mathbf{s}/d\mathbf{x}$ is a Jacobian, the matrix of derivatives of each of the texture coordinates $\mathbf{s}$ with respect to each of the screen coordinates $\mathbf{x}$. The values of $d\mathbf{s}/dx$ is computed during the scan conversion of the polygon as the perspective-corrected pixel increments. The values of $d\mathbf{s}/dy$ can be computed for each triangle using the plane equation and performing a perspective-correcting division.

The filtering of color map values can be evaluated efficiently using either a color table MIP-map or a summed area color table (Section 3.3.2).

The process (to create a MIP-map of a color table) begins with the n-element full resolution color table $\text{clut}_1[]$. Then neighboring colors in the table are averaged to create a half-resolution $n/2$-element color table $\text{clut}_2[]$. This process is repeated until a one-element color table $\text{clut}_{\lg n}[]$ results, representing the average color of the entire color table.

Given a filter width w, let $i = \lfloor \lg w \rfloor$. Then the proper resolution color table from the mip map is selected and the color indexed is returned as $\text{clut}_i[f/i]$ (or more accurately the interpolation of the values of $\text{clut}_i[f/i]$ and $\text{clut}_{i+1}[f/(i+1)]$).

Image textures are also antialiased efficiently using the summed area table [36]. A summed area table transforms information into a structure that can quickly perform integration, specifically a box filtering operation.

The summed area color table consists of a table where each entry consists of the sum of all elements in the color table including the current entry's element

$$\text{csat}[i] = \sum_{j=0}^{i} \text{clut}[j] \tag{10.14}$$

or recurrently as $\text{csat}[i] = \text{csat}[i-1] + \text{clut}[i]$. The current entry's element can be recovered by subtracting the previous summed area element from the current summed area element as $\text{clut}[i] = \text{csat}[i] - \text{csat}[i-1]$ for $i > 0$. Box filtering the color map entries for a given filter width is computed as $\text{csat}[f + w/2] - \text{csat}[f - w/2])/w$.

Special care must be taken for the cases where the support of the filter crosses the bounds of the color table. Let N be the number of entries in the color table. If $w \geq N$, then the filter returns the average of the entire color map $\text{csat}[N-1]/N$. If the color table cycles, then if $f + w/2 \geq N$

then the filter returns

$$(\mathrm{csat}[f + w/2 - N] + \mathrm{csat}[N - 1] - \mathrm{csat}[f - w/2 - 1])/w$$

whereas if $f - w/2 < 0$ it returns

$$(\mathrm{csat}[f + w/2] + \mathrm{csat}[N - 1] - \mathrm{csat}[N + f - w/2 - 1])/w.$$

If the color table is clamped, then if $f + w/2 \geq N$ then the filter returns

$$((f + w/2 - (N - 1))\mathrm{clut}[N - 1] + \mathrm{csat}[N - 1] - \mathrm{csat}[f - w/2 - 1])/w$$

otherwise if $f - w/2 < 0$ it returns

$$(-(f - w/2)\mathrm{clut}[0] + \mathrm{csat}[f + w/2])/w.$$

An alternative to performing the above computations at render time is to use the above formulae to precompute a color summed area table three times as long, ranging from $-N$ to $2N - 1$.

The derivations show that procedural textures produce aliasing artifacts from three possible places.

Quadric variation: The quadric classification changes too quickly. The magnitude of $dq/d\mathbf{s}$ is too large.

Noise variation: The noise changes too quickly. Here, the magnitude of $a_i dn(T_i \mathbf{s})/d\mathbf{s}$ is too large.

Texture coordinate variation: The texture coordinates change too quickly. The maginitude of $d\mathbf{s}/d\mathbf{x}$ is too large.

Each of these components can create a signal containing frequencies exceeding the Nyquist limit of the pixel sampling rate.

Figure 10.7 demonstrates aliasing with a zone plate constructed from the procedure rendered with an extremely harsh "zebra" color map. Analysis shows that the aliases are governed by $\nabla f = dq/d\mathbf{s} \, d\mathbf{s}/d\mathbf{x}$, with $dq/d\mathbf{s} = (100s, 100t)$. The zone plate was plotted at a resolution of 256^2 and over the unit square in texture coordinate space, hence $\partial s/\partial x = \partial t/\partial y = 1/256$. Setting the colormap filter width to $(100s + 100t)/256$ reduces the aliases to the point of being barely noticable.

Figure 10.8 illustrates texture aliasing on a torus. The centerline of the wood rings passes through the left side of the torus, creating grain of increasing frequency on the right. Hence, the filter width increases from the left to the right side of the torus, demonstrating quadric variation aliasing.

Figure 10.7. Zone plate aliased (left) and filtered (right).

The amplitude and frequency of the noise term remains constant over the torus object, and so causes a uniform increase of the filter width due to noise variation aliasing. The polygons on the silhouette of the torus have larger filter widths than their neighbors, demonstrating texture coordinate aliasing.

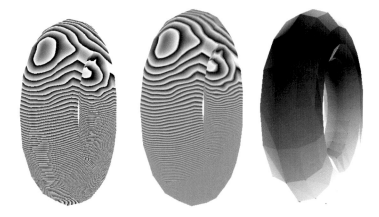

Figure 10.8.   Torus rendered with wood texture (left) is antialiased (center) using the filter widths (right) ranging from one (black) to the size of the color table (white).

10.3 Implementation

This antialiased parameterized solid texturing system has been implemented in software. The software implementation served as a stand-alone antialiasing procedural texturing shader, but could also be incorporated as a plug-in to existing software rendering systems.

The software implementation was also packaged as a utility library for OpenGL. The APST utility library used the OpenGL feedback buffer to collect the polygons transformed by OpenGL's geometry pipeline. The APST library then used its own software rasterizer to render screen-coordinate polygons with the antialiased parameterized solid textures. The resulting textured and rasterized polygons were then combined with OpenGL's non-APST rasterized polygons using a Z-buffer to negotiate visibility. Hence the APST utility library integrated parameterized solid textures into OpenGL's existing texturing, lighting and modeling system.

A complete implementation of the model can be realized in VLSI with 1.25 million gates, resulting in the image quality shown in the figures in this chapter. A reduced and approximated version of the texture synthesis model can be implemented in as few as 100,000 gates by reducing the number of noise functions to three and using existing trilinear MIP-map magnification filtering hardware to implement noise cell interpolation. The reduced-gate implementation used a 20-bit 12.8 fixed-point format, which was found not to exhibit any numerical precision artifacts on test scenes rendered at 512^2 resolution.

11

Compiling Real-Time Procedural Shaders

Compiling a shading language to run on graphics hardware is quite similar to compiling any other language for any other somewhat quirky architecture. Anyone wanting to write a shading compiler of their own should look into the vast literature on general purpose compilers, as most of it applies [3, 8, 50, 121, 122].

In this chapter, we will describe the basics of shading compiler construction to give some basis for the descriptions that follow. Our intent is to give enough background to support the coming chapters, give an idea of what current shading compilers can or cannot map efficiently to rendering hardware, and to give a starting point for those who might want to explore further.

11.1 Organization of a Compiler

Most compilers are organized in a series of passes over all or part of the program being compiled. Each of these passes performs a relatively small and understandable transformation to the program. This breakdown makes the compiler easier to write, debug, and extend.

Typically, a parsing stage converts the program text into a relatively high-level intermediate representation. Some number of passes will operate on this representation, transforming, simplifying, and optimizing the program. Then the high-level intermediate representation is converted to a lower-level intermediate form, where it is again operated on by some number of additional passes. Each intermediate representation is a step closer to the final form. Some compilers may go straight from parsing to assembly

```
f=ycomp(P/2);
for(sc=1; sc<64; sc*=2)
  f += abs(2*noise(P*sc/2)-1)/sc;
```

Figure 11.1. Source fragment.

language or something very close to it, while others work at several levels trying to squeeze as much out of the program structure as possible.

To help understand this compilation process, we present a series of examples based on the source fragment in Figure 11.1.

11.1.1 Parsing

The first stage of parsing is lexical analysis. Here, the program is broken into a series of *tokens* (Figure 11.2). Each token is a logical unit: identifier; keyword; constant; etc.

Several tools exist to create lexical analyzers, one of the most common of which is **lex** [100]. The input to lex is a description file using *regular expressions* to define the tokens. From this input, lex produces a C function that can be called by the parser. Each time the function is called, it returns another token from the source program. Lexical analysis could be done in the parser itself, but typically is not because straight lexical analysis algorithms are much faster than general parsing algorithms. Lex can't parse a full C-like language, but for finding tokens it only needs to do a couple of array look-ups for each character read.

The next logical step is to parse the series of tokens to create an internal representation of the program. Parsers can be hand-coded, or created using a parser generator like YACC or ANTLR/PCCTS [3, 132]. A common form at this stage is a tree like that in Figure 11.3. Each internal node is an operation or structural element and each leaf node is a variable reference or constant. This example shows an *abstract syntax tree* or *AST*, so called because it has already had many redundant elements removed. For example, some tree representations may insert **statement** nodes to hold each statement, **expression** nodes for expressions used as statements, and

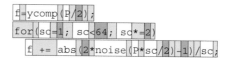

Figure 11.2. Program broken into tokens.

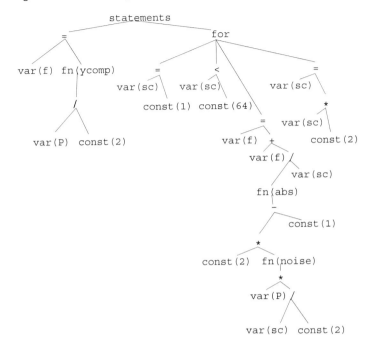

Figure 11.3. Build abstract syntax tree.

other elements indicating more details about the breakdown of the original source code.

The other feature to notice on the tree in Figure 11.3 is the addition of *node attributes* to hold extra information about the nodes. In this tree, all variables use the node type `var`, all constants use the node type `const`, and all functions use the node type `fn`. The actual variable, function or constant is found in extra data stored with the node. In the case of variables and functions, this extra data will be a reference into a *symbol table*. This table (or set of related tables) holds all identifiers used by the program, along with information about them (e.g., their type, value, points where they are defined, and points where they are used).

11.1.2 Internal Passes

Several passes may transform the AST. For example, we may perform a *constant folding* pass to evaluate any constant expressions, folding them into a single number. It is generally preferred to perform passes that prune away parts of the program or reduce its complexity as early as possible.

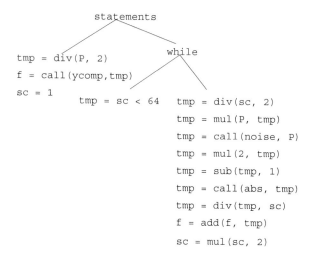

Figure 11.4. Basic blocks with control constructs.

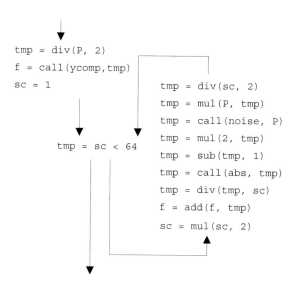

Figure 11.5. Basic blocks as nodes in a flow graph.

The intermediate form used for later stages of the compilation is more verbose, so shrinking the program early can save time and memory.

At some point, the program is transformed into a form consisting of just the control flow and linear sequences of instructions similar to Figure 11.4 or 11.5. The simple instructions in this case are just a rewrite of the tree into function-call form with temporary storage to save the partial results from one call to the next.

Both figures feature a high-level representation for the program control flow, either as control constructs as in Figure 11.4 or as a control flow graph as in Figure 11.5. These are essentially equivalent representations for use in almost all shading languages, though the flow graph can more easily represent jumps that don't fit the structured programming "nested loop and conditional" model.

Between control flow constructs of either representation, there is a linear sequence of simple instructions containing no branches or other control constructs. These blocks of instructions are called *basic blocks*. If you enter the top of a basic block, you will always proceed through the instructions to come out at the bottom. Essentially a basic block implements some number of simple expressions producing block outputs from the block inputs. Some passes at this level operate on the control flow graph, treating the blocks as untouched black boxes, while others operate on the individual blocks, ignoring all parts of the program outside.

11.1.3   Optimizations

Many shading compilers convert the shader into *Static Single Assignment* (SSA) form to for the later passes, including allocation of variables into registers or memory [23]. SSA form performs a static (i.e., compile-time) analysis to rename variables so that every variable is defined in one and only one place in the code (see Figure 11.6). In some places, the instruction stream may enter a block by more than one path. This happens in the while condition block in the middle of Figure 11.6. In these cases, there is no way to know which of several renamed variables should be used with only a static analysis. Is the value of sc going forward sc1 or sc3? Instead, we essentially punt by using a merge operator (often written $\phi(sc1, sc3)$). This says that the value of sc2 will come from one of sc1 or sc3, but we don't know which.

Even with the merge operations, SSA form is convenient for a number of basic optimizations. *Dead code elimination* is easy since it is simple to detect the unused definition code for any unused variable. This form of code elimination can propagate across merge operators as well as more ordinary operations. Eliminating one dead assignment can create several others.

```
tmp1 = div(P, 2)
f1 = call(ycomp,tmp1)              tmp3 = div(sc2, 2)
sc1 = 1                            tmp4 = mul(P, tmp3)
                                   tmp5 = call(noise, P)
                                   tmp6 = mul(2, tmp5)
      sc2 = merge(sc1, sc3)        tmp7 = sub(tmp6, 1)
      f2 = merge(f1, f3)           tmp8 = call(abs, tmp7)
      tmp2 = sc2 < 64              tmp9 = div(tmp8, sc2)
                                   f3 = add(f2, tmp9)
                                   sc3 = mul(sc2, 2)
```

Figure 11.6. Static Single Assignment form.

Dead code elimination is particularly important, not because programmers leave dead code in their production shaders, but because other optimizations that remove all uses of a variable can leave dead and unnecessary relics behind.

SSA is also a useful form for *common subexpression elimination*. If an assignment exactly matches a previous one, we use the previous variable for any future relabeling. This, too, can propagate to large swaths of code, since once the compiler has recognized that one variable matches a previous definition, it may find that a use of that variable also matches a previous definition, expanding to find all of the common uses.

A few other possible optimizations include *strength reduction, conditional constant propagation, code motion* [121, 122]. Strength reduction replaces special cases of complex operations with simpler ones, for example, x^2 with $x \cdot x$. Conditional constant propagation infers information about values within conditionals based on the conditional test results. Code motion moves common blocks of code out of loops or conditionals to reduce the number of times the common block is executed.

11.1.4 Instruction Selection

One of the final passes must choose the instructions to use to perform the program's operations. Selecting instructions effectively for shading compilers is somewhat of a black art, and we present different approaches in Chapters 13–15. Techniques used include code generation tools (see Section 11.4.2 and Chapters 13 and 14) or heuristic greedy algorithms for packing operations into rendering operations (see Chapters 14 and 15).

11.1.5   Register and Memory Allocation

Memory and register allocation is done either after or in conjunction with instruction scheduling. The choice of instructions impacts the register allocation, and the register allocation can impact the choice of instructions. Real-time shading systems tend to have very little per-pixel storage, so the algorithms used are often based on aggressive register allocation. The allocation problem is somewhat simplified for shading. A major concern of general purpose CPU allocators is effectively handling *spills*, when there are no registers left and something must be written to memory. In real-time shading systems, there may be no extra memory for spills. A shader that would spill is rejected.

SSA makes some parts of register or memory allocation easier. Instead of having variables that may be live over several sections of code (as they are assigned, used, ignored, assigned, used, ...), we have many more simple variables with short lifetimes. Each must have memory allocated at its one assignment and released after the last use. Memory allocation is complicated by the merge nodes, which must be removed and their variables assigned to a common group location.

11.1.6   Code Generation

The final stage of compilation is code generation. Generating the code by this point is usually a straightforward printing from the final intermediate form. Most of the work is in the earlier instruction assignment pass.

11.2   Intermediate Forms

As can be seen in Figures 11.1–11.6, representations for a program being compiled are quite varied. Certain optimizations and transformations are easier when some of the original structure is still present and can be done more efficiently on a high-level representation. Others can only be done at a lower level when the individual operations are exposed. Optimizations done at a high level can also reduce the size of the later lower-level representations.

Traditional compilers generally eventually end up with a linear intermediate form with simple operations, and with simple branches replacing the higher-level control constructs. This closely matches eventual target, a linear stream of assembler code for a general-purpose CPU.

Shading compilers tend to end with a hybrid representation that maintains the high-level control constructs. This matches the target for most shading compilers, a stream of low-level operations controlled by a program running on a general-purpose CPU. As with the shading classifications of Chapter 9, we categorize the output as either high-level if it is something like C code, making full use of the control constructs and features of the language, or assembly-level if it consists of a chain of simple operations.

Producing C code for portions of the shader that will run on a general purpose CPU is an attractive choice since the resulting C code can take full advantage that the native C compiler optimizations. Since the general-purpose CPU C compiler has many more users than the shading compiler, and has a longer history of development and improvement, it is generally produces better optimized code than the current fledgling shading compilers. As the shading compilers grow more sophisticated, of course they can incorporate any of techniques their older siblings already use.

In the case of pfman, the high-level shading language control constructs are compiled into equivalent C source code with embedded low-level operations (Chapter 13). OpenGL Shader also compiles to C source code with OpenGL serving as the embedded low-level operations, or it can interpret the internal representation before final code generation (Chapter 14).

Both pfman and OpenGL Shader use a final intermediate form with an assembly-level representation for operations within a basic block, but with a tree representation for the higher-level control constructs, as shown in Figure 11.4.

In contrast to pfman and OpenGL Shader, the Stanford Real-Time Shading language has no high-level control constructs. This means that its code always expands into a single basic block. Without the loop or if constructs, it can use an entirely linear stream of simple operations to represent the entire program.

The Stanford compiler can directly produce i86 code for the portions of the shader that end up running on the host CPU. This supports the idea that the evolution of shading compilers will be likely to favor representations similar to that used by traditional compilers, even for languages that support the full range of looping and comparison control constructs.

11.3   Optimization for Graphics Hardware

Beyond this type of general mapping from expressions to graphics hardware, there are shading-specific and graphics hardware specific optimizations that can be used.

11.3.1 Code Factoring

Most shaders include a loop to sum the contribution of each of the active lights. If the intensity or direction of these lights is determined by a shader, each of those light shaders will be re-executed for almost every shaded object. Pfman split each compiled shader into three parts: the part to do before any lights; the part to do for each light; and the part to do after all the lights are done. With this breakdown, it could interleave the execution of the shaders to execute the shader for each light only once (see Chapter 13).

This optimization is both shading-specific and hardware-specific. It is shading-specific because general programs don't even have the concept of lights, much less a common enough idiom of calling them to make factoring out the light computations worthwhile. It is hardware-specific because PixelFlow, the target machine for the pfman compiler, performs all shading operations on a block of pixels at one time. Performance depends only on the number of instructions executed on a block, with no dependence on the number of pixels active for each instruction. This means you have poor utilization and wasted computational resources if many pixels in the block aren't in the current shader. If you add to the number of active pixels for at least some instructions, by factoring common operations over several surfaces, you get extra computation with no penalty in performance.

Some multipass rendering passes draw an object's bounding box, using the OpenGL stencil to mask out the current object. Others copy pixels from the frame buffer to texture or back into the frame buffer to use the OpenGL operations available on pixel copy. These types of rendering passes also share the block-pixel characteristic that makes factoring common operations effective. However, a great majority of multipass rendering passes draw the object geometry. With these passes, you only pay for pixels that are in the object, so there is little advantage to the pfman-style light factoring.

11.3.2 Specializing Shaders

Shaders often have many parameters that are used to tweak the appearance of the shader (preferably an interactive process), but are not changed once the desired look is achieved. If a shading compiler has information about frozen and actively changing expressions, it can preevaluate the frozen parts of the shader while evaluating only the actively changing parts during rendering. This technique is known as shader specialization since it produces new compiled versions especially for manipulating specific parameters [62]. The frozen values in a specialized shader can be treated the same as any other constant, subject to constant folding, and improving the possibilities for using other techniques such as texture shaders for the remaining expressions.

11.4 Compiler Tools

A variety of tools make the process of creating a compiler easier. In general, these tools use an input file that is easier to understand, create, change, and debug than the program functions they replace. The tools produce C or C++ code that can be linked in with the main compiler. Tools exist for several stages of compilation, but we will focus on the beginning and end of the process.

11.4.1 Parsing

The lexical analyzer generator, lex, and the parser generators YACC and ANTLR have already been mentioned in Section 11.1.1. Together, the lexical analyzer and parser will take the program from source to an abstract syntax tree.

The input to lex is a set of regular expressions with C code to run when a matching token is found (Figure 11.7). This code can simply return a token value, but may also fill in information about the token for the parser. Lex and similar lexical analyzer generators are fast and efficient at finding tokens in the source code. The regular expressions are converted into a finite-state machine, resulting in only a couple of array look-ups for each character read [3].

The input for parser generators like YACC or ANTLR is a text description of the language grammar with C code attached to each rule to create a section of a parse tree or AST (Section 11.1.1). Figure 11.8 shows an excerpt from a shading language grammar, as it might be published in

```
surface                 return TOK_SURFACE;
uniform                 return TOK_UNIFORM;
[-+*/]                  return *yytext;      /* token = character code */
[0-9]+                  {
    yylval.i = atoi(yytext);                 /* data attached to token */
    return TOK_INTCONST;
}
```

Figure 11.7. Excerpt from a lex input file.

```
const: CONSTINT | ...
expr: const | expr * expr | ...
```

Figure 11.8. Excerpt from a language grammar.

a language specification. Figure 11.9 shows this grammar as it might be transformed into part of a YACC input file. ANTLR uses a similar syntax, but a different and sometimes more efficient parsing algorithm. Details of the YACC or ANTLR parsing algorithms are beyond the scope of this book, but can be found in the compiler literature [3, 132].

```
const
    : TOK_CONSTINT
      /* $$ = result of this rule
         $1/... = result of first component */
      { $$ = new Node(Const, $1); }
    | ...
    ;

expr
    : const
    | expr '*' expr
      { $$ = new Node(Mul, $1, $3); }
    | ...
    ;
```

Figure 11.9. Excerpt from a YACC input file.

11.4.2 Code Generation

The other main class of tools are code generator generators. These tools use a machine description file to match abstract operations to a machine instruction set. The input includes what operations are possible, but also a cost for each, which is typically derived from the execution speed of the instructions chosen. From the many possible choices, a code generation tool attempts to find the least-cost set of instructions to implement a set of abstract operations.

Two tools of particular note are lburg and iburg [51, 50]. These tools have been used in Stanford's RTSL compiler (Chapter 15) and OpenGL Shader (Chapter 14) respectively. Lburg is a tool that was developed for LCC C compiler, a full C compiler implementation described in detail a text by Fraser and Hanson [50]. Iburg is a later follow-on by Fraser, Hansen and Proebsting [51].

Both lburg and iburg are designed to find the least-cost way to assign instructions to a set of operations (or *label* the operations). They do this using a bottom-up dynamic programming algorithm. They start with a tree representation for the operations to label and a set of labeling rules with associated costs. First, the cost is computed for every possible way to label the leaf nodes. If you've got a constant, what is the cost if it is stored with the instruction? What cost if it is stored in memory? These labelings don't have to make sense in the context where the constant value is used. The choice of labeling is decided later when looking at the larger context.

The costs for labeling an internal node are found after all the children costs have been determined. For every option of how a subtree might be used, the cost is the incremental cost for that rule plus the costs found for a compatible labeling of each child.

This labeling process continues to the top of the tree—covering the whole program or basic block. At that point, you not only know the cost to label the block, but what rules to apply. A separate *reduce* pass runs rule-specific code on each node.

In the context of shading, code generation is not a process of choosing instructions, but assigning operations to parts of the graphics pipe or CPU. This can be viewed as a different aspect of the same code generation process. If the graphics hardware supports an assembly-like vertex or pixel shader extension [11, 12], the choice of a traditional code generation tool is obvious. However, even more traditional OpenGL or esoteric extensions can be handled by a traditional code generator, treating each operation as an instruction and the order and dependencies between them as a complex set of conditions on the order of instructions that can be used.

To give an idea of how this all works, Figures 11.10-11.14 walk through parts of the process of labeling a simple expression to operations at all strata of Figure 16.6. Figure 11.10 shows a sample set of rules for constant color, texture, and multiplication at different shader strata. The labels all start with lower-case letters. Labels represented are `color`, `texture`, `textureShader`, `texcoordArithmetic`, `dependentTexture`, `multitexture` and `blend`. Each label is can be matched according to several rules, either chained from another label or derived from a bit of tree. The tree structure is represented with a function-like syntax, with capitalized node ID as the function name and labels for the child subtrees as the function arguments. In this example, we use node names `Const`, `String`, `TexCoord`, and `Mul`. Finally, some of the rules are labeled with rule names. These rule names correspond to C++ classes that contain functions to determine the cost and

```
color
     : Const                                    constRule
     ;
texture
     : Lookup(String,TexCoord)                  textureRule
     | TexCoord                                 identityTexRule
     ;
textureShader
     : texture
     | color
     | Mul(color,texture)                       texShaderRule
     ;
texcoordArithmetic
     : textureShader
     | Mul(color,textureShader)                 texcoordArithRule
     ;
dependentTexture
     : Lookup(string,texcoordArithmetic) dependentTexRule
     | texcoordArithmetic                       identityTexRule
     ;
multitexture
     : dependentTexture
     | textureShader
     | Mul(color,dependentTexture)              multiTexRule
     | Mul(color,textureShader)                 multiTexRule
     ;
blend
     : multitexture
     | Mul(blend,multitexture)                  blendTexRule
     ;
```

Figure 11.10.   Example of iburg rules for combining color and texture according to Figure 16.6.

```
color(.5,.7,.9,1) * texture("texImage");
```

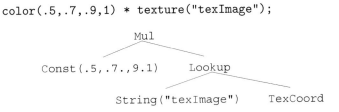

Figure 11.11. Expression and tree for labeling example.

label	rule	by way of
color	constRule	
textureShader		color
texcoordArithmetic		textureShader
dependentTexture	identityTexRule	texcoordArithmetic
multitexture		textureShader
multitexture		dependentTexture
blend		multitexture

Figure 11.12. Possible labels for Const node in Figure 11.11.

label	rule	by way of
texture	textureRule	
textureShader		texture
texcoordArithmetic		textureShader
dependentTexture		identityTexRule
dependentTexture	dependentTexRule	texture/identityTexRule
multitexture		dependentTexture
multitexture		textureShader
blend		multitexture

Figure 11.13. Possible labels for Lookup texturing node in Figure 11.11.

label	rule	by way of
textureShader	texShaderRule	
texcoordArithmetic		textureShader
texcoordArithmetic	texcoordArithRule	
dependentTexture	identityTexRule	texcoordArithmetic
multitexture		dependentTexture
multitexture		textureShader
multitexture	multiTexRule	dependentTexture
multitexture	multiTexRule	textureShader
blend		multitexture
blend	blendTexRule	blend, multitexture

Figure 11.14. Possible labels for Mul node in Figure 11.11.

to control the iburg reduce phase, where the OpenGL code is produced. Of particular note are the two instances of identityTexRule, which either uses a simple ramp texture or sets the texturing mode to pass the texture coordinates through to later stages.

Figure 11.11 shows a simple expression and its tree representation. Figure 11.12 then shows all the ways that the `Const` tree node can be labeled according to the rules from Figure 11.10. These labels range from its use as a single color, to a complete rendering to end up as a color in the frame buffer. Where several rules can produce the same label, only the one with the least cost is kept, but information is retained on the least-cost way to reach **each** of these possible label results. Similarly, Figure 11.13 shows the breakdown for the Texture node. Figure 11.14 shows the possible labels for the full expression. The multiply result could be produced as early as the textureShader stage (for use in later operations). If this is the final result of the shader, we'd reduce according to some sequence that ends up with a `blend` label to leave the answer in the frame buffer. When doing this, we rely on the rule costs to produce a one-pass result rather than rendering the constant color to frame buffer using its `blend` labeling, then multiplying by the texture through an application of the blendTexRule.

12

RenderMan

RenderMan was designed by Pixar as an interface between modeling programs and a renderer. Pixar's implementation is PhotoRealistic RenderMan renderer, which runs on a variety of UNIX platforms. Other RenderMan renderers have been written. One notable example is BMRT by Larry Gritz, which is a ray tracer instead of a scan-line renderer. It is a testament to the design of the RenderMan interface that it has not only been possible to create new RenderMan renderers, but ones that operate in a completely different way than the original REYES rendering algorithm [34, 61].

Despite all these implementations, at the time of this writing RenderMan still cannot be evaluated in real time. Nonetheless, it is still worth starting our comparisons with an off-line shading language like RenderMan's. This provides a good baseline for judging the current state of real-time shading.

The RenderMan shading language is quite high-level. It should be no surprise that it closely resembles the C programming language, as it was modeled after C. It copies C's use of {} braces for grouping statements, semicolons to end them, `if` and `for` control constructs, and other details. RenderMan does add several new language features to make writing shaders easier. A simple RenderMan shader illustrating some of these features is shown in Figure 12.1.

12.1 Shader Types

The RenderMan shading language allows user-written functions, making it a little easier to create complex shaders. The shaders themselves are defined as functions using one of several new function types. These are `displacement`, `surface`, `light`, `volume`, `atmosphere`, and `imager`, as well

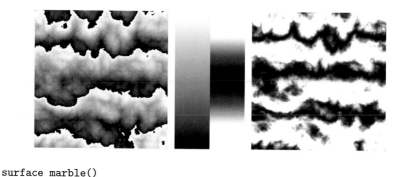

```
surface marble()
{
    float sc, f = ycomp(P/2);
    for(sc=1; sc<=64; sc*=2)
        f += abs(2*noise(P*sc/2)-1)/sc;

    Oi=Os;
    Ci=Oi * spline(mod(f,1),
        color(1.,1.,1.), color(1.,1.,1.), color(1.,1.,1.),
        color(.5,0.,.5), color(0.,0.,0.), color(.5,0.,.5),
        color(1.,1.,1.), color(1.,1.,1.), color(1.,1.,1.));
}
```

Figure 12.1.   RenderMan marble shader: grayscale turbulence, spline map to convert grayscale to marble colors, and final marble (with base color but no shading).

as the unsupported `transformation`. For more detail on these types, see Section 4.3. Each of these procedure types has access to several implicit parameters (called globals in the RenderMan documentation). These include the position and normal of the current surface sample, its position and size in the parametric space (since almost all RenderMan primitives are parametric patches), the direction of the incoming ray, and the current surface color setting.

12.2 Illuminate

Several new control constructs support light definition and use. The statements `illuminate` and `solar` are used in light procedures to control where the light falls. Perhaps more significant is `illuminance`. This new state-

```
surface ward2d(float Ks=.5, Kd=.5, Ka=.5; color specularcolor=1;
               float var_u = 0.1, covar = 0.01, var_v = 0.001)
{
    /* normalized normal, view & surface directions */
    normal Nf = faceforward( normalize(N), I );
    vector V = -normalize(I);
    vector unitU = normalize(dPdu), unitV = normalize(dPdv);

    /* inverse of covariance matrix */
    uniform float cov_det = var_u*var_v - covar*covar;
    uniform float cov_inv_uu = var_v/cov_det;
    uniform float cov_inv_vv = var_u/cov_det;
    uniform float cov_inv_uv = -covar/cov_det;

    color color_out = 0;
    illuminance(Ps, Nf, PI/2) {
        vector unitL = normalize(L);
        float N_dot_L = Nf . unitL;

        /* halfway vector: U and V components / N component */
        vector H = normalize(V + unitL);
        float Hn = H.Nf, Hu = H.unitU/Hn, Hv = H.unitV/Hn;

        /* accumulate lighting contribution using 2D Gaussian specular */
        float spec = exp(-.5 * (Hu*Hu*cov_inv_uu +
        2*Hu*Hv*cov_inv_uv +
        Hv*Hv*cov_inv_vv));

        color_out += Cl * (Kd * Cs * N_dot_L  +  Ks * specularcolor * spec);
    }

    Oi = Os;
    Ci = Os * (Ka * ambient() + color_out);
}
```

Figure 12.2.   RenderMan Shader with illuminance, implementing the Ward anisotropic shading model.

ment has the appearance of a `for` loop, and stands for an integration over all incoming light. In most cases, the lights are point-sources, so the integration degenerates to a sum of the contributions from each light. In this case, `illuminance` is really just like a `for` loop over the active lights, evaluating each light, then the body of the `illuminance` statement to accumulate the lighting contributions. Its use to implement the Ward anisotropic shading model [174] is shown in Figure 12.2. In more complex cases (e.g., with a fluorescent fixture that emits light fairly uniformly over a rectangular area), the `illuminance` statement hides the evaluation of multiple samples in the light. In this more complex case `illuminance` does act as a numerical integration operator. Within the `illuminance` loop, the `specularbrdf` and `phong` functions provide a handy shorthand for common shading models, while cases with no specialization can use `diffuse` and `specular` functions to provide the effect of a full `illuminance` loop.

12.3 Data Types

Unlike C, floating point is RenderMan's only numeric data type. There are no integer or fixed point types in RenderMan. There are, however, new composite types to represent colors, points, vectors, normals, or matrices as groups of floats. To make the typical shading tasks easier, there are several built-in operators and functions not found in typical C that operate on these new types.

The principal new math operators for points, vectors, or normals are "v1.v2" and "v1^v2". "v1.v2" returns the dot product of v1 and v2, while "v1^v2" returns the vector cross product. Most other math operations just apply the floating point version to corresponding elements. For example, "v1+v2" adds the x, y, and z components.

The basic types can be modified by either `uniform` or `varying` modifiers. Uniform values are constant across the shader, while varying values could potentially vary across the shaded surface.

12.4 Functions

There are a large number of built-in functions. Of course, there are basic math functions like `sin` and `sqrt`. Of more interest here are the shading-specific functions. We will list a wide sampling here, but for a more complete list and explanation, see one of the official RenderMan references [143, 171].

The basic math functions are extended with general functions that find particular use in shading, like `inversesqrt`, `mod`, and `clamp`. Mod may need further explanation—similar to C's `fmod`, `mod(x,y)` returns the remainder of x/y, and is useful for creating periodic patterns (e.g., in both Figures 12.1 and 12.3).

A set of step functions provide a variety of controlled transitions: `step` is a sharp transition, equivalent to that achieved by an `if` statement; `filterstep` is a smooth blended transition across the current surface sample size—`step` without the aliasing problems; and `smoothstep` gives a smooth transition over a user-defined interval. These are often used in connection with the `mix` function, which returns a weighted blend of its arguments.

RenderMan also has built-in derivative functions `Du`, `Dv`, `Deriv`. These return the derivative of an arbitrary expression with respect to the surface `u` or `v` parameterization, or with respect to another arbitrary expression. The derivatives can be computed numerically from nearby surface samples, using extra auxiliary samples, or through repeated chain-rule applications automatically computed through the shader.[1] The derivative functions are quite useful for effectively antialiasing a procedural shader or to produce constant-width surface features (like silhouette outlines). Built on these derivative operations is a `calculatenormal` function that computes a new normal for a procedurally perturbed surface position.

There are several other functions for common operations on points, vectors, or normals. For example, `length` returns the length of vector, `normalize` returns a unit-length vector in the direction of its vector argument, and `distance` returns the distance between two points. There are also a few more complex basic point and vector operations: `faceforward` to flip a vector (presumably to face toward the viewer) based on a given view and normal; `ptlined` for the distance between a point and line; and `rotate` to rotate a point around the line between two other points.

Additional functions manipulate or use matrices. A set of functions transform a point, vector, normal, or color by a matrix. Besides constructing matrices explicitly or through basic multiplication and addition, functions exist to create translation, rotation, or scaling matrices.

Finally, RenderMan provides extensive set of very shading-specific functions. Band-limited Perlin noise (`noise`) and the periodic `pnoise` are the basis of many shaders (see Section 3.6 and Chapter 10). The `cellnoise` function also provides a source of repeatable pseudo-random numbers (for example, the brick-to-brick color variation of Figure 12.3). Texture ac-

---

[1]Though a shader-writer doesn't and shouldn't need to know anything about how the derivative operators are computed.

```
surface brick(
        /* ambient and diffuse coefficients */
    float Ka = 1, Kd = 0.8;
        /* size and color of mortar and bricks */
    float b_width = 0.25, b_height = 0.1, m_width = 0.01, m_height = 0.01;
    color b_color = (0.4, 0.05, 0.05), m_color = (0.5, 0.5, 0.5);
        /* variation between individual bricks */
    float b_color_scale = 1;
        /* color swirls (low frequency noise) */
    float b_swirl = .5, b_swirl_sfreq = 10, b_swirl_tfreq = 50;
        /* graininess (high-frequency noise) */
    float b_grain = .1, m_grain = .2, b_grain_freq = 200, m_grain_freq = 200)
{

    /* compute row and column number, offset even rows by half a row */
    float ss = s, tt = t;
    float row = floor(tt / b_height);
    if (mod(row,2) < 1) ss += b_width/2;
    float col = floor(ss / b_width);

    /* compute brick coordinates, range (0,0)-(b_width,b_height) */
    ss = mod(ss, b_width); tt = mod(tt, b_height);

    /* mix factor between mortar and brick */
    float color_mix =
        (filterstep(m_width/2, ss) - filterstep(b_width - m_width/2, ss)) *
        (filterstep(m_height/2, tt) - filterstep(b_height - m_height/2, tt));

    /* shift to place each brick in a different place in noise-space */
    ss += cellnoise(col); tt += cellnoise(row);

    /* compute brick and mortar colors, then combined surface color */
    color brick = b_color
        * (1 - b_color_scale * (2*cellnoise(row,col)-1))
        * (1 - b_swirl * (2*noise(ss*b_swirl_sfreq, tt*b_swirl_tfreq) - 1))
        + (b_grain * (2*noise(ss*b_grain_freq, tt*b_grain_freq) - 1));
    color mortar = m_color
        + (m_grain * (2*noise(ss*m_grain_freq, tt*m_grain_freq) - 1));
    color surface_color = mix(mortar, brick, color_mix);

    /* final lighting */
    normal NN = normalize(faceforward(N, I));
    Ci = Os * surface_color * (Ka * ambient() + Kd * diffuse(NN));
}
```

Figure 12.3. RenderMan brick shader using noise and mod.

cess functions `texture` and `environment` allow image-based inputs to the shaders, and the related `shadow` function performs a texture-lookup into a shadow map [179]. The `spline` function gives a smooth mapping of a single scalar value to a set of colors, vectors, or other complex types (Figure 12.1). Finally, `reflect`, `refract`, and `fresnel` give directions and attenuation for rays bouncing off or through a surface, according to the formulae in Chapter 2.

13

Pfman: Procedural Shaders on PixelFlow

The pfman language was developed specifically for real-time execution on the PixelFlow graphics machine [130]. It is also a high-level C-like language, quite similar to RenderMan.

13.1 Logical Model

The logical model for PixelFlow was presented earlier to guide our initial presentation of the logical model diagrams in Chapter 4. We reproduce this diagram here for reference (Figure 13.1). We will point out this time around which procedural stages were actually implemented. Surface and light shaders were implemented and well-utilized by users of the PixelFlow system. Primitive and interpolate stages were also implemented but were not as effective, and were never really used.

13.2 The Pfman Language

Pfman shares many of RenderMan's shading features, including **uniform** and **varying** type modifiers and an **illuminance** construct for accumulating the contribution of lights in the scene. It also shares the use of separate types for vector, normal, point, color, and matrix. Since the pfman language was developed before RenderMan had all of these distinct types, the syntax chosen is slightly different. It defines vector types using arrays of simpler data types with extra attributes—**transform_as_vector float v[3]** or **float transform_as_point p[4]**. It also includes an attribute

219

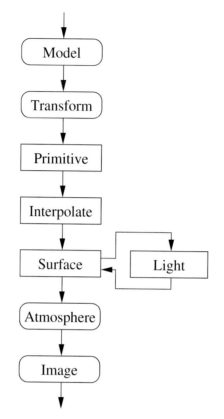

Figure 13.1. Logical model developed for PixelFlow.

unit that indicates that a vector should be normalized before it is used by the shader. This takes the place of the common idiom in RenderMan shaders of always using normalize(N) instead of N alone, since the surface normal is not guaranteed to be unit length.

13.2.1 Fixed Point

The most immediately obvious difference between pfman and RenderMan is the existence of fixed-point data types. While the PixelFlow machine could handle floating-point operations, fixed point was both faster and smaller (see Table 13.1). For real-time shading, this can make the difference between being able to use certain shaders and not being able to use them. The pfman fixed-point types include both a size and exponent, specified by a flexible notation modeled after C++ template classes: fixed<size,exponent>.

Operation	16-bit fixed	32-bit fixed	32-bit float
+	0.07 μs	0.13 μs	3.08 μs
*	0.50 μs	2.00 μs	2.04 μs
/	1.60 μs	6.40 μs	7.07 μs
sqrt	1.22 μs	3.33 μs	6.99 μs
noise	5.71 μs	—	21.64 μs

Table 13.1. Timings for fixed- and floating-point operations on PixelFlow.

The size is given in bits to give the pfman compiler more information about the range of numbers actually used[1] and thus the sizes necessary for intermediate results. For example, the sum of two eight-bit numbers could overflow into nine bits, requiring at least two bytes for intermediate results to avoid wrapping around. In contrast, if the two numbers are known to use only seven bits each, their sum can be at most eight bits long, easily fitting within a byte for both the original numbers and the sum.

The exponent is a floating-point-like scale shared across all pixels— an exponent e scales by 2^{-e}. A more natural interpretation is that the exponent gives the position of the binary point in the fixed-point number. This gives a relatively understandable interpretation of the number, as shown in Table 13.2

Fixed point is less forgiving than floating point. On the PixelFlow system, which had both, users tended to write shaders or portions of shaders first in floating point, then switch to the smaller, faster fixed-point form. In some cases, fixed point actually provides more effective precision than floating point (see Figure 13.2).

This example is zoomed in on a region of the Mandelbrot set [109], which serves as somewhat of an acid test for precision issues. It's based on an iterated complex equation:

$$z' = z^2 + c \tag{13.1}$$

specification	bit pattern	low-end	high-end (decimal)
fixed<8,0>	xxxxxxxx.0	0	255
fixed<8,8>	0.xxxxxxxx	0	$255/256$
fixed<8,4>	xxxx.xxxx	0	$15\frac{15}{16}$
fixed<8,12>	0.0000xxxxxxxx	0	$255/4096$
fixed<8,-4>	xxxxxxxx0000.0	0	4080

Table 13.2. Unsigned fixed-point numbers for pfman.

---

[1] In effect, the bit size is a poor man's approximation to interval arithmetic [4].

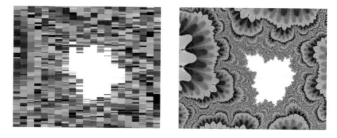

Figure 13.2.   Floating point versus fixed point. In this case, fixed point effectively provides 8 bits more precision, since a shader-wide exponent is sufficient.

The Mandelbrot set includes all points c on the complex plane that don't eventually diverge if you start with $z = 0$ and iterate forever. All points more than two units from the origin can be proved to eventually diverge, but the only way to tell if points inside that circle will diverge is to iterate the equation until they do. Thanks to this property, we can limit the fixed-point representation to cover only numbers between -4 and 4. Numbers in this range are represented by all 32 bits. Single precision floating point values cover a much larger range than necessary, using eight of the 32 bits for an exponent that is little-used in this computation. This leaves only 24 bits of precision. In most cases, when the range is not so well-bounded, it is impossible to rely on a single shader-wide exponent and still retain accuracy.

A common set of these fixed- and floating-point types are defined in a pfman standard include file. The fixed-point formats included commonly used subtypes like `unsigned fixed<16,0>` as uInt2, `fixed<15,0>` as sInt2,[2] `unsigned fixed<8,8>` as uFrac8, and `fixed<15,12>` as Short. They also include functional types, so `unsigned fixed<8,8>` is also known as Color.

A separate type, `frac<size>`, represents only fractions between zero and one, but includes its upper bound. So `frac<8>` is an 8-bit value ranging from 0 to $255/255 = 1$. While `frac` could be used in a shader to accurately represent the full range of colors, `fixed` is more flexible and thus more common.

13.2.2   Common Shader Parameters

Another noticeable difference between pfman and RenderMan is the handling of common shading parameters. RenderMan provides parameters like

---

[2]The size does not include the sign bit, so `fixed<16,0>` is actually 17 bits and would require two bytes to store.

the current position, normal, or texture coordinates as globals or implicit parameters to the shading function. Pfman requires any used parameters to be explicitly declared in the shader header. Parameters present in this list are computed for a surface when it is initially rendered, while unlisted parameters are skipped. Any shader can include `input` and `output` designators on its parameters—`input` parameters being those it wanted from previous stages and `output` parameters being those it computed for use by later stages. The only special significance of the standard set of parameters is that the standard polygon renderer outputs them. For this mechanism to work, the names of parameters between the shader that provides them and the shader that uses them must match. The standard polygon renderer uses somewhat clunky names for these standard parameters like `px_rc_cl` or `px_material_texcoord` (as compared to RenderMan's `Cl` or `s` and `t`). Since everyone wants their shaders to work with the standard polygon render, this makes names like `px_rc_cl` the de facto standard names.

13.2.3 Functions

Most pfman built-in functions are defined in include files in the pfman language itself. This includes many functions echoing the RenderMan function set like `mix` and `fresnel`. The list of functions is a fairly complete copy of the set of functions in version 3.1 of the RenderMan specification [142]. There is no `filterstep` or derivative functions, but there is a standard parameter, `px_shader_f_sqr` that gives the per-pixel texture scale factor. Together with `smoothstep`, this produces a similar result to `filterstep`. Other functions are true built-ins (like `noise`), or refer to the C library function of the same name (like `sin` or `cos`).

13.2.4 Example

For a better feel of the differences, Figure 13.3 shows a pfman shader— brick similar the RenderMan brick in Figure 12.3. A few things are worth noting in this example. The uniform parameters have default values (as do all RenderMan shader parameters), while the varying parameters do not. If the application doesn't set a parameter, it uses its default. This feature can be important for a shader with many parameters. Also, complex expressions can be put into array initializers, and these can even be used inline in an expression as an *anonymous array*.

13.3 Pfman Implementation

The pfman compiler translated a pfman shader into C++ code for the PixelFlow system's internal processors. The basic PixelFlow organization

```
#include <pftypes.h>
#include <pfman.h>
#include <pfman_excl.h>
#include "step.h"

surface brick(
        // output color
  output varying Color px_rc_co[3],
        // light color and direction inside illuminance
  varying Color px_rc_cl[3]
  varying transform_as_vector unit Short px_rc_l[3],
        // eye position
  varying transform_as_vector unit Short px_rc_eye[3],
        // surface normal, texture coordinates & area scale
  varying transform_as_normal unit Short px_material_normal[3],
  varying transform_as_texture TextureCoord px_shader_texcoord[2],
  varying TextureFSqr px_shader_f_sqr,
        // control for basic brick
  uniform float b_width = 0.25, uniform float b_height = 0.1,
  uniform float m_width = 0.01, uniform float m_height = 0.01,
  uniform float b_color[3] = {0.8,0.1,0.1},
  uniform float m_color[3] = {0.5,0.5,0.5},
        // add symmetric high frequency noise
  uniform float b_hf_mix = 1, uniform float b_hf_freq = 20,
  uniform float m_hf_mix = 1, uniform float m_hf_freq = 20,
// add low frequency to bricks
  uniform float b_lf_scale = 1,
  uniform float b_lf_u_freq = 10, uniform float b_lf_v_freq = 2,
        // color individual bricks differently
  uniform float b_color_scale = 0)
```

Figure 13.3. Pfman brick shader (continued on next page).

```
{
// find row & column
uInt1 row = px_shader_texcoord[1] / b_height;
    // fixed<17,16> since offset texcoord could exceed 1
unsigned fixed<17,16> u = px_shader_texcoord[0];
if (row % 2 < 1) u += b_width/2;
uInt1 col = u / b_width;

// compute "brick coordinates"
float st[2] = {u % b_width, px_shader_texcoord[1] % b_height};

// choose mortar or brick based on position in brick coordiantes
float duv = sqrt((float)px_shader_f_sqr);
float colormix =
    (smoothstep(m_width/2 - duv, (varying)m_width/2, st[0])
     - smoothstep((varying)(b_width - m_width/2),
                   b_width - m_width/2 + duv, st[0]))
    * (smoothstep(m_height/2 - duv, (varying)m_height/2, st[1])

        - smoothstep((varying)(b_height - m_height/2),
                      b_height - m_height/2 + duv, st[1]));

  // shift to put each brick in its own place in noise space.
  uInt1 shift[2] = {
      (uInt1)irandom((uInt2)row),
      (uInt1)irandom((uInt2)col)
  };

  // shift to put each brick at a different spot in noise space
  st += shift;

  // find brick color, mortar color, combine to full surface color
  Short brick[3] = b_color
      * (1 + b_color_scale*srandom((uInt2)(col + shift[0])))
      * (1 + b_lf_scale * snoise(b_lf_freq * st))
      + (b_hf_mix * snoise(b_hf_freq * st));

  Short mortar[3] = m_color
      + {1,1,1} * m_hf_mix *
      snoise((float[2])(m_hf_freq * px_shader_texcoord));

  float surface_color[3] = mix(mortar, brick, colormix);

  // compute vector from surface to eye and flip normal to face it
  float v[3] = normalize(px_rc_eye - getPs());
  if (px_material_normal * v < 0)
      px_material_normal = -px_material_normal;
```

Figure 13.3 (continued).

```
// accumulate diffuse colors for each light
float diffuse[3] = {0,0,0};
illuminance() {
    float l[3] = normalize(px_rc_l);
    varying float n_dot_l = px_material_normal * l;

    // no negative light on the back side of the object
    if (n_dot_l < 0) n_dot_l = 0;

    diffuse += n_dot_l * px_rc_cl;
}

// build final color (diffuse*surface_color is 'dot product')
Short color_out[3] = {
    diffuse[0]*surface_color[0],
    diffuse[1]*surface_color[1],
    diffuse[2]*surface_color[2]
};
px_rc_co = clamp(color_out, 0, 0.999)
}
```

Figure 13.3 (continued).

classified many boards into three types: renderer; shader; and frame buffer (Figure 13.4). A primitive passing through the system would be transformed and rendered on one renderer board. Each of its pixels would have surface, light, and atmospheric shaders applied on one shader board. Finally, the pixels from all shaders would be collected on a single frame buffer.

The actual machine was a collection of generic boards, assigned by software to one of these three purposes. The boards were interconnected by two networks: lower speed for geometry and control messages, and higher speed for pixel data (Figure 13.5).

Each of the boards had two CPUs and a 128 x 64 SIMD array (Figure 13.6). Uniform operations and control constructs ran on one of the general purpose CPUs, while all varying computation and pixel operations happened on SIMD array. The code running on the general CPU would produce a linear buffer of SIMD commands in the shared memory, where it would be scheduled for eventual execution. The SIMD array could access

Figure 13.4. PixelFlow physical data flow.

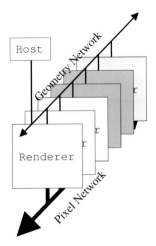

Figure 13.5. PixelFlow machine architecture.

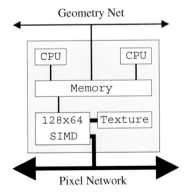

Figure 13.6. PixelFlow board architecture.

texture directly, but texture access was more expensive than computation so many PixelFlow shaders, like many RenderMan shaders, preferred computing a complex pattern to looking it up in a texture.

13.3.1 Tools

The pfman compiler used the lex and YACC parsing tools to convert the pfman shader into an internal tree representation. It was written in C++, and used a generic tree node class with specializations for the different node types. Each node included an arbitrary-length list of children, so that in later stages the linearized list of simple operations within a basic block was just stored as a statement-list-node's set of children.

Pfman didn't use any other tools for later compilation stages. Instead, each compiler pass was a virtual member function of the node class. This would traverse the tree, performing operations according to the specialized functions provided by node subclasses or sub-subclasses. Each pass-traversal function was responsible for traversing its child nodes in an appropriate order, and eventually returning a pointer to a replacement node. This use of a returned node pointer allowed a flexible set of modifications, from tree deletion (returning NULL), to simple in-place modifications (returning this), to a complete rewrite of the current node (returning a new replacement node and deleting the original).

This method does have the disadvantage that changes to the node pass structure involve touching almost every header file. Changes to the passes themselves are all expressed as C++ code, making modifications and debugging not quite as straightforward as a text input-file representation. This is countered by the complete flexibility of the traversal functions.

13.3.2 Compiler Passes

The pfman compiler used a set of simple passes to process a shader. Parsing included all the necessary scoping of symbols using a stack of nested symbol tables. With this stack, a symbol look-up at any point would look first at the innermost scope, then the next scope out, and so on until either finding a matching symbol or deciding that its undefined. The initial tree as produced by the parser represented the full shader. This was followed by a first-level pass to do simple constant folding to collapse operations that could be determined at compile time.

The next pair of passes did fixed-point type analysis, trying to find sizes for the intermediate values that would not lose precision. All fixed-point variables had to have the size and exponent defined, so that only the types for intermediate results of complex expressions had to be determined. The first step was a bottom-up pass to determine the minimum fixed-point sizes and exponents necessary to keep full input precision through the entire chain of operations. This was followed by a top-down pass to find the maximum precision that could actually make a difference to the variable result.

All later passes until code generation dealt with varying operations only. The next split the varying operations into a low-level linear form, introducing new temporaries as necessary. This was followed by a pass to convert into an SSA form (for varying computations only), so that each variable was assigned once and only once.

The SSA form was used for a dead code removal pass. It is easy to tell if a computation is never used once every variable assignment is distinct. If a variable is never used, it is safe to remove its definition, which may leave other variables unused, eventually cleaning up any code that isn't actually relevant to the final computation.

The SSA form was then used to find an accurate idea of the life of each variable for memory allocation. Memory allocation was a big concern for PixelFlow since there were only 256 bytes total SIMD memory to hold all parameters, as well as all variables used by the surface shader and light shaders as they ran. Given its critical nature and the limited total memory, the memory allocation was actually handled using a register-coloring algorithm as is done traditionally for CPU register allocation [30], with the difference that there was no memory to spill to when the register space ran out.

Finally, a code generation pass printed C++ for the uniform code (still very close to its original form) and a sequence of *EMC* instructions for the *enhanced memory controller* that controls the SIMD array. The EMC instructions are assembler-level functions (EMC_ADD(instbuf, dst, src, src, size), EMC_MUL(instbuf, dst, src, src, size), etc.) that fill the growing SIMD instruction buffer.

14

ISL: Interactive Shading Language

ISL is the multipass interactive shading language for SGI's OpenGL Shader. OpenGL Shader compiles shaders into multiple OpenGL rendering passes. The roots of OpenGL Shader lie in a prototype RenderMan renderer developed in the late 1990's at SGI.

This RenderMan implementation used multipass rendering on a software-only OpenGL. Two key extensions made a full RenderMan implementation possible on this software OpenGL when it was not possible on any actual graphics hardware of the time.

These were a form of dependent texturing (now common on low-end and mid-range hardware) and the use of floating point for all values and computations. From this basis, OpenGL Shader developed as a more limited language that could run on any OpenGL 1.2 hardware.

The concept of multipass shading (Section 9.3) is commonly described as treating each rendering pass as a complex machine instruction. In this model, the frame buffer serves as an accumulator, blending operations as the ALU, stencil, and alpha tests control conditional execution for individual pixels, and texture or *pbuffers* provide extra registers or memory.

In practice, both the RenderMan implementation and OpenGL shader actually treat OpenGL as many little instructions, affectionately called *statelets* since each is a chunk of OpenGL state handled as an atomic unit. This treatment is used to compile shaders to either multiple passes of ordinary OpenGL, or multiple passes using the NVIDIA register combiners.

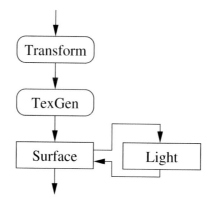

Figure 14.1. Logical model for OpenGL Shader.

14.1   Logical Model

OpenGL shader includes shading stages for surface shading and lighting, with stages proposed for texture generation and transformation. The logical model diagram for OpenGL Shader is shown in Figure 14.1 (see Chapter 4 for details on logical model diagrams). In this case, the surface shading stage handles only direct surface appearance computation. In general, the surface and light stages map into fragment operations, while the transformation and texture coordinate generation stages map into vertex operations. However, since the entire set of shaders is compiled and mapped into multiple rendering passes, this split of vertex and fragment operations isn't strictly enforced.

14.2   The ISL Language

The ISL language is lower-level in appearance than pfman or RenderMan. Most statements are of the form FB = operation. In early versions of OpenGL Shader, each statement was a rendering pass, performing some operation and storing the result in the frame buffer. In more recent versions, the statements indicate only the operations that must occur, many of which might be packed into a single rendering pass. By the time this book is published, complex expression assignments should be supported.

ISL does share several language features with both RenderMan and pfman: user-defined functions with specialized function types for shader

```
#include <microfacetbrdf.h>
#include <hdrfresnel.h>

surface brdf_with_fresnel(
        uniform string brdfP = "brdf_p.rgb";
        uniform string brdfQ = "brdf_q.rgb";
        uniform color brdfColor=color (1,0,0,0);
        uniform string env = "park.rgba";
        parameter float shaderStep = 0)
{
    // BRDF
    if (shaderStep == 0 || shaderStep == 2)
        FB = microfacetBRDF(brdfP, brdfQ,
                brdfColor);

    // Fresnel-modulated reflectance
    if (shaderStep >= 1)
        FB = hdrFresnel (env,
                "fresnelRefract.bw");
}

varying color microfacetBRDF(
    uniform string brdfP = "brdf_p.rgb";
    uniform string brdfQ = "brdf_q.rgb";
    uniform color brdfColor = color (1,0,0,0))
{
    // contribution for light 0
    FB = diffuse(0);
    FB *= texture (brdfP, 1, 3);
    FB *= texture (brdfQ, 1, 2);

    varying color a = FB;        // save results

    // Accumulate contribution for lights 1-N
    uniform float lightNum = 1;
    repeat (numdirectlights - 1) {
        FB = diffuse (lightNum);
        FB *= texture (brdfP, 1, 3+(2*lightNum));
        FB *= texture (brdfQ, 1, 2+(2*lightNum));
        FB += a;    a = FB;

        // Next light
        lightNum += 1;
    }

    // Compute viewer dependent contribution
    FB *= texture (brdfP, 1, 1);
    FB *= brdfColor;
}
```

Figure 14.2. ISL shader for combined BRDF and Fresnel in Figure 14.3, and the homomorphic factorization-based BRDF function (slighly edited for space from the one included with OpenGL Shader).

Figure 14.3.   Car model using ISL shader for paint BRDF, glossy Fresnel reflectance, and combined paint with glossy layer. (See Color Plate VIII.)

definitions; control constructs, including loops and conditionals; and type modifiers like uniform and varying to indicate the computational frequency of its data (Is it constant across a shader or can it vary from pixel to pixel?).

Figures 14.2 and 14.3 show a sample ISL shader, using two provided building-block functions. One implements the run-time portion of the homomorphic factorization technique from Section 6.6.2. The other applies a glossy layer using an environment map (Section 7.1.1).

14.2.1 Data Types

One notable difference between ISL and the previous languages is in its data types. In ISL, varying indicates values that vary across a shaded surface, just as with the other languages. Uniform, on the other hand, is used specifically for values that are known at compile time. Since a shader can be compiled multiple times during an application run, this lies somewhere between the usual use of uniform and a true constant. In ISL, variables that are constant across a surface, but can change from frame to frame are given the parameter type modifier. This was done in part because early versions of OpenGL Shader didn't allow frame-to-frame parameter changes without recompiling the shader—by the time that feature was added, the keyword uniform was already in use.

Uniform or parameter variables are always represented as floating point. Varying parameters are always represented by whatever format the graphics system supports internally. Since OpenGL Shader is designed to run on current hardware, this is generally 8-bit fixed-point fractions (or 12–16 bits on some high-end hardware), clamped to values between zero and one.

Figure 14.4 shows the results for a Mandelbrot shader using only 8-bit precision. These results are quite different than those for Figure 13.2. The area outside the set looks quite different with this shader primarily because

Figure 14.4. Mandelbrot set shader computed with only 8 bits with ISL.

precision only valued inside the -2 to 2 range is represented. Despite this compressed range, the lack of precision at the set boundary quite is visible.

14.2.2   Control Constructs

OpenGL Shader also differs in the details of its control constructs. Uniform, parameter, and varying conditional if/else statements are available, though the varying if compares a single channel of FB against a uniform or parameter value. This is shown in Figure 14.5.

```
if (FB[0] > .5) {          // compare to red
  big_red();
  if (FB[1] > param)       // nested comparison with green
    big_red_and_green(); // arbitrary list of statements
}
else
  small_red();
```

Figure 14.5. ISL code fragment showing varying if syntax.

Loops also differ. Instead of `for`, `while`, or `illuminance` loops, ISL has a single `repeat` loop taking a count of the number of times to run through the loop body. An ISL `repeat`, serving the purpose of an `illuminance` is shown in the microfacetbrdf function in Figure 14.2

14.3   OpenGL Shader Implementation

The OpenGL Shader compiler, like others described in this book, uses lex and YACC to create its parser. Like pfman, OpenGL Shader is implemented in C++ and uses a node class as the basis of its intermediate forms. OpenGL Shader's nodes contain up to four children, so lists of statements (or later linear lists of operations) are chains of `StatementList` nodes. These nodes are **not** subclassed for the individual node types, instead each node has a node type and an associated symbol in the symbol table. It is this symbol that contains the different attributes that might be associated with a node—its value if constant, its definition if a function, its location if a varying variable, etc.

14.3.1   Conversion to Linear Form

During parsing, all operations (including assignments, color indexing operations, and math operations) are converted to function calls. Most of these primitive functions are defined in an extended ISL, with access to normally hidden statelet functions. Once again, the first passes performed on the AST are to evaluate compile-time constant expressions and resolve inline function definitions. The inline function expansion converts all varying operations into a linear stream of instructions. While the style of ISL may seem to already provide a linear instruction stream in the original shader source, some fairly complex expressions are still possible. For example, the line of code in Figure 14.6 is transformed into the sequence of statements in Figure 14.7.

This is followed by an SSA conversion step (see Section 11.1), renaming variables as necessary so that every new variable is the result of a single assignment. The result is shown in Figure 14.8. Note that even the "magic" variable `FB` has been reassigned to use unique names: `t0` for the value of `FB` before this statement, and `t5` for the value following this statement.

```
FB.rgb *= texture("tname",textureMatrix,texcoordSet0);
```

Figure 14.6. A line of ISL.

```
_VVertex(_tmp,texcoordSet0);
_VXform(_tmp,textureMatrix,_tmp);
_VLookup(_tmp,"tname",_tmp);
_VMul(_tmp,_FB,_tmp);
_VMask(_FB,_FB,_tmp,8|4|2);
```

Figure 14.7. Line from Figure 14.6 expanded into assembler-like statelet pcode form.

```
_VVertex(t1,texcoordSet0);
_VXform(t2,textureMatrix,t1);
_VLookup(t3,"tname",t2);
_VMul(t4,t0,t3);
_VMask(t5,t0,t4,8|4|2);
```

Figure 14.8. ISL pcode from Figure 14.7, converted to SSA form.

14.3.2 Targeting Hardware

The heart of OpenGL Shader's optimization for the actual hardware is a pass driven by an iburg machine description (see Section 11.4.2). This pass does a forward traversal through the statements, finding costs for each statement (and hence each unique variable assignment) for all the possible places in the graphics pipeline where it could fit. For example, some points in the OpenGL pipeline where _VMul could be computed include: application of texture environment (blending texture with OpenGL lighting and color); an NVIDIA register combiner operation; a blend with blend factors $source*\text{GL\_DST\_COLOR}+dst*\text{GL\_ZERO}$; or a pixel-copy scale. Where the multiply in this example can appear depends on what was in FB immediately before this statement.

Following the iburg labeling, the *reduce* pass traverses the statements in back-to-front order, building rendering passes as it goes. At each statement, if any of the variables can be inserted inline into the budding rendering pass, they are. This leaves one less use of the original variable. The definition and computation of any variable with no uses left is removed. In essence, starting with a set of statements that could be trivially implemented as a long stream of rendering passes, we replicate operations that can be recomputed on the fly in the hopes that the pass that would have computed them in the long original version of the shader can be removed.

After rendering passes have been collected, the program is converted from SSA form back into a form with multiple assignments where necessary, and variable assignments that were not removed are allocated space in texture memory. With the ISL language as it exists as of this writing,

OpenGL Shader will never need more temporary texture storage than there are explicit varying variable definitions in the source, though it may need less. It also achieves best optimization for shaders that freely use varying variables to store simple expressions, as these can be inlined in any pass where they are used. Once ISL accepts more complex expressions, it will no longer be possible to make the same guarantees on texture memory use, since a complex expression that cannot be computed in a single pass will allocate its own extra temporary storage.

14.3.3   Emitting Code

The final OpenGL Shader code generation pass creates an internal representation of the OpenGL state changes determined by the instruction assignment pass. This form can be rapidly interpreted for run-time library use where shaders can be compiled and rendered within a single application. It can also be printed in various forms including a text dump in an *ipf file* or OpenGL C code. It can also be read from a previously printed ipf file, making translators to multiple output files easy.

15

RTSL: The Stanford Real-Time Shading Language

The *Stanford Real-Time Shading Language* (RTSL) is both higher- and lower-level than ISL. It is higher-level in that it allows arbitrary expressions as statements in the shading language, but it is also lower-level in that it doesn't have conditional or looping control constructs [146]. Its targets include multipass rendering with OpenGL, and single pass using shading extensions introduced in NVIDIA's GeForce3 and ATI's Radeon 8500.

15.1 Logical Model

The logical model for RTSL consists of just two stages: surface shader and light shader. This choice of stages is based more on purpose than the spe-

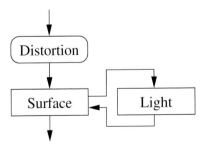

Figure 15.1. Logical model for Stanford Real-Time Programmable Shading.

cific hardware implementation, a choice that allows the same model to be applied across several hardware platforms (see Chapter 4 for an explanation of our logical model diagrams).

An extra distortion shader stage also exists, but is not fully documented. It operates as a combined transform shader, returning transformed vertex, normal and tangent directions.

Each shader can include operations across all physical stages of the actual hardware. The surface shading stage includes both interpolation or texture coordinate generation as well as the surface shading aspects of Figure 4.3.

15.2   The RTSL Language

As mentioned, you can write three types of shaders in this language: distortion; surface; and light. Code in distortion shaders can target either host or vertex shader hardware. Both surface and light may generate code for all stages of the physical hardware, from host to vertex shader to fragment shader. The Stanford system supports NT, Linux, and IRIX platforms and can target multipass ordinary OpenGL, single-pass using the NVIDIA vertex shader and register combiner extensions or ATI vertex and fragment shader extensions.

15.2.1   Computational Frequency

While the code in a shader can be targeted to different parts of the system, this targeting is not without some user intervention. Like RenderMan's uniform and varying, RTSL has data type modifiers to indicate where a computation should occur. This is called the computational frequency of the computation (see Figure 15.2). Computational frequency can take one of four values:

constant: Known at compile time and the same everywhere across the shader instance.

primitive group: Computed at run time, but constant across a group of primitives rendered at once (i.e., per glBegin in OpenGL—in previous versions of RTSL this computational frequency was known as perbegin).

vertex: Can hold a different value for each vertex.

fragment: Can hold a different value for each fragment.[1]

---

[1] As a reminder, a fragment is a rendered sample on its way to becoming part of a pixel.

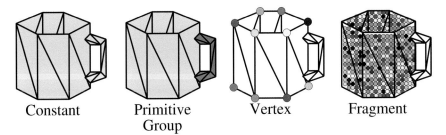

Constant   Primitive   Vertex   Fragment
                    Group

Figure 15.2. RTSL computational frequencies.

It is only possible to cast down the chain of computational frequencies from constant to primitive group to vertex to fragment. Casts from constant to primitive group or primitive group to vertex replicate the data, but casts from vertex to fragment interpolate the vertex data across each polygon to produce different values at every fragment.

Certain operations apply only to some of the computational frequencies. For example, there is only a fragment version of the texture lookup function while there is everything but a fragment version for most matrix operations. It is considered an error in the shader to try to cast values up the frequency chain or use operations of the wrong type.

In addition to the basic frequencies, some variables can be declared to be `perlight`, or left without a computational frequency at all. The compiler will attempt to infer computational frequencies for these based on the frequencies of values used to compute them, values they compute, and operations that are used.

Most code in RTSL doesn't specify the computation frequency, allowing the compiler to infer it. Even so, the code must be written with certain computational frequencies in mind. This is not really an issue caused by the Stanford language; it is a symptom of the varying capabilities and data types provided by the graphics hardware. If the hardware were more uniform in its capabilities, languages wouldn't have to choose between either lowest-common-denominator behavior or exposing certain aspects of the underlying hardware in the shading language.

15.2.2 Data Types

In addition to the different computational frequencies, there are a variety of data types in RTSL. The basic types are `float` for floating-point numbers and `clampf` for floating-point numbers clamped to a 0–1 range.

These values can be grouped together in aggregate types for three-dimensional vectors and four-dimensional homogeneous vectors (`float3`,

clampf3, float4 and clampf4). The float type can also be grouped into
3x3 or 4x4 matrices (matrix3, matrix4). Individual elements can be used
with C-style array indexing notation, and values of the aggregate types
can be built on the fly: float4 = {float, float, float, float} or
{float3, float}, matrix3 = {float3, float3, float3}.

There are also special types for Boolean true/false values (bool) and for
references to specific textures (texref). Like operations, the basic types
are valid only for the parts of the target hardware that support them. For
example, the texref type can be used only at the constant or primitive
group frequencies.

15.3 Functions

RTSL has a reasonable set of shading functions. It has common math functions like sin, cos, or pow, most of which are only available for types of
vertex frequency or above. It also includes shading functions familiar from
RenderMan, like dot product (dot()), vector normalization (normalize())
or reflection (reflect()). It has a set of matrix functions at the constant
or primitive group frequency, including invert and transpose, as well as
the common shading-specific matrix construction operations for rotation,
translation, and scaling and constructing different forms of perspective projection matrix. One matrix function of note is affine, which returns the
3 x 3 rotation and scaling subsection of a 4 x 4 matrix, stripping off any
translation or perspective.

At the fragment level, RTSL has a variety of texture access functions
for ordinary texturing, three-dimensional texturing, different forms of reflection mapping, and specular or diffuse bump mapping.

It also has some fragment-level functions designed to make mapping to
NVIDIA hardware easier. These include functions to extract portions of a
color or vector as used by the hardware:

$$
\begin{aligned}
\mathrm{rgb}(\mathrm{rgba}) &= \{\mathrm{r,g,b}\} \\
\mathrm{alpha}(\mathrm{rgba}) &= \mathrm{a} \\
\mathrm{blue}(\mathrm{rgba}) &= \mathrm{b} \\
\mathrm{select}(\mathrm{lthalf}(\mathrm{a}),\mathrm{b},\mathrm{c}) &= \left\{ \begin{array}{lll} b & : & a < \frac{1}{2} \\ c & : & a \geq \frac{1}{2} \end{array} \right.
\end{aligned}
$$

Note that red and green functions do not exist, as they are not supported by the targeted hardware.

15.3.1 Operations

In addition to the usual set of math operators (+, -, *, /), RTSL has a unique operator for blending colors. This operator is based on the flexible blending capability of OpenGL. OpenGL allows blending of a source fragment (result of the current rendering pass so far) and destination fragment (color already in the frame buffer). This blending is expressed in terms of weights to use when adding the source and destination colors. Weighting factors include zero and one, the source and destination color including alpha, the alpha channel only, and one minus each of these. Expressed in RTSL, some of the options include:

$$\text{s} \quad \text{blend}(\text{SRC\_ALPHA}, \text{ONE\_MINUS\_SRC\_ALPHA}) \tag{15.1}$$
$$\text{d} = \text{s} * \text{alpha}(\text{s}) + \text{d} * (1 - \text{alpha}(\text{s}))$$
$$\text{s} \quad \text{blend}(\text{ONE}, \text{ONE\_MINUS\_SRC\_ALPHA}) \tag{15.2}$$
$$\text{d} = \text{s} * 1 + \text{d} * (1 - \text{alpha}(\text{s}))$$
$$\text{s} \quad \text{blend}(\text{DST\_COLOR}, \text{ZERO}) \quad \text{d} = \text{s} * \text{d} + \text{d} * 0 \tag{15.3}$$
$$\text{s} \quad \text{blend}(\text{ZERO}, \text{SRC\_COLOR}) \quad \text{d} = \text{s} * 0 + \text{d} * \text{s.} \tag{15.4}$$

Blend, with its arguments, acts together as a single operator (just like + or *) operating on the color operands s and d.

The blend example in Equation 15.1 is the usual blending of color with an alpha transparency value. In this case, alpha(s) is the percentage of light reflected from the surface and 1-alpha(s) is the amount transmitted through it. Equation 15.2 is a similar blend where the source color has already been multiplied by alpha. This may be necessary, for example, if rendering with a glossy coating in a bright environment, as was done in Figure 14.3. The alpha value comes from the Fresnel reflectance equation, giving strong reflectance at glancing angles and weak reflectance when seen head-on. The blend factor for the destination color (what is seen through the glossy layer) is the same. However, the sky in this environment is ten times as bright as an 8-bit per component texture will represent, and the sun is about 100 times as bright. If the alpha blending is applied to the texture values after they've been stored in a texture, the resulting glossy layer will never show a strong reflection of the sun. Finally, Equations 15.3 and 15.4 are both simple multiplies of source and destination colors, done using blending. Another example is shown in Figure 15.3.

Figure 15.3. Teapot rendered with RTSL shader using blend operator.

```
surface shader float4
fancy (texref env, texref marblebirds, float4 uv)
{
    float4 pre_env_color = {0.5, 0.2, 0, 1};
    matrix4 tex_mat = {{2.0, 0.0, 0.0, 0.0},
                       {0.0, 2.0, 0.0, 0.0},
                       {0.0, 0.0, 1.0, 0.0},
                       {0.0, 0.0, 0.0, 1.0}};

    float4 Cenv = pre_env_color * spheremap(env);
    float4 uv_birds = tex_mat * uv;
    return texture(marblebirds, uv_birds)
        blend(SRC_ALPHA,ONE_MINUS_SRC_ALPHA) Cenv;
}
```

Figure 15.4. RTSL shader using blend operator. blend_over is a shorthand for
this common use of the blend operator.

15.3.2 Integrate

The final feature that we will discuss in RTSL is the `integrate` operator. Integrate is similar in purpose to RenderMan's `illuminance` construct. RenderMan's illuminance has the appearance of a loop, where individual light shaders are run between executions of the loop body. The RTSL integrate operator has the appearance of a function call. It also implies a loop over the lights—the only form of loop in the language. Each light shader is executed between executions of integrate's single expression argument (Figure 15.5).

```
surface shader float4
simple_diffuse(float4 diffuse_color)
{
    perlight float diffuse = dot(N,L);
    return diffuse_color * integrate(Cl * diffuse);
}
```

Figure 15.5. Source of RTSL shader using `integrate` operator.

15.4 RTSL Implementation

The RTSL compiler uses standard tools for the early stages of compilation. The lights and surfaces are combined into a single combined shader (unrolling the `integrate` loop). This combined shader is factored into a *pipeline shader* with operations for the different stages of the graphics system. The pipeline shader assumes an abstract model of the graphics system, with a single rendering pass having an unlimited number of instructions available at each stage. Only when the pipeline program is mapped to actual hardware is it split, into multiple passes for fragment processing overflows and into separate host and vertex code for vertex processing overflows.

Portions of the code that will run on the host processor are handled differently for the different processor targets. The IRIX version generates C code, runs the C compiler to produce a shared object file, and dynamically loads the shared object—all as part of a single shader compilation. The i86 version (both Linux and NT) generates Intel object code directly, avoiding the need to start up a separate C compilation process.

The different fragment back-ends also use different approaches depending on the graphics hardware target. The multipass back end makes use of existing tools, while the register combiner back end is hand-coded.

15.4.1   Multipass Back-End

The multipass OpenGL back-end uses `lburg`, the code generation tool used by the `lcc` C compiler, and a relative of the `iburg` tool used by OpenGL Shader. The costs for RTSL's `lburg` rules depend on the capabilities of the target hardware platform. Rules for extensions that exist on only some of the target platforms have target-dependent costs. If the extension is not present, the cost is set to the maximum. Lburg seeds the labeling pass with this maximum cost; any rule with the maximum cost will never be chosen, as if it didn't exist. The only time the best labeling won't beat the initial maximum cost is when there is no way to execute the given sequence of operations.

Rules exist in the multipass back-end's lburg specification for all versions of a pass that might be used. This allows great control over the building of passes, but doesn't handle NVIDIA's register combiners extension well, since the huge number of options leads to an unmanageable number of rules. This lead to the creation of a register combiner back-end.

15.4.2   Register Combiner Back-End

The register combiner back-end targets only shaders that run in a single pass through NVIDIA's register combiners [110, 146]. Since the register combiner structure is relatively complex, this back-end is hand-coded to pack shader operations into the combiners as efficiently as it can.

Register combiners provide a sequence combiner stages with temporary registers for storing results between stages. For example, the GeForce3 has eight general combiner stages. Each combiner stage has separate RGB and alpha blocks that can be used independently (Figure 15.6). These blocks naturally fit either `float3` and or `float` operations. Any `float4`

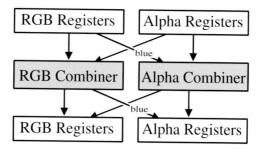

Figure 15.6. One register combiner stage

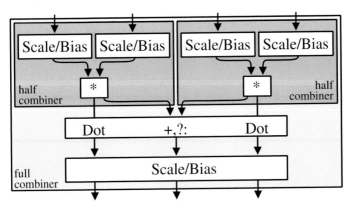

Figure 15.7. Register combiner stage as modeled by RTSL.

operations are rewritten into a pair of separate three-element and one-element operations so that they can be executed in different combiner stages if necessary.

RTSL models each combiner as two half combiners that can be combined (with certain conditions) into a full combiner. Each combiner contains several operations. The combiner inputs can be independently scaled and biased by selected powers of two. The combiner operates on signed numbers, so this allows values with a 0 to 1 range to be remapped into a -1 to 1 range. Each half of the combiner includes either a multiply or dot product. Together, the two multiply results can be accumulated, but only if neither half combiner used a dot product. It is also possible to select between the left-half and right-half combiner results based on whether an alpha register value is less than or greater than $\frac{1}{2}$. RTSL includes a lthalf() as a shorthand for this condition. The final results of half combiners and full combiner share a final scale and bias.

The back-end for register combiners uses a greedy algorithm, putting operations with the most dependencies early in the combiner chain to provide the most options for packing later operations. Interdependencies between operations in the combiners make efficient compilation difficult. For example, since output scale is shared, an output scale in one half combiner may force an countering input scale in the other half combiner, even if the two are performing completely unrelated operations.

16

ESMTL:
The Evans & Sutherland
Multitexturing Language

Procedural shaders combine a variety of local illumination and texture values to compute the color and opacity values that indicate the appearance of a surface. While in many cases, these shading procedures can be quite complex, in other cases they can be quite simple.

Recent procedural shader compilers, such as SGI's ISL (Chapter 14) and Stanford's RTSL (Chapter 15), are based on full-featured shading languages that resemble the Renderman shading language. Such tools are useful for complex procedural shaders, but when a developer wants to integrate a variety of rather simple shaders into a real-time application, these full-featured shader little-language compilers can be overkill.

The Evans & Sutherland Multitexturing Language is designed to compile simple one-liner shading expressions into real-time applications. A procedural shader in ESMTL is an expression of the surface, viewing, and lighting attributes. The shader returns an $RGB\alpha$ value that captures the appearance of the fragment. Shader expressions are functions of zero or more of the following variables: the surface normal N; the view vector V; the light vector L; the (light's) reflection vector R; and the the halfway vector H. The expression can apply a variety of operations on these attributes. The shading language takes advantage of texture shading for the evaluation of its results. For example, the shader expression

$$(.3, 0, 0) + [N.L] * (1, 0, 0) + [V.R]\hat{}9 * (1, 1, 1) \tag{16.1}$$

249

yields the shading shown previously in Figure 6.1. The ESMTL compiler creates an expression tree from the shading expression. This expression tree is then converted into multitexturing commands executed by the graphics hardware.

This shading expression uses texture shading to simulate Gouraud-interpolated Phong lighting. The texture coordinates for the texture shader are assigned per vertex as $(s = N \cdot L, t = V \cdot R)$. The remainder of the shading expression is precomputed and stored in a texture map using the formula

$$(.3, 0, 0) + s * (1, 0, 0) + t\hat{~}9 * (1, 1, 1) \qquad (16.2)$$

for s and t ranging from zero to one.

16.1 Bracketing

In the previous example, we could have set $t = (V \cdot R)\hat{~}9$ instead of $V \cdot R$. We chose not to do this because the result would have been poorly sampled. The user controls which expressions are evaluated as texture coordinates in the texture shader by bracketing them. Bracketing determines which expressions are generated as texture coordinates for a texture shader.

16.1.1 Scalar Bracketing

Bracketing a scalar value results in a one-dimensional evaluation of the result as a texture coordinate generation mode for automatically generating texture coordinates. For example, the expression

$$(.3, 0, 0) + [N.L] * (1, 0, 0) \qquad (16.3)$$

yields a one-dimensional texture map $(0.3 + s, 0, 0)$ which is texture-shaded onto the sphere by setting the texture coordinate s of each vertex of the sphere to $N \cdot L$.

Two bracketed one-dimensional expressions can be collected into a single two-dimensional texture shader, as demonstrated before in the Gouraud shading example, or one- and two-dimensional texture shaders could be combined into a single three-dimensional texture shader. The combination of independent texture shaders into a single texture shader takes more space. For example, two one-dimensional texture shaders take linear space, but their combination takes quadratic space. However, there is usually a fixed number of multitexture coordinate vectors available in a single rendering pass (currently four or six). This number does not change regardless of whether the texture coordinates are one-, two-, or even three-dimensional. The combination of independent texture shaders allows a single texturing

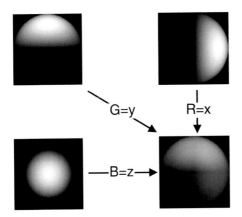

Figure 16.1. Sphere map of normal vectors. (See Color Plate XVIII.)

unit to serve multiple texture shaders, allowing more texture shaders to be applied in a given rendering pass.

16.1.2 Unit Vector Bracketing

Bracketing a unit vector (directional) quantity results in a two-dimensional projection of the quantity for reference into an environment-mapped texture shader. This projection of the unit vector quantity can be performed by using either a sphere map, cube map, or parabolic map.

A function depending solely on the unit vector quantity (and perhaps other constant values) is then precomputed for all possible unit vectors, and stored as an environment-mapped texture shader. Figure 16.1 shows the identity map implemented as an environment-mapped texture shader. It contains a sphere mapping of all possible unit vectors. (The coordinates of these vectors are displayed in RGB and assume the frame buffer is capable of representing negative values, which are clamped to zero in this image).

16.1.3 Interpolation of Bracketed Expressions

Bracketed expressions are evaluated at the vertices of the mesh and their resulting values are linearly interpolated across the polygon as texture coordinates.

The highlight is due to the term $(V \cdot R)^9 * (1, 1, 1)$. The expression $[V \cdot R]\hat{}9 * (1, 1, 1)$ sets a texture coordinate to $V \cdot R$ at each vertex, and interpolates the result of the dot product from the samples at the vertices.

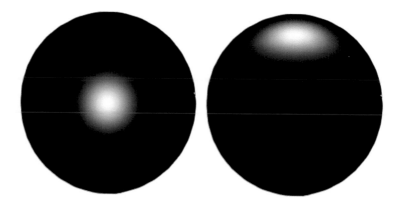

Figure 16.2. Sphere-mapped reflection vector and highlight.

This Gouraud interpolation can easily miss a highlight unless the highlight falls near one of the vertices.

The expression $(V.[R])\hat{}9*(1,1,1)$ performs a version of Phong interpolation for a fixed viewing direction (e.g., an orthographic view). It assigns a projection of the reflection vector to the texture coordinates (s,t). The texture shader is then computed from the expression $(V \cdot \mathrm{unmap}(s,t))^9(1,1,1)$, where $\mathrm{unmap}(s,t)$ returns the unit vector that would map to the point (s,t) in the texture map. This texture shader is shown in Figure 16.2 (left). This texture shader is applied to the object, the sphere in Figure 16.2 (right), by assigning the vertices of the sphere texture coordinates corresponding to the projection of the unit vector R.

Figure 16.3. Phong smooth-shaded sphere.

Figure 16.3 demonstrates Phong smooth shading on a sphere, expressed in ESMTL with the shader expression

$$(.3, 0, 0) + [N.L] * (1, 0, 0) + (V.[R])\hat{}9 * (1, 1, 1). \qquad (16.4)$$

16.2 Multipass/Multitextured Texture Shading

The shader expression will typically have more than two degrees of freedom and thus cannot be expressed as a single two-dimensional texture shader. For example, the Phong-shaded sphere in the previous section contained three degrees of freedom: one for the $[N \cdot L]$ and two for $[R]$. Hence, two texture shaders were used: a one-dimensional texture shader for the ambient and diffuse components, and a two-dimensional texture shader for the Phong specular highlight. These texture shader results are composited using multipass rendering.

The passes generated for the Phong example are:

1. $\text{tex1}[s = N \cdot L] \rightarrow \text{tex2}$

2. $\text{tex3}[s, t = \text{spheremap}(R)] \rightarrow \text{tex4}$

3. $\text{tex2} + \text{tex4} \rightarrow \text{tex5}$

Pass 1 takes the one-dimensional red ramp function texture shader generated and stored in texture #1 and applied it using $N \cdot L$ as the only texture coordinate to render a diffuse red sphere. The rendered red sphere is stored as texture #2. Pass 2 takes the highlight function rendering into the environment map stored in texture #3 and applies it to the object using a projected reflection vector for the texture as texture coordinates to place the gleam in the correct positon, and stores the result as texture #4. Pass 3 displays texture #2 on a single screen-filling polygon and adds the display of texture #4 to it, generating the final result, stored in texture #5.

Modern graphics cards support multitexturing, which makes multiple textures available in a single pass. The effect of multitexturing is to allow the combination of multiple independent renderings in a single pass. These independent renderings must be of the same model in the same pose, and in fact the only difference allowed between the renderings is the texturing (texture coordinates and texture map) of the surface.

16.3   Example: A Seeliger Skin Shader

A simple skin shader based on the Seeliger first-order approximation of diffuse reflection can be entered into ESMTL as

$$([N.L]/([N.L] + [N.V])) * (0.7, 0.4, 0.1). \tag{16.5}$$

This expresion brackets the values $N \cdot L$ and $N \cdot V$ so that the shading is computed per vertex and interpolated across the model. The quotient gives the skin a softer appearance with more light reflected near silhouette edges.

The shader is parsed into an expression tree and compiled into the following passes:

1. $\text{tex1}[s = N \cdot L] \rightarrow \text{tex2}$

2. $\text{tex3}[s = N \cdot L, t = N \cdot V] \rightarrow \text{tex4}$

3. $\text{tex2} / \text{tex4} \rightarrow \text{tex5}$

4. $(0.7, 0.4, 0.1) \rightarrow \text{tex6}$

5. $\text{tex5} \times \text{tex6} \rightarrow \text{tex7}$

This is a very simple compilation that avoids optimization for illustration purposes. For example, $[N.L]$ appears twice in the compiled output because we have not optimized common subexpressions. Moreover, the modulation by the skin's hue should be combined at an earlier stage to eliminate a modulation pass at the end.

The output and intermediate results appears in Figure 16.4. Texture #1 is a one-dimensional identity texture shader. Modern graphics cards now support a passthrough mode that allows interpolated texture coordinates to be treated as the fetched texture color. The identity texture shader is used to render $[N.L]$ at each vertex and interpolate it across the faces of the triangles, yielding the intermediate image in texture #2.

Texture #3 is the texture shader that implements the sum $s + t$ of its coordinates. Note that this sum exceeds the displayable luminance of the texture map. If the texture is clamped to $[0, 1]$, then the texture shader would need to instead store the function $(s + t)/2$ and scale the texture by two whenever it was used to avoid overflow and clamping. Texture #4 displays the sum texture shader using the coordinates $s = N \cdot L, t = N \cdot V$. The display of texture #4 is in this case saturated and clamped to one wherever $N \cdot L + N \cdot V$ exceeds one.

Figure 16.4.   Seeliger skin shader. Intermediate textures are shown above the final output.

Texture #5 displays the result of dividing texture #2 by texture #4. Quotients are currently not implemented in hardware. This operation could be performed by modulation with the inverse of the denominator, except that fixed-point representations are incapable of adequately storing the results of the multiplicative inverse. This resulting quotient is modulated by the constant texture #6 to yield the final rendering.

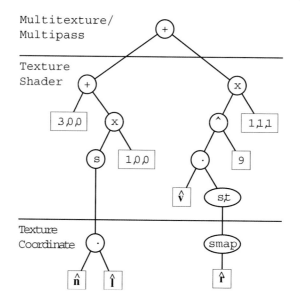

Figure 16.5. Correspondence of expression tree to shader levels.

16.4 Stratification

Shading expressions can be compiled in a variety of methods on the graphics processor. Graphics accelerators can perform operations at a variety of levels of processing. This section uses the term *strata* to describe these processing levels, and the term stratification to describe the process of breaking down a shading expression into the components that map to each graphics accelerator processing level.

Consider the Phong shading expression

$$(0.3, 0, 0) + (N \cdot L) * (1, 0, 0) + (V \cdot R)^9 * (1, 1, 1). \qquad (16.6)$$

This shader expression corresponds to the expression graph shown in Figure 16.5.

The shader expression is implemented across three levels of hardware abstraction: texture coordinate; texture shader; and multitexture/multipass.

Texture coordinate level: The bottom elements of the tree are computed as texture coordinates. These texture coordinates can be computed efficiently in the vertex shader, or even on the host if they are too complex.

In this case, the single texture coordinate of a one-dimensional texture map is set to the dot product of the normal and the light vector and the unit-length reflection vector is encoded as two texture coordinates that index into a second two-dimensional texture map.

Texture shader level: The middle elements of the tree are precomputed and stored in textures. The one-dimensional texture shader is precomputed as $(0.3, 0, 0) + s(1, 0, 0)$ for $s \in [0, 1]$. A two-dimensional texture shader is precomputed as $(V \cdot \text{unsmap}(s, t))^9 (1, 1, 1)$ for $(s, t) \in [0, 1]^2$. A correspondence is also drawn between the texture coordinates and the appropriate results of the texture coordinate level.

Multitexture/multipass level: The top elements of the tree are performed as multitexturing or multipass operations. Multitexturing operations can be performed in a single pass by combining the results of multiple fetches of texture shaders. If the number of inputs required by this level exceeds the number of multitextures, then the higher-level expressions are evaluated in multiple passes. In this example, the results of two texture shaders are added together.

It is interesting to note that the implementation of the expression tree to the graphics accelerator structure is bottom first. The most detailed levels of the expression tree are implemented in the vertex shader, which is processed first. The middle sections of the expression tree occur in the pixel shader, which is processed second. The top of the expression tree is implemented as texture and image combinations, which occur at the very end of the graphics pipeline. While it is common to draw the stages of the graphics pipeline progressing from the top to the bottom, the mapping of the expression tree to this structure inverts the expression tree, placing its leaf nodes at the top and its root at the bottom.

The Phong shading example could be compiled in a variety of manners. For example, a single three-dimensional texture shader could be used instead of two texture shaders. While this reduces the number of textures needed by the shader, the size of the three-dimensional texture shader is quite large in comparison to the alternative.

Another alternative is the encoding of the normal, light vector and view vector. These can be assigned as constant, per vertex or per pixel.

Compilers need to be aware of the resource tradeoffs available in the variety of implementations available for a given shader. These tradeoffs can sometimes be managed automatically by good optimizing compilers. However, the best implementation is often found through user intuition, and many real-time shader compilers provide mechanisms that allow the user to guide the stratification.

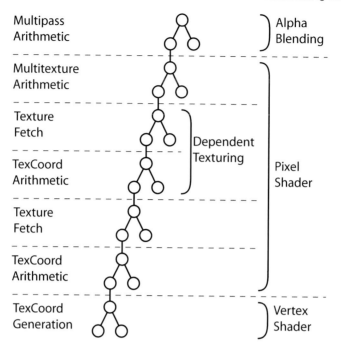

Figure 16.6. Mapping of expression trees to general shader strata.

Figure 16.6 describes the stratification into more general layers of graphics hardware.

TexCoord generation: Texture coordinate generation takes place by the application, either through the host or the vertex shader. This level assigns the texture coordinates per vertex and these coordinates are interpolated across the polygon during rasterization.

TexCoord arithmetic: Texture coordinate arithmetic occurs per pixel. The input is one or more interpolated texture coordinates at the current pixel. Its output is the location of a texture sample in one of the texture maps.

Texture fetch: The texture fetch performs a texture shading operation, by performing a look-up of a precomputed expression result. The input is current one, two, or three texture coordinates. The output is between one and four values stored in the channels of the texture map.

Dependent texturing: Dependent texturing allows the texture coordinate arithmetic and texture fetch stages to be repeated. The number of times these operations can be repeated is hardware-dependent. In this case, some of the texture coordinate are the result of previous texture fetches. This allows texture shaders to be sequenced. Texture shading allows us to encode arbitrarily complex functions as texture maps, but these maps have limited inputs. The ability to sequence texture shaders allows us to encode much more powerful expressions with more inputs.

Multitexture arithmetic: The result of the texture shaders can be combined in the pixel shaders with additional arithmetic operations. The number of pixel shader results that can be combined is limited by the total number of multitextures and the number of operations supported by the pixel shader.

Multipass arithmetic: When the complexity of the shader overruns the capability of the pixel shaders, the shader needs to be split among two or more pixel shaders. The result of each pixel shader is stored as a texture that can be redisplayed for further processing by a pixel shader. Alternatively, the results of independent pixel shaders can be combined using arithmetic operations implemented as image blending operations.

17

OpenGL 2.0

As of this writing, a proposal has been introduced for full shading language extensions to OpenGL, referred to as OpenGL 2.0 [1]. The proposal was created by 3DLabs, but has support from a large number of OpenGL ARB members. The proposal has already been through a couple of revisions. While some details of the proposal will certainly change between this writing and a final specification, most of what we describe in this chapter will still be correct by the time you read it.

Our coverage will be brief since many aspects of OpenGL 2.0 draw on previous shading systems. The OpenGL 2.0 shading language looks like a cross between C and Stanford's RTSL (Chapter 15). It differs from both in several important aspects, and these aspects are the focus of this chapter.

17.1   Logical Model

OpenGL 2.0 simplifies a number of aspects of OpenGL, replacing them with a high-level shading language. This language is used to map procedures directly onto the (current) division of hardware units. As such, the logical model diagram reflects the physical hardware organization. The stages include a high-level language for vertex and fragment processing stages as appear in DirectX (Figure 5.3). They also include a high-level interface for stages to *pack* and *unpack* pixel values as they are read in and out of the host processor. These pack and unpack shaders can map from color-mapped textures to RGB, or RGB to color-mapped on the fly, or do some forms of texture compression or decompression. The connection between these stages is shown in Figure 17.1.

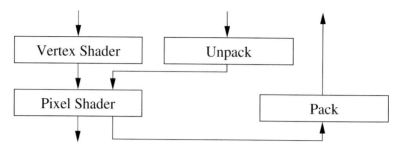

Figure 17.1. Logical model for OpenGL 2.0.

17.2 Data Types

The basic data types are int (only used in loops) and float. Vectors and matrices can be constructed from floats, vec2, vec3 and vec4 and mat2, mat3 and mat4. There is no concept of fixed-point or clamped numbers. It is assumed that these will not be an issue on future hardware supporting OpenGL 2.0, that full IEEE floating-point numbers or the equivalent will be in use at all stages of the graphics pipeline. This assumption was not possible for RTSL, which must target current hardware.

The aggregate vector and matrix types are constructed with a syntax similar to that used by RTSL. For example, a vec4 can be constructed as {float, float, float, float} or {vec3, float}. Matrices can be initialized with a long list of floats, or with a single float. The single float is cast into an identity matrix times the float value—similar to the float to matrix constructor in ISL.

Components or subvectors are accessed using a dot notation. For a vec4, v4, individual elements can be accessed using any of {v4.r, v4.g, v4.b, v4.a} or {v4.s, v4.t, v4.p, v4.q} or {v4.x, v4.y, v4.z, v4.w} or {v4.0, v4.1, v4.2, v4.3}. Arbitrary reordering or selection of subvectors is also possible using a notation that mimics the assembler-level vertex shaders [103], v4.rb = {v4.r, v4.b}. Matrix elements use two letters or numbers, with a _ as a sort of wildcard, so that m.03 is one element of a matrix, while m.0_ is a full row and m._3 is a full column.

Attached to any of these types can be one of several *type qualifiers*. These are similar to RTSL's computational frequencies: const = constant, uniform = primitive group, attribute = vertex, and varying = fragment. The subtle difference is that RTSL's computational frequencies refer to where a value is computed, while OpenGL 2.0's type qualifiers are spread across shader types. The vertex shader can read only from constant, uniform, or attribute variables, but places its results in varying variables for the fragment shader to use.

For uniform and varying values in the vertex shader only, all data types can be collected into C-style arrays, accessed with "[ ]".

17.3 Control Constructs

In a major difference from RTSL, OpenGL 2.0 has a full set of control constructs. These include if/else statements and C-style for, while, and do/while loops, all of which can be nested. Since this makes infinite loops possible. OpenGL 2.0 specifically allows an abort mechanism to break infinite loops (a concern for hardware which may otherwise lock up).

17.4 Functions

OpenGL 2.0 includes a typical set of shading functions, including common math library routines as well as vector math and shading functions. Functions were chosen according to three rules: those primitive functions that could not otherwise be expressed in the language, those common convenience functions that shaders use often, and those functions that might be accelerated by some platforms.

An example of the latter is a set of Perlin noise functions (with one-, two-, and three-dimensional versions) for building shading effects. Other real-time shading implementations have used texturing to achieve these noise functions rather than assume a built-in noise primitive. An implementation is free to choose whether to support the shading language noise function using texturing, or to use noise hardware if it is present.

Somewhat unusually for an interactive language, OpenGL 2.0 includes derivative operators Dx(expr) and Dy(expr), similar to RenderMan's Du(expr) and Dv(expr). These are expected to be computed using finite differencing. Some versions of the RenderMan Du and Dv have used finite differencing with nearby points on the same surface, providing derivatives at little extra cost (beyond a few extra border samples past the rendered edges). This method doesn't work as well in screen space since the neighboring pixels may not be part of the same object if they are beyond the object silhouette. So finite-difference computed derivatives can be expected to need extra samples, with some impact on performance. Related functions fwidth and lod return information about the size of a pixel or level in a texture map.

A final function of note is `kill(x)`, which stops processing of a fragment if $x \leq 0$. This allows shaders to include effects similar to those achieved with OpenGL's alpha, stencil, or depth tests without relying on the presence of those buffers, or managing its own auxiliary buffers.

17.5   Comparison

Having briefly outlined the OpenGL 2.0 shading langauge, how does it compare to the languages in Chapters 12-15? Certainly the language (with its complex expressions, full set of shading types and functions, and C-like control constructs) is higher-level than either ISL or RTSL, bearing more resemblance to pfman or RenderMan. Yet the logical model is taken directly from the current hardware, as described in Chapter 5.

As such, it suffers from the same mismatch from Chapter 4 between the physical organization of the hardware and the logical/functional breakdown shared by other real-time or software-based shading languages. To reiterate the conflict, say a typical technical artist[1] wants to describe a new surface appearance. Surface appearances include aspects of both vertex and fragment shading, so requires them to write shading code for both. They'd also like to use this surface appearance with a variety of procedural lights and procedural transformations.

If the vertex-shader aspects of the transformation and surface appearance are each packaged up as independent functions, a combined vertex shader can be easily created by calling them in succession. This provides a fair degree of flexibility, since these combined shaders are simple and can easily be generated at run time. Lights present a more complex problem since, like the surface appearance, they include both vertex and shader code. A single surface shader will also interact with many procedural lights in the equivalent of a RenderMan *illuminance* construct.

Fortunately, we've already got the solution, covered to some degree in every chapter in this part of the book. OpenGL 2.0 provides a fabulous cross-platform interface for the programmable aspects of the hardware. But, in the same way that RenderMan provides a more accessible shading-oriented interface to the programmability of a general CPU (or even a testbed renderer), we can use a shading language **above** OpenGL 2.0 to map the set of logical shading functions onto the physical breakdown provided by OpenGL 2.0. Since OpenGL 2.0 is that much closer to the end

---

[1]By which we mean someone who is comfortable writing shading code, but who doesn't know (or necessarily care) about the implementation differences between a software-based RenderMan renderer and hardware-based real-time shading.

shading languages, the task of creating this top-level compiler is a little simpler. Since the OpenGL 2.0 drivers will be optimized by each hardware vendor, a higher-level shading interface targeting OpenGL 2.0 will work well on a variety of platforms.

18

APIs

A shading API (application programming interface) is the interface an application uses to specify and control the shading programs run by a graphics accelerator. A detailed survey of graphics APIs is beyond the scope of this book. We will, however, present three representative and complementary examples of research-level APIs, or at least their shading subsystems. We will assume the reader is already familiar with OpenGL and DX8/9 and the various shading extensions supported by hardware vendors. The purpose of this chapter is not to act as a reference to existing APIs, but to illuminate some design choices that may influence the development of future APIs.

Two of the examples we will present support high-level shading programs written in a specialized external shading language. This is in contrast to the current machine-instruction-level OpenGL extensions used by NVIDIA and ATI to control their vertex shaders, register combiners, and fragment shaders [11, 12, 128]. Our discussion of these two APIs will focus on the integration of the shaders with the existing OpenGL API, rather than the languages themselves. The third example also starts with a low-level interface, similar in fact to that now used by ATI to specify shaders. In contrast to the use of a separate shading language with programs stored in strings or files, this API specifies instructions one function call at a time, thus avoiding the use of a parser, while making metaprogramming easier. This style of interface can make it easier to add a hierarchy of higher-level API constructs, eventually culminating in a high-level embedded shading "language" implemented by exploiting the language features of C++.

For any interface to a high-level shading language, there must be a way to tell the system about the shaders (or, as in our third example, to actually specify the shaders), a way to set shading parameters, a way to assign specific shaders to objects or lights, and a way to render using those shaders.

Our first representative example incorporates shading into the rest of the graphics API, but uses a separate shading language. Our example is PixelFlow's extensions to OpenGL. This approach is similar to that taken by OpenGL 2.0. The second example, OpenGL Shader, implements shading as a layer on top of the existing OpenGL graphics API. The third example, SMASH, extends the base API itself, as with the first example, but avoids the use of a separate parser by exploiting the capabilities of the C and C++ host languages to build an API that approaches the expressiveness of a specialized shading language.

18.1   PixelFlow

The PixelFlow shading API adds extensions to the graphics library to load shaders and set shader parameters. This API is based on OpenGL, but the shading language and the interface for specifying shaders is modeled after the RenderMan Interface [159, 171].

PixelFlow uses the OpenGL extension mechanism to add support for procedural shading. It was a requirement during the development of PixelFlow that the procedural shading extensions would have no impact on applications that did not use procedural shading, and that they fit as well as possible into the framework and philosophy of OpenGL. These extensions have been described in much more detail by Leech [97], but we will summarize them here.

Following the OpenGL standard, all of our extensions have the suffix EXT. We will follow that convention here to help make it clear what functions are already part of OpenGL and which were added. OpenGL functions also usually include additional suffix letters to indicate the operand types (f, i, s, etc.). For brevity, we will generally omit these in the text, though we will use them in the code examples.

18.1.1   Shading Parameters

Applications that do not employ procedural shading use a default OpenGL shader. This built-in procedural shader supports the standard OpenGL shading model. Parameters to the OpenGL shading model are set using the **glMaterial** call or one of a handful of other parameter-specific calls (**glColor**, **glNormal**, and **glTexCoord**). The OpenGL shading model uses a number of different color parameters (GL_AMBIENT_COLOR, GL_DIF-FUSE_COLOR, GL_SPECULAR_COLOR, or GL_EMISSIVE_COLOR). The **glColor** call can be assigned to set any one of these or the combination of ambient

```
glNormal3f(1.0, 0.0, 0.0);
glMaterialfv(GL_EMISSIVE_COLOR, white); // white is a float array
glVertex3f(0.0, 0.0, 1.0);
```

Figure 18.1. Typical OpenGL code for a vertex.

and diffuse. The other colors can still be set by **glMaterial**. Figure 18.1 shows some OpenGL code for one vertex using these calls. A triangle includes three similar vertices.

These same functions are used for setting parameters to other shaders. To handle arbitrary shading parameters, each parameter is assigned a parameter ID, which is used to identify it in the **glMaterial** call. The application can find a parameter ID using the **glMaterialParameterName-EXT** function. The **glNormal**, and **glTexCoord** functions are equivalent to using **glMaterial** with specific parameters of the shader (px_material_normal and px_material_texcoord). For example,

```
glNormalfv(normal);
glTexCoordfv(texcoord);
```

  is equivalent to

```
glMaterialfv(glMaterialParameterNameEXT("px_material_normal"),
             normal);
glMaterialfv(glMaterialParameterNameEXT("px_material_texcoord"),
             texcoord);
```

The various color parameters are equivalent to parameters named px_material_ambient, px_material_diffuse, px_material_specular, and px_material_emissive. By using parameters with these same names, user-written shaders can make use of the values that were set in the application using **glColor**, **glNormal**, and **glTexCoord**. These parameter names were chosen to avoid potential name conflicts with user-written shaders and to leave room for future extensions. All start with px_ to designate them as PixelFlow internal variables. This set of parameters also has material to designate them as material properties. In hindsight, since the set of parameters were defined before any shaders were written, it would have been easier for the users had shorter names been chosen.

18.1.2   Shader Instances

The RenderMan API allows some parameter values to be fixed when a shader function is chosen. The PixelFlow equivalent is to allow certain "bound" parameter values. A shading function along with its bound parameters together make a shader instance (or sometimes just given the

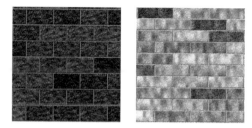

Figure 18.2. Two instances of the same brick shader. (See Color Plate XIX.)

confusing name *shader*) that describes a particular type of surface. Shader instances with bound parameter values allow us to define several surface types using the same shading function, for example, fat red bricks and thin yellow bricks (Figure 18.2, both using the brick function of Figure 13.3. We can easily choose one kind of brick or the other within the application by referring to the right shader instance.

A shader function describes how to create a certain class of surfaces, (e.g., "bricks"). To set bound parameter values, we add a **glBoundMaterialEXT** function, equivalent to **glMaterial** for bound parameters.

Shader functions are compiled in advance, but are loaded by calling the new API function **glLoadExtensionCode**. There are three new functions to create instances. The instance definition is contained in a **glNewShaderEXT**, **glEndShaderEXT** pair. This is similar to other OpenGL

```
// load the shader function
GLenum phong = glLoadExtensionCodeEXT(GL_SHADER_FUNCTION_EXT,"phong");
// create a new instance called red_phong
GLenum red_phong = glNewShaderEXT(phong);
        glShaderParameterBindingEXT(   // not bound, the default
        glGetMaterialParameterNameEXT("px_material_normal"),
        GL_MATERIAL_EXT);
    glShaderParameterBindingEXT(        // bound for this instance
        GL_DIFFUSE,
        GL_BOUND_MATERIAL_EXT);
glEndShaderEXT();

// set the bound value for the diffuse color parameter
float red[3] = .4,0,0,1;
glBoundMaterialfvEXT(red_phong, GL_DIFFUSE, red);
```

Figure 18.3. Code to create a PixelFlow shader instance.

capabilities; for example, display list definitions are bracketed by calls to **glNewList** and **glEndList**. **glNewShaderEXT** takes the shading function to use and returns a shader ID that can be used to identify the instance later. Between the **glNewShaderEXT** and **glEndShaderEXT** calls we allow calls to **glShaderParameterBindingEXT**. **glShaderParameterBindingEXT** takes a parameter ID and one of GL_MATERIAL_EXT or GL_BOUND_MATERIAL_EXT. This indicates that the parameter should be set by calls to **glMaterial** or **glBoundMaterialEXT** respectively. Figure 18.3 shows the code to create a shader instance.

The **glShaderEXT** call chooses a shader instance. This function takes a shader ID returned by **glNewShaderEXT**. Primitives drawn after the **glShaderEXT** call will use that shader instance.

18.1.3 Lights

OpenGL normally supports up to eight lights, GL_LIGHT0 – GL_LIGHT7. These lights are turned on and off through calls to **glEnable** and **glDisable**. Parameters for the lights are set by calls to **glLight**, which takes the light ID, the parameter, and the new value. All of these calls are shared for procedural lights. New light functions are loaded with **glLoadExtensionCodeEXT**, in the same way that new shader functions are loaded. New light IDs beyond the eight pre-loaded lights are created with **glNewLightEXT**.

Since OpenGL only supports eight lights, many applications reuse these lights within a frame. For example, all eight lights may be used in a single room of an architectural model. The positions and directions of the lights can be changed before rendering any polygons for the next room, giving the effect of more than eight lights, even though only eight at a time shine on any one polygon.

PixelFlow's use of deferred shading means that we cannot easily handle light changes within a frame. Each light, along with its parameter settings, is effectively a light instance in the same way that a shader with its bound shader parameters is a shader instance. This encourages a PixelFlow application to create a large number of lights, since each change in parameters requires a new light. To handle the enabling and disabling of a large set of lights, we create light groups. A new light group is created by a call to **glNewLightGroup**. Lights are enabled and disabled in the light group using the normal **glEnable** and **glDisable** calls. Within the frame we use **glEnable** with a light group ID to switch the active set of lights. Light groups may be a useful shorthand on other systems, but their primary purpose is to make light changes within a frame possible on PixelFlow.

18.2   OpenGL Shader

OpenGL Shader has taken a different tack from PixelFlow or OpenGL 2.0. Instead of making the shading API part of the graphics library, it is a separate library written on top of the graphics library. This has the advantages of working on current and future releases of OpenGL without requiring shading extensions and establishing a logical separation between shading language compiler and its target, just as the interface for programming a CPU is (usually) not only one high-level language. OpenGL Shader compiles the textual ISL language into commands for the underlying graphics library, which can be ordinary OpenGL, or can include shading extensions. For this type of compilation, assembler-level shading extensions are the most logical and useful [110].

It would seem that building an API on top of the graphics library might restrict the applications that use it, by requiring a specific scene graph[1] to store geometry, so that it can be rendered multiple times, or by passing all calls through new library interfaces. This latter approach of using one-for-one replacement graphics library calls is the one taken by the Stanford Real-Time Shading System, though even in that case, the library is designed to look like an OpenGL replacement. The call replacement is a necessary step if you want to operate on top of current graphics libraries without playing unportable tricks with the shared library loading order tricks.

18.2.1   Callbacks

Instead of placing those burdens on the application designers, the OpenGL Shader API relies on callbacks for non-shading operations that are normally under an application's control. There is one callback for drawing geometry and another for binding textures. These application-provided functions are used by OpenGL Shader, so the application can still manage its geometry and texture paging without interference from the shading library.

The texture binding callback receives the string texture name as specified in the shader and an anonymous data pointer for application-specific data. An application might use the data pointer, for example, to store a hash table of loaded textures. If a texture is already loaded, the callback just needs to call the **glBindTexture** function to make it active. The texture callback returns the number of dimensions in the texture so the internal shading code can know which OpenGL calls to make to turn it on

---

[1]A scene graph is a data structure that stores geometry, transformations, and other information about the scene [46].

and off later. The texture name is just a string, generally assumed to be a texture file name, but the application is free to use it as a base for flipping through a sequence of video frames, as an atlas texture, or as the first in a stack of files building a three-dimensional texture.

The geometry drawing callback also passes through an anonymous data pointer, typically used to point to the piece of scene graph being shaded. In addition, it has the number of multitexture units it is using if multitexture support is enabled, and a texture coordinate set ID number for each. The application can generate or switch between sets of texture coordinates based on this number.

When drawing an unshaded object, the application is on its own. When drawing a shaded object, the application calls OpenGL Shader, which will set some OpenGL state, possibly call for a texture load, then the geometry callback. Then it will set different state for the next pass and call the geometry callback again. This repeats until the object is fully shaded. After the shaded object has been rendered, control returns to the application.

18.2.2 Class Hierarchy

OpenGL Shader is implemented as a set of classes in a C++ library. The most basic class is **islShader**, which holds the source for a shader and provides interfaces for querying and setting parameters.

Two lists of **islShader**s, one for stacked surface effects and one for lights, are collected in an **islAppearance**. This contains everything you need to know about the appearance of an object. The stacked surface shaders are only of limited use, but can provide a means for adding decals or a glossy Fresnel reflective coat as separate shader effects on top of any other ISL shader. When using fog, it is just the last of these surface shaders.

The set of surfaces and lights in an **islAppearance** can be compiled by applying the **islCompileAction**. In order to fit cleanly into an application with its own graphical interface, all compiler errors are reported back through an error class, each including shader or file, line number, type of error, and the error message.

The top of the hierarchy is **islShape**. The class **islShape** holds information about both geometry (callback and application data) and appearance. A single **islAppearance** can be used for several shapes. A shaded object is drawn by applying the **islDrawAction** to an **islShape**.

An application can load and compile the shaders in advance, or update them on the fly. It may render any number of objects without shaders, intermixed with shaded objects. For each shaded object it applies an **islDrawAction** to the appropriate **islShape**.

18.3   SMASH

SMASH is an API for a real-time graphics system currently under development at Waterloo. This API is OpenGL-like, but an experimental approach was taken with the design of this API rather than attempting to make it strictly compatible. It is unlikely that SMASH will ever be adopted wholesale by a mainstream vendor; it is more of a testbed for API design ideas.

We will explain SMASH via a sequence of examples. SMASH is intended as a low-level API, and so our initial examples will look suspiciously like assembly language programs, although with virtualized storage resources. However, unlike string-based shader language interfaces, the base SMASH API is type- and syntax-checked at the time of compilation of the host language, and features of the host language can be used to manipulate shader programs conveniently and directly. In particular, modularity and control constructs in the host language can be "lifted" into the shader language, and this rapidly lets us build higher-level abstractions. We will refer to this style of API as a *metaprogramming* API.

The SMASH shader sub-API gives a way for the application program to build a shader program on the fly. On-the-fly (just-in-time) compilation is supported so that shaders can be optimized dynamically by the host program. Since current technology for optimized compilation of shader programs onto existing graphics hardware can complete in less than a second for a single-pass shader that uses all available resources, and current accelerators are not (yet) optimized to be compilation targets, just-in-time compilation appears to be reasonable [146], and has many advantages.

SMASH supports a stack-and-register expression language. Once a shader definition has been opened, individual API calls are used to add individual instructions to it; when a shader definition is complete, it is closed and then the driver compiles it. Other API calls exist to manage shader definitions, set compilation options, activate and deactivate a current shader, let the system know which shaders will be used in the near future (to optimize performance by pipelining shader loading), and so forth.

It should be emphasized that the abstract model of programming that SMASH uses is meant to be an efficient and flexible way to *specify* programs to an optimizing backend from front ends of various kinds. We most emphatically do *not* mean to imply that implementation of SMASH programs will necessarily use exact stack machine semantics, although a literal implementation is a convenient way to build a software interpretor for SMASH.

Storage for a shader program takes the form of a stack containing n-tuples of real numbers (with each tuple possibly being of different dimensionality) and a set of registers, also holding n-tuples. Conceptually the stack, the number of registers, and the length of items is unbounded. We do not define limits on registers, stack size, or shader length since the compiler may well optimize the shader and reduce the amount of memory needed. However, once a shader has been closed, the system can be queried to determine if the shader will be implemented using hardware acceleration or not.

As with OpenGL, SMASH will fall back to a software implementation if hardware acceleration is not feasible—although of course this may not result in the desired performance, since software implementation of fragment shaders will also require software rasterization.

Arithmetic operations act on the stack, popping operands off and pushing results on. For each operation simple rules determine the dimensionality of the result given the dimensionality of the arguments; many operations come in several forms that differ only in the dimensionality of the operands expected. For instance, multiplication will multiply elementwise tuples of the same dimensionality, but if given a scalar and an n-tuple as an argument, will multiply the scalar by every element of the n-tuple and generate a new, scaled n-tuple. The dimensionality of the tuples are fixed at compile time and so this overloading will not incur any performance penalty during execution of the shader.

Load and store instructions can pop data off the stack and put it in a register, can just copy the top of stack to a register, and finally can retreive data from a register and push it on the stack. Registers contain tuples of arbitrary lengths, but like stack items, these lengths are fixed at compile time. Registers can be allocated and deallocated in a stack-based fashion to facilitate use of nested scopes.

It is assumed that the back-end optimizes away unnecessary data movement operations and dead code, so programmers are free (and should be encouraged) to write "readable" code rather than trying to perform these relatively trivial optimizations manually.

The stack machine architecture proposed enables a simple metaprogramming API and in particular permits the semantics of the host language to be used for modularity. Due to the stack-based nature of SMASH's execution and register allocation model, there is little potential for naming conflicts; what remains can be resolved using the namespace and scope mechanisms of the host language.

For instance, shader "macros" can simply be wrapped in host language functions that emit the necessary sequence of shader operations inline into an open shader definition; likewise scoped names can be given to registers by naming their identifiers using scoped variables in the host language.

18.3.1 Definition

Definitions of shader programs are opened by the following call:

`SMshader` **smBeginShader()**

which returns an opaque identfier of type `SMshader` that can be used later to refer to the shader. Shader identifiers can be allocated only by the system, unlike the case in OpenGL with texture object identifiers.

Open shader definitions are closed, and compilation initiated on the current shader program, by the following call:

smEndShader()

At most one shader definition can be open at any one time.

Calls that can be used inside an open shader definition and *only* inside an open shader definition include the word **Shader**.

After calling **smEndShader** the system should be queried to determine if the shader program can be implemented using hardware acceleration and if so, how many resources it will consume. This can be done using the call

`SMdouble` **smShaderResources(**`SMshader` *s* , `SMenum` *r* **)**

with various values of the resource identifier *r*. To determine if a shader will be implemented using hardware acceleration, the resource `SM_SHADER_ACCEL` can be queried; a value greater than or equal to 100 indicates full hardware acceleration, a value less than that indicates that some fraction of the shader had to be performed with software assistance. Other resource tokens can be used to determine determine other metrics of performance, such as the number of passes, using resource `SM_SHADER_PASSES`. Of course, nothing beats benchmarking; the values returned by this call are meant only to be rough guides.

18.3.2 Activating Shaders

Shaders are made active using the following call:

smShader(`SMshader` *s* **)**

The active shader is also called the "current" shader. There can be only one active shader at a time.

Activating a shader also automatically activates and loads any associated texture objects. To maximize performance, shaders that share textures should be used in sequence; the system will detect this and avoid reloading an already loaded texture object.

To permit preloading of shader programs before they are actually used, the calls

smNextShader(SMshader *s*)
smNextShaders(SMsizei *n*, SMshader* *ss*)

hint to the system that the indicated shader(s) will be used in the near future and that the system should prepare to switch to them. When multiple shaders are hinted the ones with the lowest index in the array will be used the soonest. Whenever a hint call is made of either type it supercedes all previous hints. These calls should be made immediately after a call to **smShader** to maximize the time available for preparation. Violating a hint or omitting hints is not an error, but may reduce performance. Note that loading shaders is a fairly heavyweight process, since it potentially involves loading several textures.

18.3.3 Deleting Shaders

Finally, shaders can be deleted using

smDeleteShader(SMshader *s*)
smDeleteShaders(SMsizei *n*, SMshader* *ss*)

Deleting a shader does *not* delete any texture objects it uses. It is not mandatory to delete shader objects, but it may save resources.

18.3.4 Saving and Restoring Precompiled Shaders

The "shader object" abstraction is used because non-trivial compilation may be needed to map a shader program onto a given implementation, and also to permit fast switching between shaders when drawing a scene. However, while the intention is that compilation should be fast enough to take place during load time, very complex shaders might benefit from compilation during installation. Once a shader has been compiled for a particular graphics accelerator, a platform-dependent, opaque byte stream can be recalled, saved for later use, and restored using the following calls:

SMsizei **smShaderSize**(SMshader *s*)
smGetShaderProg(SMubyte* *prog*, SMshader *s*)
SMbool **smSetShaderProg**(SMint *s*, SMubyte* *prog*)

Storage for the array passed to **smGetShaderProg** must be allocated by the application program. If a byte stream has been previously stored, at load time the program needs only to check if the graphics hardware configuration has changed, since such precompiled byte streams are not intended to be portable. The **smSetShaderProg** call returns false if the shader could not be loaded—typically because it was compiled for a different platform. In that case, it must be respecified.

18.3.5   Executing Shaders

Shaders are normally executed during rendering of primitives. However, a shader can also be executed explicitly using the following call:

smExecShader(SMdouble p [4])

This executes the active shader, using the parameters on the parameter stack, at position p (specified using homogeneous coordinates) in model space—the point p is transformed, in the same way a vertex would be, by the current modelview matrix. Results must be read back using the following call:

smGetExecShaderColor(SMdouble c [4])

Right now shaders have only one result, a color. However, as we add possible outputs, for instance, to the view-space position to support displacement shaders, we can easily add more result functions. Executing shaders explicitly can be used for test purposes, but can also be used to sample points from textures or access other internal state accessible to shader programs.

18.3.6   Shader Programming Calls

Shader programming calls issue instructions into an open shader definition, and can be divided into declarations and operations.

Declarations control how the shader is implemented, define and allocate registers to hold intermediate results, and control how the shader interfaces with the outside world. Operations can be divided into categories: stack manipulation (for instance, pulling items out of the middle of the stack to support shared subexpressions, swapping items in the stack); arithmetic; comparisons (discontinuous functions that return 0 or 1, optionally with smooth transitions for antialiasing); logical operations; component manipulation; and register load/store. Operations cannot act directly on registers.

Parameter declaration and access

SMASH sets up parameters for binding to vertices using a parameter stack, rather than named parameters. Parameters for a shader must be declared in the order they are expected to appear on the parameter stack or in a parameter array. While it is not mandatory, for readability parameters should be declared before any other shader operations are specified.

Declaration is done with the following calls:

```
SMparam smShaderDeclareParam(SMuint n)
SMparam smShaderDeclareColor(SMuint n)
SMparam smShaderDeclareTexCoord(SMuint n)
SMparam smShaderDeclareNormal(SMuint n)
SMparam smShaderDeclareCovector(SMuint n)
SMparam smShaderDeclarePlane(SMuint n)
SMparam smShaderDeclareTangent(SMuint n)
SMparam smShaderDeclareVector(SMuint n)
SMparam smShaderDeclarePoint(SMuint n)
```

Declaration establishes both the type and the dimensionality n of the parameter. The type is used currently only for type-checking, but the dimensionality determines the size of the tuple pushed on the stack for parameter access operations. The opaque identifier returned by each call should be assigned to a variable with an evocative name for later reference.

Parameters are accessed with the following calls, which push a copy of the parameter onto the evaluation stack of the shader program itself:

```
smShaderGetParam(SMparam p)
smShaderGetColor(SMparam p)
smShaderGetTexCoord(SMparam p)
smShaderGetNormal(SMparam p)
smShaderGetCovector(SMparam p)
smShaderGetPlane(SMparam p)
smShaderGetTangent(SMparam p)
smShaderGetVector(SMparam p)
smShaderGetPoint(SMparam p)
```

Register allocation

Registers hold untyped tuples. They are allocated with the following call; the parameter n is the dimensionality:

```
SMreg smShaderAllocReg(SMuint n)
```

As with parameters, the opaque identifier returned by this call should be assigned to a host language variable with a useful name. It will be required later to refer to the register.

To facilitate use of subscopes, the call

smShaderBeginBlock()

records the current register allocation state, and the call

smShaderEndBlock()

restores the register allocation state in a last-in, first-out fashion; in other words, it deallocates all registers allocated since the last nested **smShaderBeginBlock** call.

To store a value in a register, one of the following calls should be used:

smShaderStore(SMreg r**)**
smShaderStoreCopy(SMreg r**)**

The **smShaderStore** call pops the value from the front of the execution stack and puts the item in the indicated register. If the dimensionalities do not match an error is generated. The **smShaderStoreCopy** call just copies the item from the front of the stack into the register but does not pop it.

To retreive an item from a register, the following call pushes it onto the execution stack.

smShaderLoad(SMreg r**)**

The value stored in the register is not disturbed.

Stack manipulation

For some stack manipulation instructions, items on the stack are referred to by integer offsets from the "front" of the stack. The 0th item is the item on the front of the stack, the 1st item is the next item on the stack, and so forth.

The drop operation discards k items from the front of the stack: The items dropped can be of any dimensionality, and need not all have the same dimensionality.

smShaderDrop(SMuint k**)**

The **smShaderPop** operation is just **smShaderDrop** with an implied argument of one. It is provided for consistency with "pop" operations defined elsewhere in the API.

The **smShaderDup** operation pulls any item out of the stack and pushes it onto the front. The original is not deleted, so the rest of the stack is not disturbed:

smShaderDup(SMuint k)

The **smShaderPush** operation is just **smShaderDup** with an implied operand of zero; it makes a copy of the item on the front of the stack.

Component manipulation

Each item on the stack is a tuple of elements. Component manipulation instructions permit items to be constructed from and decomposed into elements.

Conceptually, items are pushed onto the stack *highest element first*. This is important to understand since several operations in this section treat the execution stack as a sequence of elements, not items. For instance, if we push items (a_0, a_1, a_2), (b_0, b_1), and (c_0, c_1, c_2, c_3) onto the execution stack, in that order, then considered as a sequence of elements the execution stack will look like

$$a_2, a_1, a_0, b_1, b_0, c_3, c_2, c_1, c_0$$

Elements are numbered starting at the "front" or extreme right. In this example, c_0 would have element index 0, c_1 would have element index 1, b_0 would have element index 4, a_1 would have element index 7, and so forth.

The extraction operation permits direct access to items, and so can be used to assemble a new item from arbitrary elements of other items. The output of an extract operation can have a different dimensionality from any of its inputs. In fact, the dimensionalities of the inputs are basically ignored, but do have to be considered to compute the element indices. There are several versions of this operation; one general version that requires an array parameter, and several others with a fixed number of integer parameters for dimensionality 1 through 4:

smShaderExtract(SMsizei k, SMuint* e)
smShaderExtract1(SMuint ...)
smShaderExtract2(SMuint ...)
smShaderExtract3(SMuint ...)
smShaderExtract4(SMuint ...)

The extract operation does not disturb the existing items on the stack but generates a new item by pulling out the indicated elements and pushing the newly constructed item onto the stack.

The **smShaderSwap** operation exchanges the 0th and 1st item on the stack. Swapping the two bottom elements does *not* change any of the element indices of items higher on the stack, since the total number of elements on the bottom of the stack for the first two items will remain the same.

The **smShaderRev** operation reverses the order of elements in an item. Like the swap operation, it does not change the element indices of elements higher in the stack.

The **smShaderJoin** and **smShaderCat** operations join two items together into one by concatenating their elements. The join operation does this without changing the element indices, but this makes it seem like the second operand (on the front of the stack) is concatenated to the *left* of the first operand. The concatenate operation **smShaderCat** is equivalent to a swap followed by a join and has semantics more consistent with the arithmetic operators.

Finally, the split operation, invoked with

smShaderSplit(SMuint k)

splits all the elements of the item on the front of the stack and makes two new items of lower dimensionality. In pseudocode:

POP $(a_0, a_1, \ldots a_{k-1}, a_k, \ldots a_{n-1})$
PUSH $(a_k, a_{k+1}, \ldots a_{n-1})$
PUSH $(a_0, a_1, \ldots a_{k-1})$

The results will be of dimensionality k and $n - k$ if the input is of dimensionality n. The parameter k must be greater than or equal to 1 and less than or equal to $n - 1$. Note that if k is 1, then a scalar will be placed onto the front of the stack. If k is equal to $n - 1$ then the second item on the stack will be a scalar. To be consistent with the ordering of elements, the item on the front of the stack will be drawn from the *lower*-indexed elements of the item that was originally on the front of the stack.

Each new item must have at least one element; the parameter k must vary between 1 and n.

This operation does not change the element indices of any element on the stack, it just reclassifies elements into different items. A join operation reverses a split.

Constants

Constants may be pushed onto the execution stack with the following calls:

smShaderParam{**1234**}{**sifd**}(T p ...)
smShaderColor{**1234**}{**sifd**}(T p ...)
smShaderTexCoord[{**1234**}from]{**1234**}{**sifd**}(T p ...)

smShaderNormal{3}{sifd}(T p ...)
smShaderCovector{3}{sifd}(T p ...)
smShaderPlane{34}{sifd}(T p ...)
smShaderTangent{3}{sifd}(T p ...)
smShaderVector{23}{sifd}(T p ...)
smShaderPoint[4from]{234}{sifd}(T p ...)

These operations work exactly like corresponding parameter specification functions for vertices in immediate mode, except they push items onto the shader execution stack, not the parameter stack. Transformations are also applied as with the parameter specification functions, but these transformations are applied using the transformation matrices in effect at the time the shader is specified, *not* when the shader is run.

If you want to transform something explicitly using the transformations in effect at the time the shader is executed, use the transformation access and matrix multiplication operators.

Environment access

The shader may depend on information like model-space position, view-space position, view direction, and device-space position. These can be accessed with the following calls:

smShaderGetViewVec()
smShaderGetViewPos()
smShaderGetModelPos()
smShaderGetDevicePos()

The last actually returns a three-dimensional item containing the integer pixel position relative to the origin at the lower-left corner of the output image, and the depth value used for Z-buffering. The depth alone can be accessed with

smShaderGetDepth()

Under perspective using our usual conventions, the view vector and the view positions are negations of one another, but this is not necessarily always the case. In an orthographic view, for instance, the view vector is constant. The **smShaderGetViewVec** call uses the projection matrix to compute the correct view vector, by first back-projecting the eye point, then (if it is located at a finite position) subtracting the view-space position from it. It does *not* normalize the vector to unit length; the length of the view vector will be the distance to the eye from the point being rendered, in the viewing coordinate system. If the eye point is at infinity, as with an orthographic projection, then the view vector is set up to point in the correct direction but is not guaranteed to be of unit length.

Buffer access

The current value of the target pixel in the destination buffer can be obtained with the following call:

smShaderGetBuffer()

This pushes value of the destination sample in the destination buffer onto the execution stack.

This permits a simple interface to compositing operations, a fixed set of which are usually implemented at the end of the fragment pipeline on current accelerators. However, use of this feature followed by complex processing of buffer contents may force multipass execution of the shader.

Texture look-up

Texture accesses can be invoked by the following call:

smShaderLookup(SMtexture t**)**

This call takes the item off the front of the stack and uses it as a texture coordinate for a texture look-up in texture object t. The dimensionality of the item must match the dimensionality declared for the texture object, and the texture object must have been previously defined.

Arithmetic operations

For arithmetic operations, the execution stack should be visualized as a list written left-to-right, with the front (top-of-stack) item on the extreme right. Binary operators go between the two items on the right of this list. For non-commutative operators, the item on the front of the stack (item position 0) is the *right* operand and the item at position 1 is the *left* operand.

Arithmetic operators are overloaded on the dimensionality of their arguments. Two-operand arithmetic operators generally operate in one of three modes:

vector: $(\mathbf{R}^n, \mathbf{R}^n) \mapsto \mathbf{R}^n$.

In this case the two operands have the same dimensionality, and the operation is applied elementwise. Specifically, if $\oplus$ is the operator,

POP $(b_0, b_1, \ldots, b_{n-1})$
POP $(a_0, a_1, \ldots, a_{n-1})$
PUSH $((a_0 \oplus b_0), (a_1 \oplus b_1), \ldots, (a_{n-1} \oplus b_{n-1}))$.

The result will have dimensionality n.

left scalar: $(\mathbf{R}^1, \mathbf{R}^n) \mapsto \mathbf{R}^n$.

In this case the first operand (the second item on the stack, or equivalently the one just behind the front of the stack) is a scalar, and is applied to all elements of the second vector as the left operand of the operation.

Specifically, if $\oplus$ is the operator,

POP (b_0)
POP $(a_0, a_1, \ldots, a_{n-1})$
PUSH $((a_0 \oplus b_0), (a_1 \oplus b_0), \ldots, (a_{n-1} \oplus b_0))$.

The result will have dimensionality n.

right scalar: $(\mathbf{R}^n, \mathbf{R}^1) \mapsto \mathbf{R}^n$.

In this case the second operand (the front of the stack) is a scalar, and is applied to all elements of the second vector as the right operand of the operation, resulting in an output of the same dimensionality as the first operand.

Specifically, if $\oplus$ is the operator,

POP $(b_0, b_1, \ldots, b_{n-1})$
POP (a_0)
PUSH $((a_0 \oplus b_0), (a_0 \oplus b_1), \ldots, (a_0 \oplus b_{n-1}))$.

The basic two-operand arithmetic operators are invoked by the following calls:

smShaderMult()
smShaderDiv()
smShaderAdd()
smShaderSub().

The following unary operations are also defined:

smShaderNeg()
smShaderRecip()
smShaderSqrt()
smShaderRecipSqrt()
smShaderSq()
smShaderRecipSq()
smShaderProjDiv()
smShaderSum()
smShaderProd().

The **smShaderNeg** (negation), **smShaderSqrt** (square root), **smShaderRecipSqrt** (reciprocal square root), **smShaderSq** (square), **smShaderRecipSq** (reciprocal square), and **smShaderRecip** (reciprocal) calls operate on every element of a tuple separately, generating a new tuple of the same dimensionality.

The **smShaderProjDiv** call performs homogeneous normalization, multiplying every element of a tuple by the reciprocal of its last element. It generates a new tuple of dimensionality one less than its input tuple.

The **smShaderSum** call sums all elements in a tuple and generates a scalar. Likewise, **smShaderProd** forms the product of all elements in a tuple and outputs a scalar.

Transformations and matrices

The transformation matrix in effect at the time the shader is executed can be pushed onto the stack with the following call:

smShaderGetMatrix(SMenum *m*)

where *m* is one of SM_MODELVIEW, SM_TEXTURE, or SM_PROJECTION. This call pushes 16 elements onto the stack in row-major order. If for some reason you want only a submatrix, use an **smShaderExtract** operation to extract the elements you want; dead-code removal will eliminate the extra data movement if it is possible.

To push the inverse or adjoint of a standard matrix, use one of the following calls, each of which also pushes 16 elements:

smShaderGetInvMatrix(SMenum *m*)
smShaderGetAdjMatrix(SMenum *m*).

Note that the inverse is the the adjoint divided by the determinant. The determinant can be obtained separately:

smShaderGetDetMatrix(SMenum *m*).

Using these calls will likely be cheaper than computing an inverse explictly. Note as well that these will be the matrices in effect at the time the last vertex in the current triangle was specified.

To multiply a vector by a matrix or a matrix by a vector, use

smShaderMultVecMatrix()
smShaderMultMatrixVec().

The first operation treats the left operand as a row vector; the second operation treats the right operand as a column vector. The

smShaderMultMatrix(SMuint r, SMuint c**)**

operation multiplies matrices together and outputs a new matrix of the given numbers of rows r and columns c. The inner dimensions of the factors are inferred from their sizes and the size specified for the output matrices. This works on matrices of any size.

Square matrices can be inverted. This operation uses Cramer's rule to generate a closed-form expression, so it should not be used for matrices much larger than four dimensions:

smShaderInvMatrix().

In some situations, i.e., for projective geometry operations where constant scale factors cancel, the adjoint can be used in place of the inverse:

smShaderAdjMatrix().

Again, if you want only some elements of the inverse or the adjoint, use an extraction operation and the optimizer will get rid of the extra unused computations.

The determinant of a matrix can also be computed:

smShaderDetMatrix().

Matrices equivalent to the transformation calls defined for the immediate mode interface are also supported. Like the calls that manipulate the immediate-mode matrix stacks, these calls generate a matrix and postmultiply it onto an existing matrix:

smShaderRotateMatrix()
smShaderTranslateMatrix()
smShaderScaleMatrix().

The other parameters for these calls are located on the execution stack. For **smShaderRotateMatrix**, the stack should contain a 4×4 matrix, a scalar angle, and a three-dimensional unit-length axis vector. These will be popped off and replaced with a transformed matrix. The **smShaderTranslateMatrix** call expects an $n \times n$ matrix and an $(n-1)$-dimensional vector, generates a translation matrix, and postmultiplies it by the given matrix. The **smShaderScaleMatrix** call expects an $n \times n$ matrix and an n-dimensional vector, generates a diagonal scale matrix, and postmultiplies it by the given matrix. If the scale vector is of length $n-1$, the last scale factor is taken to be 1. Note that **smShaderMult** can be used for uniform scaling.

Finally, the identity and an arbitrary constant matrix can be loaded onto the execution stack. These calls do not replace the item on the bottom of the stack, they push on new items:

smShaderLoadIdentityMatrix(
    SMuint r, SMuint c)
smShaderLoadMatrixd(
    SMuint r, SMuint c ,
    SMmatrixd m).

Obviously, matrix operations can potentially use a lot of resources, although in the end they just boil down to a sequence of arithmetic and extraction operations.

Geometric operations

Geometric operations perform standard operations on vectors and points. While easily definable in terms of basic arithmetic and element manipulation operations, defining them explicitly is helpful to both the programmer and possibly the compiler.

They are given as follows:

smShaderDot()
smShaderCross()
smShaderLen()
smShaderSqLen()
smShaderRecipLen()
smShaderRecipSqLen()
smShaderNorm()
smShaderDist()
smShaderSqDist()
smShaderRecipDist()
smShaderRecipSqDist().

The **smShaderDot** operation computes a dot (or inner) product. It works on tuples of any dimensionality, and produces a scalar. The **smShaderCross** operation computes a cross product. It takes two three-tuples as input and produces a three-tuple as output.

The **smShaderLen** operation computes the Euclidean length of a tuple; it operates on tuples of any dimension. The **smShaderSqLen** operation computes the squared Euclidean length of a tuple; the **smShaderRecipLen** operation computes the reciprocal of the Euclidean length of a tuple; the **smShaderRecipSqLen** operation computes the reciprocal of the squared Euclidean length of a tuple. Like the **smShaderLen** operation, these work on tuples of any dimensionality.

The **smShaderNorm** operation normalizes a tuple to unit length, and works on tuples of any dimensionality. The **smShaderDist** operation computes the Euclidean distance between two tuples of any dimensionality, and **smShaderSqDist**, **smShaderRecipDist**, and **smShaderRecipSqDist** compute the square, reciprocal, and squared reciprocal of that value.

Standard mathematical functions

The SMASH API defines a number of standard mathematical functions. Ultimately, functions equivalent to most built-in RenderMan shading language functions will be defined to make the conversion of RenderMan shading programs to SMASH shaders easier. Note that most of these "built-ins" will probably be implemented as macros and so will not require extra support from the driver. They will be defined, however, in case an accelerator *would* want to provide direct support.

To evaluate trigonometric functions, use the following calls, which work elementwise on tuples:

smShaderSin()
smShaderArcSin()
smShaderCos()
smShaderArcCos()
smShaderTan()
smShaderArcTan()
smShaderArcTan2() .

The **smShaderArcTan2** call takes two tuples of the same dimensionality as arguments. The elements of the first are interpreted as $r\sin(\theta)$ values, the second as $r\cos(\theta)$ values. Angles are always measured in radians.

Noise

Randomness is a critical component of many shaders. SMASH provides the following noise generation calls:

smShaderHash()
smShaderVNoise()
smShaderPNoise().

The **smShaderHash** function computes a hash value between zero and one, based on each element of its input tuple. This value will appear random, but will be repeatable.

The **smShaderVNoise** function computes value noise between zero and one. At each point on a grid with unit spacing, a hash value will be computed, and then over the cell linear interpolation will be performed. The input is a multidimensional index into the grid. This noise is inexpensive, but will not look as nice as Perlin noise. Its cost will also grow exponentially with dimensionality as the number of vertices at the corners of each cell grows.

The **smShaderPNoise** function computes derivative-continuous Perlin noise bounded over $[0, 1]$ with a unit-cell spacing. This will look nicer than value noise but may be more expensive to compute.

Different platforms may use different hash functions and noise generators, so application developers should not expect features generated by noise functions to be consistent across platforms.

Discontinuities

The following functions results in hard discontinuties, and so should be used with care:

smShaderMax()
smShaderMin()
smShaderClamp()
smShaderAbs()
smShaderSgn()
smShaderStep()
smShaderFloor()
smShaderCeil()
smShaderSelect().

The **smShaderMax** operation compares two tuples elementwise and keeps the larger of each element. If a scalar and a tuple are compared, the scalar is first replicated to the same dimensionality as the tuple. The **smShaderMin** operation is similar, but keeps the smaller of each element. The **smShaderAbs** operation computes the elementwise absolute value of each element of a tuple. The **smShaderClamp** operation limits each element in its input to the range $[0, 1]$. The **smShaderSgn** operation computes the elementwise signum function of each element of a tuple (i.e., the output is -1 if the element was negative, zero if it was zero, and one if it was positive). The **smShaderStep** function is a step function, returning zero for negative or zero values and one for positive values. The **smShaderFloor** function finds the largest integer less than or equal to each element of its input. The **smShaderCeil** function finds the smallest integer greater than or equal to each element of its input.

Finally, the **smShaderSelect** function is used as a kind of "if statement". It takes three arguments: two items of the same dimensionality and a scalar. If the scalar is negative or zero, the first item is taken, otherwise the second item is taken.

Versions of the previous functions with soft transitions are also provided, and are important for writing antialiased shaders. They all take an additional scalar argument on the stack, which should be the width of the transition region. The exact functions used are implementation-dependent but should be derivative-continuous:

smShaderSMax()
smShaderSMin()
smShaderSClamp()
smShaderSAbs()
smShaderSSgn()
smShaderSStep()
smShaderSFloor()
smShaderSCeil()
smShaderSSelect() .

Discarding fragments

The following calls consume a single scalar from the execution stack:

smShaderRejectOpen()
smShaderRejectClosed()

For **smShaderRejectOpen**, if that value is positive and greater than or equal to zero, then the fragment is retained. Otherwise, if the value is negative, the fragment is rejected. For **smShaderRejectClosed**, if that value is strictly positive, then the fragment is retained. Otherwise, if the value is negative or zero, the fragment is rejected.

These operations always execute at the highest frequency level available; if you use them inside a subshader, they will be "pushed down" to a finer level. Multiple rejections are permitted in a shader. A fragment is rejected if *any* rejection test passes.

Indicating results

Every shader has to call the function that sets the output color:

smShaderSetColor().

The input tuple can be one-, two-, three-, or four-dimensional. A one-dimensional item will be interpreted as a luminance and the alpha will be set to one. A two-dimensional item will be interpreted as a luminance plus alpha. A three-dimensional item will be interpreted as an opaque RGB color (alpha of one). A four-dimensional item will be interpreted as an RGBA color.

18.3.7   Subshaders

Often parts of a shader can be evaluated at low resolution and interpolated, and when this is possible, it will generally be a performance win. The simplest example is the evaluation of "smooth" parts of a shader at vertices, such as the diffuse irradiance. The results of these per-vertex evaluations can then be interpolated to fragments, where the shader computation can be completed using the rest of the shader.

The mechanism SMASH uses to specify subshaders permits a shader first to be written at the finest resolution level available and tested. Then, to identify a part of the shader program which can be evaluated at a lower resolution, wrap the desired subexpressions in the following calls:

smBeginSubShader(SMenum *level* **)**
smEndSubShader().

Currently, *level* must be one of:

```
SM_CONSTANT
SM_PRIMITIVE
SM_VERTEX
SM_SUBVERTEX
SM_FRAGMENT
SM_SAMPLE.
```

Constant shaders are defined and evaluated once at shader definition time. Primitive shaders are defined for every **smBegin/smEnd** block. Vertex shaders are evaluated at each vertex of a primitive. Subvertex shaders are evaluated at the vertices of primitives that are subdivided internally (i.e., subdivision surfaces, displacement maps). Fragment shaders are evaluated at every pixel fragment. Finally, the finest level of detail may be the sample, in the case of multisampled antialiasing. On systems without multisampling the fragment and sample levels will be identical. By default, shaders are evaluated at the finest possible level.

Subshaders cannot depend on any result computed at a finer level of detail, but otherwise the evaluation semantics are unchanged. Note that to implement SMASH shaders in their full generality, *all* resolution levels need to support identical sets of operations, including, for instance, texture lookups at vertices. While it would be possible to limit the operations that can be used at each level, and such shaders would be forward-compatible with more general systems [146], such restrictions are undesirable as they could be a source of portability problems and complicate programming.

The syntax given above for subshaders can be extended to other purposes. For instance, part of a shader could be identified for automatic approximation using a particular technique, or part of a shader could be identified for tabulation and storage in an unnamed texture object.

18.3.8 Base Example

Now for the examples. We will use as a running example an implementation of a two-term, single light source, separable reflectance model [83, 114]. We will assume that four parabolic hemicube maps are defined to hold the factors of the two-term separable BRDF approximation. This gives, for example, a good approximation of brushed metal using the Poulin/Fournier reflectance model [83, 145]. The variables a, b, c, and d will be predefined to hold the appropriate texture object identifiers. The values stored in a, b will be unsigned fixed-point values over $[0, 1]$, but will require a common scaling three-color aAB to represent values over a wider range. The values stored in c and d will also be over $[0, 1]$ but will represent *signed* factors over a potentially wide range, and so will require biases of bC and bD and another common scaling three-color of aCD. The pointers aAB, bC, bD, and aCD will refer to appropriate predefined three-element arrays. Because of this biasing and scaling, several operations will be required in the shader simply to "unpack" these textures.[2]

---

[2]We may modify the texture API in the future to include scaling and biasing as part of the definition of texture objects. For now, and for the purposes of this example, we will state these operations explicitly.

In the following sections, we will implement a separable BRDF shader expression for a single point source. We will start with the simplest and lowest-level metaprogramming technique, the macro, and then work up to higher-level shader programming techniques.

18.3.9 Macros

Macros are implemented using host language functions that emit shader operations as side effects; they are lifts of the procedure modularity concept into the shader language from the host language. This lets us use the naming scope mechanism of the host language, with a little bit of help from the API, to strongly encapsulate shader modules.

The following conventions are used for writing macros:

- Pass operand(s) and result(s) on the stack.

- Consume all parameters.

- Leave undisturbed any values higher on the stack than the macro's parameters.

- Use **smShaderBeginBlock** before issuing any other shader operations and issue **smShaderEndBlock** afterwards. The **smShaderBeginBlock** call pushes the current number of registers allocated onto a stack; calling **smShaderEndBlock** at the end of the macro definition restores the count of the number of registers allocated by popping it from the stack. This encapsulates register allocation and usage.

  We suggest using registers for storing intermediate results to enhance readability. In the example we also show how to name registers; by wrapping shader definitions in host language scope blocks that match the register allocation and deallocation blocks, register names can be limited in scope and so isolated from the rest of the program.

With these conventions, macros are syntactically indistinguishable from built-in API calls. This is an important and useful feature, as it permits macros to be used to enhance portability while providing a growth path for the API.

If a particular hardware vendor wants to provide a hook to some special feature of their hardware (say, bump-mapped environment maps, a new noise function, whatever), they should first write a "compatibility macro" using the standard operators guaranteed to be available on all implementations. Then, in the driver for their particular system, the standard instructions would be replaced with an appropriate hook into the special feature. User-level programs would not change, and would not even have to be recompiled if a dynamically linked library is used for the required macro package. If precompiled shaders are used, this still works if compilation takes place upon installation; of course, every time the program runs, it should make sure it is using the same graphics subsystem for which it was installed.

On the other hand, if some set of utility macros comes into wide use, a hardware vendor can add explicit support for these macros to their hardware. In any case, all shaders can be portable across all hardware that supports the base shader instruction set.

Certain macro packages may have initializers that declare and initialize texture objects or other information. For instance, "math" macros to implement special functions via table look-up might be useful. An implementation could support a set of useful, "built-in" macros of this nature (as well as other useful, more specific macros, such as the orthonormalization macro used in this example). Because of the need to allocate hidden texture objects, the use of "specified" texture object identifiers (and shader identifiers) is *not* supported. A programmer *must* use system-allocated identifiers, and their internal structure is opaque. While shader and texture identifiers are guaranteed to take the same amount of space as a pointer, they are not to be considered equivalent to pointers (or integers), and an implementation should not depend on their exact value, range, or internal structure.

A shader defined using macros is shown in Figures 18.4 through 18.7. The function `FrameVector` defined in Figure 18.4 outputs shader instructions that generate texture coordinates for a separable BRDF approximation, given a unit-length light source vector, a unit-length normal, and a tangent on the stack. The normal and a tangent are *not* assumed orthonormal. This permits the use of a constant "global" tangent along the axis of a surface or near-surface of revolution, a handy technique to add tangents to objects that don't have them as part of their definition.

The **smShaderDup** and **smShaderExtract** operations used in this example, as well as register store and load operations, will usually be zero cost after compilation and optimization, but they are convenient in this case to specify the data flow. To reiterate, the SMASH API just specifies an expression tree which will be rebuilt inside the driver, then an internal mapping onto the implementation architecture will take place, with its own specific optimization algorithms. For instance, for processor-based shaders, register allocation will be performed to minimize the total storage required to implement the specified expression, and scheduling will reorder the operations to maximize usage of the processor's functional unit(s).

```
/** Compute coordinates of normalized vector relative to frame.
 * in: â, b̂, ĉ: frame vectors normalized to unit length
 * out: p⃗: surface texture coordinates (3D hemisphere map index) */
void
FrameVector () { // â, b̂, ĉ, v⃗
  // Save register allocation state
  smShaderBeginBlock(); {
    // Allocate new registers
    SMreg v = smShaderAllocReg(3);
    SMreg a = smShaderAllocReg(3);
    SMreg b = smShaderAllocReg(3);
    SMreg c = smShaderAllocReg(3);
    // Put arguments into registers
    smShaderStore(v);        // â, b̂, ĉ
    smShaderStore(c);        // â, b̂
    smShaderStore(b);        // â
    smShaderStore(a);        // <empty>
    // Compute coordinates of v⃗ relative to â, b̂, ĉ
    smShaderLoad(c);         // ĉ
    smShaderLoad(v);         // ĉ, v⃗
    smShaderDot();           // (ĉ·v⃗)
    smShaderLoad(b);         // (ĉ·v⃗), b̂
    smShaderLoad(v);         // (ĉ·v⃗), b̂, v⃗
    smShaderDot();           // (ĉ·v⃗), (b̂·v⃗)
    smShaderLoad(a);         // (ĉ·v⃗), (b̂·v⃗), â
    smShaderLoad(v)          // (ĉ·v⃗), (b̂·v⃗), â, v⃗
    smShaderDot();           // (ĉ·v⃗), (b̂·v⃗), (â·v⃗)
    smShaderJoin();          // (ĉ·v⃗), ((â·v⃗), (b̂·v⃗))
    smShaderJoin();          // p⃗ = ((â·v⃗), (b̂·v⃗), (ĉ·v⃗))
    // Release registers
  } smShaderEndBlock();
} // return p⃗
```

Figure 18.4. Definition of a macro to project a vector against a frame. This is basically a $3 \times 3 \times 3$ matrix-vector product, but with the matrix assembled from three vectors. Note that the driver can easily ignore any extraneous data movements, i.e., the movement of the arguments to and from registers.

18.3.10 Textual Infix Expressions

A stack-based shading language can sometimes be inconvenient, particularly if complex data flow requirements must be specified. The addition of registers to the programming model makes it unnecessary to use the stack for intermediate results. However, it is also relatively easy to define some conventions for a simple textual language for shader expressions that can be compiled on-the-fly to shader operations. By implementing some functions in a utility library to give string names to parameters, texture objects,

```
/** Orthonormalize one vector against a normalized vector
 * in: t⃗: target vector; unnormalized
 *     b̂: base vector; normalized to unit length
 * out: v̂: orthonormalized target vector */
void
Orthonormalize () { // t⃗, b̂
  // Save register allocation state
  smShaderBeginBlock(); {
    // Allocate and name registers
    SMreg b = smShaderAllocReg(3);
    // Store base vector
    smShaderStore(b);        // t⃗
    // Orthonormalize
    smShaderDup(0);          // t⃗, t⃗
    smShaderLoad(b);         // t⃗, t⃗, b̂
    smShaderDot();           // t⃗, (t⃗·b̂)
    smShaderLoad(b);         // t⃗, (t⃗·b̂), b̂
    smShaderMult();          // t⃗, (t⃗·b̂)b̂
    smShaderSub();           // v⃗ = t⃗ − (t⃗·b̂)b̂
    smShaderNorm();          // v̂ = v⃗/|v⃗|
  // Release registers
  } smShaderEndBlock();
} // return v̂
```

Figure 18.5. Definition of a macro to orthonormalize one vector against another.

and registers, this can be made convenient, yet we can freely intermix such string-based infix expressions and macro or base API calls.

Here are the conventions and functions we propose for the smu utility library:

- The **smuBeginTexture** function wraps **smBeginTexture** but, in addition, inserts a string name into a symbol table. Square brackets will be used after a texture object name in a string-based shader expression to indicate texture lookup.

- The special names %i refer to the ith item on the stack.

- The special names #i refer to the ith element on the stack.

- The comma operator can be used to concatenate items. In particular, this permits the formation of items out of individual elements.

- Parameters can be referred to by names defined in **smuShaderDeclare*** calls. These calls differ from their **smShaderDeclare*** namesakes in that only a string name is associated with the parameter.

```
/** Compute coordinates of halfvector and difference vector relative
 * to local surface frame.
 * in:  n̂: normal covector; normalized to unit length
 *      ū: tangent vector; may be unnormalized, non-orthonormal
 *      l̂: light vector; normalized to unit length
 * out: p̂: half vector surface coords (3D hemisphere map index)
 *      q̄: difference vector surface coords (3D hemisphere map index) */
void
HalfDiffSurfaceCoords () { // n̂, ū, l̂
  // Save register allocation state
  smShaderBeginBlock(); {
    // Allocate and name registers
    SMreg h = smShaderAllocReg(3);
    SMreg t = smShaderAllocReg(3);
    SMreg s = smShaderAllocReg(3);
    SMreg n = smShaderAllocReg(3);
    SMreg tp = smShaderAllocReg(3);
    // Compute normalized half vector ĥ
    smShaderGetViewVec();     // n̂, ū, l̂, v̄
    smShaderNorm();           // n̂, ū, l̂, v̂
    smShaderAdd();            // n̂, ū, h̄ = l̂ + v̂
    smShaderNorm();           // n̂, ū, ĥ
    smShaderStore(h);         // n̂, ū
    // Generate full surface frame from n̂ and ū
    smShaderSwap();           // ū, n̂
    smShaderStoreCopy(n);     // ū, n̂
    Orthonormalize();         // t̂
    smShaderStoreCopy(t);     // t̂
    smShaderLoad(n);          // t̂, n̂
    smShaderSwap();           // n̂, t̂
    smShaderCross();          // ŝ = (n̂ × t̂)
    smShaderStore(s);         // <empty>
    // Orthonormalize t̂ against ĥ
    smShaderLoad(t);          // t̂
    smShaderLoad(h);          // t̂, ĥ
    Orthonormalize();         // t̂'
    smShaderStore(tp);        // <empty>
    // Coordinates of ĥ relative to (t̂, ŝ, n̂)
    smShaderLoad(t);          // t̂
    smShaderLoad(s);          // t̂, ŝ
    smShaderLoad(n);          // t̂, ŝ, n̂
    smShaderLoad(h);          // t̂, ŝ, n̂, ĥ
    FrameVector();            // p̂ = ((t̂·ĥ), (ŝ·ĥ), (n̂·ĥ))
    // Coordinates of v̄ relative to (t̂', ŝ', ĥ)
    smShaderLoad(tp);         // p̂, t̂'
    smShaderLoad(h);          // p̂, t̂', ĥ
    smShaderDup(1);           // p̂, t̂', ĥ, t̂'
    smShaderCross();          // p̂, t̂', ŝ' = (ĥ × t̂'))
    smShaderLoad(h);          // p̂, t̂', ŝ', ĥ
    smShaderGetViewVec();     // p̂, t̂', ŝ', ĥ, v̄
    FrameVector();            // p̂, q̄ = ((v̄·t̂'), (v̄·ŝ'), (v̄·ĥ))
  // Release registers
  } smShaderEndBlock();
} // return p̂, q̄
```

Figure 18.6.   A macro to compute texture coordinates for a separable BRDF
approximation using the reparameterization proposed by Kautz and McCool [83].

```
/** Local reflectance model using two-term separable BRDF approximation.
 */
SMshader sepbrdf = smBeginShader(); {
    // allocate and name parameters
    SMparam C = smShaderDeclareColor(3);
    SMparam L = smShaderDeclareVector(3);
    SMparam T = smShaderDeclareTangent(3);
    SMparam N = smShaderDeclareNormal(3);
    // Allocate and name registers
    SMreg p = smShaderAllocReg(3);
    SMreg q = smShaderAllocReg(3);
    // Compute surface coordinates (using vertex shader)
    smBeginSubShader(SM_VERTEX);
        smShaderGetNormal(N);          // n̂
        smShaderGetTangent(T);         // n̂, t⃗
        smShaderGetVector(L);          // n̂, t⃗, l̂
        HalfDiffSurfaceCoords();       // p̂, q⃗
    smEndSubShader();
    // Put interpolated surface coordinates in registers
    smShaderStore(q);                  // p̂
    smShaderStoreCopy(p);              // p̂
    // Compute BRDF
    smShaderLookup(a);                 // a[p̂]
    smShaderLoad(q);                   // a[p̂], q⃗
    smShaderLookup(b);                 // a[p̂], b[q⃗]
    smShaderMult();                    // ab = a[p̂] * b[q⃗]
    smShaderColor3dv(aAB);             // ab, α
    smShaderMult();                    // AB = ab * α
    smShaderLoad(p);                   // AB, p̂
    smShaderLookup(c);                 // AB, c[p̂]
    smShaderColor3dv(bC);              // AB, c[p̂], β1
    smShaderAdd();                     // AB, bc = c[p̂] + β1
    smShaderLoad(q);                   // AB, bc, q⃗
    smShaderLookup(d);                 // AB, bc, d[q⃗]
    smShaderColor3dv(bD);              // AB, bc, d[q⃗], β2
    smShaderAdd();                     // AB, bc, bd = d[q⃗] + β2
    smShaderMult();                    // AB, bcd = bc * bd
    smShaderColor3dv(aCD);             // AB, bcd, γ
    smShaderMult();                    // AB, CD = bcd * γ
    smShaderAdd();                     // f  =  AB + CD
    // Compute irradiance and multiply by BRDF
    smBeginSubShader(SM_VERTEX);
        smShaderGetVector(L);          // f, l̂
        smShaderGetNormal(N);          // f, l̂, n̂
        smShaderDot(N);                // f, (l̂·n̂)
        smShaderParam1d(0);            // f, (l̂·n̂), 0
        smShaderMax();                 // f, s = max((l̂·n̂), 0)
        smShaderGetColor(C);           // f, s, c
        smShaderMult();                // f, e = s * c
    smEndSubShader();
    smShaderMult();                    // f * e
    // Set output fragment color
    smSetColor();                      // <empty>
} smEndShader();
```

Figure 18.7. Top level of the definition of a shader that implements a two-term separable approximation to a BRDF assuming a single directional light source.

- Registers can also be referred to by names defined in a **smuShader-AllocReg** call, which differs from **smShaderAllocReg** in that only a string name is associated with the register. Assignments can also be made to registers using the "=" operator at the beginning of an expression; this executes a **smShaderStore** operation, so the result is *not* left on the stack after an assignment.

- Arithmetic infix operators act on n-tuples using the same dimensionality rules as the associated operators **smShaderMult**, **smShaderDiv**, **smShaderAdd**, **smShaderSub**, and **smShaderNeg**. Other operators have the same name as those in the shader language proper but take extra arguments for their operands, use all lower case, and drop the `smShader` prefix. The vertical bar is used to indicate a dot product and the circumflex is used to indicate a cross product. Operator precedence is the same as in C for compatibility with operator-overloaded utility libraries in C++; for dot and cross product to work as expected, it is suggested that they always be enclosed in parentheses.

- All names (i.e., for texture objects, parameters, and registers) share a common name space. However, a name defined by the user will take preference over those of built-in functions. More precisely, built-in functions are defined in an outermost "system" scope, and names defined by the user are automatically in a name scope nested inside the system scope. The functions **smuShaderBeginBlock** and **smuShaderEndBlock** push and pop register allocation and environment frames and so create scopes and subscopes for names.

- The functions **smuShaderAllocReg** and **smuShaderDeclare*** return identifiers just like **smShaderAllocReg** and **smShaderDeclare***. If you use *just* the infix operators you can ignore these return values. If they are retained they should be assigned to `SMreg` and `SMparam` variables with the same names as the strings used in the infix expressions.

Finally, the utility function

smuShaderExpr(`char* ` *string*)

converts an expression given in the string argument into an appropriate sequence of base API calls to execute the operations specified in the string. An example is shown in Figure 18.8, using our running example of a separable BRDF reconstruction for two terms and one light source.

```
/** Local reflectance model using two-term separable BRDF approximation.
 * Uses infix expression compiler to simplify expression of the shader.
 */
SMshader sepbrdf = smBeginShader(); {
    // allocate and name parameters
    SMparam C = smuShaderDeclareColor(3,"C");
    SMparam L = smuShaderDeclareVector(3,"L");
    SMparam T = smuShaderDeclareTangent(3,"T");
    SMparam N = smuShaderDeclareNormal(3,"N");
    // Allocate and name registers
    SMreg p = smuShaderAllocReg(3,"p");
    SMreg q = smuShaderAllocReg(3,"q");
    // Compute surface coordinates using macro
    smBeginSubShader(SM_VERTEX);
        smShaderGetNormal(N);
        smShaderGetTangent(T);
        smShaderGetVector(L);
        HalfDiffSurfaceCoords();
    smEndSubShader();
    // Put interpolated surface coordinates in registers
    smShaderStore(q);
    // Another (silly) way of doing the above
    smuShaderExpr("p = %0");
    // Compute BRDF
    smShaderColor3dv(aAB);
    smuShaderExpr("%0*a[p]*b[q]");
    smShaderColor3dv(bD);
    smShaderColor3dv(bC);
    smShaderColor3dv(aCD);
    smuShaderExpr("%0*(c[p]+%1)*(d[q]+%2)");
    // Compute irradiance and multiply by BRDF
    smBeginSubShader(SM_VERTEX);
        smuShaderExpr("C*max((L|N),0)");
    smEndSubShader();
    smShaderMult();
    // Set output fragment color
    smSetColor();
} smEndShader();
```

Figure 18.8. A rewrite of the example shader to use the textual infix expression compiler defined in the utility library and named parameters and registers. We still show only the main shader here and still use the macros defined earlier.

18.3.11 Textual Shading Languages

The above approach uses only a small part of a compiler; thus, macros and infix expressions can be freely mixed. A complete textual shading language could also be defined. Because of the common back-end compiler and extensive support for optimization expected in the driver, however, this can be a simple syntactic transformation. The transformation can be done on the fly, or by using a separate program. Syntax analysis and transformation can be easily implemented using the yacc/lex or the bison/flex compiler-compiler systems, for example.

Following the initiative of the group at Stanford [146], a type system can be used to distinguish quantities to be computed at different levels of detail (i.e., vertices versus fragments). The textual language should also have the capability to explicitly set precision requirements.

18.3.12   Object-Oriented Toolkits

You can also lift object-oriented modularity constructs into the shader language. For instance, you can build a shader expression graph from object instances, and then provide a function to "walk" the graph in postfix order and emit appropriate base API calls. Garbage collection is essential in this case to avoid insanity—fortunately, since only DAGs are required, this can be implemented using a reference-counting "smart pointer" or "handle" class in C++.

The running example implementing the separable BRDF is repeated in Figure 18.9 using a very simple set of object constructors; the **SmExpr** classes are in fact reference-counting "smart pointer" classes that, once initialized with a pointer to an object, start tracking references to those objects. Whenever the last reference is removed from an object, the smart pointer "releasing" the object automatically deletes it.

By wrapping object constructors in functions that take handles (smart pointers) and dynamically allocate new nodes but return such handles rather than pointers, we can simplify the syntax for defining each new expression node. Reference-counted garbage collection also permits the use of nested expressions, so we can avoid having to declare and name all the intermediate expression nodes. We can also use a namespace to simplify the names for the constructor functions and other parts of the SMASH API. Consider the example given in Figure 18.10.

Finally, if we use operator overloading for these constructor functions, we can use simple expressions to specify shading expressions. An example is given in Figure 18.11. Although it looks similar to the RenderMan shading language, this "shading language" differs from the use of a textual shading language, since operator overloading is fully type- and syntax-checked in the host language at compile time, while we retain all the power of metaprogramming (i.e., programmer-controlled specialization). The only things really missing are specialized constructs such as RenderMan's `illuminate`, but we can easily use alternative approaches to support equivalent functionality. In the case of `illuminate`, a utility library function could be implemented that executes a (host language) `for` loop over light sources and

```
/** Local reflectance model using two-term separable BRDF approximation.
 * Builds up DAG as a C++ data structure. */
SMshader sepbrdf = SmBeginShader(); {
    // allocate and name parameters
    SmExpr nC = new SmShaderDeclareColor(3,"C");
    SmExpr nL = new SmShaderDeclareVector(3,"L");
    SmExpr nT = new SmShaderDeclareTangent(3,"T");
    SmExpr nN = new SmShaderDeclareNormal(3,"N");
    // Compute surface coordinates using macro
    SmExpr nseq = HalfDiffSurfaceCoords(nN,nT,nL);
    SmExpr nvsc = new SmSubShader(SM_VERTEX,nseq);
    SmExpr nvp = new SmIndex(nseq,0);
    SmExpr nvq = new SmIndex(nseq,1);
    // Compute BRDF
    SmExpr na = new SmShaderLookup(a,nvp);
    SmExpr nb = new SmShaderLookup(b,nvq);
    SmExpr nalpha = new SmShaderColor3dv(aAB);
    SmExpr nab = new SmShaderMult(na,nb);
    SmExpr nAB = new SmShaderMult(nalpha,nab);
    SmExpr nbeta1 = new SmShaderColor3dv(bC);
    SmExpr nbeta2 = new SmShaderColor3dv(bD);
    SmExpr ngamma = new SmShaderColor3dv(aCD);
    SmExpr nc = new SmShaderLookup(c,nvp);
    SmExpr nd = new SmShaderLookup(d,nvq);
    SmExpr nalpha = new SmShaderColor3dv(aAB);
    SmExpr nbeta1c = new SmShaderAdd(nc,nbeta1);
    SmExpr nbeta1d = new SmShaderAdd(nd,nbeta2);
    SmExpr ncd = new SmShaderMult(nbeta1c,nbeta1d);
    SmExpr nCD = new SmShaderMult(ncd,ngamma);
    SmExpr nf = new SmShaderAdd(nAB,nCD);
    // Compute irradiance and multiply by BRDF
    SmExpr nz = new SmShaderParam1d(0);
    SmExpr ndot = new SmShaderDot(nL,nN);
    SmExpr nmax = new SmShaderMax(ndot,nz);
    SmExpr nC = new SmShaderGetColor(C);
    SmExpr ne = new SmShaderMult(nC,nmax);
    SmExpr nve = new SmSubShader(SM_VERTEX,ne);
    SmExpr nfe = new SmShaderMult(nf,nve);
    // Traverse and compile DAG
    SmShaderCompile(nfe);
    // Set color
    smSetColor();
} SmEndShader();
```

Figure 18.9.   The shader DAG can be expressed using a data structure built up object by object. The **SmShaderCompile** function propagates subshader information, then traverses the DAG and emits the appropriate shader instructions for each node. We assume that submacros have been redefined to take and return DAGs.

```
/** Local reflectance model using two-term separable BRDF approximation.
 * Builds up DAG as a C++ data structure, but uses smart pointers and
 * constructor functions.  Also assumes a namespace to reduce the
 * length of names. */
SMshader sepbrdf = beginshader(); {
    // allocate and name parameters
    Expr C = declarecolor(3);
    Expr L = declarevector(3);
    Expr T = declaretangent(3);
    Expr N = declarenormal(3);
    // Compute surface coordinates using macro
    Expr sc = subshader(VERTEX,HalfDiffSurfaceCoords(N,L,T));
    // Access elements of returned sequence
    Expr nvp = index(sc,0);
    Expr nvq = index(sc,1);
    // Compute BRDF
    Expr f = add(
      mult(
        mult(lookup(a,nvp),lookup(b,nvq)),
        color3dv(aBC)
      ),
      mult(
        mult(
          add(lookup(c,nvp),color3dv(bC)),
          add(lookup(d,nvq),color3dv(bD))
        ),
        color3dv(aCD)
      )
    );
    // Compute irradiance and multiply by BRDF
    Expr e = subshader(VERTEX,
      mult(
        C,
        max(
          dot(L,N),
          param1d(0.0)
        )
      )
    );
    // Multiply irradiance by BRDF
    Expr fe = mult(f,e);
    // Traverse and compile DAG
    fe->compile();
    // Set color
    setcolor();
} endshader();
```

Figure 18.10. Functional specification of shader using constructor functions. A C++ name space can be used to make the names of the constructor functions less verbose without polluting the global name space.

```
// wrap constants and texture identifiers
// (would really do at point where textures defined)
Color<CONST> alpha(3,aBC), beta1(3,bC), beta2(3,bD), gamma(3,aCD);
Texture A(a), B(b), C(c), D(d);

/** Local reflectance model using two-term separable BRDF approximation.
 * Builds up DAG as a C++ data structure, but uses smart pointers,
 * constructor functions, and operator overloading. */
Shader sepbrdf = beginshader(); {
    // allocate and name parameters
    Color C(3);
    Vector L;
    Tangent T;
    Normal N;
    // Compute surface coordinates using macro
    Expr<VERTEX> p, q;
    HalfDiffSurfaceCoords(p,q,N,L,T);
    // Compute BRDF
    Expr f = alpha*A[p]*B[q] + gamma*(C[p]+beta1)*(D[q]+beta2);
    // Compute irradiance and multiply by BRDF
    Expr<VERTEX> e = C*max((L|N),0.0));
    Expr fe = f*e;
    // traverse and compile DAG
    fe->compile();
    // Set output fragment color
    setcolor();
} endshader();
```

Figure 18.11. Functional specification of shader using constructor functions that are bound to overloaded operators. Operators act on operator trees (shader expressions), not data. There are several templated subclasses of smart pointers to handle declarations, subshaders, etc. The declarations shown at the top would usually be handled at the point of definition.

that calls previously registered function pointers to invoke shader macros for each light, then issues shader instructions to accumulate the results. If C++ is used instead of C, such an approach is to be preferred over the use of the **smuShaderExpr** function.

The statements where we "wrap" constants and texture objects (using smart pointer subclasses that automatically invoke the appropriate constructor functions) could be omitted if we did this at the point of declaration of the constants and texture objects. Wrapping in the case of texture objects is necessary for the use of operator overloading of the square bracket operator for the `lookup` operation. We also add wrapping functionality to other subclasses of the smart pointer type to help declare parameters. Likewise, subshader and type attributes can be set using template parameters to the smart pointer classes. Registers are not required; the host language provides equivalent functionality through the use of variables, and the compiler can detect sharing and allocate registers internally to describe this sharing to the API.

The main point of all these programming examples is that several syntaxes and approaches to programming shaders are possible, but do *not* need to be built into the base API. Syntax is a type of user interface: a linguistic one. Several such user interfaces are possible for specifying shaders, and are appropriate for different kinds of users at different times. In fact, although we gave no examples, visual interfaces to programming shader specifications are also possible and for many users desirable.

By providing a basic, low-level API, SMASH does not force use of a particular high-level shader language but hopefully enables the straightforward implementation of a variety suited to different purposes and users. At the same time, a standard C++ utility library can be provided that gives nearly all the expressiveness of a specialized textual shading language.

Part IV

And Beyond

This final part explores the developments in graphics hardware we expect to see over the next few years, and how the ideas covered in this book will apply if and when our expectations become reality.

19

Predicting the Present

This book describes numerous methods for using (and misusing) existing features in graphics hardware to implement and accelerate advanced shading algorithms. But graphics hardware is a fast-moving area and the features that were available at the time of this writing may be outdated by features available to the reader. This chapter provides some context on both what our assumptions were about the direction shading hardware was going, and how the concepts of the book will apply and adapt to this brave new world: the ever changing present.

Over the same time frame covered in this chapter, general-purpose CPUs will also likely evolve. It may even be that graphics accelerators and CPUs will become indistinguishable. However, at the moment, GPUs have certain specialized features, such as a deep texture prefetch pipeline and hardware implementation of rasterization algorithms. These specialized computational resources give them a large performance advantage over general-purpose CPUs for graphics operations that will probably persist for at least the next few years.

19.1 Predicting the Recent Past

At the time this book was written (the beginning of 2002), support for procedural shading in graphics accelerators was in a state of flux.

Real-time procedural shading was first demonstrated on custom hardware at the University of North Carolina, Chapel-Hill, then on commercial graphics hardware by SGI through multipass rendering. The popularity of real-time shading took off when NVIDIA added advanced multitexturing in the GeForce2, then direct support for procedural shading in consumer-level hardware with floating-point per-vertex computations and integer per-pixel computations (with some limited extensions to the range and precision of per-pixel computations) in the GeForce3. Along with these capabilities came many extensions to OpenGL to support them. NVIDIA also introduced many other changes to the conceptual model of the accelerator and to the API, such as a new mechanism for specifying smooth surfaces efficiently. Many of these extensions make other parts of OpenGL obsolete.

In August 2001, ATI Technologies responded with their own vertex and fragment shading system, but with a different set of OpenGL API extensions to interface with it. ATI also has their own mechanism to extend the geometry capabilities of their accelerators.

In order to address the danger of a fragmented OpenGL API, a proposal for OpenGL 2.0 was floated, spear-headed by 3DLabs, that included a standard built-in shading language based in part on Stanford and SGI's shading languages. If a high-level language can be agreed upon, not only will it be easier to implement the techniques described in this book, but it will also free the hardware designers from an overly restrictive conceptual model. However, striking the right balance between ease of use and control of the hardware will be a very difficult design task.

Information on the DX9 API from Microsoft, which includes Direct3D, was also made public in late 2001. This unofficial advance information (actually, a presentation given by Microsoft [116]) included indications of significant advances in support for shaders beyond that available in DX8. Since Microsoft bases Direct3D features on the expected features of next-generation hardware, it's pretty clear that these features will probably be available on hardware accelerators sometime soon.

19.2   Increasing Range and Precision

Fully programmable floating-point computations are already available from several vendors, including ATI and NVIDIA, at the vertex level. Limited hardware support for fragment-level floating point is available in pixel copy operations on SGI's hardware and in the texture shader[1] operations on NVIDIA's GeForce3 and later GPUs. In neither case is this precision carried through to the fragments written into the frame buffer. However, we

---

[1]The term "texture shader" has been used to describe arithmetic on texture coordinates that occurs before a fetch operation (or in place of a fetch operation). Perhaps a better term for this is "texture coordinate shading" or better yet "texture coordinate arithmetic." This differs from our use of "texture shader" as a method for storing and retrieving precomputing shading computations in the texture memory.

expect graphics accelerators with fully programmable floating-point *fragment* shading units to appear soon. They will probably already be available by the time you read this.

The Microsoft DX9 proposed feature set for Direct3D, which of course is not yet official, includes both floating point programmable fragment shading capabilities as well as floating-point texture and buffer storage formats. The inclusion of floating point buffers and textures is important, since it means that it will be possible to implement multipass algorithms with full floating-point precision. Half-precision 16-bit floating point formats are also specified to save on bandwidth when 32-bit single precision is not needed. The fragment shaders will be also capable of writing to multiple outputs, which will again make it easier to write complex multipass shaders. Finally, this proposal also states that the programming model of the fragment unit will use an instruction set similar to that of current vertex shading units, with the addition of texture lookup operations. This will help simplify compilers, as compilers can target a common instruction set.

As mentioned above, floating point is already available on a per-fragment level in the NVIDIA GeForce3, in the "texture shader" units. Unfortunately, this unit is not programmable, and the floating-point computational capabilities in this unit cannot be used for programming arbitrary computations. One of the main limitations of the GeForce3 architecture is that all values must be quantized to eight bits before being written to the destination buffer, and textures cannot hold more than 16 bits of precision (and that only with particular and specialized storage modes that are not directly compatible with values written to buffers). So, while floating-point computations already exist at the fragment level in current accelerators, floating-point values cannot be passed between stages of a multipass shader.

Higher fully programmable range and precision, specifically 16-bit fixed point (one sign bit, 3-bit integer, 12-bit fraction), is also now available from ATI in the Radeon 8500. While better than the 8 bits plus sign available on the GeForce3, it's still not quite enough for many shading operations. For example, the results of these computations are used for dependent texture lookups. The GeForce3 uses floating point computation for all texture address computations, since dependent texturing takes place in the floating point texture shading units of the GeForce3. In some circumstances, for example extreme projective distortion with repeated textures, the large dynamic range of floating point is mandatory. Because of this, the implementation of some effects will be easier on one system than another, with no clear advantage to either. The GeForce3 will be fabulous at certain things (those for which the floating-point texture shader unit is suitable,

like bump-mapping) but not others (such as procedural Phong lighting).
The ATI Radeon 8500 will be good for many tasks, but is limited by the
limited precision and range.

Why do we want floating point? Simple: While 8 bits is (almost) adequate to represent the result of a shader computation, if correctly gamma
corrected, it is *not* adequate for intermediate values. This is because
mathematical operations that scale up a value will also enlarge the "gaps"
between input quanta. This can happen with simple scaling by values
greater than one, but it can also happen with nonlinear operations where
the derivative is greater than one. If the precision is just barely adequate
to avoid the perception of gaps, then *any* such scale will reveal them. You
don't need anything as complex as the Mandelbrot shader in Figure 14.4
to reveal precision limits. Also, floating-point values have greater precision
near zero, which is usually where we need it perceptually when representing
color.

Even to implement something as simple as the Phong lighting model,
which has a large nonlinearity in the form of an exponentiation, high precision is needed to avoid visible contouring. An example is given in Figure 19.1. In this figure, we compare a procedurally evaluated lighting
model with one evaluated using values stored in a texture map. Even
though the procedural lighting model uses only a small exponent (because
we must evaluate exponentiation by repeated multiplication) the nonlinearity causes severe contouring artifacts. The texture-based lighting does
not suffer from these defects, even though the values in the texture map
are only 8-bit. This is because values stored in the texture map are interpolated, so we can afford to use a higher exponent. As we have discussed
earlier, texture-based lighting of this nature can also be antialiased simply
by MIP-mapping the texture and turning on normal texture filtering.

However, the advantages of texture-based lighting may be temporary.
The programming model used for this example—the register combiner extensions from NVIDIA—use an abstraction of operating on numbers between $[0, 1]$. When an accelerator with floating-point fragment computations becomes available (from NVIDIA, anyway), it is likely that the same
register combiner program will run with higher precision and the procedural lighting model here will not show any contouring. Therefore, one can
consider the current accelerators as "prototyping systems." Procedural
lighting models will run, but they probably won't look pretty until you get
the higher precision of future floating-point fragment computation units.

Lighting and reflectance models based on texture access have bandwidth, storage, and performance penalties that procedural models do not.
It should theoretically be possible to switch between procedural lighting

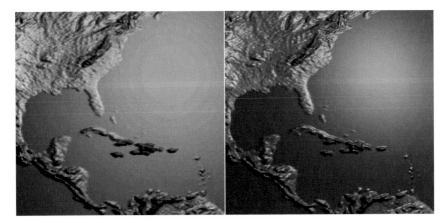

Figure 19.1.   Precision effects in the evaluation of lighting models. Left: a bump-mapped surface with the Blinn-Phong lighting model evaluated using 8-bit precision in the register combiners of the GeForce3. Notice in particular the contouring around the highlight. Right: the same bump-mapped surface, but with the lighting model computed from stored texture values. Computing the lighting model in advance on the host means that we can use higher precision computations. This implementation also keeps most of the computation in the texture shading unit, so higher-precision normals (16-bit) can be used and combined with the half-vector using floating-point operations. Finally, the lighting model on the right uses a higher Phong exponent than the model on the left, which (a) can't use a large exponent due to limits in the number of register combiner operations available and (b) would look even worse with a large exponent (and a larger nonlinearity).

models faster than between texture-based lighting models, assuming that the procedures can be represented more compactly than the corresponding texture values and the programs used to combine them. Whether this theoretical advantage becomes a real advantage depends on whether the hardware vendors support loading of programs in a manner which is at least as efficient as the loading and caching of texture samples, and whether a given application *requires* rapid switching between multiple shaders.

Light in real scenes also has a huge dynamic range. If we want to compute using physical units, we need a representation that can handle this range conveniently. We need to ultimately apply some tone-mapping operation to compress this range to something viewable on the display device. However, we still need that range for intermediate results if we wish to perform physically based computations.

Finally, more advanced applications of programmable shaders might involve manipulation of geometry, not just color information. For instance, a fragment shader might be written to evaluate a partial differential equation over a discretized grid to simulate the motion of cloth. To render the results, the image computed by the fragment shader needs to be reinterpreted as a polygon mesh. If both geometry and color use a common data format, such advanced applications become easier.

When we say floating point, we mean single-precision IEEE floating point. It is unlikely that double-precision floating point will appear in the near future, unless (or until) graphics accelerators start being used for applications that would demand it, such as advanced physical simulation.

19.3   Real-Time RenderMan versus Real-Time Toy Story

RenderMan was used to render the scenes in Pixar's *Toy Story*, as well as in other movies by Pixar. It is interesting to note that RenderMan was originally conceived as a hardware API ([99]), although it has drifted from this heritage and today is used mostly[2] as an interface to non-real-time software renderers.

We are getting close to the point at which we can equal or surpass the rendering quality of the scenes in *Toy Story* on real-time systems. With the addition of floating-point computation in the graphics accelerator, it will be possible to create a complete accelerated RenderMan implementation [138]. However, the shaders used for RenderMan software rendering are not necessarily the shaders you would write for real-time rendering. The RenderMan shaders for software rendering can be thousands of lines of code, and tend to use much more computation as compared to real-time shaders that perform better with texture-based algorithms. We are very close to "real-time RenderMan" for some shaders, but not necessarily the exact shaders used in a movie like Toy Story.

Systems like RenderMan are also a moving target. For instance, hardware graphics accelerators have not matched recent developments in Pixar's internal rendering engines, such as deep shadow maps [104], necessary for rendering antialiased shadows in hair. Efficient support for deep shadow maps would require a new type of texture with variable-sized texels; not an impossibility, but not likely in the near future on commodity hardware, either. Certain effects in *A Bug's Life* were ray-traced through a separately running ray tracer: Again, not an impossibility in real-time systems, but

---

[2] A hardware implementation exists, the ART system, but it is not real-time.

currently not the first method of choice, either. This is just one use of a recent RenderMan feature that allows shaders to call arbitrary C library code—this code can do anything.[3] Needless to say, hardware acceleration won't help with those kinds of shader operation.

Advances in many other areas are also needed to match the quality of animation and the sheer complexity of the models used for movies. For games in particular, effective real-time physical simulation, collision detection, and behavioral animation algorithms are needed to establish more than a simple canned animation, but a believable world you can interact with.

On the other hand, real-time demonstrations of certain scenes from *Final Fantasy* were being rendered on hardware accelerators at SIGGRAPH 2001. The rendering wasn't up to the quality of the movie, but you had to know what to look for to spot the differences.

The other issue that will probably change in the near future is the distinction between multipass and multitexturing shader implementations. As explained earlier, in a multipass system, intermediate results are stored in the frame buffer (or in copies of the frame buffer) and each pass accomplishes only a small amount of work, using for instance a single compositing operation per pass. In a multitexturing system, a larger amount of work is accomplished in a single pass, using multiple texture look-ups and some kind of programmable system to combine results, such as NVIDIA's register combiners.

At first, multitexturing systems could do only a few operations on every pass with a very limited number of texture look-ups. Therefore, they were thought of as ways to combine passes in a multipass system. However, systems were available in late 2001 that could perform (up to) 12 texture lookups from (up to) six textures in a single pass and perform (up to) 16 operations on these values. This is enough that one pass would be enough for many interesting effects.

Internally, many of these systems use a recirculating pipeline. This means that the actual fragment shader hardware might only provide, say, six texture look-ups and eight operations. However, if more are required, the partially-processed fragment could be sent back to the start of the pipeline and processed again with another six texture look-ups and eight more operations. In order for this to work, the hardware needs to be able to switch quickly between two contexts, so both fragments in their first and second passes can be processed efficiently.

This approach can be easily extended to multiple passes, as long as the memory is available to store all the different programs and states needed

---

[3]Even ftp to a live camera on the South Pole if that's what you want.

for each different fragment processing context. A natural extension of this would be to use a cache for programs, and use a prefetching architecture similar to what is currently being used for texture samples [80]. Then it would be possible to dynamically switch between a large number of shader programs and contexts, although there would of course be consequences in texture cache coherency if this were pushed too far.

Recently, a paper by Stanford proposed a multipass alternative that would store fragments in a buffer, in the same order as they would be written to the frame buffer [111]. These fragments could then be read out and sent back through the fragment unit as many times as necessary, each time with a different fragment program. There would be two ways to do this: with fragments identifying the pixel to which they were targeted; or with rerasterization of the geometry to generate the same sequence of pixel addresses. If the former approach were used, depth testing could be done at some point to discard fragments that were not visible on the front surfaces of objects, to avoid expending effort shading them.

This can also be done with a recirculating buffer approach, as long as a conditional "fragment kill" operation is available to the fragment shader, and the depth buffer can be accessed from the fragment shader (as a texture, for instance).

Use of a fragment buffer is slightly different from the use of a recirculating pipeline. First, a fragment buffer uses external memory, and so incurs a bandwidth usage penalty. Also, there is a memory management issue: The lengths of fragment buffers can be unbounded.

However, only one fragment shader program is used at a time with the fragment buffer approach, and so the cost of the fragment shader hardware is reduced, and texture coherence can be improved. A recirculating pipeline would require more hardware to store multiple contexts, and may suffer from lower texture coherence.

The bottom line is that both recirculating pipelines and fragment buffers make it possible to have long fragment shader programs with many operations, and arbitrarily long dependent texture lookup chains.

With recirculating pipelines, it is even possible to have efficient conditional execution. Suppose there was a register that you could conditionally write to at the end of a fragment shader "basic block" that would indicate which of several fragment shader subprograms and texture contexts to use for the next basic block. This would permit both selective execution and looping, while maintaining the long fragment shader pipeline needed for efficient texture look-up.

To implement looping, request either the same context as the current block or (if the loop is terminating) the context of the basic block following the loop.[4] For conditional execution, write (conditionally) one of two possible contexts to follow the current context. The current vertex and fragment shaders already include the equivalent of conditional assignments, so this would not be a huge leap at the API level. Unfortunately, this would also scramble fragment order, and so would require new synchronization primitives, and it would play havoc with texture cache coherence—but it's possible.

19.4 Render to Texture

Another feature that will make it easier to implement multipass shaders is also in the works. Several vendors have recently introduced extensions that permit direct rendering into a texture, which can then be used in a later pass. The system still needs to make sure that all fragments destined for a buffer are actually written to it before it is read as a texture.

Direct rendering to textures is very useful, as it provides an efficient means to pass intermediate results from one pass to a later one. Why was this not possible before? First, on some systems, textures and buffers were stored in completely different memory systems. Newer systems use a unified memory architecture that makes the actual unification of buffer and texture types possible. However, there is another issue: buffer pixels are usually organized in scanline order to make it easier to read out scanlines for sending to a video display. In contrast, textures are usually organized into blocks, to improve spatial locality and so texture cache coherency. In order to render directly to a texture, the compositing unit has to be able to swizzle (rearrange) pixels into the texture block-order before writing them into the buffer. This requires a relatively small amount of hardware, but without that special hardware the rearranging needs to be done on the host, an expensive proposition.

Some systems (notably SGI IR and VPro graphics) do not support directly rendering to a texture, but do support fast (hardware-accelerated) copying of a buffer to a texture, including generation of the MIP-map levels. The latter operation is important for applications like environment mapping; if the host is involved in generating the MIP-map, then the cost of performing the operation must include not only the swizzling, but also the copy to and from the host. For use as intermediate values in multipass shaders, MIP-map generation is not necessary as the values will be read

---

[4]When describing this to someone, the question was asked "What happens if you write an infinite loop on the GPU?" The answer: "The same thing that would happen if you wrote an infinite loop on the CPU." Or alternatively: "Don't do that." An API call to reset the GPU would come in handy, though, and/or a watchdog timer.

back from a "texture" aligned with the pixel grid of the final destination buffer.

19.5   Virtualizing Resources

Current hardware accelerators typically support fixed numbers of different kinds of resources: texture units; shader operations; memory; matrix stack depth; and so forth.

There will probably be some effort expended on virtualizing these resources. This is desirable from a high-level programming point of view to improve portability. Ideally, when you write a shader program, you would like not to worry about the number or kind of operations available on the hardware. Certainly it is best to avoid situations like pfman, where the memory limits depend on the exact run-time combination of surface and light shaders. It's easy enough to take these things into account when writing a shader for a single target platform; the real problem arises when you want to write a portable shader that will run on a number of platforms.

Unfortunately, this is a difficult problem, since there might be a significant cost to virtualizing a resource. For real-time applications, there is also the problem of "performance cliffs": a shader implementation might slow down dramatically when using $N + 1$ rather than N texture units. Ultimately, what is needed is more research into smart shader compilers and/or shader language features that can target performance goals by approximating shaders or using alternative implementations (for instance, by being smart enough to sample part of a shader and using a spare texture map look-up rather than using one more computational operation, or vice versa [62]). Doing this right will require both extensive research by shader compiler implementors and probably some support from hardware vendors.

19.6   Transparency and Order
Independence

Today, in order to implement transparency on a hardware accelerator, polygons must be sorted in a back-to-front order and possibly split to resolve cyclic dependencies. This effectively replaces the Z-buffer hidden surface algorithm with Painter's algorithm, at least for transparent surfaces. However, even with this extra effort, refraction cannot be handled correctly.

It is possible that some kind of order-independent transparency support will appear soon on a hardware accelerator. In such a system, polygons with alpha values attached would ideally just be thrown at the hardware in any old order, and it would do "the right thing" (although perhaps more efficiently for some orders than others).

Many techniques have been developed that would support this. A recent paper [181] showed how a recirculating pipeline or fragment-buffer-like architecture could be used to sort fragments by depth. It is also possible to find the nth surface using multipass algorithms [44] and use that to implement order-independent transparency, although at a significant cost. A-buffer algorithms, either approximate or exact, can also be implemented in hardware [26], although at a larger memory and memory-management cost than is currently considered acceptable, though it is not out of the question for a hardware implementation [119].

There are several complications. First, all fragment shader operations should be completed before a fragment is combined with others, as the fragment shader computes the color and transparency of a fragment (and perhaps even its depth). This implies at least a conceptual single-pass (multitexturing) shading model. Secondly, the current conceptual models of hardware include the idea that fragments arrive at the target buffer in the same order that the primitives that generated them were sent to the hardware.

The ordering constraint was in fact originally specified in order to make it possible to implement, among other things, Painter's algorithm and multipass shading. However, if we sort fragments by depth, then of course we will be violating this ordering. In general, it would be nice to loosen the constraint of absolute synchronization anyway, for performance reasons [42]. Some of the extensions suggested above for recirculating pipelines, especially conditional execution of fragment shader's basic blocks, would also potentially change the order in which fragments are written to a destination buffer. Therefore, rather than enforcing strict ordering for everything, future systems will probably include explicit synchronization and permit limited (but controllable) reordering. Normally, in most algorithms we will only need to control the ordering between coarse-grained steps of a rendering algorithm, since the need for fine-grained ordering will be eliminated by the development of more advanced shading systems.

19.7 The GPU as a Supercomputing Co-Processor

The point of using a graphics accelerator in the first place will be to obtain significantly higher performance than that possible on a general-purpose

CPU. We are finding that, as the GPU becomes more programmable and its performance acceleration continues to outpace that of the CPU, limiting the GPU to polygonal rasterization and shading is a suboptimal use of available resources.

The GPU is evolving into a general streaming parallel processor, optimized for data-dependent non-conditional execution. Algorithms that require a lot of conditional execution do not map well onto currently available graphics hardware.

Current graphics accelerators have been compared to a vector processor (the vertex shading unit) followed by an array processor. The vertex shading unit processes a stream (vector) of vertices. Then, the rasterizer is an address generation unit, the texture unit is an array access unit, the fragment shader performs element computations, and finally the compositor writes, conditionally, results back to another array. Currently barriers exist that make it hard to, for instance, feed array results back through the input of the vertex (vector) unit. We predict that these barriers will (eventually) go away, and the feature set of graphics accelerators will actually simplify as they converge onto an orthogonal set of common operations and data formats.

Still, graphics accelerators are best suited to massively parallelizable algorithms that can execute in a SIMD mode. Such algorithms have predictable data access patterns that will best exploit the specialized memory-access units available in graphics accelerators. There are many computations in graphics, however, that don't directly compute colors that fall into this category. Solution of large systems of partial differential equations, for instance, are highly regular and parallelizable. Such systems show up in the simulation of cloth, water, and flexible solids. Global illumination involves the solution of large linear systems. This is also a well-studied problem amenable to parallelization.

Several researchers have implemented a ray tracer using the programmable features of graphics hardware [27, 148]. These early GPU ray tracers show not only the flexibility of the GPU as a general-purpose processor but also its limitations. For example, GPU ray tracers tend to implement "all-pairs" intersections between all rays and all triangles, and even these early implementations have required some form of spatial partitioning to reduce this per-ray linear complexity. Advanced CPU-based ray tracers use conditional execution to exhibit a per-ray logarithmic execution time, but the GPU is not yet that advanced.

As the GPU evolves into a more general purpose processor, many more will want to exploit its performance on an increasingly vast array of applications. While the specific details of this book may become outdated as new features emerge, the general principles it outlines are fundamental and timeless, and these principles will serve as the stepping stones for this new "multipass" style of programming and computing, at least for those of you who now have the skill to use them.

Bibliography

[1] 3DLABS. *OpenGL 2.0 Shading Language White Paper*, 1.1 ed., December 2001.

[2] ABRAM, G. D., AND WHITTED, T. "Building block shaders." In *Computer Graphics (Proc. SIGGRAPH '90)* 24(4): 283–288(1990).

[3] AHO, A. V., SETHI, R., AND ULLMAN, J. D. *Compilers: principles, techniques, tools.* Boston: Addison-Wesley, 1986.

[4] ALANDER, J. "On interval arithmetic range approximation methods of polynomials and rational functions." *Computers and Graphics* 9(4): 365–372(1985).

[5] AMANATIDES, J. "Algorithms for the detection and elimination of specular aliasing." In *Proceedings of Graphics Interface*: 86–93(May 1992).

[6] AMBURN, P., GRANT, E., AND WHITTED, T. "Managing geometric complexity with enhanced procedural models." In *Computer Graphics (Proc. SIGGRAPH '86)* 20(4): 189–195 (1986).

[7] APODACA, A. A., AND GRITZ, L. *Advanced RenderMan: Creating CGI for motion pictures.* San Francisco: Morgan Kaufmann, 2000.

[8] APPEL, A. W. *Modern Compiler Implementation in C: Basic Techniques.* Cambridge: Cambridge University Press, 1997.

[9] ASHIKHMIN, M., PREMOZE, S., AND SHIRLEY, P. "A microfacet-based BRDF generator." In *Proceedings of SIGGRAPH 2000, Computer Graphics Series, Annual Conference Series*, pp. 65–74. Reading: Addison-Wesley, 2000.

[10] ASHIKHMIN, M., AND SHIRLEY, P. "An anisotropic phong BRDF model." *journal of graphics tools* 5(2): 6–74(2000).

[11] ATI. *Pixel Shader Extension*, 2000. Specification document, available from http://www.ati.com/online/sdk.

[12] ATI. *Vertex Shader Extension*, 2001. Specification document, available from http://www.ati.com/online/sdk.

[13] BANKS, D. "Illumination in diverse codimensions." In *Proceedings of SIGGRAPH 94, Computer Graphics Series, Annual Conference Series*, pp. 327–334. New York: ACM Press, 1994.

[14] BARR, A. H. "Global and local deformations of solid primitives." In *Computer Graphics (Proc. SIGGRAPH '84)* 18(3): 21–30(1984).

[15] BATTKE, H., STALLING, D., AND HEGE, H.C. "Fast line integral convolution for arbitrary surfaces in 3D." In *Visualization and Mathematics*, edited by H. C. Hege and K. Polthier, pp. 181–195. Heidelberg: Springer-Verlag, 1997.

[16] BENNIS, C., VÉZIEN, J.-M., IGLÉSIAS, G., AND GAGALOWICZ, A. "Piecewise surface flattening for non-distorted texture mapping." In *Computer Graphics (Proc. SIGGRAPH '91)* 25(4): 237–246 (July 1991).

[17] BISHOP, G., AND WEIMER, D. M. "Fast Phong shading." In *Computer Graphics (Proc. SIGGRAPH '86)* 20(4): 103–106(Aug. 1986).

[18] BLINN, J. F. "Models of light reflection for computer synthesized pictures." In *Computer Graphics (SIGGRAPH '77 Proceedings)* 11(2): 192–198(July 1977).

[19] BLINN, J. F. "Simulation of wrinkled surfaces." In *Computer Graphics (Proc. SIGGRAPH '78)* 12(3): 286–292(Aug. 1978).

[20] BLINN, J F. "A Generalization of Algebraic Surface Drawing." *ACM Transactions on Graphics* 1(3): 235–256 (1982).

[21] BLINN, J. F., AND NEWELL, M. E. "Texture and reflection in computer generated images." *Communications of the ACM* 19: 542–546(1976).

[22] BORN, M., AND WOLF, E. *Principles of Optics: Electromagnetic Theory of Propagation, Interference, and Diffraction of Light*, 6th ed. Cambridge: Cambridge University Press, 1980.

[23] BRIGGS, P. *Register Allocation via Graph Coloring*. Ph.D. thesis, Rice University, Apr. 1998. TR92-183.

[24] BROCKELMANN, R. A., AND HAGFORS, T. "Note on the effect of shadowing on the backscattering of waves from a random rough surface." *IEEE Transactions on Antennas and Propagation* 14: 621–626(Sept. 1966).

[25] CABRAL, B., OLANO, M., AND NEMEC, P. "Reflection space image based rendering." In *Proceedings of SIGGRAPH '99, Computer Graphics Proceedings, Annual Conference Series*, pp. 165–170. Reading: Addison-Wesley Longman, 1999.

[26] CARPENTER, L. "The A-buffer, an antialiased hidden surface method." In *Computer Graphics (Proc. SIGGRAPH '84)* 18(3): 103–108(July 1984).

[27] CARR, N. A., HALL, J.D., AND HART, J.C. *The Ray Engine*, University of Illinois DCS Tech Report #R-2002-2269, March 2002.

[28] CARR, N. A., AND HART, J. C. "Meshed atlases for real-time procedural solid texturing." *ACM Trans. on Graphics* 21(2): (Apr. 2002). (To appear.)

[29] CATMULL, E. "A subdivision algorithm for computer display of curved surfaces." Tech. Rep. UTEC-CSc-74-133, University of Utah, Salt Lake City, Dec. 1974.

[30] CHAITIN, G. J., AUSLANDER, M. A., CHANDRA, A. K., COCKE, J., HOPKINS, M. E., AND MARKSTEIN, P. W. "Register allocation via coloring." *Computer Languages* 6(1): 47–57(1981).

[31] CIGNONI, P., MONTANI, C., ROCCHINI, C., AND SCOPIGNO, R. "A general method for recovering attribute values on simplified meshes." In *IEEE Visualization '98*, edited by D. Ebert, H. Hagen, and H. Rushmeier, pp. 59–66 (Oct. 1998).

[32] COHEN, J., OLANO, M., AND MANOCHA, D. "Appearance-preserving simplification." In *Proceedings of SIGGRAPH 98, Computer Graphics Proceedings, Annual Conference Series*, pp. 115–122. Reading: Addison-Wesley, 1998.

[33] COOK, R. L. "Shade trees." In *Computer Graphics (Proc. SIGGRAPH '84)* 18(3): 223–231(1984).

[34] COOK, R. L., CARPENTER, L., AND CATMULL, E. "The REYES image rendering architecture." In *Computer Graphics (Proc. SIGGRAPH '87)* 21(4): 95–102(1987).

[35] CROW, F. C. "A more flexible image generation environment." In *Computer Graphics (Proc. SIGGRAPH '82)* 16(3): 9–18(1982).

[36] CROW, F. C. "Summed-area tables for texture mapping." In *Computer Graphics (Proc. SIGGRAPH '84)* 18(3): 207–212(1984).

[37] DEBEVEC, P. E. "Rendering synthetic objects into real scenes: Bridging traditional and image-based graphics with global illumination and high dynamic range photography." In *Proceedings of SIGGRAPH 98, Computer Graphics Proceedings, Annual Conference Series*, pp. 189–198. Reading: Addison-Wesley, 1998.

[38] DEBEVEC, P. E., AND MALIK, J. "Recovering high dynamic range radiance maps from photographs." In *Proceedings of SIGGRAPH 97, Computer Graphics Proceedings, Annual Conference Series*, pp. 369–378. Reading: Addison-Wesley, 1997.

[39] DIEFENBACH, P., AND BADLER, N. "Pipeline rendering: Interactive refractions, reflections and shadows." In *Displays: Special Issue on Interactive Computer Graphics* 15(3): 173–180(1994).

[40] DOGGETT, M., AND HIRCHE, J. "Adaptive view dependent tessellation of displacement maps." In *Proc. of Graphics Hardware*: 59–66(2000).

[41] EBERT, D. S., MUSGRAVE, F. K., PEACHEY, D., PERLIN, K., AND WORLEY, S. *Texturing and Modeling: A Procedural Approach*, second ed. San Diego: Academic Press, 1998.

[42] ELDRIDGE, M., IGEHY, H., AND HANRAHAN, P. M. "Pomegranate: A fully scalable graphics architecture." In *Proceedings of SIGGRAPH 2000, Computer Graphics Proceedings, Annual Conference Series*, pp.443–454. Reading: Addison-Wesley, 2000.

[43] ENGLAND, N. "A graphics system architecture for interactive application-specific display functions." *IEEE CG&A* 6(1): 60–70(January 1986).

[44] EVERITT, C. *Interactive Order-Independent Transparency*, NVIDIA OpenGL Applications Engineering White Paper, 2002.

[45] FLEISCHER, K., AND WITKIN, A. "A modeling testbed." In *Proceedings of Graphics Interface '88*: 137–137. Canadian Inf. Process. Society, 1988.

[46] FOLEY, J. D., VAN DAM, A., FEINER, S. K., AND HUGHES, J. F. *Computer Graphics, Principles and Practice, Second Edition*. Reading: Addison-Wesley, 1990.

[47] FOURNIER, A. "Filtering normal maps and creating multiple surfaces." Technical Report Imager 92/1, Imager, Computer Science, University of British Columbia, 1992.

[48] FOURNIER, A. "Normal distribution functions and multiple surfaces." In *Graphics Interface '92 Workshop on Local Illumination*: 45–52(May 1992).

[49] FOWLES, G. R. *Introduction to Modern Optics*, 2 ed. Mineola: Dover Publications, 1989.

[50] FRASER, C. W., AND HANSON, D. R. *A Retargetable C Compiler: Design and Implementation*. Redwood City: Benjamin/Cummings, 1995.

[51] FRASER, C. W., HANSON, D. R., AND PROEBSTING, T. A. "Engineering a simple, efficient code generator generator." In *ACM Letters on Programming Languages and Systems* 1(3): 213–226(Sept. 1992).

[52] GLASSNER, A. S. "Normal Coding." In *Graphics Gems*, edited by A. Glassner, pp.257–264. San Diego: Academic Press, 1990.

[53] GLASSNER, A. S. "Spectrum: An architecture for image synthesis research, education, and practice." In *Developing Large-scale Graphics Software Toolkits — SIGGRAPH 1993 Course Notes* (Aug. 1993).

[54] GOEHRING, D. AND GERLITZ, O. *Advanced Procedural Texturing Using MMX Technology*, Intel, 1997. (Intel MMX Technology Application Note, http://developer.intel.com/software/idap/resources/technical_collateral/mmx/proctex

[55] GOOCH AND GOOCH. *Non-Photorealistic Rendering*. Natick: A K Peters, 2001.

[56] GOOCH, A., GOOCH, B., SHIRLEY, P. S., AND COHEN, E. "A non-photorealistic lighting model for automatic technical illustration." In *Proceedings of SIGGRAPH 98, Computer Graphics Proceedings, Annual Conference Series*, pp.447–452. Reading: Addison-Wesley, 1998.

[57] GOOCH, B., SLOAN, P. P., GOOCH, A., SHIRLEY, P., AND RIESENFELD, R. "Interactive technical illustration." In *ACM Symposium on Interactive 3D Graphics*: 31–38(1999).

[58] GREEN, M., AND SUN, H. MML: A language and system for procedural modeling and motion. In *Proceedings of Graphics Interface 88*: 16–25 (1988).

[59] GREENE, N. "Applications of world projections." In *Proceedings of Graphics Interface '86*: 108–114(May 1986).

[60] GREGER, G., SHIRLEY, P., HUBBARD, P., AND GREENBERG, D. "The irradiance volume." *IEEE CG&A*, 18(2): 32–43 (1998).

[61] GRITZ, L., AND HAHN, J. "BMRT: A global illumination implementation of the renderman standard." *journal of graphics tools* 1(3): 29–47(1996).

[62] GUENTER, B., KNOBLOCK, T., AND RUF, E. "Specializing shaders." In *Proceedings of SIGGRAPH 95, Computer Graphics Proceedings, Annual Conference Series*, pp. 343–350. Reading: Addison-Wesley, 1995.

[63] HAEBERLI, P., AND SEGAL, M. "Texture mapping as a fundamental drawing primitive." In *Fourth Eurographics Workshop on Rendering*: 259–266(June 1993).

[64] HALL, R. A., AND GREENBERG, D. P. "A testbed for realistic image synthesis." *IEEE CG&A* 3: 10–20(November 1983).

[65] HANRAHAN, P., AND LAWSON, J. "A language for shading and lighting calculations." In *Computer Graphics (Proc. SIGGRAPH '90)* 24(4): 289–298(Aug. 1990).

[66] HART, J. C., CARR, N., KAMEYA, M., TIBBITTS, S. A., AND COLEMAN, T. J. "Antialiased parameterized solid texturing simplified for consumer-level hardware implementation." In *Proceedings of SIGGRAPH '99, Computer Graphics Proceedings, Annual Conference Series*, pp. 45–53, Reading: Addison-Wesley Longman, 1999.

[67] HART, J. C. "Perlin Noise Pixel Shaders." In *Graphics Hardware 2001*, edited by Kurt Akeley and Ulrich Neumann, pp. 87–94, New York: ACM Press, 2001.

[68] HART, J. C., SANDIN, D. J., AND KAUFFMAN, L. H. "Ray tracing deterministic 3-D fractals." In *Computer Graphics (Proc. SIGGRAPH 89)* 23(3): 289–296(1989).

[69] HECKBERT, P. S. "Survey of texture mapping." In *IEEE CG&A* 6(11): 56–67(1986).

[70] HEDELMAN, H. "A data flow approach to procedural modeling." In *IEEE CG&A* 3(1): 16–26(January 1984).

[71] HEIDRICH, W. "A model for anisotropic reflections in OpenGL." In *Conference abstracts and applications: SIGGRAPH 98*, pp. 267–267. New York: ACM Press (1998).

[72] HEIDRICH, W. *High-quality Shading and Lighting for Hardware-accelerated Rendering*. Ph.D. thesis, Universität Erlangen-Nürnberg, 1999.

[73] HEIDRICH, W., DAUBERT, K., KAUTZ, J., AND SEIDEL, H. P. "Illuminating micro geometry based on precomputed visibility." In *Proceedings of SIGGRAPH 2000, Computer Graphics Proceedings, Annual Conference Series*, pp. 455–464. Reading: Addison-Wesley, 2000.

[74] HEIDRICH, W., KAUTZ, J., SLUSALLEK, P., AND SEIDEL, H.-P. "Canned lightsources." In *Rendering Techniques '98 (Proceedings of Eurographics Rendering Workshop)* (1998).

[75] HEIDRICH, W., AND SEIDEL, H. "Efficient rendering of anisotropic surfaces using computer graphics hardware." In *Image and Multi-dimensional DSP Workshop (IMDSP)* (1998).

[76] HEIDRICH, W., AND SEIDEL, H. P. "View-independent environment maps." In *Eurographics/SIGGRAPH Workshop on Graphics Hardware*: 39–45(1998).

[77] HEIDRICH, W., AND SEIDEL, H. P. "Realistic, hardware-accelerated shading and lighting." In *Proceedings of SIGGRAPH '99, Computer Graphics Proceedings, Annual Conference Series*. Reading: Addison-Wesley, 1999.

[78] HEIDRICH, W., SLUSALLIK, P., AND SEIDEL, H. "Sampling procedural shaders using affine arithmetic." In *ACM Transactions on Graphics* 17(3): 158–176(July 1998).

[79] HEIDRICH, W., WESTERMANN, R., SEIDEL, H. P., AND ERTL, T. "Applications of pixel textures in visualization and realistic image synthesis." In *ACM Symposium on Interactive 3D Graphics* (1999).

[80] IGEHY, H. ELDRIDGE, M. AND HANRAHAN, P. "Parallel texture caching." In *Proceedings 1999 Eurographics/SIGGRAPH Workshop on Graphics Hardware*, pp. 95–106, New York: ACM Press, 1999.

[81] JENSEN, H. W., MARSCHNER, S. R., LEVOY, M., AND HANRAHAN, P. "A practical model for subsurface light transport." In *Proceedings of SIGGRAPH 2001, Computer Graphics Proceedings, Annual Conference Series*, pp. 511–518. Reading: Addison-Wesley, 2001.

[82] M. KAMEYA, M. AND HART, J.C. "Bresenham Noise." In *SIGGRAPH 2000 Conference Abstracts and Applications, Computer Graphics Annual Conference Series*, New York: ACM SIGGRAPH, 2000.

[83] KAUTZ, J., AND MCCOOL, M. "Interactive rendering with arbitrary BRDFs using separable approximations." In *Tenth Eurographics Workshop on Rendering*: 281–292(June 1999).

[84] KAUTZ, J., AND MCCOOL, M. D. "Approximation of glossy reflection with prefiltered environment maps." In *Proc. Graphics Interface*: 119–126 (2000).

[85] KAUTZ, J., AND SEIDEL, H. P. "Towards interactive bump mapping with anisotropic shift-variant BRDFs." In *Graphics Hardware 2000*: 51–58(Aug. 2000).

[86] KAUTZ, J., AND SEIDEL, H. P. "Hardware accelerated displacement mapping for image based rendering." In *Proc. of Graphics Interface*: 61–70(2001).

[87] KAUTZ, J., VÁZQUEZ, P.-P., HEIDRICH, W., AND SEIDEL, H.-P. "Unified approach to prefiltered environment maps." In *Rendering Techniques (Proc. of the Eurographics Workshop on Rendering)*: (2000).

[88] KELLER, A. "Instant radiosity." In *Proceedings of SIGGRAPH 97, Computer Graphics Proceedings, Annual Conference Series*, pp. 49–56. Reading: Addison-Wesley, 1997.

[89] KNOLL, T. *Filter Module Interface for Adobe Photoshop*, Adobe Photoshop developers kit, 1990.

[90] KOLB, C. E. *Rayshade User's Guide and Reference Manual*, January 1992.

[91] KUCHKUDA, R. "An introduction to ray tracing." In *Theoretical Foundations of Computer Graphics and CAD F40*, pp.1039–1060. Springer Verlag, 1988.

[92] KYLANDER, K., AND KYLANDER, O. S. *Gimp: The Official Handbook*. The Coriolis Group, 1999.

[93] LAFORTUNE, E., FOO, S. C., TORRANCE, K., AND GREENBERG, D. "Non-linear approximation of reflectance functions." In *Proceedings of SIG-GRAPH 97, Computer Graphics Proceedings, Annual Conference Series*, pp. 117–126. Reading: Addison-Wesley, 1997.

[94] LAFORTUNE, E., AND WILLEMS, Y. "Using the modified Phong reflectance model for physically based rendering." Tech. Rep. CW197, Dept. Comp. Sci., K.U. Leuven, 1994.

[95] LARSON, G. W., RUSHMEIER, H., AND PIATKO, C. "A visibility matching tone reproduction operator for high dynamic range scenes." In *IEEE Transactions on Visualization and Computer Graphics* 3(4): 291–306(Oct. 1997).

[96] LARSON, R. D., AND SHAH, M. S. "Method for generating addresses to textured graphics primitives stored in RIP maps." US Patent 05222205, 1993.

[97] LEECH, J. "OpenGL extensions and restrictions for PixelFlow." Tech. Rep. TR98-019, Department of Computer Science, University of North Carolina, 1998.

[98] LEFFLER, S. J., REEVES, W. T., AND OSTBY, E. F. "The Menv modelling and animation environment." In *Journal of Visualization and Computer Animation*1(1): 33–40(August 1990).

[99] LEVINTHAL, A. AND PORTER, T. "Chap – A SIMD Graphics Processor." *Computer Graphics* 18(3): 77–82 (July 1984).

[100] LEVINE, J. R., MASON, T., AND BROWN, D. *lex & yacc*, second ed. O'Reilly & Associates, 1992.

[101] LÉVY, B., AND MALLET, J.-L. "Non-distorted texture mapping for sheared triangulated meshes." In *Proceedings of SIGGRAPH 98, Computer Graphics Proceedings, Annual Conference Series*, pp. 343–352. Reading: Addison-Wesley, 1998.

[102] LEWIS, R. "Making shaders more physically plausible." In *Eurographics Workshop on Rendering*: 47–62(June 1993).

[103] LINDHOLM, E., KILGARD, M. J., AND MORETON, H. "A user-programmable vertex engine." In *Proceedings of SIGGRAPH 01, Computer Graphics Proceedings, Annual Conference Series*, pp. 149–158. Reading: Addison Wesley, 2001.

[104] LOKOVIC, T., AND VEACH, E. "Deep shadow maps." In *Proceedings SIGGRAPH 2000, Computer Graphics Proceedings, Annual Conference Series*, pp. 385–392. Reading: Addison-Wesley, 2000.

[105] MA, S. D., AND LIN, H. "Optimal texture mapping." In *Proceedings of the European Computer Graphics Conference and Exhibition* (Nice, France, Sept. 1988), P. Duce, D.A.; Jancene, Ed., North-Holland, pp. 421–428.

[106] MAILLOT, J., YAHIA, H., AND VERROUST, A. "Interactive texture mapping." In *Proceedings of SIGGRAPH 93, Computer Graphics Proceedings, Annual Conference Series*, pp. 27–34. New York: ACM Press, 1993.

[107] MALZBENDER, T., GELB, D., AND WOLTERS, H. "Polynomial texture maps." In *Proceedings SIGGRAPH '01, Computer Graphics Proceedings, Annual Conference Series*, pp. 519–528. Reading: Addison-Wesley, 2000.

[108] MAMMEN, A. "Transparency and antialiasing algorithms implemented with the virtual pixel maps technique." *IEEE Computer Graphics and Applications* 9(4): 43–45(July 1989).

[109] MANDELBROT, B. *The Fractal Geometry of Nature.* San Francisco: Freeman, 1977.

[110] MARK, W. R., AND PROUDFOOT, K. "Compiling to a VLIW fragment pipeline." In *Graphics Hardware 2001*, edited by K. Akeley and U. Neumann, SIGGRAPH/EUROGRAPHICS. New York: ACM Press, 2001.

[111] MARK, W. R., AND PROUDFOOT, K. "The F-Buffer, a rasterization-order FIFO buffer for multi-pass rendering." In *Graphics Hardware 2001* edited by K. Akeley and U. Neumann, SIGGRAPH/EUROGRAPHICS, pp. 57–64. New York, ACM Press, 2001.

[112] MARUYA, M. "Generating a texture map from object-surface texture data." In *Computer Graphics Forum, Proceedings of Eurographics 95* 14(3): 397–406(Aug. 1995)

[113] MCCOOL, M. D., ANG, J., AND AHMAD, A. "Homomorphic factorization of BRDFs for high-performance rendering." In *Proceedings SIGGRAPH '01, Computer Graphics Proceedings, Annual Conference Series*, pp. 171–178. Reading: Addison-Wesley, 2001.

[114] MCCOOL, M. D., AND HEIDRICH, W. "Texture shaders." In *Proc. Eurographics/SIGGRAPH Workshop on Graphics Hardware*: 117–126(1999).

[115] MICROSOFT. *DirectX Graphics Programmers Guide*, DirectX 8.1 ed. Microsoft Developers Network Library, 2001.

[116] MICROSOFT. *DX9*, 2001. Microsoft Meltdown 2001 presentation, available at www.microsoft.com/mscorp/corpevents/meltdown2001/ppt/DXG9.ppt.

[117] MILENKOVIC, V. "Rotational polygon overlap minimization." In *Proceedings of the 13th International Annual Symposium on Computational Geometry (SCG-97)*, pp. 334–343. New York: ACM Press, 1997.

[118] MILLER, G., AND HOFFMAN, R. "Illumination and reflection maps: Simulated objects in simulated and real environments." In *SIGGRAPH '84 Course Notes – Advanced Computer Graphics Animation* (July 1984).

[119] MOLNAR, S. *Image-Composition Architectures for Real-Time Image Generation*. Ph.D. thesis, University of North Carolina, Chapel Hill, 1991.

[120] MOLNAR, S., EYLES, J., AND POULTON, J. "PixelFlow: High-speed rendering using image composition." In *Computer Graphics (Proc. SIGGRAPH '92)* 26(2): 231–240(July 1992).

[121] MORGAN, R. *Building an Optimizing Compiler*. Woburn: Digital Press, 1998.

[122] MUCHNICK, S. S. *Advanced Compiler Design and Implementation*. San Francisco: Morgan Kaufmann, 2000.

[123] MUSGRAVE, F. K., AND MANDELBROT, B. B. "Natura ex machina." In *IEEE Computer Graphics and Applications* 9(1): 4–7(Jan. 1989).

[124] NADAS, T., AND FOURNIER, A. "GRAPE: An environment to build display processes." In *Computer Graphics (Proc. SIGGRAPH '87)* 21(4): 75–84, 1987.

[125] NEUMANN, L., NEUMANN, A., AND SZIRMAY-KALOS, L. "Reflectance models with fast importance sampling." In *Computer Graphics Forum*, edited by D. Duke, S. Coquillart, and T. Howard, 18(4): 249–265. Eurographics Association, 1999.

[126] NEWELL, M. *The Utilization of Procedure Models in Digital Image Synthesis*. Ph.D. thesis, University of Utah, 1975.

[127] NORTON, A., ROCKWOOD, A. P., AND SKOLMOSKI, P. T. "Clamping: A method of antialiasing textured surfaces by bandwidth limiting in object space." In *Computer Graphics (Proc. SIGGRAPH '82)* 16(3): 1–8 (1982).

[128] NVIDIA. *NVIDIA OpenGL Extensions Specifications*, March 2001.

[129] OLANO, M. *A Programmable Pipeline for Graphics Hardware*. Ph.D thesis, University of North Carolina at Chapel Hill, 1999.

[130] OLANO, M., AND LASTRA, A. "A shading language on graphics hardware: The PixelFlow shading system." In *Proceedings of SIGGRAPH 98, Computer Graphics Proceedings, Annual Series*, pp. 159–168. Reading: Addison-Wesley, 1998.

[131] O'NEILL, B. *Elementary Differential Geometry*. San Diego: Academic Press, 1966.

[132] PARR, T. J., AND QUONG, R. W. "ANTLR: A predicated-LL(k) parser generator." In *Software — Practice and Experience* 25(7): 789–810(July 1995).

[133] PEACHEY, D. "Solid texturing of complex surfaces." In *Computer Graphics (Proc. SIGGRAPH '85)* 19(3): 279–286(July 1985).

[134] PEDERSEN, H. K. "Decorating implicit surfaces." In *Proceedings of SIGGRAPH 95, Computer Graphics Proceedings, Annual Conference Proceedings*, pp. 291–300. Reading: Addison Wesley, 1995.

[135] PEDERSEN, H. K. "A framework for interactive texturing operations on curved surfaces." In *Proceedings of SIGGRAPH 96, Computer Graphics Proceedings, Annual Conference Series*, p. 295–302. Reading: Addison Wesley, 1996.

[136] PEERCY, M. "Linear color representations for full spectral rendering." In *Proceedings of SIGGRAPH 93, Computer Graphics Proceedings, Annual Conference Series*, pp. 191–198. New York: ACM Press, 1993.

[137] PEERCY, M., AIREY, J., AND CABRAL, B. "Efficient bump mapping hardware." In *Proceedings of SIGGRAPH 97, Computer Graphics Proceedings, Annual Conference Series*, pp. 303–306. Reading: Addison-Wesley, 1997.

[138] PEERCY, M. S., OLANO, M., AIREY, J., AND UNGAR, P. J. "Interactive multi-pass programmable shading." In *Proceedings of SIGGRAPH 2000, Computer Graphics Proceedings, Annual Conference Series*, pp. 425–432. Reading: Addison-Wesley, 2000.

[139] PERLIN, K. "An image synthesizer." In *Computer Graphics (Proc. SIGGRAPH '85* 19(3): 287296(1985).

[140] PERLIN, K., AND HOFFERT, E. M. "Hypertexture." In *Computer Graphics (Proc. SIGGRAPH '89)* 23(3): 253–262(1989).

[141] PHONG, B. T. "Illumination for computer generated pictures." In *Communications of ACM* 18(6): 311–317(June 1975).

[142] PIXAR. *The RenderMan Interface, version 3.1*, September 1989.

[143] PIXAR. *The RenderMan Interface, version 3.2*, July 2000.

[144] POTMESIL, M., AND HOFFERT, E. M. "The Pixel Machine: A parallel image computer." In *Computer Graphics (Proc. SIGGRAPH '89)* 23(3): 69–78(1989).

[145] POULIN, P., AND FOURNIER, A. "A model for anisotropic reflection." In *Computer Graphics (Proc. SIGGRAPH '90)* 24(4): 273–282(Aug. 1990).

[146] PROUDFOOT, K., MARK, W. R., HANRAHAN, P., AND TZVETKOV, S. "A real-time procedural shading system for programmable graphics hardware." In *Proceedings of SIGGRAPH 01, Computer Graphics Proceedings, Annual Conference Series*. Reading: Addison-Wesley, 2001.

[147] PRUSINKIEWICZ, P., LINDENMAYER, A., AND HANAN, J. "Developmental models of herbaceous plants for computer imagery purposes." In *Computer Graphics (Proc. SIGGRAPH '88)* 22(3): 141–150(1988).

[148] PURCELL, T. J., BUCK, I., MARK, W. R., AND HANRAHAN, P. "Ray Tracing on Programmable Graphics Hardware." In *Proceedings of SIGGRAPH 02, Computer Graphics Proceedings, Annual Conference Series*. Reading: Addison-Wesley, 2001.

[149] RAMAMOORTHI, R., AND HANRAHAN, P. "An efficient representation for irradiance environment maps." In *Proceedings of SIGGRAPH 2001, Computer Graphics Proceedings, Annual Conference Series*, edited by Eugene Fiume, pp. 497–5000. Reading: Addison-Wesley, 2001.

[150] RAMAMOORTHI, R., AND HANRAHAN, P. "A signal-processing framework for inverse rendering." In *Proceedings of SIGGRAPH 2001, Computer Graphics Proceedings, Annual Conference Series*, edited by E. Fiume, pp. 117–128. Reading: Addison-Wesley, 2001.

[151] REEVES, W. T. "Particle systems – A technique for modeling a class of fuzzy objects." In *ACM Transactions on Graphics* 2(2): 91–108(April 1983).

[152] RHOADES, J., TURK, G., BELL, A., STATE, A., NEUMANN, U., AND VARSHNEY, A. "Real-time procedural textures." In *Proceedings of 1992 Symposium on Interactive 3D Graphics*, special issue of *Computer Graphics* 25: 95–100(1992).

[153] RUBIN, S. M., AND WHITTED, J. T. "A 3-dimensional representation for fast rendering of complex scenes." In *Computer Graphics (Proc. of SIGGRAPH '80* 14(3): 110–116(1980).

[154] SAMEK, M. "Texture mapping and distortion in digital graphics." *The Visual Computer* 2(5): 313–320(1986).

[155] SANDER, P. V., SNYDER, J., GORTLER, S. J., AND HOPPE, H. "Texture mapping progressive meshes." In *Proceedings of SIGGRAPH 2001, Computer Graphics Proceedings, Annual Conference Series*, pp. 409–416. Reading: Addison-Wesley, 2001.

[156] SCHILLING, A., KNITTEL, G., AND STRASSER, W. "Texram: A smart memory for texturing." In *IEEE CG&A* 16(3): 32–41(May 1996).

[157] SCHLICK, C. "A customizable reflectance model for everyday rendering." In *Eurographics Workshop on Rendering*: 73–84(June 1993).

[158] SEDERBERG, T. W., AND PARRY, S. R. "Free-form deformation of solid geometric models." In *Computer Graphics (Proc. SIGGRAPH '86)* 20(4): 151–160(1986).

[159] SEGAL, M., AND AKELEY, K. *The OpenGL Graphics System: A Specification (Version 1.2.1)*, 1999.

[160] SHEFFER, A., AND ÜNGÖR, A. "Efficient adaptive meshing of parametric models." In *Proceedings of the Sixth Symposium on Solid Modeling and Application (SSMA-01)*, edited by D. C. Anderson and K. Lee, pp. 59–70. New York: ACM Press, 2001.

[161] SLOAN, P. P., MARTIN, W., GOOCH, A., AND GOOCH, B. "The lit sphere: A model for capturing NPR shading from art." In *Proc. Graphics Interface*: 143–150(2001).

[162] SLUSALLEK, P., PFLAUM, T., AND SEIDEL, H. P. "Implementing renderman—practice, problems and enhancements." In *Computer Graphics Forum* 13(3): 443–454(1994).

[163] SLUSALLEK, P., STAMMINGER, M., HEIDRICH, W., POPP, J. C., AND SEIDEL, H. P. "Composite lighting simulations with lighting networks." In *IEEE CG&A* 18(2): 22–31(Mar. 1998).

[164] SMITH, B. "Geometrical shadowing of a random rough surface." In *IEEE Trans. Ant. and Propagation AP* 15(5): 668–671(Sept. 1967).

[165] SNYDER, J. M., AND KAJIYA, J. T. "Generative modeling: A symbolic system for geometric modeling." In *Computer Graphics (Proc. SIGGRAPH '92)* 26(2): 369–378(1992).

[166] SOUCY, M., AND LAURENDEAU, D. "Multiresolution surface modeling based on hierarchical triangulation." In *Computer Vision and Image Understanding* 63(1): 1–14(1996).

[167] STALLING, D., ZÖCKLER, M., AND HEGE, H. C. "Fast display of illuminated field lines." In *IEEE Transactions on Visualization and Computer Graphics* 3(2): 118–128(Apr. 1997).

[168] TANNENBAUM, D. C., TANNENBAUM, P., AND WOZNY, M. J. "Polarization and birefringency considerations in rendering." In *Proceedings of SIGGRAPH 94, Computer Graphics Proceedings, Annual Conference Series*, pp.221–222. New York: ACM Press, 1994.

[169] TRUMBORE, B., LYTLE, W., AND GREENBERG, D. P. "A testbed for image synthesis." In *Eurographcs '91*, edited by W. Purgathofer, pp. 467–480. North-Holland, 1991.

[170] TRUMBORE, B., LYTTLE, W., AND GREENBERG, D. P. "A testbed for image synthesis." In *Developing Large-scale Graphics Software Toolkits— SIGGRAPH 1993 Course Notes* (Aug. 1993).

[171] UPSTILL, S. *The RenderMan companion: A Programmer's Guide to Realistic Computer Graphics.* Reading: Addison-Wesley, 1990.

[172] VAN OVERVELD, C. W. A. M., AND WYVILL, B. "Phong normal interpolation revisited." *ACM Transactions on Graphics* 16(4): 397–419(1997).

[173] VOORHIES, D., AND FORAN, J. "Reflection vector shading hardware." In *Proceedings of SIGGRAPH 94, Computer Graphics Proceedings, Annual Conference Series*, pp. 163–166. New York: ACM Press, 1994.

[174] WARD, G. "Measuring and modeling anisotropic reflection." In *Computer Graphics (Proc. SIGGRAPH '92)* 26(2): 265–272(July 1992).

[175] WATT, A., AND WATT, M. *Advanced Animation and Rendering Techniques: Theory and Practice.* Reading: Addison-Wesley, 1992.

[176] WESTLUND, H. B., AND MEYER, G. W. "Applying appearance standards to light reflection models." In *Proceedings of SIGGRAPH 01, Computer Graphics Proceedings, Annual Conference Series*, pp. 501–510. Reading: Addison-Wesley, 2001.

[177] WHITTED, T., AND WEIMER, D. M. "A software testbed for the development of 3D raster graphics systems." In *ACM Transactions on Graphics* 1(1): 43–57(January 1982).

[178] WILKIE, A., TOBLER, R. F., AND PURGATHOFER, W. "Combined rendering of polarization and fluorescence effects." In *Rendering Techniques 2001: 12th Eurographics Workshop on Rendering*: 197–204(2001).

[179] WILLIAMS, L. "Casting curved shadows on curved surfaces." In *Computer Graphics (Proc. SIGGRAPH)* 12(3): 270–274(Aug. 1978).

[180] WILLIAMS, L. "Pyramidal parametrics." In *Computer Graphics (Proc. SIGGRAPH '83)* 17(3): 1–11(July 1983).

[181] author = WITTENBRINK, C.M. "R-Buffer: A Pointerless A-Buffer Hardware Architecture." In *Graphics Hardware 2001*, edited by Kurt Akeley and Ulrich Neumann, pp. 73–80, New York: ACM Press, 2001.

[182] WOLFF, L. B., AND KURLANDER, D. J. "Ray tracing with polarization parameters." *IEEE CG&A* 10(6): 44–55(1990).

[183] WYVILL, G., AND KUNII, T. L. "A functional model for constructive solid geometry." *The Visual Computer* 1(1): 3–14(July 1985).

[184] ZÖCKLER, M., STALLING, D., AND HEGE, H. C. "Interactive visualization of 3D-vector fields using illuminated streamlines." In *Proceedings of IEEE Visualization '96, San Francisco*: 107–113(Oct.1996).

Index